A THEOLOGY OF PREACHING AND DIALECTIC

A THEOLOGY OF PREACHING AND DIALECTIC

Scriptural Tension, Heraldic Proclamation and the Pneumatological Moment

Aaron P. Edwards

LONDON • NEW YORK • OXFORD • NEW DELHI • SYDNEY

T&T CLARK
Bloomsbury Publishing Plc
50 Bedford Square, London, WC1B 3DP, UK

BLOOMSBURY, T&T CLARK and the T&T Clark logo are trademarks of
Bloomsbury Publishing Plc

First published in Great Britain 2018

A catalogue record for this book is available from the British Library.

A catalog record for this book is available from the Library of Congress.

ISBN: HB: 978-0-5676-7856-0
ePDF: 978-0-5676-7857-7
eBook: 978-0-5676-7859-1

Typeset by Newgen KnowledgeWorks Pvt. Ltd., Chennai, India
Printed and bound in Great Britain

To find out more about our authors and books visit www.bloomsbury.com
and sign up for our newsletters.

CONTENTS

PREFACE

This book would not have happened were it not for a God who speaks. I have often reflected on how different my life might have been had I not responded – semi-reluctantly – to the call to follow Him at the age of sixteen. Many more moments of semi-reluctant following have come since that time, in which the God who speaks has continued to speak, redirect, reassure, disturb, comfort, challenge, fortify and divert in all sorts of ways.

One such unintentional diversion involved my reluctant ascent (or descent) into academia via a PhD at the University of Aberdeen from 2011–2014, which formed the basis for this book, though much revised. Although I now find myself somewhat surprisingly *in* academia as a faculty lecturer and programme leader at Cliff College, I am still trying to work out what academia is actually *for* in its modern manifestation. Fewer and fewer people care about academic theology anymore, within or beyond the Church. What is most unsettling about this stark reality is that most of them are probably right to do so. Pastors, let alone congregants, simply do not have time for it. It would be derided as a 'luxury' but even that would suggest too positive a connotation. Modern academic theologians exist within a system that may as well have been purposely designed to produce no lasting fruit for the kingdom of God. We have been preoccupied (not always intentionally) with pleasing other masters. In doing so, we have proven to be utterly hopeless at multitasking and thus have all too frequently neglected our chief call and commission. As such, the vast majority of our theological works are excellently erudite, excellently rigorous, but – as far as the actual mission of the Church is concerned – excellently useless. This book, like most academic books, is not likely to be read by all that many people, but it is hoped that those who do read it will find it may yet be of some use to the task of Christian proclamation, however indirectly. If it isn't, it probably isn't worth a moment (pneumatological or otherwise) of your time, and was probably a significant waste of my own.

I hope that this book proves not to have been a waste of time, since it was not only my time that was spent. I owe so much thanksgiving to my wonderfully supportive wife, Molly, who has brought such enduring comfort from despair on many occasions throughout the thinking, writing, rethinking and rewriting process, and who has herself had to put up with not only many late nights but many melodramatic laments on the state of academia. I am also incredibly grateful to my four splendid young children, Isabelle, Malachi, Miriam, and Rebekah, who have been an unremitting source of childish delight and distraction upon many occasions when I have returned home from the office with a headful of footnotes. This book may have been finished far more quickly (but far more miserably) were it not for their unwavering demands for various games in which I was forced to play the role of a goblin or a snake or some other such creature, usually culminating with me being dramatically felled by the victorious infants and sent crashing down onto the lounge floor, only to miraculously resuscitate in order to repeat the process several times over.

Goblins aside, I am also much obliged to the Arts and Humanities Research Council for their generous funding, which – during my PhD – instigated overseas research trips to the Søren Kierkegaard Research Centre in Copenhagen (2012), St. Olaf's College in Northfield, Minnesota (2012) and two AAR conferences in Chicago (2012) and Baltimore (2013). Thanks also to The Bible Society, whose initial financial support was indispensable, and to the academic journals who published some of my articles along the way which directly or indirectly contributed to the tenor of this project: *Theology, International Journal of Systematic Theology, The Expository Times, Literature and Theology, Scottish Bulletin of Evangelical Theology, Harvard Theological Review, Theology Today, International Journal of Philosophy and Theology* and *Toronto Journal of Theology*. None of these articles has been exactly republished in the present work as such, though a handful of chapter subsections bear some resemblance in content to select article sections.[1]

During the infancy of this project, David Clough of Chester deserves special mention for sacrificing many hours of his time – many years ago – sitting with me in Binks café, offering general advice and support. Within the illustriously grey walls of Aberdeen's Divinity department, there are too many people to name. The fellow students with whom I shared offices, seminars, coffees and a 6:30am football pitch were a curious, perplexing and wonderful bunch of people. Most of them hailed from across the pond, so getting to know (and argue with) them was something of a cultural education in itself, as well as being a lot of fun. I am, of course, deeply grateful to my Doktorvater, Tom Greggs, who was exceptionally supportive, challenging and encouraging, especially of an ambitiously constructive project which often threatened to ascend to the heavens. Academically speaking, I certainly wouldn't have gotten very far at all without his wisdom and guidance. I also particularly enjoyed the kind warmth, good humour and theological rigour of others within the Aberdeen faculty who did not carry the burden of supervising me: Phil Ziegler, whose conversational interestedness was matchless; Paul Nimmo, who would be terrifying if he wasn't so kind; Don Wood, whose

---

1. I.1 and I.4.i – 'Preacher as Balanced extremist: Biblical Dialectics and Sermonic Certainty', in *The Expository Times* 126:9 (June 2015), pp. 425–35; II.1–3 and II.6 – 'The Paradox of Dialectic: Clarifying the Use and Scope of Dialectics in Theology', in *International Journal of Philosophy and Theology* 77:4–5 (November 2016), pp. 273–306; III.4 – 'The Strange New World of Confidence: Barth's Dialectical Exhortation to Fearful Preachers', in *Scottish Bulletin of Evangelical Theology* 32:2 (Autumn 2014), pp. 195–206; III.5.iii – 'Life in Kierkegaard's Imaginary Rural Parish: Preaching, Correctivity, and the Gospel', in *Toronto Journal of Theology* 30:2 (Fall 2014), pp. 235–46; IV.2.iv – 'Thus Saith the Word: The Theological Relationship between Biblical Exposition and Prophetic Utterance in Preaching', in *The Expository Times* 125:11 (August 2014), pp. 521–30.

intimidatingly ponderous silences were a constant spur to immediately rethink whatever one had just said; Brian Brock, whose call for radical discipleship in the modern world was a beacon and a catalyst; Russell Re Manning, who – despite his unfortunate Tillichian infection – was always such a welcoming and stimulating conversationalist; and the late John Webster, whose cheerful theological obstinacy was so outlandishly reassuring in the midst of contemporary academia. I'm sure he had a lot to do with what made theology at Aberdeen so rich and so unique, especially by his perpetual insistence that theology is, indeed, about God.

I would also like to acknowledge the many great preachers I have heard since I was sixteen, particularly within the *newfrontiers* family of churches, who brought the Word to bear upon life so efficaciously and purposefully in the power of the Spirit. Such preachers exemplified a firm-yet-dialectical grasp of what biblically faithful preaching ought to entail, never ceasing to exchange God's unwavering Word for cultural acclaim, and yet never ceasing to bring fresh bread. In many ways such sermons were probably the indirect catalysts of what eventually culminated – however unexpectedly – in this very academic book about a very unacademic subject. Although such preaching is rare indeed in most pulpits today, such moments still give me hope that God is not yet finished with his heralds because he is not yet finished with his people.

And we also thank God constantly for this, that when you received the word of God, which you heard from us, you accepted it not as the word of men but as what it really is, the word of God, which is at work in you believers.

– 1 Thess. 2:13[1]

There is a place for doubt, for the dialectic of Yes and No, for the attitude of perhaps and perhaps not, for hesitation whether things might be so. But this place is merely the forecourt where we think we are dealing with possibilities… But [Easter] makes it impossible for us to be *ceaselessly* and therefore *hesitantly* occupied with these possibilities.

– Karl Barth[2]

1. Scripture quotations are from the ESV® Bible (The Holy Bible, English Standard Version®), copyright © 2001 by Crossway, a publishing ministry of Good News Publishers. Used by permission. All rights reserved.

2. Karl Barth, *Church Dogmatics* [hereafter *CD*], 4 vols. in 13 pts., ed. G. W. Bromiley and T. F. Torrance (Edinburgh: T & T Clark, 1956–75), IV/3, p. 288 (emphasis added).

INTRODUCTION

How does the preacher know the one thing God wants to say *now* based upon the many things God wanted to say *then*? Preachers and theologians throughout history have grappled with a perennial and unavoidable problem in Christian proclamation: the task of interpreting apparently oppositional emphases within Scripture alongside the task of declaring the clear and authoritative 'Word of God' from the contemporary pulpit. It is not that the preacher has been forced to concede that the Bible 'contradicts' itself as such, but simply that the diversity within the Bible complexifies the assertive proclamation of any *singular* biblical truth in any singular moment of time. If one wants to do business with the Bible theologically, then one cannot assume the path will be entirely straightforward. The wisest preachers have always admitted that their peculiar handbook – lying thumbed and thumped on the surfaces of hundreds of thousands of pulpits across the globe – will never cease to surprise them.

It should come as no surprise to preachers that the Bible should be perpetually surprising, because it is not a solely human word. Its source and authority lie elsewhere, and this 'elsewhere' seems like nowhere else we have ever known. As such, whichever way we wish to describe Scripture's nature or function in proclamation, we know at least two things: it does not always arrive in the way it *ought* to, and yet (like a good wizard) it always arrives precisely when it *means* to. Surprise, however, is not without its problems. Surprise means preachers cannot be wholly reliant on any particular form, mode or expectation in advance of the event. Indeed, surprise seems far too open to contingency – hence why many preachers try their best to make do without it. Their Bible does not sit in the way they might prefer it to sit if they had seated it themselves, and so they opt for simpler alternative solutions, often by either overemphasizing certainty or overemphasizing ambiguity. Both solutions are dangerously 'safe' solutions because they create convenient sermonic straitjackets into which Scripture's member-texts can be crammed, however uncomfortably. Both solutions are an abdication of the unavoidable problem. However, although the classic stereotype of the overly certain pulpiteer often appears the more abhorrent of the two, it is seldom noticed how the gravitation to ambiguity and the failure to proclaim Scripture with acute confidence may be far worse, for it threatens to anaesthetize the Christian pulpit altogether.

The apparent failure of twenty-first century Western preaching to emulate the great preachers of Christian history – not only in their numerical and social impact but in their emphatically humane confidence – is the result of a complicated matrix of factors which cannot be discussed in any great detail here. Such pulpit hesitancy as there is today appears to be a consequence of preacherly indecisiveness borne of a sceptical philosophical, sociological and political climate which has long since shed its verbal attachment to metanarratives – and with it, the possibility of declaring any hint of certainty. This climate plays its part, no doubt, in causing preachers to draw back from the precipice of confidence, but it is not 'the postmodern condition' itself which causes the perennial problem of preaching. The problem was there long before Lyotard and Foucault were pitching their tents against the Apostle Paul's in the mid-late-century haze of anti-totalitarian revolt. The problem has been there since the very beginning of Christian preaching, rooted in Scripture itself. It is Scripture which proves the preacher's greatest stumbling block, seemingly failing to deliver the linear lucidity expected of it. This is because Scripture appears to present the preacher with theological truths in a variety of forms which cannot be reconciled in any truly totalizing scheme. To say that Scripture cannot be 'totalized' usually sounds as though one is a fully paid-up member of the postmodern party (whatever that might mean) so it is important to clarify what is meant by it.

Scripture *is* 'totalizing' in that it speaks of – and is itself the purveyor of – transcendently authoritative truths which speak to the whole condition of humanity from its temporal inception to its eternal destination. But in another sense, Scripture is 'anti-totalizing' by the form in which it happens to convey those truths, which do not follow the pattern one might expect. Although, as will be argued, Scripture's message is fundamentally unified, no preacher or theologian can possess any singular system by which they may declare any one thing in Scripture without at least some reference to one of its voluminous dialectical counterparts. For every text there lurks a potential counter-text. And yet even to set it up via such a binary undersells the complexity, because some texts do not have counter-texts in the same way as others do. Some do not seem to have any at all, while others seem to have several. Indeed, individual texts (or aspects within texts) can be interpreted and emphasized in multifarious ways, even from preachers who agree on the same core doctrinal principles. Nor is it even evident that Scripture is meant to be imagined via a dialectical schema of oppositional emphases in the first place. But neither is it possible to say that Scripture's texts are knitted together in a 'totally' systematic way, like a mechanized circuit board. And because of such convolutions, the problem remains implanted in the very heart of preaching. To put the problem more fundamentally: preaching *from* biblical texts necessarily means preaching *against* biblical texts. Not always, and not uniformly, but nonetheless unavoidably. To attend to this unavoidable problem is to attend to – and affirm – the reality of Scriptural tension, or: biblical dialectics.

However, to grapple with biblical dialectics alone only responds to this *one* side of the problem. Indeed, to only do this would be distinctly *un*dialectical in itself. The other side of this problem is indeed that Christian preachers *do* have a commission to proclaim the Word of God as 'heralds' in light of the resurrection, announcing the eschatological reality of the returning king. Thus, when preachers preach they are actually called to preach with the utmost confidence, declaring the very Word of God to their hearers. And their 'script' for this impossibly heraldic task remains the same: the surprising and unstraightforward canon of Holy Scripture. As noted, Scriptural tension is easily ignored in favour of outright 'certainty' in proclamation. Such preaching may indeed be effective in particular moments but ultimately fails to convey the fullness of the biblical message, usually forcing non-compliant texts into ideological pigeonholes.[3] However, *ceaseless* attention to the dialectical multivocity of Scripture without equivalent emphasis upon heraldic and unambiguous proclamation is equally problematic. The pulpit cannot be silent: somehow, something must be said on Sunday.

If preachers believe that Scripture does speak both clearly *and* dialectically, an important question emerges: which particular emphasis should preachers proclaim, and how might they proclaim it decisively in the face of its dialectical counterparts? This study argues for the significance of both the dialectical and the heraldic task in biblical proclamation, whereby the preacher may be freed to think dialectically without losing their heraldic confidence, and to speak heraldically without losing their dialectical awareness. We will see that the preacher cannot escape the dialectical problem of attending to Scriptural multivocity, but that – ultimately – this problem cannot become the final word for preaching. Proclamation, it will be shown, involves far more than decisions over rhetorical emphasis. Indeed, proclamation must be understood as a unique pneumatological moment which addresses its context with the *necessary* Word of God in all its objective contingency. This is what it means for preaching to be 'heraldic', allowing us to reinterpret the dialectical complexity within Scripture not as a hindrance to faithful heraldic proclamation but as a vital element of it, demonstrating Scripture's multivalent pneumatological authority as variously 'useful' and uniquely authoritative in different ways and moments (2Tim. 3:16).

It will be seen that, through a pneumatological account of heraldic preaching, we may understand preaching as the event in which the preacher is used by the Spirit to bring the message of Scripture to the hearer with authority and confidence; and that it may do so regardless of those tangential counter-emphases – however exegetically legitimate – which might also have been proclaimed simultaneously. Such a conjunction of dialectical negotiation and heraldic confidence is not

---

3. This is not to say we cannot read Scripture through any overarching lens but that preachers must be restrained in the kinds of systematic certainty they claim for their readings of Scripture wherever it threatens to undermine canonicity. Chapter I will negotiate the importance of biblical theology in this debate, whereby we do indeed read the entirety of Scripture through the overarching lens of the Gospel of Jesus Christ. This could be seen as an 'ideological pigeonhole' too, but not an inappropriate one, since it is this kerygmatic conception which has always remained consistent in the formation, foundation, and function of biblical canonicity itself.

determined by irrational fideism but by attentive hearing to Word and Spirit, whose utterance is received and proclaimed in faith. The aim of this book is to offer a theological grounding for the faithful rendering of Scripture's dialectical complexity *and* its intrinsic gravitation towards heraldic proclamation. As a result, it is hoped that preaching may be better understood theologically by comprehending its heraldic task as a perpetually dialectical corrective within a distinct pneumatological moment.[4]

A distinctive aspect of this work consists in conjoining two points of doctrinal enquiry together: theological dialectics and heraldic preaching. Given that these two concepts are rarely uttered in the same breath (and even appear, sometimes, as incompatible concepts), a serious discussion of their interrelationship is lacking. Although this book focuses upon both 'dialectic' *and* 'preaching', preaching will retain greater freight within this pairing, since it invokes the decisive culmination of the dialectical problem. Preaching, in other words, is where the rubber hits the road when it comes to what one believes about theological dialectic. Where the problem might be debated ad infinitum by biblical scholars and systematicians within the academy, preachers do not possess this luxury. Indeed, as this very sentence is read, there are hundreds of thousands of preachers worldwide currently thinking about or delivering a sermon derived from the content of Scripture. This urgency should not be a cause for superficial doctrinal reflection in favour of ill-informed practice, but it should demonstrate something of the uniqueness of the preaching task when it comes to relating preaching *to* theological dialectics. Preaching is not only the cause of theological thinking – in that theology owes its very existence to Gospel proclamation – but preaching is also the *end* of theological thinking, where theological work bears its fruit, or indeed, goes to die. It is the vital conjunction of the two concepts – a theology of dialectic *with* a theology of preaching – which animates this book.

There are significant gaps within both homiletical and theological literature which warrant this approach. In the first instance, not many theologians in the contemporary era have written upon a theology of preaching in extensive detail, particularly not within the field of systematic theology itself. Indeed, where preaching is considered, it is often seen as a secondary concern, either as a sub-set of the doctrine of Scripture, the channel for the practical application of doctrine(s), or as a mere form of rhetorical communication. As such, although there is a wealth of systematic theology regarding the various doctrines which might be preached in the pulpit, there has been insufficient theological reflection upon the doctrine of preaching itself. In other words, there is a vital need not for more teaching *for* preaching, but for more teaching *about* preaching. One reason this neglect tends to occur is that preaching already possesses its own specialist field of enquiry, 'homiletics'. As such, systematics tends to get on with its own

---

4. 'Corrective' here does not necessarily mean 'rebuke' (contra, say, 'encouragement') but it refers to *dialectical* correctivity: the oppositional reactionary movements between differing polar emphases.

specified doctrinal work, safe in the knowledge that preaching is well accounted for. However, as is well known, the vast majority of contemporary homiletical approaches are overwhelmingly freighted towards the technical, practical element of preaching: 'how does one *do* preaching?', rather than the conceptual: 'how does one *understand* preaching?'[5] Indeed, preaching is usually seen as a practice of applied theology rather than something which warrants its own theological reflection.[6] This is not to deny the importance of these practical questions within homiletics but to say that the conceptual questions are also necessary and severely lacking. Where homiletics often contains theological overtones within a wider practical vision, this book attempts to convey practical overtones within a wider theological vision. Although this theme appears inherently 'practical' in its orientation, it remains a 'systematic' proposal because its concern lies, primarily, with how we may understand dialectic and heralding theologically in the first instance. Where it is applicable to the preacher's practical task, the particularities of *how* this task should be done are less important here than the theological lens through which this task is conceived.

The sources used for this undertaking are necessarily various. This is because the attempt here is not to understand one thinker's approach in particular, but to harness a variety of useful reflections upon both dialectic and preaching within the constructive argument. It will be evident, of course, that a cluster of thinkers are drawn upon more frequently than others, whose volume and variety requires something of an introduction in itself. In particular, Karl Barth's thought will be engaged frequently, not only because of his 'dialectical' theology but also because of his theological conceptions of preaching, which he considered the primary foundation for theology itself.[7] Despite these prevailing emphases in his theological project, however, Barth never wrote a specifically focused work upon the nature of dialectics in conjunction with heraldic proclamation.[8] Wherever this book agrees with Barth, it attempts to do justice to the unapplied aspects of his

5. This prevalence, it will be argued, stems from the hugely influential 'New Homiletic' of the 1970–80s. See Chapter III.

6. As will be seen throughout this study there are, of course, notable exceptions to this, including the work of Willimon, Jacobsen, Kay, Lischer, Pasquarello, Allen, and others, where attempts have been made to reflect upon preaching's theological nature. However, most of these approaches remain situated *within* the field of homiletics itself, not systematic theology. Beyond Barth, the concern for preaching as a 'practical science' (rather than preaching as befitting doctrinal reflection itself) tends to prevail.

7. Barth, *CD* I/1, pp. 74–7.

8. There is, of course, Barth's oft-noted *Homiletics* book. However, the 1991 English version by which this is known was not translated from an equivalent German text but compiled from collated student notes taken from Barth's 1932–3 homiletics seminars in Bonn. This material does not delve with any particular detail into the interaction of dialectic and preaching itself, but rather sets out some theological foundations and practical applications of one's preaching method.

thinking regarding the unique authority of preaching alongside the simultaneous inescapability of dialectical theological speech. For this reason, Barth's voice will appear more prominent than others, even though this is by no means a study of Barth's thought per se. Other thinkers who appear frequently include other sometime adherents to the dialectical theology 'school' such as Emil Brunner and Paul Tillich, particularly regarding aspects of preaching as 'encounter' and the 'moment', which are important for how I describe what preaching seeks to do. Another key interlocutor is one of the purported inspirations behind the dialectical theology movement, Søren Kierkegaard. This is not only because Kierkegaard spoke so often of 'paradox' and 'dialectic' within his corrective theological project, but also because he contributes to the modern conception of 'moment' and because his inimitably iconoclastic homiletical voice still offers much to the 'post-Christendom' preaching situation.

There will be a particular emphasis, too, upon Reformation approaches to Scripture and preaching, especially via Martin Luther and John Calvin, whose thought often punctuates the ways in which Scriptural authority and interpretation are approached. Contrastingly, voices from the Catholic tradition such as Thomas Aquinas and Yves Congar also prove extremely helpful on the role of prophecy and discernment in pneumatological preaching. Indeed, the role of the 'prophetic' has sometimes been neglected within Protestant theology due to its prevalent emphasis upon the *written* Word of God.[9] Modern and contemporary voices from within the Reformed tradition (such as John Webster, G. C. Berkouwer and Timothy Ward) are consulted, in addition to key twentieth-century voices behind biblical theology (such as C. F. D. Moule, Rudolf Bultmann and Brevard Childs) while considering the canonicity, clarity, illumination and efficacy of Scripture. These concepts play a vital role in the interaction between dialectics *in* Scripture and the preacher's interpretative theological confidence.

It has also been important to highlight the examples of many preachers who illuminate how heraldic preaching has functioned, including George Whitefield, Charles Spurgeon, P. T. Forsyth, James Stewart, David Martyn Lloyd-Jones and William Willimon. It barely needs saying that the greatest theological insights on preaching have often come from those who have been great preachers themselves. This is especially the case with preacher-theologians who, like Augustine, Luther, Calvin, Barth, Bonhoeffer, et al., have seen their practice of preaching as so closely intertwined with their practice of theology. It has often been observed that the best theology, that which is most faithful to the Church's mission and to its

9. This is not to discount the overt Protestant emphasis on the *preached* Word of God, as with the oft-cited Second Helvetic Confession, where the preaching of the Word of God *is* the Word of God. See Arthur C. Cochrane (ed.), *Reformed Confessions of the 16th Century* (London: SCM, 1966), p. 225. Although the Protestant tradition maintains a high view of 'preaching', this is not always specified in terms of 'prophecy', which can sometimes be seen, incorrectly, in revelatory competition to the authority and sufficiency of Scripture, rather than as a charism which may be complexly entwined with the Scriptural message.

divine commissioner, always keeps at least one eye on the pulpit. The fact that contemporary systematic theology spectacularly fails in this regard has been one of the many causes for the oft-bemoaned Church-academy gulf and, subsequently, the tragic neglect of theology in the contemporary Church. Thus, the engagement with both theologians *and* preachers in this book illuminates this need to sketch a systematic theological approach to preaching which bears its practice in mind without becoming a thoroughly 'practical' account of preaching per se.

It is obvious that no argument can encapsulate every facet within its chosen field of enquiry. Although this book appears to take a broad approach in its implied scope, it should not be seen as an attempt to encapsulate 'dialectic' and 'heraldic preaching' in their entirety, but as an exercise in dialectical and systematic theology. A potential pitfall within this, of course, is the danger of a superficial engagement with either 'dialectic' or 'preaching' within this broader schema. A more sustained focus upon one or the other might allow for more in-depth descriptive reflection. However, this is not the goal of this project, which attempts to explore the relatedness of these two concepts. As such, this undertaking attempts a different kind of approach to that which might treat one doctrinal locus in isolation. In this part-synthesizing method, it is hoped that the argument for 'heraldic preaching' is clarified by its conversation *with* 'dialectic', which acts as the problematization for a straightforward approach to preacherly confidence.

Another possible problem could be the wide array of sources used, as noted above. Although a potentially eclectic range offers variety, there is greater potential to apply aspects of a thinker's thought overly selectively, and beyond their immediate context. This, however, is an inherent constraint of any 'constructive' project, whereby elements of thought-schemes may be pieced together to serve and buttress the prevalent dogmatic claims. It is, of course, intended that none of the sources used has been misapplied or misappropriated beyond the initial intentions of their thought, even where only minor aspects of their respective projects are engaged. Where it has been impossible to convey all distinctive nuances of each thinker, this displays another necessary limitation of any constructive theological project.

The structure of the work is composed of four distinct chapters, each addressing the four vital thematic concerns within the argument: I. Scripture; II. Dialectic; III. Proclamation; IV. Pneumatology.

Chapter I outlines Scripture's simultaneous propensity towards both dialectic and preaching, through its Gospel-founded 'clarity' and its dialectical complexity. Having introduced the inseparable connection between preaching and Scripture (I.1), it is argued that the proclaimed Gospel is an inherent foundation of New Testament canonicity itself (I.2.i–ii), rendering Scripture as inherently 'preachable' since canonicity finds its *telos* in Gospel proclamation (I.2.iii). Although there are different ways of identifying what the Gospel meant for the early Church, its primary tenets inform Scripture's reception as a theologically coherent text (I.2.iv–v). This claim is supplemented by consulting Reformation accounts which locate Scriptural clarity in the Gospel message, further demonstrating that Scripture is received by the Church through the lens of proclamation, not dialectical ambiguity (I.3). This canonical propensity towards expository heraldic proclamation is complexified (though not nullified) by dialectical variety *within* Scripture, affecting any given sermon. Even with the presuppositions of clarity and unity, Scripture's simultaneous diversity problematizes the expository preaching task (I.4.i). An overt example of this is found – illustratively – in the Grace-Works dynamic between Paul and James (I.4.ii), which may be variously interpreted. It will be found that there is a kind of dialectical tension between the concepts of 'dialectic' and 'clarity' themselves with which the preacher must wrestle in the task of biblical expository preaching.

Having outlined Scripture's double propensity towards dialectical ambiguity *and* clear Gospel proclamation, Chapter II sketches the complexity of dialectical method itself, seen variously in both the philosophical and theological traditions. Although 'dialectic' is a difficult term to pin down precisely, it will be seen that some primary tenets include the rejection of *singular* propositions and the radical openness between two strands of interactive truth (II.2.i). The way in which such polarity interactions occur, however, remains complexly various. Philosophical dialectic will be distinguished from theological dialectic by the differing aims and presuppositions behind each method, with a particular focus upon the dialectical theology school of the 1920s (II.2.ii). Dialectic will also be delineated from a similar concept, 'paradox', which also endures various expressions (II.3.i). Constructive exemplifications of theological paradox will then be explored via Meister Eckhart and G. K. Chesterton (II.3.ii), and the complexity of *both* concepts via Kierkegaard (II.4.i). Paradox, it will be seen, retains dialectical emphases but is better seen as a *type* of dialectic rather than an outright method itself. The ambiguity between the two terms is further illuminated by a relatively recent debate between John Milbank and Slavoj Žižek ('Paradox or Dialectic?'), in which two vastly different approaches to 'contradiction' are seen as the maintenance and/or harmonization of dialectical tension (II.4). Given Hegel's prevalence in modern dialectical theory (and his recurrence within the Milbank-Žižek debate), Hegelian dialectic will be reconsidered through his nuanced conception of contradiction, where antitheses are not necessarily synthesized into a new polarity but retain a sense of tension *within* sublation (II.5). Through these varying accounts of dialectical complexity, it will be seen that it is not straightforward to speak of 'dialectic' without reference to its variety. The chapter will then conclude by identifying four primary dialectical modes in which the problem of contradictory polarities may be approached (II.6): 1. paradoxical dialectic; 2. harmonized dialectic; 3. hierarchical dialectic; 4. antagonistic dialectic. These modes may interlink and do not exhaust every dialectical possibility, but they do serve as a platform from which we may speak of dialectical variety within the canon, clarifying what kinds of dialectic preachers will encounter.

Following this outline of different dialectical modes, Chapter III connects the concept of dialectic to 'heraldic' preaching, which requires a certain form of dogmatic confidence usually denied by dialectics (III.1–2). The identification of preaching as 'heraldic' is defined and then brought into dialogue with contemporary homiletical thought (particularly, the 'New Homiletic'), which tends to highlight listener consciousness and deliberate ambiguity, while repudiating traditional preacherly authority (III.3.i). A more nuanced conception of the heraldic model will then be offered which incorporates some of the New Homiletic's hesitancies regarding authoritarian abuse without losing the important emphasis on heraldic decisiveness in the midst of biblical dialectics. This will be further clarified by a conceptual theological grounding for 'confidence' in heraldic preaching, based upon the notion of preaching as a commissioned event in which the preacher is simultaneously aware of the impossibility and necessity of the preaching task (III.4). Having outlined this nuanced foundation for 'heraldic preaching', a clearer, more specified view is gained regarding *why* preaching is complexified by dialectics. This will be applied to various dialectical sermonic possibilities in light of the aforementioned dialectical modes (II.6) and mapped onto the illustrative Grace-Works dialectic (I.4.ii). These applications will indicate possible avenues of heraldic-yet-dialectical variety in the pulpit, invoking a recalibration of the nature of preaching as a 'contingent dialectical corrective', helpfully exemplified in Kierkegaard's corrective approach to Lutheran justification (III.5.ii–iii). The nature of heraldic confidence, it will be concluded, necessitates the nature of contingent dialectical correctivity.

Having outlined the nature of heraldic preaching and shown its relatedness to the varying modes through which Scriptural dialectics may be interpreted, Chapter IV provides an account of how such dialectically corrective decisiveness is possible, via pneumatology (IV.1). The 'prophetic' function of preaching is illuminated, outlining legitimate ways to speak of the Spirit's revelatory activity alongside biblical exposition (IV.2). This prophetic conception is then applied to dialectical 'decisiveness', detailing decisive variety between different Scriptural emphases (IV.3.i) and highlighting the Spirit's role in maintaining interpretative conviction via Scriptural 'illumination' (IV.3.ii). This leads to a theological account of how such decisiveness may be attained in practice, through faithful preacherly and congregational 'discernment' (IV.3.iii). Faith-attained decisive 'peace' is hoped for, despite the potential 'restlessness' invoked by dialectics (IV.3.iv). The penultimate section then introduces two important elements in the *purpose* of pneumatologically prophetic preaching: 'encounter' (IV.4.i) and 'manifestation' (IV.4.ii). These distinctive elements tentatively differentiate 'preaching' from 'teaching', suggesting a new theological lens through which the preacher's decisiveness connects to the Spirit's *specific* work in the preaching event. Understanding this pneumatological dimension recalibrates the dialectical 'problem' because it becomes possible to see that preaching is not burdened with dialectical reconciliation in every sermon. The final section culminates this discussion of preaching's uniqueness with the concept of the 'pneumatological moment' (IV.5). Different conceptions of 'moment' in preaching are distinguished (IV.5.i–ii) before it is argued that the 'pneumatological moment' is a *created* moment into which the hearers are drawn to receive the specific Scriptural emphasis deemed prophetically necessary. It will be seen that the Spirit is at work in multifarious ways in the preaching event, within and beyond our interpretative scope. Furthermore, the Spirit's prophetic 'timeliness' in rendering the Word *present* for the hearer is simultaneously tethered to the 'fixed' content of Scripture (IV.5.iii). The preaching moment is nonetheless Scriptural and not at the mercy of preacherly whims, congregational wants, or the transient urgencies of the *Zeitgeist*. It will thus be concluded that heraldic proclamation is genuinely 'expository', 'dialectical', 'pneumatological' and 'kairotic'.[10]

As noted, it will be evident that the entirety of this study carries an absence of an overt focus upon the 'practical' aspects of preaching. Although practical concerns are of vital importance, a 'science' of practice is not always the best way to assist practice. It has been necessary here – indeed, it is one of the novel aspects of this work – to refrain from driving at the issue *through* the practical but to spend time at a distance from practice in order to better inform the practical task *theologically*. Ultimately, I believe this will be of greater benefit *to* the practice of preaching, allowing preachers to consult the various pathways of application as their own peculiar personalities, contexts and congregations allow. Pointers will be provided in the conclusion, however, into ways in which the practical aspects might be explored further on the back of what has been established theologically. The discipline of maintaining a predominantly conceptual focus also helps to outline the distinctive aspects of both dialectic and heraldic preaching both in isolation and conjunction. By relating these concepts together, this work hopes to offer something of a clarion call towards a theological *re*claiming of preacherly confidence both in and through dialectical method; that is, not merely a dialectical theological reflection upon preaching but also a homiletical reflection upon dialectical theology. It is hoped that this will benefit the systematic theologian who has neglected the place of preaching within theology, as well as benefitting the preacher who has neglected (or struggles with) the task of interpreting Scriptural dialectics. Ultimately, it is also hoped that preachers are better resourced to speak as confident heralds in spite of their necessary incompetence for this paradoxical task, and to do so alongside – indeed, with the help of – the variously dialectical nature of Scriptural theology.

10. Where Chapter III introduces 'heraldic' as the primary category, these other elements ('expository', 'dialectical', 'pneumatologically prophetic', and 'kairotic') are not separate from the heraldic motif but emanate from it, since it will be argued that the heraldic is the source of the preacher's theological identity (see III.1–2).

Chapter I

CANONICITY, CLARITY, DIALECTIC: THE PROBLEMATIC TASK OF EXPOSITORY PREACHING

1. *Introduction: Preaching and Scripture*

How do we understand, theologically, the task of preaching from biblical texts which appear to refute one another? It is well noted that particular texts within the Bible appear to present not only 'diverse' teachings, but teachings which appear to be irreconcilable into a clear system or whole. This is a unique problem for expository preaching, whereby the primary 'content' for the sermon is seen, demonstrably, in the exposition of the biblical text. Although not unique to Protestantism,[1] this conception of preaching was heavily re-emphasized in the Reformation and has continued throughout the Protestant tradition. Such preaching relies upon the presupposition of Scriptural authority and clarity, necessitating that textual exposition remains its central task: 'There has to be absolute confidence in holy scripture. If preachers are content to make their sermons expositions of scripture, that is enough.'[2] Preaching, then, is dependent upon a foundational understanding of Scripture's vocal unity rather than its incongruity. However, the 'dialectical' problem for preaching arises when one attends to the particularities of the biblical texts themselves. If Scripture is to be seen as authoritative in its particular elements *and* its entirety, then biblical preaching is faced with the complexifying problem of attending to these problematic tensions which exist *between* different texts of Scripture. Although there are many ways of speaking of 'dialectic',[3] this dialectical 'problem' refers to the apparently competitive doctrinal emphases between biblical texts. In essence, Scripture appears to be unified *and* diverse; clear *and* complex; univocal *and* plurivocal. This is what appears – at least on the surface – to be deeply problematic for biblical expository preaching.

---

1. It should be noted, for example, that most medieval sermons 'were based on Scripture, and were intended to explain Scripture or communicate some scriptural truth to their audience'. Fran van Liere, *An Introduction to the Medieval Bible* (Cambridge: Cambridge University Press, 2014), p. 215.

2. Karl Barth, *Homiletics*, trans. Geoffrey W. Bromiley and Donald E. Daniels (Westminster: John Knox Press, 1991), p. 76.

3. See II.6.

Although this chapter will approach this issue theologically, its complexity is borne out of the reality of the historical and contemporary *practice* of preaching itself. The regular task of preaching through the Bible necessitates that this problem of conflicting Scriptural passages is encountered by any preacher who upholds Scripture as the authoritative source for Christian preaching. Eventually, the preacher will be met with a text they cannot reconcile easily with another, which will require an articulated theological judgement in the pulpit. Karl Barth notes this same dilemma which he faced as a full-time preacher in Safenwil:

> I sought to find my way between the problem of human life on the one hand and the content of the Bible on the other. As a minister I wanted to speak to the *people* in the infinite contradiction of their life, but to speak the no less infinite message of the *Bible*, which was as much of a riddle as life.[4]

The fact that Scripture appears to be something of a 'riddle' (apparently contradictory and complex rather than simple and unified) complicates this preaching task. As noted, this tension is faced, in particular, by the preacher who upholds Scripture as *the* primary theological content for their sermons.[5]

This chapter, then, will attempt to identify and evaluate the tension between the unified, clear message of Scripture and the theological dialectics which exist *within* Scripture. Some approaches to this problem tend towards an over-dependence on the 'dialectical' nature of Scripture, whereby theological tension itself is proclaimed rather than the necessary particularities (and even, extremes) of each text.[6] Conversely, ignoring the dialectical tension between Scriptural texts in favour of certain extremities or simplistic harmonizations devalues the full sense of biblical revelation in which unity, clarity *and* dialectic exist. In order to navigate this tension appropriately, a robust account of both 'canonicity' and 'clarity' will be given *prior* to the dialectical problem itself. It will be seen that these two concepts provide the necessary precursors and guiding parameters

---

4. Karl Barth, 'The Need and Promise of Christian Preaching', in *The Word of God and the Word of Man*, trans. Douglas Horton (London: Hodder & Stoughton, 1928), pp. 97–135 [100]. Although there is a newer critical edition of these essays (*The Word of God and Theology*, trans. Amy Marga (London: T&T Clark, 2011)), Horton's older translation is preferred here due to its prevalent impact upon the Anglophone reception of dialectical theology in the twentieth century.

5. The 'form' of the sermon itself is not of primary concern here. Expository preaching may involve eclectic styles and need not necessitate a monotonous verse-by-verse mode to the exclusion of other forms of expository proclamation (see III.3.i); 'expository' here merely means that the sermon's theological content is demonstrably textual and not derived primarily from some other source, even if other sources might be incorporated *within* this primary exposition.

6. This is seen, for example, in much of the preaching within early 'dialectical theology' (see II.2.ii).

for interpreting Scriptural dialectics. In order to introduce the problematic relationship of dialectic to expository preaching, we must first outline why this may be called 'problematic' at all: namely, because of the assumption that Scripture is itself a unified rather than an inherently fragmented text.

2. *The Proclaimed Gospel and Early Canonicity*

How can the preacher declare, authoritatively, that Scripture teaches something which appears to counteract another Scriptural teaching? The task of ascertaining a truly 'Scriptural' voice in preaching is problematized by this, but not to the extent that expository preaching should be thought impossible. The Bible, though full of various tensions, retains enough of a unified emphasis through the message of the Gospel, which can be said to permeate each tension. The dialectics of Scripture should be seen not *simply* as one voice warring against another in isolation, but as particular nuances of tension *within* the overall message. This message may rightly be said to preside over the vocal volume of each polarity within the canonical whole. We will see this borne out in the following account of the emergence of proto-canonical unity in the early Church, through the unifying proclamation of the Gospel.

i. *The Received Unity of Scripture*

The preacher's problem with biblical dialectics begins with the larger question of biblical unity. Are the texts of Scripture theologically unified to the extent that a *single* message might be preached, or is the preacher to choose from a collation of scattered messages in perpetual dialectical conflict? If Scripture does contain diverse theological incongruities, we might also ask: why is Scripture received by the Church and preached by the Church as a supposedly unified text? At the outset, this univocal reception of Scripture should inform any discussion of its diversity. Indeed, Scriptural unity is inherent within its very identity as canon: 'No matter how great its inner diversity, this set of writings is to be taken as mirroring in a wholeness of its own the unity of the church's own identity.'[7] This means, of the sixty-six canonical books which comprise the Old and New Testaments, there must be an overall thematic thread which connects each book into *one* book.[8] Although there are varieties of genre and purpose within the particular texts, such

---

7. David Kelsey, *Uses of Scripture in Recent Theology* (London: SCM, 1975), p. 106.

8. Many challenge the notion that this unifying thread should denote *one* message: 'It is very uncertain whether any single theme or concept stands at the apex of biblical theology. Many believe that the complete lack of consensus demonstrates that a cluster of ideas, rather than a single theme, unites all the others.' Grant R. Osborne, *The Hermeneutical Spiral: A Comprehensive Introduction to Biblical Interpretation* (Downers Grove: IVP, 1991), p. 282. Kelsey, for example, argues for 'three distinct but complexly and inseparably interrelated

as history, law, poetry, wisdom, prophecy, narrative, proposition or parable, we may say that the individual texts of Scripture are subservient to their identity as a necessary part of the canon.[9] Their inclusion in the canon presupposes that there is some kind of connection within each text that warrants its canonical status. The reasoning behind these connections between the canonical books, of course, involves a variety of complex historical and theological issues.[10] Arguing for the *historical* validity of the canon is not of primary concern here (though the historical canon is, of course, affirmed); rather, our focus will be the *theological* locus which connects these apparently divergent texts.

In large portions of hermeneutical and biblical scholarship, Scripture's *disunity* has often been emphasized as being competitive with its unity: 'The canon as a collection becomes more problematical when one sees how varied are the writings that have been included.'[11] In addition, some critiques centre upon the assumptions of a certain *kind* of unity based upon the Bible's modern presentation:

> The Bible in any of the forms it is encountered in the modern world gives out the strongest possible signals of unity, coherence, and closure. All the books have the same typography, the same style of translation, a consistent pagination, and a fixed order: features that arouse strong expectations that the contents will be

plots' regarding creation, consummation and reconciliation. David Kelsey, *Eccentric Existence: A Theological Anthropology*, Volume One (Louisville: Westminster John Knox Press, 2009), p. 152. Such an approach introduces an unnecessary complexity to the notion of canonicity as rooted in the Gospel message, even as the Gospel contains various facets. As will be seen, it is not impossible to speak of 'the Gospel' as a broadly implicated but singular message, and hence, as a unifying *kerygma* – especially when we imagine there has always been something *specifically* 'good' about 'the good news'.

9. When speaking of canonical unity here, there will be a necessary focus upon the New Testament. This is not just for the sake of brevity but also because it is the Gospel (and the ensuing proclamation of the New Testament Church) upon which the view of the Bible's *entire* unity is built; that is, the unity of Old *and* New Testaments rather than the unity of the Old Testament alone. The focus here is upon why *these* New Testament texts, which later became 'canonical', came into use as additionally authoritative to – and interpretative of – the existing Old Testament canon. See Westerholm: 'The early Christians were convinced that the scriptures of Israel were only correctly understood when Christ was seen at their center. Conversely, Christ himself was understood in the light of Israel's scriptures.' Stephen Westerholm and Martin Westerholm, *Reading Sacred Scripture: Voices from the History of Biblical Interpretation* (Grand Rapids: Eerdmans, 2016), p. 42.

10. 'The determination of the canon rested upon a dialectical combination of historical and theological criteria.' Bruce M. Metzger, *The Canon of the New Testament: Its Origin, Development, and Significance* (Oxford: Clarendon Press, 1987), p. 254. The connection of texts to apostolicity and the *regula fidei* are other such historical factors.

11. John Reumann, *Variety and Unity in New Testament Thought* (Oxford: Oxford University Press 1991), p. 281.

a single 'work'. One of the first and most obvious effects of historical criticism is that it disappoints all such expectations.[12]

It is true that the unity of Scripture is not always as straightforward as it may appear, and that Scriptural 'diversity' cannot be rejected outright. However, this should not be framed in a way which pits unity *against* diversity. Indeed, even to call this collection of varied texts 'the Bible' presupposes a unity which is not simply an indirect by-product of the printing press, but a direct result of its consistent recognition as 'canon' in the history of the Church's preaching and teaching. It is not wildly inappropriate, then, to presuppose this unity as the basis for assessing any accompanying disunity. Although historical canonical validation is not the key issue here, it will be helpful nonetheless to reference its importance as an exemplification which informs how we conceive of the canon theologically.

ii. *Theological Canonicity*

The reason historical canonical reception is less immediately relevant to the preaching task is because the preacher receives Scripture *as* canon rather than having to ascertain the parameters of its authority themselves. A theology of canon need not necessarily argue the case for historical canonicity itself but aims to highlight the canon's theological and homiletical implications, presupposing its received authority. This is why the canon need not be renegotiated in every era of the Church. Indeed, a doctrine of divine inspiration locates the canon within a theological trajectory and not strictly upon historical acts of human judgement, as John Calvin famously says: 'a most pernicious error widely prevails that Scripture has only so much weight as is conceded to it by the consent of the church. As if the eternal and inviolable truth of God depended upon the decision of men!'[13] Similarly, Barth asserts: 'We cannot think that the Church can give authority to a sacred writing, but only that it can establish its authority.'[14] The role of the Church is crucial to the 'economic' sense of canonicity as a functional recognition of its authority, but not *as* its authorization itself. The larger dogmatic concern locates historical canonicity within the encompassing event of divine inspiration via the Holy Spirit.

It is true, then, that when we speak of the historical (or human) nature of the canonical process, we are merely demonstrating *how* divine inspiration elevated these texts from 'human-making' to the 'Word of God', as in John Webster's account: 'The texts of the canon are human realities annexed by divine use.'[15] Here

---

12. John Barton, *The Spirit and the Letter: Studies in the Biblical Canon* (London: SPCK, 1997), p. 151.

13. John Calvin, *Institutes of the Christian Religion*, 2 vols., ed. J. T. McNeill (Philadelphia: Westminster Press, 1960), vol. 1, p. 75.

14. Barth, *CD* I/1, p. 474.

15. John Webster, 'The Dogmatic Location of the Canon', in *Word and Church: Essays in Christian Dogmatics* (Edinburgh: T & T Clark, 2001), pp. 9–46 [31].

we have a theological foundation for presuming that the Bible is in every way as God intended it to be – no more, nor less – while also avoiding the perspective which either elevates the texts to an ontologically divine status or relegates them to entirely human realities.[16] In whichever way they were received, these texts have been received by the Church as inspired by God – indeed, as the very Word of God. Equally, the ecclesial reception of these texts as divine address is not, in itself, a determinant of their inspiration or authority: 'The "decision" of the church...has noetic but not ontological force, acknowledging what Scripture is but not making it so.'[17] The locus of Scripture's authority (and its ensuing clarity and unity) ought to be seen primarily in the divine activity rather than the ecclesial activity.[18] We

16. It is worth noting here an insightful critique of Webster's conception of Scriptural ontology. D. A. Carson, a biblical scholar who more than most has remained as committed to the theological task as to the historical, notes that the antithesis Webster sets up between the inspired canonical 'process' and the final canonical 'product' is potentially misleading, questioning why an emphasis on the inspired 'product' necessarily divinizes the biblical text. This is particularly pertinent in light of a passage such as 2Tim. 3:16, which *does* refer to the inspired 'product', not the process. See D. A. Carson, *Collected Writings on Scripture* (Nottingham: IVP, 2010), pp. 253–4. This is not to say that Webster's emphasis need be seen as actually misleading, but simply that it could be especially open to polemical misapplication in order to entirely discount the historical process *or* the authority of the final Scriptural text. Both process and product may actually be affirmed and related within God's activity of inspiration, whereby the authority of the text can be upheld without collapsing it into God's being or treating the received text as a deistic 'replacement' for God's ongoing revelatory activity.

17. John Webster, *Holy Scripture: A Dogmatic Sketch* (Cambridge: Cambridge University Press, 2003), p. 63.

18. Such a theological rendering of Scriptural unity often evokes the connection between God's own consistently unified being and his revealed Word, which can be purported to undermine any such enquiry of 'tension' within the canon. See, for example, Zwingli: 'But God is one, and he is a Spirit of unity, not of discord. Hence we may see that his words have always a true and natural sense.' Ulrich Zwingli, 'Of the Clarity and Certainty of the Word of God', in G. W. Bromiley (ed.), *Zwingli and Bullinger* (The Library of Christian Classics, Volume XXIV) (London: SCM, 1953), p. 87. However, it is perfectly plausible that a unified and self-consistent God could inspire what appears to the finite creature as a non-unified or what *we* might term an 'inconsistent' text. Divine inspiration does not *necessarily* connote a unified Bible. It is true that God has indeed revealed that he is faithful, truthful, consistent, and not 'double-tongued', and that such attributes *may* indicate that the inspired Bible *ought* to be unified; but, crucially, this should not lead to the presumption of a particular *kind* of Scriptural unity which conforms to our creaturely expectations. Indeed, God's infinitude renders the possibility of a kind of dialectical unity which finite beings are incapable of comprehending. We have reason to believe, however, that Scripture is unified because its content is bound to the message – and person – through which it was first mediated to the Church and that which the Church continues to proclaim, as will be seen.

have reason, then, to be cautious of any appeal to the 'history' of the canon in what aims to be a distinctly theological account of Scriptural unity.[19]

However, despite these dogmatic cautions, this does not mean that historical canonical criteria cannot act as a helpful indicator to the constitution of biblical unity. After all, the process of canonization itself exists to highlight and affirm the kind of unity between the individual texts which justifies their conformity into *one* text. Although we need not lean too heavily upon the early Church decision-making processes themselves, their indicative merit is evident in echoing the similarly kerygmatic concerns of the Reformers' rendering of Scriptural clarity, which underpins our approach to biblical dialectics. What, then, were the *theological* verifications for proto-canonization?

iii. *Gospel and Canon*

It is widely accepted that the primary unifying foundation upon which the early Church was united was the Gospel message: 'Whatever judgement we may form of the Christianity of the earliest times, it is certain that those who discerned the limits of the canon had a clear and balanced perception of the gospel of Jesus Christ.'[20] This 'clear and balanced perception' (however perceived) meant that the texts of the canon ought to comprise some kind of unity, even if not uniformly so. Indeed, this unity, even in its points of differentiation, ought not to contradict the message that was consistently preached and lived-out among the earliest congregations (the *regula fidei*).[21] Daniel P. Fuller recognizes this not only as a historical criterion for canonicity but as an ongoing indication for perceiving Scriptural unity:

> When we wish to interpret some affirmation coming from early Christianity not merely as an isolated phenomenon, but as an actual biblical text, as part

19. The symbiotic relationship between history and theology is itself too complex to be investigated here, but it should be borne in mind whenever theology appears to be pitted *against* history, as might appear to be the case in this chapter. Rather, the emphasis on the theological here is merely to say that the argument for what Scripture *is* can never be understood in 'atheological' historical terms. At root, Scripture is only Scripture as we know it because of its distinctly theological properties, as a primary aspect of God's revelation of Himself. The fact that this revelation occurs *in* history is, of course, an obvious indicator of the inseparability of history from this revelation, but even here it is clear that the theological remains *prior*. If we mean to account for a God who enters history in revelation, then history itself must first be understood theologically rather than theology being understood historically.

20. Reumann, *Variety and Unity in New Testament Thought*, p. 287.

21. Metzger points to the importance of 'the congruity of a given document with the basic Christian tradition recognized as normative by the Church'. Metzger, *The Canon of the New Testament*, p. 251.

belonging to a totality, we must call upon salvation history as a hermeneutical key, for it is the factor binding all the biblical text together.[22]

It appears that the Gospel is itself the 'canon' by which the canonical books were measured and recognized: 'The Christian church responded to this literature as the authoritative word of God, and it remains existentially committed to an inquiry into its inner unity because of its confession of the one gospel of Jesus Christ.'[23] This means that only the Gospel can provide the perspective from which to interpret Scripture's theological unity. Consequently, this also applies to any assessments of the internal dialectics within the canon. For this reason, it is necessary to sketch a proper foundation of the relationship between the Gospel and the Canon. What is meant, though, by 'the Gospel'?

The Gospel usually refers to the proclamation of the 'good news' of Jesus Christ, the message preached and taught by the first apostles, by which the early Church was gathered. It is this same Gospel which we may say is anticipated in the revelation of the Old Testament, unifying the two testaments. As Barth says, New Testament revelation serves to 'bring fully to light what revelation in the Old Testament had always brought to light only in the form of a pointer'.[24] Of course, there are many potential theological interpretations of the Gospel's primary 'content'. Attempting to define 'the Gospel' itself can lead into a mire of caveats. For the purposes of this particular attempt at 'theologizing' canonicity, the Gospel can be broadly defined as the message of salvation for sinful humanity to be ultimately reconciled to God through the perfect life, atoning death and victorious resurrection of Jesus Christ. Such a summative formulation attaches the Gospel to an ongoing proclaimed message in which the Church was formed and continued to function, pertaining to 'the appearing of our Saviour Christ Jesus, who abolished death and brought life and immortality to light *through the gospel*' (2Tim. 1:10).[25] It is this Gospel message from which the Scriptural texts emanated and through which they were attested in the early recognition of a latent canon of

---

22. Daniel P. Fuller, 'Biblical Theology and the Analogy of Faith', in Robert A. Guelich (ed.), *Unity and Diversity in New Testament Theology: Essays in Honor of George E. Ladd* (Grand Rapids: Eerdmans, 1978), pp. 195–213 [208].

23. Brevard S. Childs, *Biblical Theology of the Old and New Testaments: Theological Reflection on the Christian Bible* (Minneapolis: Fortress Press, 1993), p. 8.

24. Barth, *CD* I/1, p. 320.

25. Emphasis added. Although there are specific functions of *how* the Gospel is 'Good News' (forgiveness of sins, Christ's power over death, hope of eternal reconciliation, restoration of the kingdom of God, etc.), these are not the primary issues here in defining how this message shaped biblical-theological canonicity. This is because not all canonical texts contain overt connections to *all* of the Gospel's implications; rather, the texts of the proto-canon 'rang true' with the preached message that humanity is reconciled to God through Jesus Christ. It is too large a question to discuss here the 'definitive' or 'exclusive' content of the Gospel, but it is helpful to note that Paul saw the basic message of Christ's

texts. It was, after all, the preaching of the Word that gathered the Church, rather than an agreement over canonical books: 'The earliest Christians did not trouble themselves about criteria of canonicity; they would not have readily understood the expression.'[26] Rather, they would have understood the Gospel that bound them together as the Church – not just in one context but throughout 'the whole world' (Col. 1:5–6) – to which these 'new' Scriptural texts attested. Later 'criteria' in the officializing of canonization reflected back upon the theological moves of the Church to use various Scriptural texts in their daily life and worship, coalescing with this Gospel they had received.[27]

On this, Luther and Calvin were in agreement that the unity of the Scriptural texts was dependent upon whether 'they all together preach and stress Christ',[28] that 'if [the Scripture] shows forth Christ, it is the word of life.'[29] To 'show Christ' was to hearken back to the proclaimed Gospel of the early Church in which the differing texts of the New Testament originated. Again, we can see that it is not the texts that led to the canonization of the Gospel, but the Gospel that led to the *latent* canonization of the texts. Bruce M. Metzger relates this widespread acceptance of a latent canon among the churches of various widespread cultures as being of particular significance in the 'remarkable' collation of New Testament unity.[30] Barth also hints at the notion of a latent canon that was accepted through general textual recognition long before the canon was officialized:

> For the obvious core of the history of the Canon is this, that within the various churches, and with all kinds of vacillations, particular parts of the oldest tradition have gradually been distinguished and set apart from others...a process which proper and formal canonisation by synodic resolutions and the like could only subsequently confirm. At some time and in some measure...these very writings, by the very fact that they were canonical, saw to it that they in particular were later recognised and proclaimed to be canonical.[31]

sin-atoning death, burial and resurrection 'in accordance with the scriptures' as being 'of first importance' (1Cor. 15:3–4). Such tenets are 'primary' not only for one specific context but for all Christians; this is the basic message Paul had himself 'also received' (1Cor. 15:3) and it remains at least *indicative* for our basic grasp of the message which unified both Church and canon.

26. F. F. Bruce, *The Canon of Scripture* (Downers Grove: IVP, 1988), p. 255.

27. It should also be recognized that such 'moves' were not *entirely* ecclesial in their agency but may also be seen as part of the 'God-breathed' process of inspiration in recognizing the kerygmatic context of the texts, thus refusing to separate the textual content of the Gospel from the revelatory activity of the Spirit (cf. 1Thess. 1:5).

28. Martin Luther, *Luther's Works*, in 55 vols., vol. 6, ed. Jaroslav J. Pelikan and Helmut T. Lehmann (Philadelphia and St. Louis: Concordia Publishing House, 1955–1986), p. 478.

29. Calvin, *Institutes*, vol. 1, p. 95.

30. Metzger, *The Canon of the New Testament*, p. 254.

31. Barth, *CD* 1/2, p. 475.

The canonical texts were appointed *as* canonical and thus became recognizable as such through their ongoing proclamation. Again we see the pervasive functionality of Scripture as useful in the life of the Church because it corresponded with the proclaimed Gospel the early Church had received. This Gospel permeated this evolutionary process towards a recognizably 'fixed' canon:

> Christianity did not begin as a scriptural religion. The faith of the earliest Christians was evoked by and focused on a person, Jesus of Nazareth, and he was apprehended not in written texts but in the preaching about him as the crucified and risen Messiah, and in the charismatic life of the Christian community.[32]

Even if it might be a category error to claim that Christianity was not originally 'scriptural' (not least because the earliest Christians' apprehension of the person of Christ was mediated through his fulfilment of Old Testament revelation), the significance of the Church's earliest proclamation does highlight the distinctly kerygmatic foundations of New Testament canonicity. We have seen, so far, that the reception and acceptance of canonicity exhibits definitive parameters of theological unity *in* the Bible from which a preacher might preach authoritatively *from* the Bible. This assumes that the Bible does indeed demonstrate an appropriate kind of theological unity, not in the correlation of each text to a strictly repetitive uniformity but in the centrality of the textually pervasive Gospel message.

iv. *The Content of the* Kerygma

The connection between early Church preaching and canonical formation provides a helpful foundation from which to map the relationship of canonicity to contemporary preaching, which underpins our engagement with biblical dialectics. The relationship between proclamation and canon, however, is complex: how is first-century proclamation meant to inform present-day proclamation?

a. *Encounter as* Kerygma.

In the modern biblical-theological tradition, the importance of 'proclamation' to Scripture's theological unity has been particularly emphasized by Rudolf Bultmann. His distinct focus upon the kerygmatic force of theology has been vastly influential in the interplay between different theological and historical schools of thought. For Bultmann, the concrete situation of proclamation is the primary factor in the reading and preaching of Scripture. The Bible is seen as both divine *address* and divine *encounter*: 'The Bible is transmitted through the church as a word addressing us.'[33] It is impossible, for Bultmann, to locate any inherent unity of the New Testament canon in a merely objective sense, since it can be encountered

32. Harry H. Gamble, *The New Testament Canon: Its Making and Meaning* (Philadelphia: Fortress Press, 1985), p. 57.
33. Rudolf Bultmann, *Jesus Christ and Mythology* (New York: Scribner, 1958), pp. 78–9.

only through the present-day ongoing *kerygma* in which it was birthed and continues to 'live'. Bultmann locates this *kerygma* specifically within the early Church preaching of the message of salvation, which he unpacks through various kerygmatic passages from the New Testament: 'Salvation has become available through preaching, the "word of truth," the "Gospel" (Col. 1:5; Eph. 1:13)…consequently, this "word" of preaching must be kept alive in the Church (Col. 3:16).'[34] The task of proclaiming the Gospel, then, becomes vital in the ongoing use of the Bible in the Church and, indeed, for ongoing ecclesial formation: '[The pastoral epistles] know the importance of the Gospel as the proclaimed word by which salvation was and continues to be revealed and know what importance preaching has for the Church.'[35] The primacy of the task of preaching in canonical formation *and* ongoing prophetic witness is demonstrably important for Bultmann.

Yet in Bultmann's account there is an observable overstatement of subjectivity regarding what the Gospel actually is: 'The statements of kerygma are not universal truths but are personal address in a concrete situation.'[36] For Bultmann, the *kerygma* has no fixed content beyond the individual's existential encounter with the preached Word. The content of this encounter may differ vastly from the *kerygma* preached in the early Church itself, which serves as more of a foundation of the *kerygma* than a depository of its primal content. If the Gospel itself is dependent upon a plethora of oscillating forms and receptions in the ever-unfolding kerygmatic encounter of proclamation, this renders the task of locating Scripture's clarity within 'the Gospel' extremely problematic. In making this subjective move, it seems that Bultmann's overall concern is to avoid an inappropriately speculative theology ('the isolated reflection of thought').[37] Bultmann wants to emphasize the event of proclamation itself over the notion of its theological content. His countermove is to focus upon the primacy of the existential. However important this corrective might be, Bultmann overemphasizes the particularity of the contextual reception of the Gospel above its ever-present elements. Bultmann is right, however, to focus upon the formation of the canon as emanating from the 'concrete situation' of the divine address to believers in a particular context. This is significant and – as we have seen – plays a key role in illustrating the historical process towards latent kerygmatic canonization. Yet we can still say there is a universal truth to this *kerygma* even if it may be existentially received and collated in diverse settings and with diverse emphases.

b. *Encounter and* Kerygma.
Gerhard Ebeling, Bultmann's student, responded to his mentor's position with a distinction between two separate forms of *kerygma*: 1. the *kerygma* of history, and 2. the *kerygma* of event. The *kerygma* of history is that which was proclaimed

34. Rudolf Bultmann, *Theology of the New Testament*, vol. 2, trans. Kendrick Grobel (London: SCM, 1955), p. 141.
35. Bultmann, *Theology of the New Testament*, p. 185.
36. Ibid., p. 240.
37. Ibid., p. 241.

in the texts of the New Testament and formed the basic content of the historical proclamation, whereas the *kerygma* of event connotes the essence of proclamation as divine 'address'.[38] This second notion of *kerygma* is Bultmann's primary concern, the ongoing encounter with the living Word of God.[39] But more helpful to the present discussion is the first notion, the historical *kerygma*, particularly in its role in shaping New Testament theological unity. Ebeling is keen to maintain, however, that when we speak of this form of proclamation, it is not just 'the mere repetition of kerygmatic formulae'.[40] He wants to avoid the idea that the 'form' of the early Church's proclamation, in all its linguistic expressions and contextual nuances, *is* the *kerygma*. Rather, he wants to show that *kerygma* is that which is proclaimed *now*, beyond the trappings of exclusive first-century categories. Bultmann would also assert this, of course, but Ebeling differs by maintaining that those earliest kerygmatic expressions continue to remain essential to the content of the *kerygma* today even if it is not bound by them through monotonous formal repetition.

This understanding of the *kerygma* allows for a dialectical diversity of expression in the Gospel while retaining a central emphasis: 'The kerygma does indeed allow, as the diversity of the New Testament well shows, a great variety in the different Christological forms in which it is presented.'[41] Ebeling goes on to extend this to say that such diversity is essential to the nature of the *kerygma* because of the need for a 'present-day' kerygmatic encounter throughout all generations spanning multifarious contexts: '[The *kerygma*] not only allows this [diversity], but it is necessary that, since it is to be proclaimed throughout history, it should be expressed with the help of differing Christologies.'[42] There are indeed clusters of varied kerygmatic expression in the New Testament, each of which comprises facets of the *kerygma*, that it might be proclaimed in various situations and cultural climates, rather than through one narrow form. However, Ebeling provides the caveat that these different expressions are not without necessary parameters and key identifiers, tied explicitly to Jesus Christ:

> Even if one can speak of Christology as being variable in its form, it still seems to be a mark of the constant of the self-understanding of faith, that the faith is faith in Jesus Christ…directed to the Christological kerygma, and which accepts this kerygma as its own confession.[43]

---

38. Gerhard Ebeling, *Theology and Proclamation: A Discussion with Rudolf Bultmann*, trans. John Riches (London: Collins, 1966), pp. 40–1.

39. This 'existential' emphasis, though partially critiqued here, remains essential to a robust theology of proclamation, and will be further applied later via Brunner and Barth (see IV.4).

40. Ebeling, *Theology and Proclamation*, p. 47.

41. Ibid.

42. Ibid.

43. Ibid., p. 48.

This provides a platform which allows the force of Bultmann's kerygmatic emphasis without isolating early Church kerygmatic content from present-day proclamation.

c. *Kerygmatic Norm.*

C. H. Dodd's account of *kerygma* was also significantly different when compared to Bultmann's. Dodd's definition of *kerygma* was based not on the 'event' of preaching but on its content: 'a proclamation of the facts of the death and resurrection of Christ in an eschatological setting which gives significance to the facts'.[44] Where, for Bultmann, 'preaching' is the *kerygma*, Dodd asserts that Scripture is the *kerygma*, precisely because it contains that which *was* proclaimed in the first-century apostolic period. If Scripture's unity is to be founded in the Gospel, it must be seen not only as hearkening back to a 'concept' of proclamation, but to a defined 'content'. For Dodd, it is the unity of Gospel content that creates both latent and 'official' canonicity.

As noted earlier, the idea of 'criteria of canonicity' as conceived in later Church councils was not a particular concern in the earliest ecclesial traditions. However, this does not mean that there was no understanding or constitution of 'authoritative' texts which had congruence with the preached Word: 'The "faithful sayings" in the Pastorals, though not representing in any sense a "canon," betray an instinct for classification into true or false'.[45] What was thought to be 'true' teaching, then, as opposed to 'false' teaching, was that which could be aligned with what had already been received in the proclaimed testimony of the existent Church, through the *kerygma*: 'in accordance with the gospel of the glory of the blessed God with which I have been entrusted' (1Tim. 1:11). Indeed, the pastoral epistles offer an example of this proclaimed Gospel as being the centre around which 'sound doctrine' (Titus 1:9; 2:1) or 'sound words' (1Tim. 6:3; 2Tim. 1:13) were taught: 'Remember Jesus Christ, risen from the dead, the offspring of David, as preached in my gospel' (2Tim. 2:8). This notion of 'soundness' in one's message or teaching (which we see explicitly and repeatedly throughout the epistles) can often be abused by interpreters to qualify whichever perspective they happen to prefer. Yet it seems clear that where Paul uses the concept of 'soundness' here he is grounding it upon his apostolic authority, by which he can highlight those teachings or 'words' which *do* accord with the apostolic Gospel; indeed, as C. F. D. Moule notes: 'The sense of responsibility for receiving, preserving, and handing on the authentic Christian Gospel is strikingly strong throughout the epistles'.[46] This is the same 'criterion' by which New Testament Scripture (as the authoritative basis for such doctrine) would later be canonized and therefore be seen as theologically unified. There was 'a commonly recognised norm of Christian confession forming itself on the basis

---

44. C. H. Dodd, *The Apostolic Preaching and its Developments* (London: Hodder & Stoughton, 1936), p. 18.

45. Metzger, *The Canon of the New Testament*, p. 252.

46. C. F. D. Moule, *The Birth of the New Testament* (London: A & C Black, 1981), p. 232.

of the apostolic *kerygma*'.[47] This, of course, presupposes that it is indeed possible to define the parameters of this *kerygma*.

d. *Kerygmatic Variety.*

It is also important to recognize that the texts which eventually came to comprise the New Testament are consistent in their message not because they teach the 'same' message in every sense but, primarily, because they 'ring true' alongside the content of the Gospel message; as Barth says of Scripture:

> It is true by being true. It does not lie behind us but before us. Thus and only thus can we refer to it as to the decision against the relative validity and in favour of the absolute validity of the Bible as the Word of God, as the authentic and supreme criterion of Church proclamation.[48]

Where the aforementioned pastoral epistles demonstrate this 'trueness' with explicit references to 'the gospel' or the work of Christ, other 'sound' texts articulate different aspects of the message, or act as supplementary exhortations to Christian living which may be harmonized with it. An example of this could be seen in Paul's advice to the Colossians regarding evangelism: 'Walk in wisdom towards the outsider, making the best use of the time. Let your speech always be gracious, seasoned with salt, that you may know how you ought to answer each person' (Col. 4:5–6). Such 'covert' connections to the Gospel can be illuminated when juxtaposed with clear summative affirmations of the basic content of the Gospel in other texts, such as: 'The saying is trustworthy and deserving of full acceptance, that Christ Jesus came into the world to save sinners' (1 Tim. 1:15). This is a clear expression of one key function of the Gospel, which shows an element of its substantial core: salvation from sin. This core is the proclaimed testimony of Jesus Christ's death and resurrection.

Identifying the Gospel within such Christological parameters stops the *kerygma* from becoming simply *any* kind of proclamation which may fluctuate from generation to generation. This has often been seen as the danger within Bultmann's position. Again, Moule is helpful here: 'The criterion of faithfulness to the apostolic *kerygma* did in fact admit within the canon only those writings which kept sufficiently close to the Christ-event to achieve this coherence.'[49] The *kerygma* (and, in turn, canonicity) is tied to an explicit focus upon Jesus Christ and who he is *for* humanity.

This does not mean, of course, that all texts followed the very same emphatic expression of the Gospel message in order to be considered 'sound'. It is clear that the proclaimed Gospel had a number of facets of expression alongside the foundational tenets. We see different writers focusing on different aspects of the message. Peter, for example, focuses upon resurrection and eschatological blessing: 'he has caused

47. Ibid., p. 206.
48. Barth, *CD* I/1, p. 265.
49. Moule, *Birth of the New Testament*, p. 217.

us to be born again to a living hope through the resurrection of Jesus Christ from the dead, to an inheritance that is imperishable, undefiled, and unfading, kept in heaven for you' (1Pet. 1:3–4). This is a different kerygmatic expression from Paul's emphasis upon grace in the conquest of sin: 'In him we have redemption through his blood, the forgiveness of our trespasses, according to the riches of his grace, which he lavished upon us' (Eph. 1:7–8). Again, this contrasts with John's emphasis upon the triumph of divine revelation: 'This is the message we have heard from him and declare to you: God is light; in him there is no darkness at all' (1John 1:5). Such texts are united as being summative statements about the Gospel message despite their vastly differing emphases. These texts were accepted both in early ecclesial contexts *and* later councils as being in 'sound' accordance with the proclaimed message of Jesus Christ:

> Any estimate of Jesus which did not acknowledge his historical existence and his real death would be out; so would any which did not acknowledge the transcendent aliveness of Jesus and the continuity between the transcendent Lord and Jesus of Nazareth, and the decisiveness of his fulfilment of God's plan of salvation as Christians read it out of the Scriptures of the Old Testament.[50]

This is especially relevant for understanding the *kerygma* since it is the proclamation of not only *who* Jesus is, but who he is *for* the Church in particular. This is what makes such proclamation 'good news' for the Church.

e. Kerygma *and* Didachē.

We have seen that the plurivocal expression of the univocal Gospel message provides a hermeneutical key for intertextual Scriptural unity. These different texts and expressions point to the same message. Yet one of the keys to the problem of dialectics in Scripture relates to those texts which do *not* appear to contain this overtly kerygmatic element. These more didactic texts are generally seen as comprising a tenet of the Gospel's 'application'. Moule speaks of a 'merged *kerygma-and-didachē*'[51] in which the proclamation of the Gospel fed into the catechetical instruction and teaching of the Christian life. Hence, even the ecclesial instructions of the epistles are founded in and referential to the *kerygma* out of which the New Testament *didachē* material emanates. The teachings of the New Testament for the Church remain utterly dependent upon the Gospel in order to function as genuine *didachē* of the *kerygma*, since this is what gives the *didachē* its identity and functional content. What may be seen in those overtly didactic texts is an underlying assumption of the Gospel, even if the Gospel is not 'proclaimed' as such within the confines of the text itself: '[Given that] the congregation, by definition, knew and had accepted the *kerygma*, the speaker is more likely to have devoted himself to drawing out its ethical consequences.'[52] The *didachē*, then, could be seen as

---

50. Ibid., p. 206.
51. Ibid., p. 186.
52. Ibid., p. 41.

taking the form of the instructional homily which succeeds the *kerygma*. Again, this pattern is always a necessary supplementary aspect of the Gospel: 'The homily would most naturally follow the line of exhortation to the congregation to *become* what, thanks to the Gospel-proclamation, they essentially *were*.'[53] When configuring New Testament canonicity, then, these more covertly kerygmatic texts become essential to the full expression of the Gospel precisely by deviating from the tone and content of the overtly kerygmatic texts.

This caveat, however, does not abolish the dialectical problems that remain between some of these texts, but it lends flexibility to the idea that the proclaimed Gospel provides the focal point for New Testament theological unity. Such flexibility was not always seen in some of the Reformers' approaches to New Testament diversity, particularly Luther's conception of the (didactic) Epistle of James. Yet the Reformers do uphold this connection of Scripture's unity to the Gospel, even if it led Luther to a certain hyperbole regarding these 'non-Gospel' texts, as will be seen. Before we turn to the Reformers, however, we will observe briefly the vital connection between canonicity and Scriptural 'clarity.' Both concepts together form the basis upon which the preacher may preach and, subsequently, the responsible basis from which we might approach biblical dialectics.

v. *The Relationship between Canonicity and Clarity*

It has been seen that the historical decisions to include or exclude particular texts from the canon either informally (*regula fidei* in the early Church) or formally (later Church councils) exemplify the theological reality that these texts were unified precisely because their content was in accordance with the Gospel's unifying message. Despite the various historical criteria for canonicity, the Gospel can be seen as a primary 'yardstick' by which Scripture can be ascertained. The very notion of a 'canon' immediately implies a kind of unity by the very fact that some texts were included and others excluded. To speak of a 'unified' canon, however, does not necessarily imply a 'clear' canon. The function of canonicity merely outlines the boundaries of theological unity and diversity, without requiring any sense of how such theological content might be *perceived*. Evidently, these are two different concepts: canonicity suggests that the individual books of the Bible belong together, that they are theologically related because of their relationship to a primary message; clarity, however, states that this message is a *lucid* message, demonstrably comprehensible and ascertainable from the individual texts within the canon. It is evident, then, that canonicity and clarity are both related to the Gospel message: canonicity plays the precursory role in the identification of theological unity *between* the biblical texts, whereas clarity demonstrates the explicitness of that unity *from* the unified biblical text(s).

The same foundation for the canonicity of Scripture (the proclaimed Gospel) is also used by the Reformers to argue for the clarity of Scripture. The reason these two concepts are relevant to the problem of dialectic and preaching is that they are

53. Ibid.

both challenged by the existence of dialectics within Scripture. A unified canon is challenged by inherent dialectics within its boundaries because canonicity itself rests upon a unity which some dialectics or paradoxes seem to undermine. So too with the clarity of Scripture: if the meanings of individual texts are ascertainable on the *basis* of a 'Gospel hermeneutic', then an incongruity between two texts which appear to teach different things may become deeply problematic, whereby the meaning of any one text could become *un*clear because its anchoring in a singularly clear message has become questionable.

Irreconcilable theological content within Scripture is a problem for both canonicity and clarity, and both remain foundational for preaching. As will be seen, the 'clarity' of Scripture becomes a more concrete issue for the preacher than for 'canonicity' because it relates to whether or not these texts can be *preached* with interpretative authority (rather than simply whether or not these texts belong together, formally or conceptually). Having now sketched the relationship between canonicity and clarity in the scope of the broader problem of dialectic, we will proceed to the Reformers' accounts of the clarity of Scripture.

3. *The Clarity of Scripture as Dialectical Precursor*

It has been asserted that expository preaching rests upon the content of Scripture for its primary sermonic content. Challenges to the way in which this sermonic content is construed involve not only whether this content holds together as a theologically unified collection, but whether or not it is even possible to speak *from* the Bible with definitive clarity. Are these texts interpretable for use in the pulpit, or do they remain ambiguous? And if there are indeed remnants of ambiguity, how does this affect the way a preacher might *proclaim* these biblical texts? It is this problem that led to the Reformers' need for theological *clarity* regarding the clarity of Scripture: 'Holy Scripture is an ancient book, a very large book with many perplexing passages. How sense is to be made out of individual passages and the Holy Scriptures as a whole is the problem of the clarity of scripture.'[54] It will be argued here that, prior to our dialectical engagement with Scripture, the primary task is to emphasize a *clear* Bible *from which* we can speak of biblical dialectics, because it is only upon this basis that dialectical tensions can have any meaning. If Scripture is *only* dialectical (rather than clear *and* dialectical), the question of dialectic as a 'problem' for preaching becomes irrelevant because there would be no basis upon which to chasten or govern any apparently contradictory emphases.

i. *The Reformation Emphasis*

We focus here upon the Reformation accounts of the clarity of Scripture not only because of the extent to which the Reformation revolved around debates over

---

54. Bernard Ramm, *Protestant Biblical Interpretation* (Grand Rapids: Baker Book House, 1970), pp. 97–8.

the nature and interpretation of Scripture,[55] but also because of the significance of preaching within such debates. It was, in one sense, the task of preaching that led to the Reformers' urgency over the importance of Scriptural clarity. The proclamation of the Word was a primary Reformation activity, as is often noted: '[Calvin] understood the delivery of sermons as among his most important duties;'[56] 'Luther was first and foremost a preacher.'[57] It was the Word *proclaimed* rather than the Word *written* which took precedence (although one would not want to divorce the two, as such). Such preaching was heavily reliant upon the assumption of the clarity of Scripture, since Scripture's clarity was the very reason it could be expounded before the congregation. The Reformers, of course, did not believe that Scriptural clarity entailed a rejection of the activities of interpretation and exposition:

> There have been debased versions of the doctrine of the clarity of Scripture which confuse *claritas* with immediacy and therefore think of interpretation as a curse from which we have to be redeemed. But neither the Reformers nor the Protestant dogmaticians construe clarity in that way; nor do they fail to emphasize that clarity does not disqualify the activities of interpretation.[58]

The articulation of the clarity of Scripture, then, initiates a call towards the proper ordering of how the preacher conceives of Scripture as an interpretable possibility in order to comprehend and – most importantly – to *preach* its content.

It is important to see the Reformers' concern not only from the context of the ongoing necessity of regular biblical preaching but from the wider Reformation agenda for the restoration of the Gospel message to the Church: '[*sola Scriptura's*]

---

55. Such debates were not only driven by confrontations with ecclesiastical authority, but more specifically a transition from the Medieval inheritance of Scriptural exposition. Ocker, however, has argued that this movement was less revolutionary than is often seen. See Christopher Ocker, *Biblical Poetics Before Humanism and Reformation* (Cambridge: Cambridge University Press, 2008), pp. 184–219. The Reformers were certainly not ignorant of their Medieval exegetical forebears but it is not inappropriate to say there was indeed a genuine exegetical revolution in the Reformation, catalysed especially by the Wittenberg circle, consisting not in bringing the Bible *to* the Church as such, but in distinguishing its unique authority from other aspects of ecclesial worship.

56. Dawn DeVries, 'Calvin's preaching', in Donald K. McKim (ed.), *The Cambridge Companion to John Calvin* (Cambridge: Cambridge University Press, 2004), pp. 106–24 [106].

57. A. Skevington Wood, *Captive to the Word: Martin Luther, Doctor of Sacred Scripture* (Exeter: The Paternoster Press, 1969), p. 86.

58. John Webster, 'On the Clarity of Holy Scripture', in *Confessing God: Essays in Christian Dogmatics* II (London: T & T Clark, 2005), pp. 33–67 [61]. See also, Heppe: 'The perspicuity of Scripture does not exclude its need for exposition.' Heinrich Heppe, *Reformed Dogmatics*, trans. G. T. Thomson (Eugene: Wipf and Stock, 2007), p. 33.

purpose was to show the church that it needed to turn toward the gospel of Scripture itself again and again in the midst of all human traditions.'[59] The Reformation account of *sola Scriptura* provides the platform within which clarity (or 'perspicuity') resides; this, in turn, is linked to the clarity of the Gospel message *within* canonical Scripture: 'The Reformation doctrine of perspicuity did not aim at the clarity of the words as such, but at the message, the content of Scripture.'[60] The following account of the clarity of Scripture serves as the prolegomena for engaging with Scriptural dialectic in tension *with* Scriptural clarity. This tension appears to be problematic to the task of clear and authoritative preaching from individual biblical texts, and we will see that the Reformers offer an important starting point *from which* the preacher may engage with canonical dialectical tensions. This Reformation emphasis urges that preaching must engage primarily with that which is clear before that which is *unclear*. Ignoring this necessary starting point *prior* to engaging in biblical dialectics undermines the task of challenging (and being challenged by) these dialectics in preaching. We will see that dialectic itself cannot be prioritized ahead of that which has been clearly revealed. This is because such revelation is not esoteric; it contains the vital *purpose* of proclamation within it.

ii. *Distinctive Foci*

Each of the key Reformers, although united in their connection between Scriptural clarity and the Gospel, contributes distinctive emphases to the conception of how such clarity functions.

a. *Luther: Clarity as Priority.*

Luther's belief in the clarity of Scripture was a primary driving-force in the Reformation task of restoring Scripture to the hands of the congregation: 'No greater mischief can happen to a Christian people, than to have God's Word taken from them, or falsified, so that they no longer have it pure and clear.'[61] For Luther, the ecclesial control of Scriptural interpretation had muted Scripture's voice and meaning, not only regarding falsifications but also a general overemphasis upon Scriptural ambiguities, which had become exaggerated to the point of absurdity: 'Who will maintain that the town fountain does not stand in the light because the people down some alley cannot see it, while everyone in the square can see it?'[62] In contrast, Luther sought to redress this imbalance and called for the need to emphasize the Bible's overwhelming clarity and unity before emphasizing its more ambiguous statements or diverse emphases. His primary reasoning for this is that the Gospel's clarity points us to Scripture's clarity.

59. G. C. Berkouwer, *Holy Scripture* (Grand Rapids: Eerdmans, 1975), p. 313.

60. Ibid., p. 274.

61. Martin Luther, *Table Talk*, trans. William Hazlitt (Grand Rapids: Christian Ethereal Classics Library, 2004), p. 18.

62. Martin Luther, *The Bondage of the Will*, trans. J. I. Packer and O. R. Johnston (Grand Rapids: Fleming H. Revell, 1997), p. 72.

The importance of Gospel-derived clarity, for Luther, is also evident in his oft-misunderstood approach to canonicity. Despite his notorious views regarding a small number of canonical books (most famously, James), it can be said that Luther 'treated Scripture as a homogenous whole'.[63] His views on peripheral canonical books are often viewed out of context from his overall view of the Bible's unified theological message:

> Every theological student knows that Luther dismissed [James] as an epistle of straw. What is not so generally realized is that Luther wrote differently on other occasions about James, and that if the actual context of the offending reference is consulted a rather different construction is placed upon his observation.[64]

Luther's 'straw' reference occurs only in pre-1537 editions of his *Preface to the New Testament*, where Luther is attempting to distinguish 'the true and noblest books of the New Testament'.[65] The 'true and noblest' are those most important for a new believer to know all they need regarding the Gospel. It is on this note that Luther says: 'St. James's epistle is really an epistle of straw, compared to these others, for it has nothing of the nature of the gospel about it.'[66] Yet it is important to note that Luther nonetheless *included* James (and other 'borderline' books) within his translation of the New Testament. For Luther, such 'Gospel-lacking' books remained canonical.

We might see these more 'questionable' books as having something of a covert witness to the Gospel rather than an overt proclamation (as with the aforementioned *kerygma-didachē* distinction). Suffice to say, this opinion of Luther's did not create a formal 'canon within the canon' as is often thought, even if an informal hierarchy is evident (the 'noblest' books being those which display *overt* Gospel content). It must be remembered, as Wood notes: 'When Luther spoke about "all Scripture" he intended…to indicate all canonical Scripture. He had his own opinions about [some books] but he did not quarrel with others who accepted them.'[67] It might be seen, then, that Luther's views on canonicity, though peculiar and systematically obscure, do not contradict his affirmations of the clarity and unity of Scripture. We ought to critique his attitude to James not because it deviates from orthodox canonicity, but because it refuses to be open to the functional fullness of canonicity in the practice of preaching. James may be no-less-essential to the Gospel message if allowed to function as an instructive and corrective text where necessary.[68] With Luther's near-perpetual emphasis upon justification by faith alone, this corrective was not deemed to be necessary. Yet it should be maintained that, for Luther, those books which did not coalesce as neatly with the 'nature of the Gospel' (as

63. Skevington Wood, *Captive to the Word*, p. 149.

64. Ibid., p. 155.

65. Luther, *Luther's Works* 35, p. 361.

66. Ibid., p. 362.

67. Skevington Wood, *Captive to the Word*, p. 158.

68. See Kierkegaard's 'correction' of Lutheran justification (III.5.iii).

he would have preferred) were still included in the canon and read in light of the accompanying Gospel-centred texts. Even here, we see the same principle of Scriptural 'light' (Gospel clarity) dictating the approach to Scriptural 'darkness' (dialectical ambiguity).

Luther's account of canonicity, then, is inseparable from his view of Scripture's clarity, even with the aforementioned tensions. For Luther, the Bible is sufficiently 'clear' to the extent that he would never counsel a believer to interpret it without seeing its overall theological narrative: 'Read the Scriptures in order from beginning to end so as to get the substance of the story in your mind.'[69] Luther not only saw Scripture through this narratival lens, but saw that the 'substance of the story' is itself the Gospel and person of Jesus Christ: 'The view that Holy Scripture interprets itself, but also that Christ is its decisive content, is the presupposition underlying Luther's conviction that Scripture is "clear." '[70] The content of the Gospel was seen in a variety of ways through different texts, yet always through this prevailing lens of Jesus Christ as the content of this good news. The Gospel is the pattern in which the Bible finds its unity, and hence, its clarity.

For Luther, because the Bible, as a whole, portrayed the Gospel message throughout, there had to be a necessary consistency to this narrative: 'Holy Scripture is in excellent agreement with itself and is uniformly consistent everywhere.'[71] Such statements can easily be misunderstood as displaying a naïve ignorance towards the simultaneous ambiguities within Scripture. Luther was, of course, aware of this counterpoint: 'His stress on the oneness of Scripture did not lead him to ignore its obvious divergences.'[72] However, for Luther, the *urgent* need was to 'set aside the obscure and cling to the clear'.[73] This was as much a pastoral urge as a theological one, highlighting the importance of clarity *over* ambiguity. But this was not an entirely contextual emphasis since his view stemmed primarily from a reading of Scripture that saw the Gospel as its primary content and thus, the reception of the Gospel as the first point of clarity: 'The Scriptures are common to all and are clear enough in respect to what is necessary for salvation.'[74]

However, in the same sentence, Luther also adds that the Scriptures 'are also obscure enough for inquiring minds'.[75] Scriptural obscurity is not in competition with clarity, but the order between them becomes apparent:

---

69. Martin Luther, 'To George Spalatin. January 18, 1518', in Theodore G. Tappert (ed.), *Luther: Letters of Spiritual Counsel* (The Library of Christian Classics, Volume XVIII) (London: SCM, 1953), p. 112.

70. Bernhard Lohse, *Martin Luther's Theology: Its Historical and Systematic Development*, trans. Roy A. Harrisville (Edinburgh: T&T Clark, 1999), p. 193.

71. Luther, *Luther's Works* 3, p. 247.

72. Skevington Wood, *Captive to the Word*, p. 152.

73. Luther, *Luther's Works* 32, p. 217.

74. Ibid.

75. Ibid.

> I certainly grant that many passages in the Scriptures are obscure and hard to elucidate, but that is due, not to the exalted nature of their subject, but to our own linguistic and grammatical ignorance; and it does not in any way promote our knowing all the contents of Scripture.[76]

Even without access to the meanings of these obscurities, for Luther there is an overwhelming amount of clarified content which must be received *first*, leaving obscurity to those 'enquiring minds'. To relegate Scripture's interpretability to the exclusively 'enquiring mind' then, was seen by Luther as a gross mishandling of the overwhelmingly clear message of Scripture. The necessity of clarity is overstressed precisely because it must be the first port of call for the interpreter and preacher of Scripture. To become enraptured in the Bible's unclarity *before* grasping the significance of its clarity would misrepresent it and ultimately paralyse the preaching task.

Scriptural ambiguities, then, were not discounted but seen in light of Scripture's principal clarity, where they take on a different meaning, turning upon the fallible interpreter: '[For Luther] the failure to understand the Scripture clearly is not due to an imperspicuous Scripture, but rather to an imperspicuous understanding of a perspicuous Scripture by finite and sinful humanity'.[77] A symptom of the perpetual emphasis upon Scriptural obscurity is less a problem within the text as a problem within the exegete. With the presupposition that Scripture *is* clear, apparent obscurities can be seen only *through* this clarity:

> For what solemn truth can the Scriptures still be concealing, now that the seals are broken, the stone rolled away from the door of the tomb, and that greatest of all mysteries brought to light – that Christ, God's Son, became man, that God is Three in One, that Christ suffered for us, and will reign for ever? And are not these things known, and sung in our streets?[78]

Even with such a triumphant Gospel emphasis, Luther did not deny the paradoxical expressions through which Scriptural theological truth is conveyed. Some of Luther's detractors could agree with him regarding the prevalence of Gospel clarity, but not in its particular matters of doctrine. Responding to Erasmus' claim that the Bible is obscure on key matters of doctrine, Luther responds: 'Scripture confesses the Trinity of God and the humanity of Christ and there is nothing here of obscurity or ambiguity. But how these things can be, Scripture does not say (as you imagine), nor is it necessary to know'.[79] If God has revealed paradoxical doctrine precisely *as* paradoxical, the ensuing inaccessibility of apprehending the scope of such divine truth is inherently 'revelatory', and remains a *clear* revelation

---

76. Luther, *The Bondage of the Will*, p. 71.

77. Richard Edwards, *Scriptural Perspicuity in the Early English Reformation in Historical Theology* (New York: Peter Lang, 2008), p. 79.

78. Luther, *The Bondage of the Will*, p. 71.

79. Luther, *Luther's Works* 33, p. 28.

even without resolution.[80] This is not equatable with stating the content of such doctrine as 'unclear'. We know, for example, that Jesus is both human and divine without knowing *how*. But we still know, with emphatic clarity, that this paradoxical doctrine is maintained within Holy Scripture and is wholly congruent with the Gospel message. This, for Luther, was the essential difference between obscurity and clarity in Scripture.

b. *Zwingli: Clarity as Recognition.*

Although Luther is known as the catalyst for *sola Scriptura*, Ulrich Zwingli (1484–1532) is thought to have been the first Reformer to emphasize the clarity of Scripture, in particular.[81] In Zwingli's preaching, his close expositions of Scripture served to highlight its inherent unity and clarity:

> By introducing sequential interpretation of the Bible, Zwingli demonstratively placed the Bible in front of the established church traditions. The scriptures no longer merely occurred as citations that were embedded in traditional liturgy whose centre was the administration of the churchly sacraments; instead, they became the primary place to encounter God. Moreover, at the same time, Zwingli's continuous exegesis made it clear that *God's Word* is not composed of selected passages, but from the entire Bible.[82]

Like Luther, Zwingli's pastoral commitment to demonstrating the significance of Scriptural clarity is something of a polemical necessity in his context (though not *merely* contextual, of course). Zwingli felt that the clarity of Scripture ought to be reclaimed in his own day precisely because it was something inherently true of the Bible that had been subsequently downplayed, or in some cases entirely forgotten.[83]

His famous sermon *Of the Clarity and Certainty of the Word of God* (1522) is his most notable theological engagement with the clarity of Scripture. With regard to the sermon, Opitz notes a common misconception about what Zwingli means by 'clarity': 'What Zwingli has in mind with this clarity is not a rejection of philology. For him, it is much more about the theological dimension of the Bible – about the Bible as the location where God speaks.'[84] For Zwingli, the issue is not the

80. See 'paradox' (II.3).

81. Richard A. Muller, *Post-Reformation Reformed Dogmatics: The Rise and Development of Reformed Orthodoxy, ca. 1520 to ca. 1725, Volume Two: Holy Scripture: The Cognitive Foundation of Theology* (Grand Rapids: Baker Academic, 2003), p. 322.

82. Peter Opitz, 'The Authority of Scripture in the Early Zurich Reformation (1522–1540)', in *Journal of Reformed Theology* 5:3 (2011), pp. 296–309 [298].

83. This was a feature of the Reformation more broadly, reflected in the transformation of church architecture and furnishings to emphasize the increasing centrality of biblical preaching in the service, which had previously been a peripheral (and merely 'optional') aspect of congregational worship. See Robert Whiting, *The Reformation of the English Parish Church* (Cambridge: Cambridge University Press, 2014), pp. 182–93.

84. Opitz, 'Authority of Scripture', p. 301.

comprehension of linguistic etymologies; clarity relates solely to the message of divine address in Scripture. The message that God wants to convey as he speaks through Scripture is not ambiguous or contradictory; it is abundantly clear and trustworthy. As with the other Reformers, Zwingli locates the Gospel as the proper 'context' for the interpretation of Scripture. For him, to engage the particularities of biblical passages without reference to Scripture's overarching message leads to unnecessary obscurities:

> Oh you rascals – you are not instructed or versed in the Gospel, and you pick out verses from it without regard to their context, and wrest them according to your own desire. It is like breaking off a flower from its roots and trying to plant it in a garden. But that is not the way: you must plant it with the roots and the soil in which it is embedded. And similarly we must leave the Word of God its proper nature if its sense is to be the same to all of us.[85]

For Zwingli, the 'proper nature' of the Word of God is that which emanates from the heart of Scripture, the very Gospel which draws people *to* Scripture. It is too simplistic, therefore, to highlight the unclarity of Scripture through the exegesis of isolated comparative texts. Because the Gospel has *caused* Scriptural formation, it cannot be divorced from these Gospel 'roots' at any particular point.

Again, Zwingli's stance could easily appear blindsighted to the more problematic canonical texts. However, Zwingli maintains – like Luther – that a 'dark' passage also provides a clear, revelatory function: 'Even discourse that appears to be veiled can in the end stand in the service of God's revelation, because it prompts people to want to know God's truth.'[86] A revealed obscurity within the framework of Gospel-rooted clarity does not make the entirety of Scripture unclear or contradictory, but the existence of the mysterious elements alongside the clarity propels the believer to faith, inducing further dependence upon God.[87]

For Zwingli, the element of subjective faith in the Word of God becomes essential to the reception of its clarity, and there is even a 'taste'-related aspect to the reception of Scripture's unity:

> Consider a good strong wine. To the healthy it tastes excellent. It makes him merry and strengthens him and warms his blood. But if there is someone who is sick of a disease or fever, he cannot even taste it, let alone drink it, and he marvels that the healthy is able to do so. This is not due to any defect in the wine, but to that of the sickness. So too it is with the Word of God.[88]

---

85. Zwingli, 'Clarity and Certainty', p. 87.
86. Opitz, 'Authority of Scripture', p. 302.
87. See Kierkegaard's emphasis on paradox and faith (II.4.i.b).
88. Zwingli, 'Clarity and Certainty', p. 75.

This is congruent with Luther's emphasis on the inescapability of the exegete's sinful nature and creatureliness, which continually limits our reception of Scriptural clarity. The Bible is presupposed to be clear because of its relation to the Gospel, thus dictating the lens through which apparent disunity is seen. But this lens can be seen only if there is faith in Scripture's clarity, as mediated by the Spirit: 'The Spirit is… for Zwingli, the bridge between biblical narrative and personal experience.'[89] The dialectical situation of textual obscurity is brought about by the creator-creature distinction and the subsequent need for divine illumination by the Spirit. The text alone cannot 'convince' one of its clarity, yet it can nonetheless be spoken of as clear. This is only possible when there is a prerequisite belief in the authority of Scripture in accordance with the internal witness of the Spirit. The dialectic of Word and Spirit is crucial to Zwingli's notion of clarity and unity in the Bible. Paradoxically, we may see that it is possible to speak of Scripture's objective clarity only by nature of subjective faith. But this faith itself emanates *from* the Gospel message of Scripture *through* the witness of the Spirit. Zwingli's account of the Spirit in the recognition of Scripture's clarity was also heavily influential upon Calvin's approach.

c. *Calvin: Clarity as Revelation.*

As a second-generation Reformer, Calvin's doctrine of the clarity of Scripture drew upon that of his predecessors: 'Calvin was able to take up both Zwingli's relational definition of God's Word and Spirit as well as Bullinger's argumentation for the authority of scripture.'[90] Calvin pointed to the self-authenticating (*autopistia*) nature of Scripture, urging against cogent arguments for *why* one ought to believe and accept its unity, clarity and authority. He appealed to the Spirit's work in the believer to bring the recognition of Scripture's clarity to light: 'The Word will not find acceptance in men's hearts before it is sealed by the inward testimony of the Spirit.'[91] This does not mean that Scripture cannot be shown to be clear as such, but that such demonstrable 'clarity' becomes irrelevant if one is not able to recognize it by the Spirit:

> Yet they who strive to build up firm faith in Scripture through disputation are doing things backwards…even if anyone clears God's Sacred Word from man's evil speaking, he will not at once imprint upon their hearts that certainty which piety requires.[92]

Calvin sought not to 'defend' the Bible but merely to proclaim it and trust the internal witness of the Spirit to generate a conception of its authority. This is

89. Opitz, 'Authority of Scripture', p. 302.
90. Ibid., p. 309.
91. Calvin, *Institutes* 1, p. 79.
92. Ibid.

often seen as the unique mark of Calvin's account of Scriptural clarity.[93] Yet even within this notion we find a Zwinglian echo, where the Spirit's witness is linked to the subjective realm of 'taste' rather than the 'external' properties of the text. The text is clear to those for whom it is clear, and it can be shown to be clear only to those who have the ability to savour it: 'Those for whom prophetic doctrine is tasteless ought to be thought of as lacking taste buds.'[94] Similarly to Barth's notion of Scripture being 'true because it is true', Calvin affirms Scripture's ability to make itself clear by virtue of its very being: 'Scripture exhibits fully as clear evidence of its own truth as white and black things do of their colour, or sweet and bitter things do of their taste.'[95] The internal witness of the Spirit is the mode of access to this knowledge of Scripture's truthfulness. This too, we might say, is related to the reception of the Gospel in the believer, by which one is 'sealed' upon conversion: 'In him you also, when you heard the word of truth, the gospel of your salvation, and believed in him, were sealed with the promised Holy Spirit' (Eph 1:13). Word and Spirit, for Calvin, implies the reception of the Gospel followed by the indwelling witness of the Spirit through which one is able to receive Scripture as both clear and unified.

This explicit link to the Gospel message ensures that the notion of 'taste' cannot become *merely* subjective. Like other Reformers before him, Calvin assumed outright that the canonical text was unified by virtue of its reflection of Jesus Christ: 'For we see a number that have turned over the Scripture leaf by leaf and are able to give a good account of it, but, even so, they do not know what is its main thrust, for their aim is not directed at our Lord Jesus Christ.'[96] This 'main thrust' is similar to what Luther called the 'substance of the story' – at all junctures, the direction of Scripture's overarching narrative points to this same Gospel. Calvin's handling of Scripture reflects this presupposition of such unified clarity: 'Calvin does not isolate passages and expound on them. His exegetical work is marked by his emphasis on the unity and harmony of Scripture.'[97] Calvin maintains in both belief and practice that Scripture cannot be read aside from its message. Indeed, Calvin is not a mere doctrinal 'extractor' of Scripture; his sole exegetical aim is to point to Jesus Christ: 'By the exposition of the contents of Scripture [Calvin] wishes to proclaim to his countrymen this living Lord; nothing

93. 'The special contribution of Calvin to the doctrine of Scripture is not so much that he emphasized its self-convincing character – for others had done that before him in different words – but that he explained the acknowledgement of the authority of Scripture through the inner witness of the Holy Spirit.' Henk van den Belt, 'Heinrich Bullinger and Jean Calvin on the Authority of Scripture (1538–1571)', in *Journal of Reformed Theology* 5:3 (2011), pp. 310–24 [324].

94. Calvin, *Institutes* 1, p. 83.

95. Ibid., p. 76.

96. John Calvin, *Sermons on the Epistle to the Ephesians*, trans. Arthur Golding (Edinburgh: Banner of Truth Trust, 1973), p. 423.

97. Edwards, *Scriptural Perspicuity*, p. 88.

more.'[98] This is because Jesus Christ is the centre and thread-line of Scripture, the bearer of Scripture's unity and clarity. Calvin's articulation of the relationship between Word and Spirit is complementary: the believer is drawn closer to Christ *through* the self-authenticated Scripture *via* the internal testimony of the indwelling Spirit.

For Calvin, Scripture is clear because Christ sends the Spirit who illuminates the Word. Thus, it is 'objectively' clear, but this clarity is only accessible subjectively through the work of the Spirit. Consequently, those who trust that Scripture is clear, in practice, find that it *is*: 'Anyone, therefore, who opens his eyes with the obedience of faith shall know by experience that Scripture has not been called *light* in vain.'[99] Calvin's notion of the 'experience' of Scripture's clarity is especially pertinent for the preacher.

iii. *Scriptural Clarity and Expository Preaching*

As noted, it is the act of preaching itself which catalysed the Reformers' conceptions of Scriptural clarity. This task did not sidestep the need for interpretation; rather it suggested the need for it, precisely for the sake of the pulpit. For Calvin, the task of expounding Scripture in its totality was of chief importance: '[Calvin] assumed that his whole theological labour was the exposition of Scripture.'[100] This is clearly evident in his writings: 'One cannot read Calvin's *Institutes* or *Commentaries* without noting his exegetical style and what it reveals of his doctrine of the perspicuity of Scripture.'[101] The clarity of Scripture is the basis for such rigorous exposition; if Scripture is indeed clear, interpretation becomes the task of bringing the inherent clarity to light. Calvin's homiletical approach actively demonstrates this position: 'Calvin's preaching was of one kind from beginning to end: he preached steadily through book after book of the Bible.'[102] This was not simply a systematic approach to the biblical books but a close reading of each book's particulars: 'Calvin's intention…was to expound each passage. Usually this entailed the continuous exposition of sentence by sentence, sometimes of clause by clause.'[103]

This expository method was not, of course, invented by Calvin. Systematic expositions of biblical texts were already present in some of the fathers, such as John Chrysostom and Augustine, as well as in the medieval period in the homilies

98. Wilhelm Niesel, *The Theology of Calvin*, trans. Harold Knight (Cambridge: James Clarke & Co., 2002), p. 29.

99. John Calvin, *Commentaries*, ed. and trans. Joseph Haroutunian (Louisville: Westminster John Knox Press, 2006), p. 97.

100. John Dillenberger, *John Calvin: Selections from His Writings* (Atlanta: Scholars Press, 1975), p. 14.

101. Edwards, *Scriptural Perspicuity*, p. 87.

102. John Piper, *John Calvin and His Passion for the Majesty of God* (Nottingham: IVP, 2009), p. 47.

103. T. H. L. Parker, *Calvin's Preaching* (Edinburgh: T & T Clark, 1992), p. 132.

of Anselm, Bernard of Clairvaux, Bonaventure and Aquinas. Calvin was merely 'taking up the tradition of the later Fathers and of the medieval tradition'.[104] But it is clear that Calvin was bringing the exposition of Scripture to the forefront, accentuating the fact that Scripture is indeed worthy of such close rendering. We might even see this deliberate accentuation of exposition as a partially polemical move. Calvin sought to overemphasize what had been previously underemphasized: 'Calvin had to win people over to become Bible Christians'.[105] It would be misleading, however, to assume this polemical element was Calvin's *primary* motivation behind his preaching method. Ultimately, this was what he believed was necessary in order to give Scripture its rightful place in the life of the Church. Calvin was 'not enslaved by his method',[106] he simply believed it was commensurate with Scriptural clarity, allowing the *sensus plenior* to speak and conveying its vital truth to his congregations by expounding it.

Such homiletical emphases, of course, characterized the Reformation as a whole. Luther was also a prolific preacher, delivering over 4,000 sermons in his lifetime: 'Luther's preaching ministry was remarkable, his productivity prodigious – almost miraculous'.[107] The expository style often associated with Calvin also characterized Luther's preaching: 'With Luther came what many interpreters call a totally new form of the sermon: the expository sermon'.[108] Of course, this was not a totally 'new' form of the sermon, but it did belie new foundational presuppositions. For Luther, the clarity of Scripture meant that the preacher can only preach 'the Word of God' if the text of Scripture forms the substance of the sermon. Thus, unlike previous versions of expository preaching, Luther's method presupposed Scripture's clarity to such an extent that the pure content of the sermon could be nothing more than exposition:

> The salient feature of Luther's preaching was its biblical content and reference. It was subject to Scripture throughout...His preaching was never merely topical... it was always a move from the text to men. The matter never determined the text: the text always determined the matter.[109]

This high view of the text was a result of the clarity and authority of Scripture. The content of the Bible (whole and parts) was deemed to be that which congregations

104. Ibid., p. 80.

105. Ibid., p. 127.

106. Ibid., p. 136.

107. Fred W. Meuser, 'Luther as Preacher of the Word of God', in Donald K. McKim (ed.), *The Cambridge Companion to Martin Luther* (Cambridge: Cambridge University Press, 2003), pp. 136–148 [136]. See also Robert Kolb, *Martin Luther and the Enduring Word of God: The Wittenberg School and Its Scripture-Centred Proclamation* (Grand Rapids: Baker, 2016), pp. 174–208.

108. Meuser, 'Luther as Preacher', p. 140.

109. Skevington Wood, *Captive to the Word*, p. 89.

needed most imperatively. This did not mean Luther's sermons simply involved dry commentary upon each passage (his well-known 'exaggerative' style suggests far more than a mere lecture upon the text), but it did mean that the sermon's theme and truth ought to be evidently taken from the chosen text: 'The text is to control the sermon…The sermon is to follow the flow, language, and dynamic of the text, and not impose its own direction or dynamic from without.'[110]

Such an approach would not have been possible without the undergirding belief that Scripture does not contradict itself. The text in each passage could be expounded and proclaimed because it was unified and clear enough to be interpreted in accordance with the message of Scripture. As noted, for both Luther and Calvin, the Gospel of Jesus Christ is the primary interpretative key. Difficult or 'dark' passages are dealt with in reference to the Gospel as the primary theme in Scripture (even if, as with Luther, this involves the necessity of the Law as prolegomena to the Gospel). The 'plain sense' of a given passage must always be filtered through the Christ-hermeneutic. This could also, of course, lead to a potential weakness in Luther's preaching: 'One of the captivating and frustrating things about Luther is that everything he knew about Christ had a way of creeping into his treatment of almost any text.'[111] Although he stressed a strict anchoring of the sermon to the text, there was a tendency for this Christ-hermeneutic to flatten any textual particularity. This was less true of Calvin's preaching, who was not as prone to turn each text into a Gospel message,[112] even though he also believed in reading Scripture through a Christocentric lens.

The motivations behind the Reformers' expository methods were undoubtedly an outworking of their belief in the clarity and unity of Scripture. Scripture and Gospel are seen as mutually related, grounding and informing one other, resulting directly in the prominence of expository preaching:

[Calvin] preached in the way he did because he believed what he did. It is clear that the single-minded concentration on the Holy Scriptures could come only from a particular view of the Bible. No-one would spend so much time on a book to which he did not attach an extraordinary importance.[113]

This 'particular view', as we have seen, echoes that of Luther and Zwingli as well as the majority of the other Reformers; that is, Scripture is clear enough to exposit in detail and has a singular message which always points to Christ. The message of Scripture is not hidden or obscured, even if there are obstacles to it; it is '[not]

110. Meuser, 'Luther as Preacher', p. 140.

111. Ibid., p. 139. This is, of course, an exaggeration, though not without some foundation. See Kolb, *Martin Luther and the Enduring Word of God*, pp. 125–28.

112. '[Calvin] is always careful to treat the authors in their historical context of living before the Incarnation…there may be little or no mention of Jesus or the Gospel in a sermon.' Parker, *Calvin's Preaching*, p. 92.

113. Ibid., p. 1.

beyond our reach'.[114] For preaching, this is a fundamental presupposition. It is from this basis that we can adequately engage with the inherent problem of theological dialectics within Scripture in a way that both challenges and aids the theological task of preaching.

iv. *The Gospel and the Passage*

Does it follow, then, that all passages of Scripture serve for 'proclamation'? It is not immediately obvious that every passage ought to be preached in the same way, as though each text contained the same *kind* of content. We ought to be cautious, as Timothy Ward notes, of 'over-extending' the clarity of Scripture to the extent that the Bible becomes 'a compendium of divine teaching, out of which doctrine can be mined and pieced together in systematic fashion'.[115] Such a construal, he adds, nullifies the key point of seeing Scripture as 'God's communicative act in which he presents to us his covenant promise fulfilled in Christ'.[116] Scripture is not a mere doctrinal depository; it is God's revelation of *Himself* to His people. But 'all' Scripture is nonetheless 'useful for teaching' (2Tim. 3:16), even if this is not *all* that it is. Each passage of Scripture will communicate something different in different ways and with different intentions, without deviating from the kerygmatic narrative. Although it is important to recognize (but not overemphasize) different literary 'genres' within Scripture, *any* passage of Scripture ought to be hermeneutically applicable to this message, even where its basis appears tangential to an overt 'proclamation'.[117] Given that canonicity itself is only possible *because* of this overarching and passage-unifying message, then it corresponds that each passage taken in 'isolation' in a preaching moment can be *re*connected to this overarching narrative without entirely neutralizing its particular textual emphases.

Of course, it is *in* the particular emphases of each text that the question of dialectic threatens to challenge this overarching hermeneutic, as will be seen. From the outset, however, it must be maintained that Scriptural clarity and unity necessitate that any passage may be proclaimed *through* the lens of the Gospel, to which it continually bears witness. This reflects Jesus' own figuration of Scripture's overarching purpose: 'You search the Scriptures because you think that in them you have eternal life; and it is they that bear witness about me' (John 5:39).[118] Such

114. Berkouwer, *Holy Scripture*, p. 274.

115. Timothy Ward, *Words of Life: Scripture as the Living and Active Word of God* (Downers Grove: IVP, 2009), p. 124.

116. Ibid.

117. The history of expository preaching in the Reformed tradition bears witness to this. Even the apparently 'redundant' prefaces of Paul's epistles receive numerous sermons in and of themselves, as preachers such as D. Martyn Lloyd-Jones were known to spend several years expositing a short epistle in the pulpit. It is also a practice seen in the enthusiastic exegetes of the Patristic era, particularly Origen. See Westerholm and Westerholm, *Reading Sacred Scripture*, pp. 97–100.

118. See also Luke 24:27.

a hermeneutical key should not be seen as a 'proof text', not least because it does not specify how each texts fits this lens – the 'how' certainly differs from passage to passage, even where it may be said that 'not every passage chosen by a preacher or assigned by the lectionary contains preachable content worthy of the descriptor "good news." '[119] However, it is not that each passage must itself proclaim this news directly, but rather that each passage plays a part in telling the full story of this news, even at its darkest or bleakest moments. Thus, the Christ-hermeneutic of John 5:39 may be acknowledged in the general sense that the overarching message of Scripture should always form the initial backdrop to Scripture's interpretation and proclamation in any of its individual parts. The connection made earlier between canonicity and proclamation was not just a historical occurrence which happened to determine the canon's parameters; this connection remains intrinsic to the ongoing proclamation of these canonical texts today. We will now see how such a connection may be engaged by the 'dialectical' elements which exist when individual passages appear in contrast.

4. *Dialectic and Scripture*

We have established that Scriptural unity and clarity form the essential bedrock to responsible Scriptural interpretation and proclamation. However, even with this conceptual touchstone, there is no apparently ideal method for navigating the apparent dialectical tension between Scripture's many passages and doctrinal emphases. Given that the term 'unity and diversity' often frames this issue,[120] there are a number of factors which ought to be considered when approaching the 'diversity' of Scripture, lest it really become an issue of 'diversity' rather than diversity *within* unity.

i. *Approaching Scriptural Diversity*

a. *Navigating Contradiction.*
It is often asserted that, despite a perceived overarching unity between the texts of the Bible through congruence with the Gospel message, the individual texts

119. O. Wesley Allen, Jr., 'Doing Bible: When the Unfinished Task of Historical Theology Pushes the Envelope of Canonical Authority', in David Schnasa Jacobsen (ed.), *Homiletical Theology in Action: The Unfinished Theological Task of Preaching* – The Promise of Homiletical Theology, Volume 2 (Eugene: Cascade, 2015), pp. 131–46 [134].

120. The widespread use of this terminology is partially due to the significance of James D. G. Dunn's seminal work, *Unity and Diversity in the New Testament: An Inquiry into the Character of Earliest Christianity* (London: SCM, 1977). See also the influence of F. C. Baur (1792–1860), who proposed the hugely influential, oft-contested argument proposing a quasi-Hegelian 'synthesis' of two dialectically competitive 'schools' within the New Testament ('Pauline' and 'Petrine'). See F. C. Baur, *Paul, the Apostle of Jesus Christ*, 2 vols, trans. Allen Menzies and Eduard Zeller (London: Williams and Norgate, 1873; 1875).

themselves represent more conflict than unity: 'Books and voices within books are still struggling to eradicate each other, offended by each other's presence within the canon.'[121] Such a reading does not see the diversity within Scripture as merely 'obscure' (as though we fail to understand *how* particular texts fit together) but as genuinely antithetical to other theological emphases within the canon. Although the claim is often exaggerated, we have reason to admit there is apparent tension between some teachings, making it difficult to say what the Bible *singularly* says on any singular subject. This plurality of voices and doctrinal positions within Scripture represents a 'dialectical' problem for canonicity, clarity and preaching.

Some, of course, overstate this problem: 'This is, or should be, the scandal of every introductory Bible course, in seminary and in parish: The Scriptures are chock-full of embarrassing, offensive, and internally contradictory texts, texts we do not wish to live with, let alone live *by*.'[122] Such a view suggests not only that these pluralities are difficult to navigate, but that they abolish the very idea of canonical unity. Because of the obvious diversity of writers, contexts, literary genres, historical periods and theological engagements within Scripture, such a low view of biblical unity is certainly possible as an initial observation. Yet it has also been widely noted that one must ensure that 'diversities' do not become overstated as outright 'contradictions'.[123] Anthony C. Thiselton urges 'a measure of caution against equating a plurality of voices with logical inconsistency'.[124] Although we would not want to downplay the problematic nature of the inherent diversity, identifying genuine contradiction is not always a straightforward task. Metzger argues that the tensions are merely a reflection of differing contexts of authorship:

> The homogeneity of the canon is not jeopardized even in the face of tensions that exist within the New Testament. These tensions, however, must not be exaggerated into contradictions as a result of giving inadequate consideration to the divergent situations in the early Church to which the writers addressed themselves.[125]

It is apparent that canonical unity need not be immediately threatened by apparent diversity given the necessary conditions of diversity in which it was formed.

121. Hugh Pyper, 'The Offensiveness of Scripture' (paper presented at the *Society for the Study of Theology* Annual Conference, April 2011), p. 10.

122. Ellen F. Davis, 'Critical Traditioning: Seeking an Inner Biblical Hermeneutic', in Ellen F. Davis and Richard B. Hays (eds.), *The Art of Reading Scripture* (Michigan: Eerdmans, 2003), pp. 163–80 [177].

123. For some caveats regarding 'contradiction', see II.3–5.

124. Anthony C. Thiselton, 'Canon, Community and Theological Construction', in Craig G. Bartholomew and Anthony C. Thiselton (eds.), *Canon and Biblical Interpretation* (Milton Keynes: Paternoster Press, 2006), pp. 1–32 [25].

125. Metzger, *The Canon of the New Testament*, p. 280.

Some commentators tend to claim a contradiction whenever there is an apparent dissimilarity between two biblical perspectives within texts, though such swift judgement is not always warranted.

b. *Maintaining Unity.*

It is quite possible that the very concept of Scriptural diversity may actually contribute to the depth of its unity: 'Once open to the rich diversity of the Bible, we shall see that it is not a collection of disconnected statements.'[126] Indeed, by overstating the negative implications of such diversity through a supposedly overwhelming plethora of irreconcilable contradictions, such approaches may prove too simplistic an interpretation of Scripture. This is deeply ironic given that such accounts are usually presented as offering greater 'complexity'. However, by not seeing the complex relatedness of clarity *and* dialectic, a singular extremity of focus upon 'ambiguity' emerges, distorting the way dialectic actually functions within the canon. This also belies an insufficient understanding of Scripture's ecclesial reception throughout history, as C. Stephen Evans notes: 'Many contemporary writers think that the actual New Testament is so diverse as to be full of contradictions. Clearly, neither the early church nor the church through the ages has thought this was so, and I believe myself it is an exaggeration.'[127] Richard Bauckham, similarly, argues for an initial rendering of unity above inconsistency:

> The church's reading of Scripture has usually presupposed its narrative unity, that is, that the whole of the Bible – or the Bible read as a whole – tells a coherent story. Any part of Scripture contributes to or illuminates in some way this one story, which is the story of God's purpose for the world.[128]

The Church's reception of the Bible's unity is itself a sufficient initial prolegomena for approaching Scripture as a unified rather than contradictory text. While we do not want to ignore the complexities which challenge this, it is important to outline the parameters of what is meant by the observable theological tensions within Scripture *before* responding to them. Otherwise, we let the 'critical' side frame the boundaries of a debate which, in reality, only exists in any conceivable sense *because of* the inherited acceptance of Scripture *as* unified and clear.

c. *Identifying Superficiality.*

To avoid the dangers of inappropriate claims to contradiction, then, we ought to exemplify what we do *not* mean by a genuine theological tension within

126. Paul D. Hanson, *The Diversity of Scripture: A Theological Interpretation* (Fortress Press: Philadelphia, 1982), p. 4.

127. C. Stephen Evans, 'Canonicity, Apostolicity, and Biblical Authority: Some Kierkegaardian Reflections', in *Canon and Biblical Interpretation*, pp. 146–66 [152].

128. Richard Bauckham, 'Reading Scripture as a Coherent Story', in *The Art of Reading Scripture*, pp. 38–53 [38].

Scripture, since it may be seen that some of these notable 'tensions' exist at a relatively superficial level, especially within the same flow of teaching within a passage. This is evident, for example, in Paul's apparently double-tongued charge to the Galatians to 'bear one another's burdens' (Gal. 6:2) and to 'bear their own load' (Gal. 6:5). Paul's two instructions appear to contradict one another, but not in a way that cannot be resolved by appeal to authorial context. Regarding this particular construct, D. A. Carson notes it is 'easy to find *formal* inconsistencies and contradictions in the New Testament', but equally easy to show their authorial and contextual consistency.[129] Here, Paul is presenting a rhetorical form of paradox (see II.3.i.a) in that he wants the Galatians to love each other in two particular ways (by not giving burdens *and* by actively taking others' burdens). Notably, of course, it is not presented as a univocal argument; for everyone to *totally* obey one side of this charge (everyone carrying everyone's burdens so that no one could carry their own) necessitates that the other side of the charge cannot be *totally* obeyed simultaneously. However, an absence of linear logic does not mean the exhortation is inherently inconsistent in what it intends to achieve: love of neighbour over self. This means the teaching is not intended to be obeyed in a 'total' sense, even as both charges are issued as equally necessary within the overall purpose of the charge.

Even such a small example demonstrates the need to be cautious about overly simplistic claims to theological contradiction or inconsistency. This is not to adopt an excessively defensive stance from the outset, but rather to treat the particular problem of Scriptural tensions alongside the aforementioned presuppositions of Scriptural unity and clarity with one eye always on the pulpit. This is because Scripture is itself a product of proclamation and – contrary to the inheritance of modern historical criticism – should not be treated in isolation from proclamation. There are, of course, far more problematic tensions between Scriptural teachings which could be engaged. We are not here attempting to engage with each and every possible 'dialectical' interaction within Scripture, but to offer a theological account of engaging with dialectic in relation to preaching. Approaching this problem requires a clear assessment of what a supposed 'contradiction' is, alongside its sibling categories of dialectic and paradox, which will be approached in the next chapter. Before this, however, we can still argue that Scriptural dialectics may be assumed *within* the unity and clarity of the canon, and although they do not nullify canonicity, they problematize any straightforward approach to clear and authoritative preaching.

d. *Embracing Dialectic.*

Despite the possibility of exaggerated claims, it cannot be denied that the Bible contains many varieties of unresolved tension, which can be called 'dialectics'.

---

129. D. A. Carson, 'Unity and Diversity in the New Testament: The Possibility of Systematic Theology', in D. A. Carson and John D. Woodbridge (eds.), *Scripture and Truth* (Grand Rapids: Baker Books, 1995), pp. 65–95 [86].

Such tensions are not necessarily meant to be abolished, they simply exist within the canon.[130] Barth, whose thought regarding the concept of dialectic will be seen more closely in the next chapter, based much of his dialectical theology upon the premise that Scripture presents antithetical doctrinal expressions which remain beyond our comprehension precisely *because* they are revealed by God in this way:

> It is the peculiarity of Biblical *thought and speech* that they flow from a source which is above religious antinomies. The Bible treats, for instance, of both creation and redemption, grace and judgement, nature and spirit, earth and heaven, promise and fulfilment...[I]t enters now upon this and now upon that side of its antitheses, but it never brings them pedantically to an end...it never hardens, either in the thesis or in the antithesis; it never stiffens into positive or negative finalities. It always finds as much and as little in the Yes as in the No; for the truth lies not in the Yes and not in the No but in the knowledge of the beginning from which the Yes and the No arise...It is through and through dialectic.[131]

For the early Barth in particular, the apparent tension between Scriptural teachings is unavoidable and ought to be embraced as a means by which God chooses to communicate his Word.[132] Where the human subject may yearn to solve these antinomies into static unities of thought, Scripture itself never 'hardens' or 'stiffens' into 'finalities'. Seeing this dialectical aspect as intrinsic to Scripture's nature (even alongside its canonicity and clarity) is essential to approaching such tensions theologically. The point is to hear the Word of God *as* the Word of God rather than to dissolve the apparent tension into either a Yes or a No. This approach refuses to allow for the human propensity to 'solve' such tensions (harmonization having been a particularly cherished method among Patristic and Medieval exegetes, from Origen to Augustine to Aquinas),[133] an approach where such tensions may be allowed to exist within – and *as* – the canon.

For the preacher seeking to hear the unique message of a particular text, this means laying aside the supposed requirement to hear each biblical message simultaneously or harmoniously. To do so would be to refuse to hear what God *actually* wants to communicate through his Word in exchange for a totalizing system. Barth exemplifies this regarding the two covenants of Ex. 19–20 and Jer. 31: 'We obviously cannot listen to both at the same time...a systematic conspectus

---

130. The language of 'contradiction' can be used in a number of ways to describe such tensions, but is probably too freighted a term to use without qualification, due to the unhelpful connotations of its challenge to the concept of canonicity itself.

131. Karl Barth, 'Biblical Questions, Insights, and Vistas', in *The Word of God and the Word of Man*, trans. Douglas Horton (London: Hodder & Stoughton, 1928), pp. 51–96 [72–3].

132. This must be nuanced, of course, since dialectic is by no means the *only* way God chooses to communicate. See II.2.ii.b.

133. See Westerholm, *Reading Sacred Scripture*, pp. 76–7, 139, 182.

of both is impossible. Hence we can only listen either to the one or the other at the one time.'[134] Observing such dialectics within Scripture is not always to approach them *as* contraries (although this may sometimes be appropriate), but to accept the possibility of each text's unique voice *within* its wider canonical context. This is demonstrated by the sharp-edged approach of the Old Testament prophets:

> The prophets admittedly surprise us by the abrupt one-sidedness with which at one moment they relentlessly speak only of judgment to come and at another they speak unrestrainedly only of coming redemption…There can thus be no system of prophetic utterance. It was either threat or promise. In this very one-sidedness it sought to be God's Word. To understand it there was and is needed what is called faith…namely, the perception either way of what is not said.[135]

To hear the texts of the canon 'one-sidedly' is not to abandon their connectedness to the Gospel in which their unity (and clarity) is founded, but to temporarily choose to incorporate two *kinds* of hearing. The particularity of a text must be heard in its fullness without attempting to simultaneously hear its canonical 'opposite'. But this one-sided hearing is not permitted to be *entirely* one-sided precisely because canonicity necessitates that 'what is not said' must also be perceived even as it is not *fully* 'heard' at that moment: 'The other can be heard only indirectly, in faith.'[136]

To conceive of Scriptural dialectical tensions in this way, of course, is really only to restate the problem regarding how the *preacher* must face these tensions in a variety of ways. We have thus far ventured only a brief introduction to the nature of dialectics within canonical Scripture and the way in which these may be perceived. The mechanics of how these dialectical problems may relate to preaching will come in Chapters III and IV. Before attempting, in Chapter II, to give an account of the conceptuality and methodology behind 'dialectic', we will highlight one biblical problem, in particular, with which expository preaching is faced: Paul-James. This illustrative example will lend a sense of concreteness to the dialectical 'problem' for the pulpit.

ii. *Concretizing the Preacher's Problem: Paul-James*

Although biblical dialectics might be problematic to the *concept* of biblical unity and clarity in general, this problem is felt most acutely by the preacher. Before the expectant congregation, the preacher not only needs to find a way of theologizing these dialectics but must also find a way of speaking something *particular* in their midst. Biblical-theological tensions between opposing texts serve to undermine any *one* thing the preacher might wish to say. Undoubtedly, one of the most

---

134. Barth, *CD* I/1, p. 180.
135. Ibid.
136. Ibid.

notorious expressions of doctrinal 'incongruity' in the New Testament exists between Paul and James (as Luther well knew). At a general level, this might be seen as an example of the Law-Gospel dynamic throughout Scripture, whereby, as Richard Lischer notes: 'The preaching of the gospel – whether from the Old or New Testament – is always dialectical.'[137] But what *kind* of 'dialectical' is it? Observing the Paul-James dialectic by way of illustration may not give us insight into *all* possible biblical dialectics, but it does offer a concrete exemplification of the kind of problem the preacher may encounter. As will be seen, this particular dialectic may be conceived in a variety of ways, which heightens its applicability when approaching other canonical conflicts more broadly.[138]

a. *The Basic Incongruity.*

Although one could speak of biblical 'paradoxes' in a conceptual sense (such as the parallel teachings of human responsibility and divine sovereignty, or the doctrines of the hypostatic union or the Trinity), the Paul-James relationship represents an incongruity between two very clear, resolute affirmations of doctrinal truth which are rooted in particular *texts* of Scripture: Paul on justification by faith (Rom. 4:1–25; Gal. 2:15–21) and James on justification by works (Jam. 2:14–25). This heightens their apparent problematization of expository preaching in particular, which attempts not to exposit a 'doctrine' per se, but the doctrine inherent within a particular text. Where two texts appear in explicit conflict, this makes the incongruity all the more stark because one observes a *precise* rhetorical contrast. For Paul: 'We know that a person is not justified by works of the law but through faith in Jesus Christ...by works of the law no one will be justified' (Gal. 2:16). For James: 'You see that a person is justified by works and not by faith alone' (Jam. 2:24). Evidently, Paul is as determined that justification *cannot* include works as James is determined that justification *must* include works. There is a double polemic, which necessitates a dialectical relationship between the two. Both draw apparently opposing conclusions from the situation of the faith of Abraham. In Romans, Paul states the absurdity of the suggestion that Abraham could be justified by works: 'For if Abraham was justified by works, he has something to boast about, but not before God... "Abraham believed God, and it was counted to him as righteousness."' (Rom. 4:2–3). Abraham's righteousness is borne not from his obedience in the Isaac command, nor any other works, but by his faith. This, Paul says, is the *only* foundation of his righteousness. In contrast, James reads Abraham's situation entirely differently:

> Was not Abraham our father justified by works when he offered up his son Isaac on the altar? You see that faith was active alongside his works and faith was

---

137. Richard Lischer, *A Theology of Preaching: The Dynamics of the Gospel* (Eugene: Wipf & Stock, 2001), p. 33.

138. This wider application will become more evident when we come to establish various dialectical 'modes' in Chapter II and consequently apply them homiletically to Paul-James in Chapter III.

completed by his works...'Abraham believed God, and it was counted to him as righteousness'...You see that a person is justified by works and not by faith alone. (Jam. 2:20–24)

We see how Paul and James have interpreted the same scenario, and indeed the same Old Testament quotation (Gen. 15:6), to formulate seemingly opposing doctrines of justification. It is clear, then, that there is an incongruity between the two 'polarities' of Paul and James. For a preacher to attempt to preach *either* or *both* of these texts, a number of possible interpretations may be possible in dealing with this problem.

b. *Alternative Conceptions.*

Although we have seen how Paul and James can be seen as starkly incongruous in emphasis, this is not the only way to interpret them. When approaching Paul and James simultaneously, the preacher is forced to consider their *method* of engaging such an extreme case of diversity, whereby simplistic resolution of the conflict appears problematic: 'James and Paul appear to be addressing different questions from very different perspectives which should not be easily harmonized.'[139] Given that there is evident complexity which renders Paul and James neither easily reconcilable nor easily divorced, we must evaluate how these two polarities are, in fact, related. In what ways can the relationship between Paul and James be seen as 'a dialectic'?

If one were keen to critique canonical unity, it would be easy to label the Paul-James dynamic as an outright contradiction, rendering the very presence of *both* within the canon as 'impossible'. As noted, canonicity itself necessitates this dilemma. If one of these teachings were *outside* the canon, there would be no need to speak of the two 'dialectically'. Yet their 'impossible' coming-together *within* the canon emphasizes their incongruity. Neither polarity seems willing to allow for the presence of the other. In the aforementioned texts, at least, Paul disallows works to play any role in justification (even via application), and James disallows justifying faith to exist isolated from works. Where the Pauline texts appear to separate faith and works, James appears to assert that they are ontologically *in*separable. The contextual extremity of each position is what renders them, in this basic sense, incompatible: each polarity emphasized at the *expense* of the muted opposite.

However, there are other elements within this dynamic that allow for the Paul-James dynamic to be conceived in other ways, too. It is not absolutely impossible, for example, in a different moment, to 'harmonize' Paul and James. This would entail showing that there is a definite trueness to both teachings because, in isolation, neither is a *fully* 'canonical' truth. Seen together, the partiality of each polarity becomes a fuller picture. Thus, one could say, Paul proclaims one facet of justification, and James proclaims another: 'If the "faith of Abraham" is used by Paul to teach that people are justified by grace through faith and by James to teach that faith without works is dead, it does not necessarily follow that the two authors

139. Childs, *Biblical Theology*, p. 547.

are ignorant of the other's work or in disagreement with it[140] This allows for Paul and James to be referring to two sides of the same 'coin' regarding the applicability of the faith of Abraham.

As legitimate a reading as this is, however, one must also admit that it assumes that *neither* Paul's nor James' emphases *in* those particular texts are *fully* 'true' in total isolation, since they mask their canonical opposites. The harmonizing approach is useful, but cannot resolve the homiletical problem per se. This is because it effectively neutralizes the particularities of *each* text, creating a kind of hypertext in which the extremes of 'faith-without-works' and 'faith-through-works' are nullified into something which resembles neither emphasis in its fullness. Even knowing, for example, that Paul is happy to encourage 'works' in other texts (Eph. 2:10; Tit. 2:14), his emphasis in Romans and Galatians deliberately masks this element. For preachers approaching these texts, to resort to a harmony too quickly might severely inhibit the full proclamation of either emphasis in its fullest force.

In addition, we might also see Paul-James in a different kind of relationship whereby each text builds upon an *assumption* which is not emphasized directly within their own emphasis.[141] Here, each emphasis acts correctively rather than comprehensively, even if Paul's 'faith' polarity might carry heavier freight within the corrective schema.[142] This would mean that the proclaimed 'Gospel' emphasis lays the foundation into which more applicatory material can be taught for the outworking of that doctrine or as a counterweight to its misuse. Indeed, Luther may have been the first to see James in this light, as a directly 'homiletical' text applying the *kerygma* to the lives of a congregation.[143] Indeed, if the preacher were to see James *in light of* the Gospel, we may well see how Luther (and any other preacher) could happily affirm James' canonical value while upholding the Gospel as the prerequisite key to canonical unity.

We have seen, then, that there are a number of ways in which Paul-James may be seen as 'dialectical', exemplifying other dialectical relationships between seemingly opposing Scriptural emphases. For the preacher, this serves as concrete exemplification of the complexity which lies at the heart of expository preaching, in which individual passages of Scripture are to be preached not only in relation to the other texts of the canon and the Gospel, but in such a way that its *own* voice is amplified. Where a multitude of dialectical 'options' may be available to the preacher, the problem sketched here remains a pregnant problem for every pulpit situation because *every* canonical text bears at least some relationship to its canonical others. Even where harmonizations may bring a sense of cohesion and contingent clarity, there remains a perpetual sense of canonical tension which can only be truly 'resolved' by the actual preaching of these texts, not *merely* as isolated texts but as canonically connected texts.

---

140. Carson, 'Unity and Diversity', p. 88.
141. See '*Kerygma* and *Didachē*' (I.2.iv.e).
142. On 'correctivity' see III.5.ii–iii.
143. See Moule, *Birth of the New Testament*, p. 41.

5. *Conclusion: Engaging Dialectic with Clarity*

This chapter has built an important foundation regarding how biblical dialectics might be approached theologically. We have seen the vital connection between preaching and Scripture, and between canonicity, clarity and the proclaimed Gospel. We now have an appropriate framework from which to begin our investigation into the problematic nature of dialectical obscurity or ambiguity, knowing that the first focus for the preacher ought to be Scriptural 'light' rather than Scriptural 'darkness', and canonical unity rather than canonical fragmentation. Indeed, the concepts of canonicity, clarity *and* dialectic are mutually essential. Where canonicity and clarity form a kind of conceptual 'system' of parameters, this appears to downplay or minimize dialectics. The concept of univocity often appears to outweigh the simultaneous existence of plurivocity, resulting in dialectics becoming easily ignored, glossed over, or quickly harmonized. Although superficial contradictions within Scripture can be legitimately resolved, there are significant instances in which this is not possible in any complete sense, as seen illustratively in some conceptions of Paul-James. Tensions such as this continue to challenge expository preaching. However, the existence of these dialectical tensions *within* an undergirding of clarity and canonicity should be maintained, whereby neither conception annihilates the other.

In this way, one may see an operative dynamic between these concepts: to take clarity seriously one must take canonicity seriously, and to take canonicity seriously one must take dialectic seriously, because Scripture effectively canonizes tension. However, merely 'embracing' dialectic must never become an endpoint in itself or Scripture might not be seen as interpretable at all, internally corrupted by its inappropriate divisions. The preacher, for whom this problem is acute, upholds the clarity of Scripture as essential for the task of expository biblical proclamation. The 'problem' of biblical dialectic for the preacher actually stems from a full appreciation of canonicity, since all preaching which occurs in earshot of Scripture's *other* emphases necessitates the reality that difficult or problematic texts will be encountered. This problem should not be ignored by the preacher, nor feared, but might actually be welcomed. The Paul-James dialectic, as outlined above, is a concrete theological and practical problem for any preacher seeking to declare the truth of either text while avoiding self-contradiction. Yet it has been the task of this chapter to outline the necessity of canonicity, clarity *and* dialectical tension within the overarching 'system'.

Thus far we have not seen *how* the preacher engages with this problem, nor, in fact, how the preacher might find that 'dialectic' may also be an entirely *necessary* element of the heraldic task. This chapter has merely sketched the problem and suggested ways of approaching it, but it is not altogether clear what lies behind dialectics in a theological sense, nor how such tensions should be categorized or interpreted. The following chapter, then, will explore various approaches within the theological tradition of engaging the problem of theological tension.

Although this chapter has used the word 'dialectic' quite freely, there are different ways in which dialectics function and different ways in which they are potentially problematic for the preacher. In order to clarify how we might engage with the problem of dialectic and preaching, we must first interpret the different ways in which one may perceive and understand dialectical problems in a distinctly theological way.

Chapter II

DIALECTIC, PARADOX, CONTRADICTION: THE PARADOXICAL LEGACY OF THEOLOGICAL DIALECTIC

1. *Introduction: Towards Terminological Clarity*

The previous chapter outlined an important foundation for any theological approach to dialectic in relation to preaching: the unity and clarity of canonical Scripture. As noted, however, various instances of what we might call 'dialectic' occur when one attempts to interpret and preach a singular passage of Scripture. The problem for preaching is that of apparent 'contradiction' *between* two oppositional doctrinal emphases. 'Dialectic' and 'paradox' are concepts within theological thought and speech which attempt to give voice to – and engage with – the problem of contradiction. Yet it is not altogether clear what the differences are between these complex terms. Both paradox and dialectic have been used variously and defined differently in the theological tradition, causing significant obfuscation over what they actually refer to. The expressions of 'either/or' and 'both/and' are often used, for example, to refer to 'dialectic' *or* to 'paradox', connoting the tension or simultaneity within a propositional truth. Such categorizations, of course, are somewhat simplistic. Both 'both/and' *and* 'either/or' could be used to refer to a number of different dialectical forms, and neither expression states how the polarities interact *specifically*. The primary goal of this chapter, then, is to clarify this terminology so that we have a sense of clarity regarding what dialectic means, what it consists of, what lies behind it, and how it may function within theological speech.

One of the primary reasons that apparent contradiction is deemed problematic for preaching is the residual condition of *ambiguity* for theological speech. Can we speak of Scriptural truths in the midst of – or only in isolation from – their canonical 'opposites'? Roy Sorensen, in a study on *Vagueness and Contradiction* (2001) highlights the problem of ambiguity as the necessary result of what lies *between* two clear propositions: singular focus upon one proposition eliminates ambiguity, where simultaneous focus upon both creates and upholds ambiguity.[1]

---

1. Roy Sorensen, *Vagueness and Contradiction* (Oxford: Clarendon Press, 2001), p. 121.

If one is to engage with *two* or more propositions (as with an apparent 'contradiction'), the result is often either 'ambiguity' or 'extremism'.[2] The preacher may veer to either one of these while using biblical texts as their homiletical basis. Yet a fuller understanding of dialectic will allow for a more robust sense of conviction in spite of the vague 'no-man's-land' between two clear statements of truth. Although dialectic is, in some sense, inescapable from ambiguity in its essence,[3] affirming the realities of theological dialectic for Christian doctrine does not mean affirming outright ambiguity. Simultaneously, to take a critical stance towards dialectic should not invoke the impulsion towards extremism to escape the potentiality of ambiguity in Christian preaching. Here we will attempt to map a fuller understanding of the role of dialectic for theological speech whereby dialectic may be embraced *without* – by default – leading to ambiguous preaching. In order to affirm this, some important terminological clarification is required within this 'dialectical' foundation.

There is an avalanche of complexity surrounding 'dialectic' as a concept, especially in relationship to the sibling concepts of 'paradox' and 'contradiction'. The task of navigating through this complexity will be approached in three primary ways: 1. Delineating the broad definitional tenets for each term in both philosophical and theological usage; 2. Demonstrating some key ways in which dialectic and paradox have been used, providing an account of why each is theologically necessary; 3. Establishing variety within the concept of 'dialectic' through the outlining of four primary dialectical modes. To attain the clarity of these primary modes, of course, will first require an account of some of these uses through an extensive analysis of significant thinkers from the theological and philosophical tradition. These include as varied a range as Meister Eckhart, G. W. F. Hegel, Søren Kierkegaard, G. K. Chesterton and Karl Barth. Before addressing these particular uses or clarifying their particular functions, however, we will attempt to reintroduce the concept of philosophical and theological dialectic in its broadest possible sense.

---

2. He adds that propositions in themselves (i.e. 'extreme' polarities) are fundamentally *clear* in what they state: 'Propositions may be vague but can never be ambiguous.' Sorensen, *Vagueness and Contradiction*, p. 121.

3. Even the early Barth admitted an inherent weakness in the dialectical method regarding ambiguity. See Karl Barth, 'The Word of God and the Task of Ministry', in *The Word of God and the Word of Man*, trans. Douglas Horton (London: Hodder & Stoughton, 1928), pp. 183–217 [210]. See also Kierkegaard's criticisms of the passionless dialectical reflection of his age, where polarity distinctions could be sidestepped via 'a feat of dialectics' which 'reduces the inward reality of all relationships to a reflective tension which leaves everything standing but makes the whole of life ambiguous'; 'dialectical complications are difficult to root out, and it requires even better ears to track down the stealthy movement of reflection along its secret and ambiguous path'. Søren Kierkegaard, *The Present Age*, trans. Alexander Dru (London: The Fontana Library, 1969), pp. 45, 50 (emphasis removed).

2. *Dialectic*

i. *Defining Dialectic*

Dialectic is a term which is owned, claimed, defined and reinterpreted by numerous thought schools, both theological and philosophical. Hegel, the dialectician *par excellence*, whose dialectical method is usually seen as 'the notion of dialectic at its modern point of origin',[4] believed dialectic to have originated with the Greek philosophers Zeno and Plato, though even this is difficult to ascertain.[5] What most schools would likely agree upon is that dialectic (at root) connotes the act of reflection upon some form of contradiction in the midst of conversational or conceptual incongruity. Of course, this might merely trace the term, in a sense, to the very origins of human thought and speech itself. However, although various uncertainties perpetually revolve around the term, it is still possible to arrive at a sense of clarity as to what this term denotes in both its broader and more specific uses.[6]

a. *Philosophical Dialectic.*

At an abstract philosophical level, 'dialectic' connotes the freedom of formulations of thinking. In dialectical thinking, no singular mode of thought or conclusion is necessarily preferred: 'What separates a dialectical theory of knowledge and reality from other variants of historicism and relativism is a particular kind of radical "openness" – a dialectical openness which preserves the tension between the relative and the absolute.'[7] The notion of 'openness' is a helpful key to understanding the different forms of dialectic, as will be seen. Dialectic is not concerned with immoveable formulations or propositions of thought but, as Hegel said of all dialectical methods, their aim is 'to totter what is firmly fixed'.[8] It is for this reason that dialectic has often been referred to as 'the algebra of revolution'.[9] Indeed, many modern applications of dialectic (such as Marxist adaptations of Hegel) point towards the breaking down and reorienting of fixed 'propositions' (or 'establishments') in the social and political sphere. The fact that dialectic has such

---

4. Michael Rosen, *Hegel's Dialectic and Its Criticism* (Cambridge: Cambridge University Press, 1982), p. ix.

5. Andries Sarlemijn, *Hegel's Dialectic*, trans. Peter Kirschenmann (Dordecht: D. Reidel Publishing, 1975), p. 27.

6. It barely needs mentioning, of course, that this cannot hope to be comprehensive, nor even entirely chronological, nor is there any apology for not including every single niche dialectician of the last three thousand years. But it is hoped that by noting various flashpoints in how dialectic has been seen and used, some kind of a pattern may emerge.

7. Scott Warren, *Emergence of Dialectical Theory: Philosophy and Political Inquiry* (Chicago: University of Chicago Press, 2008), p. 16.

8. Sarlemijn, *Hegel's Dialectic*, pp. 34–6.

9. See John Rees, *The Algebra of Revolution: The Dialectic and the Classical Marxist Tradition* (London: Routlege, 1998).

wide-ranging applications beyond the realm of speculative thought, however, does not render its general philosophical meaning inaccessible. Even in such so-called political dialectics, there is this same notion of the radical openness to the counterpoint of singular proposition.

Along this line, Theodor W. Adorno renders dialectic as the inescapable reality facing *all* human thought: 'Dialectics is the consistent sense of non-identity. It does not begin by taking a standpoint. My thought is driven to it by its own inevitable insufficiency.'[10] It would be simplistic, of course, to draw comparisons with so-called postmodern suspicions of objective truth here, which – though sharing a dialectical cadence – do not reflect the specific aims of dialectical method as such. Dialectic in its purest sense (if such a term is possible) is not necessarily concerned with 'tottering' objective truth itself, but in calling all propositions of *singularity* into question because of the simultaneous existence of their necessary countertruths. Correspondingly, dialectic also has etymological roots in the meaning of 'deliberation' over an idea or decision.[11] Here, we may see more specifically what dialectical 'openness' might mean: one 'deliberates' because one is *uncertain* over a singular proposition or decision. In this sense, all dialectic – in some way or other – involves the problematic reflection upon opposing or differing polarities of (subjective *or* objective) truth.

Beyond this basic schema, however, there are many divergences and types of philosophical dialectic. Dmitri Nikulin attempts to clarify the difference between dialectic and its related concept, 'dialogue', but admits that it is difficult to assert the fixed origins of either term: 'It is not ultimately clear where each of them belongs in the traditional division of philosophy, the sciences, and art.'[12] It is not only the situating of the term that is problematic, but the very definition of it. For example, one might point to the 'Socratic dialectic' of conversing, questioning and enquiring; the 'Thomist dialectic' of catechetical question-and-answer;[13] the 'Kantian dialectic' of antinomy;[14] or the 'Hegelian dialectic' of oppositional sublation. Even with the aforementioned tenet of 'openness' governing all dialectical enquiry, each of these methods uses the word 'dialectic' in a radically different sense.

As noted, a core tenet of the dialectical method is a kind of 'conversation' between opposing polarities. At a general level, this essential conversational characteristic is true of the dialectical methods of Socrates, Origen, Abelard, Aquinas, Hegel,

---

10. Theodor W. Adorno, *Negative Dialectics*, trans. E. B. Ashton (London: Routlege, 1996), p. 5; Adorno also speaks of the 'immanent contradiction' in all human thinking. Ibid., p. 146.

11. Sarlemijn, *Hegel's Dialectic*, p. 27.

12. Dmitri Nikulin, *Dialectic and Dialogue* (Palo Alto: Stanford University Press, 2010), p. 10.

13. See Thomas S. Hobbs, *Dialectic and Narrative in Aquinas: An Interpretation of the Summa contra gentiles* (Notre Dame: University of Notre Dame Press, 1995), pp. 23–30.

14. See Jonathan Bennett, *Kant's Dialectic* (Cambridge: Cambridge University Press), pp. 114–17.

Kierkegaard and many others: 'All dialectic springs from a contradiction; etymologically it originates in dialogue, in assertion and contradiction.'[15] Indeed, a connection between opposing polarities would be impossible without *some* notion of a conversational relationship, whether conflicting or resolved. Hermann Diem has called this conversational element the 'most original and simplest form of dialectic'.[16] In all dialectics there must be at least two differing forces or polarities which must (on some level) become related, even through conceptual radical difference. Polarity tension is a significant aspect of such relationship: 'Dialectic moves by grappling with opposites, particularly at the moment of their alleged coincidence.'[17] Although dialectic necessitates oppositional divergence, there is no uniform way in which such conversational 'grappling' occurs. Within this lack of uniformity, it becomes even more complicated to distinguish between philosophical and theological dialectic, though not impossible.

b. *Theological Dialectic.*

There are, certainly, oversimplistic ways of rendering the distinction between philosophical and theological dialectic: 'Unlike philosophical thinking, theological dialectic refuses to resolve contradictions; instead, it strives to keep them in creative tension with each other.'[18] It is incorrect, of course, to say that philosophical dialectic *always* seeks to 'resolve'. This view purports the misguided notion that 'philosophy' is concerned primarily with dissolving contradictions into logical coherence, whereas 'theology' – because it has a transcendent dimension – is more comfortable with leaving unresolved contradictions 'in God's hands'. In reality, both philosophical and theological dialectics may resolve *or* maintain apparent contradictions, though there may be specific 'schools' within each discipline which emphasize a particular response to contradiction as *the* way of defining dialectics. As noted, all dialectics involve some sense of tension between concepts, doctrines or propositions, even in a harmonizing process. If a concept is to be called 'dialectical' at all, it must contain *some* kind of internal opposition (otherwise it is eo ipso 'undialectical').

What can be said of the distinction, however, is that philosophical dialectic (broadly conceived) requires no direct correspondence to an absolute *telos* which governs the oppositional conflicts of conceptual reality.[19] Thus, philosophical

---

15. Theodor Haecker, *Søren Kierkegaard*, trans. Alexander Dru (London: Oxford University Press, 1937), pp. 30–1.

16. Hermann Diem, *Kierkegaard's Dialectic of Existence* (Westport: Greenwood Press, 1978), pp. 10–11

17. Nikulin, *Dialectic*, p. 11.

18. Donald G. Bloesch, *A Theology of Word and Spirit: Authority and Method in Theology* (Illinois: IVP, 1992), p. 77.

19. Of course, many modern philosophical ventures maintain universal being or reason as their governing philosophical *telos*, which connotes a 'concept' of God, as evident in Hegel's 'Absolute' or 'Spirit' (see II.5), or in Kant's 'unity of the end to which all the parts relate and in the idea of which they all stand in relation to one another'. Immanuel Kant, *Critique*

approaches to dialectic aim at comprehending these quandaries of human thought as they become observable in all realms of life, whereas theological approaches to dialectic remain tethered to the implications of divine revelation, as T. F. Torrance notes: 'In dialectical thinking we let our knowledge, our statements, or our theological formulations be called into question by the very God toward whom they point.'[20] For the philosopher, however, there is a virtually parameterless variety in how dialectic may be used and imagined.[21] For this reason, dialectic within philosophy remains a perpetually insecure concept, as in Maurice Merleau-Ponty's recalibration:

> Dialectic is not the idea of a reciprocal action, nor that of opposites and their sublation. Dialectic is not a development which starts itself again, nor the cross-growth of a quality that establishes as a new order a change...these are consequences or aspects of the dialectic. But taken in themselves or as properties of being, these relationships are marvels, curiosities, or paradoxes. They enlighten only when one grasps them in our experience...[Dialectic] provides the global and primordial cohesion of a field of experience wherein each element opens onto the others.[22]

Here we see the claim that dialectical thinking is not a 'method' as such but an effervescent emanation of reality itself – the dialectics are discovered ad hoc, 'in our experience', and remain perichoretic within the 'primordial cohesion' of unfolding universal reality. Again, this provides one example of how philosophical dialectic attempts to account for the universality and particularity of reality (in various ways), meaning that its dialectical conflicts carry a different freight, are interchangeable, in constant flux, and become self-reflective of the dilemma of human language. This is why philosophical dialecticians have an entirely different task in how they apprehend and articulate dialectical realities, as Adorno states:

> The task of dialectical cognition is not, as its adversaries like to charge, to construe contradictions from above and to progress by resolving them...Instead, it is up to dialectical cognition to pursue the inadequacy of thought and thing, to

---

of Pure Reason, trans. Norman Kemp Smith (New York: St. Martin's, 1929), p. 833. However, this still differs radically from the theologian's task of interpreting dialectics *within* divine revelation and relating them back *to* the God who revealed them. Furthermore, in theology, God is not a universal 'concept' but a person through whom the theologian's theology is perpetually informed.

20. T. F. Torrance, *Karl Barth: An Introduction to His Early Theology, 1910–1931* (London: SCM, 1962), p. 88.

21. This is not to say theological dialectic does not contain such variety but that philosophical dialectic is virtually infinite in its possible conceptions of where dialectic may lead.

22. Maurice Merleau-Ponty, *Adventures in the Dialectic*, trans. Joseph Bien (London: Heinemann, 1974), pp. 203–4.

experience it in the thing...[N]o single thing is at peace in the unpacified whole. The aporetical concepts of philosophy are marks of what is objectively, not just cogitatively, unresolved.[23]

It is not that the theological dialectician is not also 'experiencing' these aporias within the 'inadequacy' of human thought, but merely that such rational aporias are specifically located. The theologian is not trying to come to terms with the 'unpacified whole' of universal reality itself, but attempting to articulate that which *God* would have them know and say. The theologian responds to dialectics because they are given, seeking to interpret theological revelation as the *telos* of each encountered dialectic without necessarily accounting for how *all* aporias fit together. The philosophical dialectician – particularly in the ever-expansive philosophical climate of the twentieth century and beyond – insists upon no such *necessary* parameters. As a result, the very concept and meaning of dialectic within philosophical discourse is forever under dialectical investigation itself.[24]

Although we might well observe the boundless crossovers and splinters within and between the two disciplines, it is important to maintain that theological dialectic does not have a prior commitment to 'openness' per se, nor a universal anxiety about singular propositions, but a perpetual awareness of the transcendent subject matter of which it speaks. Although there are different types of theological dialectic, and different ways of being a 'dialectical theologian', the fundamental reason for the necessity of dialectical thinking is ever-present: the creator-creature distinction. The deference of all human theological articulations to the qualitatively distinct nature of God is what catalyses the need to speak in reference to uncertain oppositional polarities. It is this fundamental conviction which undergirded the emphases of the famously short-lived 'school' of dialectical theology. We will now recount something of how this school of thought came about, and what theological and conceptual distinctions lay behind its emphases.

23. Adorno, *Negative Dialectics*, p. 153.

24. Wolfe notes, for example, that Martin Heidegger's early interest in dialectical theology and its nineteenth-century sources – such as Kierkegaard, Dostoevsky and Overbeck – differed precisely on 'the conviction of a methodological gulf between theology and philosophy' which altered how one interpreted the restless tone of such thinkers: 'Karl Barth, keenly aware of the fundamental difference between Heidegger's anthropocentric and his own theocentric approaches, was careful to frame that difference not as a competition but as evidence that philosophy and theology operated on different paradigms with little mutual input.' Judith Wolfe, *Heidegger's Eschatology: Theological Horizons in Martin Heidegger's Early Work* (Oxford: Oxford University Press, 2013), pp. 92, 107. Reflecting on Heidegger's work later on, Barth saw it as just one more example of philosophy's shrouded attempt at 'patronising' and 'conditioning' theological thought. See Barth, *CD* I/1, p. 39.

ii. 'Dialectical' Theology

a. *The Crisis of Yes and No.*

Dialectical theology is one of the most notable movements in theological history to offer a sustained engagement with the problem of contradictory realities within revelation. It emerged in the aftermath of the First World War among a new generation of theologians keen to cast off their theological upbringing in anthropocentric liberalism. The advent of the 1920s inaugurated a seismic shift in theological thought in Europe, often referred to as the 'Theology of Crisis'. Previous certainties regarding what God was 'for' or 'against', particularly in the political sphere, came under intense scrutiny. In the aftermath of the war, which in Germany had begun with such abundant theological optimism (the will of God having been conflated with the will and 'progress' of human thinking), emerging voices began to herald the cataclysmic destruction of these ideals. In September 1919, Barth's Tambach conference appeared to summon a new era for theological speech, invoking the fervent discursiveness of likeminded theologians with an ear for theological tension.[25] 'Dialectical theology' opposed the idealism of the Zeitgeist by speaking of 'the brokenness of our human thinking, which cannot reconcile but only articulate contradictory statements'.[26] These dialectical theologians – including Barth, Emil Brunner, Friedrich Gogarten, Rudolf Bultmann and Eduard Thurneysen – became something of a (temporarily) likeminded collective, particularly through their various contributions to *Zwischen den Zeiten* ('between the times'),[27] the newly founded journal which aptly captured the theological restlessness of the movement. The notion of dialectical theology as an organized 'movement', of course, was strongly resisted by Barth himself: 'So far as Thurneysen, Gogarten, and I really may be said to form a "school" in the familiar sense of the word, our work is superfluous';[28] 'The "new" theology came not from any desire of ours to form a school or to devise a system; it arose simply out of what we felt to be the "*need and promise of Christian preaching.*"'[29] The connection of the roots of dialectical theology to preaching, of course, is important. Barth maintained that it

25. Chalamet shows how at least an embryonic form of this dialectical attuning was already inculcated in both Barth and Bultmann under Willhelm Herrmann's influence: 'In Herrmann's classroom, they learned not so much to conciliate both sides of the spectrum but to articulate these in their utmost radicality, preserving each side's grain of truth...He taught Bultmann and Barth how to maintain these tensions, how to speak about God hidden in his revelation, about God's judgement and grace.' Christophe Chalamet, *Dialectical Theologians: Wilhelm Herrmann, Karl Barth and Rudolf Bultmann* (Zürich: TVZ, 2005), pp. 13–14.

26. Ibid., p. 12.

27. Ibid., p. 177.

28. Barth, 'The Need and Promise of Christian Preaching', in *The Word of God and the Word of Man*, p. 98.

29. Ibid., p. 100.

was the very act and ongoing expectation of biblical proclamation – which he and Thurneysen felt so intensely in their rural pastorates – that catalysed the 'revolution' towards dialectical thinking. Indeed, preaching forces the theologian to reflect upon the constraints of revelation most acutely.[30]

The necessary restlessness of this 'theology of crisis' critiqued any certainty that one placed outside of God: 'Dialectical theology had as its fundamental contention that every theological position had to be denied because it was not, and could not be, authentically theological.'[31] The inherent paradox within such an enterprise (holding a 'fundamental contention' which denies the possibility of a 'fundamental contention') was not a case of mere logical slackness, but was embraced as theologically essential. Even in its self-definition, dialectical theology struggled to find a statically adequate affirmation for its own theological speech. This was, of course, a sharp and necessary reaction to the previous generation which had all-too-easily affirmed that human thinking had inherent access to God-speech, declaring God to be in favour of their own affirmations. The primary focus of dialectical theology, then, was not upon God's unequivocal Yes to humanity, but his No.[32] In its initial phases, dialectical theology was, indeed, predominantly negative: God was seen not as immanently reconciled with humanity but *wholly other*.[33]

This emphasis came in the midst of a particular rereading of Scripture, and was thus grounded in divine revelation itself rather than speculative thought upon the limits of human reason.[34] This is what separates dialectical theology from a dialectical 'method' per se, as Eberhard Jüngel notes: 'Barth does not seek to reach behind revelation by transcendental questioning, but rather sees himself induced

---

30. See also a recent argument for an alternative conception of Barth's own 'dialectical' motivations in David W. Congdon, 'Dialectical Theology as Theology of Mission: Investigating the Origins of Karl Barth's Break with Liberalism', in *International Journal of Systematic Theology* 16:4 (Oct 2014), pp. 390–413.

31. Robert P. Scharlemann, 'The No to Nothing and the Nothing to Know: Barth and Tillich and the Possibility of Theological Science', in *Journal of the American Academy of Religion* 55:1 (1987), pp. 57–72 [61].

32. This critical stance, of course, did not obscure the simultaneous 'Yes' to which God's 'No' to humanity was oriented, as seen in this sermon: '*No and Yes* can be said of us, *No and Yes* is the truth of our lives. In God there is no opposition to us. In God we persevere, for in Him is stimulus, life, hope. There is nothing but Yes and No in God, only because of the Yes.' Karl Barth and Eduard Thurneysen, 'The Great "But"', in *Come Holy Spirit*, trans. George W. Richards, et al. (Edinburgh: T & T Clark, 1934), pp. 13–23 [23].

33. Barth would later come to repeal the 'wholly other' concept as essentially 'corrupt' and 'pagan' when used to refer to God in such an exclusive manner. Barth, *CD* IV/1, p. 186.

34. Notably, Dostoevsky also saw Scripture itself as the primary source for the reason/revelation dialectic. See P. H. Brazier, *Dostoevsky: A Theological Engagement* (Eugene: Pickwick, 2016), pp. 90–2.

to make his inquiry on the ground of revelation.'[35] In returning to the primacy of Scriptural revelation, Barth and Thurneysen made a key 'discovery' which pointed to the essential distinction which bookmarked their dialectical theology: human finitude and divine humanity:

> We have found in the Bible a new world, God, God's sovereignty, God's glory, God's incomprehensible love. Not the history of men, but the history of God! Not the virtues of men but the virtues of him who hath called us out of darkness into his marvellous light! Not human standpoints but the standpoint of God![36]

Following this radical return to the authority and prophetic immediacy of Scripture, Barth wrote his famous *Römerbrief* (1919). The much-revised 1922 edition of this work (notably published 400 years after Luther's 1522 commentary on Romans) catapulted Barth's theological revolution to a new level. It became known not only as that 'bomb on the playground of theologians,'[37] but also as 'the brightest flower of that exotic plant of the 1920s, Dialectical Theology'.[38] Barth's theological exegesis of Romans imagined a new world in which human optimism was countered by God's prevailing sovereignty: 'All human activity, negative and positive, is radically questionable and insecure.'[39] This focus upon the 'insecurity' of human thought carries a distinctly theocentric emphasis. For Barth, this was not simply a preferred dialectical 'method', it was the necessary theological implication of the great separation between humanity and God, whose sovereignty represented 'the final security of insecurity'.[40] This gave Barth's message a distinctly iconoclastic character: '[For Barth,] Paul's letter to the Romans presented an idol-breaking critique of every merely human strategy of salvation.'[41] Barth's message emphasized the 'critical' dialectical aspect over the positive: the 'No' over the 'Yes'.

35. Eberhard Jüngel, *God's Being is in Becoming: The Trinitarian Being of God in the Theology of Karl Barth*, trans. John Webster (Edinburgh: T & T Clark, 2004), p. 73.

36. Karl Barth, 'Barth to Thurneysen, 11 November 1918', in *Revolutionary Theology in the Making: Barth-Thurneysen Correspondence, 1914-1925*, trans. James D. Smart (Richmond: John Knox Press, 1964), p. 45.

37. See Kevin J. Vanhoozer (ed.), *Dictionary for the Theological Interpretation of the Bible* (Grand Rapids, Baker Academic, 2005), p. 700; Karl Adam, 'Die Theologie der Krisis', in *Hochland* 23 (1926), pp. 271–86 [276]. Notably, Adam's famous comment referred to the earlier edition of 1919. See Paul Brazier, 'Barth's First Commentary on Romans (1919): An Exercise in Apophatic Theology?' in *International Journal of Systematic Theology* 6:4 (2004), pp. 387–403 [387–8].

38. Colin Brown, *Karl Barth and the Christian Message* (London: Tyndale, 1967), p. 19.

39. Karl Barth, *The Epistle to the Romans*, trans. E. C. Hoskyns (London: Oxford University Press, 1933), p. 294.

40. Ibid., p. 293.

41. Gary Dorrien, *The Barthian Revolt in Modern Theology: Theology without Weapons* (Louisville: Westminster John Knox Press, 2000), p. 53.

But this did not mean that the No was the sole focus of dialectical theology. Rather, forsaking the *exclusive* Yes with an *emphasis* on the No, it became not a theology of No but a theology of Yes-and-No: 'The knowledge which the Bible offers and commands us to accept forces us out upon a narrow ridge of rock upon which we must balance between Yes and No, between life and death, between heaven and earth.'[42]

This fundamental concern with the danger of one-sidedness also existed in Brunner's dialectical theology, in spite of his increasingly different presuppositions.[43] Indeed, there were many differing caveats, perceived implications and divergences between the dialectical theologians in regards to where such theology should ultimately *lead*.[44] Nonetheless, the fixation upon the 'Yes-and-No' (however it functioned) was always the fundamental root from which the school of 'dialectical theology' had grown. The vastly revised distinction between God and human thinking led to the impossibility of saying *either* the Yes *or* the No – theological speech now needed to reflect an awareness of the tension between *both*, whether 'realistic' or 'idealistic'.[45] What, though, is the nature of this tension? What actually *occurs* in the hinterland between the Yes and No?

Most definitions of dialectical theology tend towards the non-harmonization of polarities, exemplified in Bruce L. McCormack's description: 'A method which calls for every theological statement to be placed over against a counter-statement, without allowing the dialectical tension between the two to be resolved in a higher synthesis.'[46] It should be noted, though, that dialectic is not averse to polarity resolution as well as tension, as in Chalamet's definition: 'The presence of resolved or unresolved tensions between two contradictory theological aspects.'[47]

42. Barth, 'Biblical Questions, Insights, and Vistas' in *The Word of God and the Word of Man*, p. 58.

43. See Cynthia Bennett Brown, *Believing Thinking, Bounded Theology: The Theological Methodology of Emil Brunner* (Cambridge: James Clarke & Co., 2015), p. 183; David Andrew Gilland, *Law and Gospel in Emil Brunner's Earlier Dialectical Theology* (London: T&T Clark, 2015).

44. McGrath notes this variety: 'The term "dialectical theology" was used in several different senses by those emphasising the priority of divine revelation. It is historically improper to suggest that Barth was the proper claimant to the notion of "dialectical theology", with others deviating from, or fundamentally misunderstanding, its essential content. From the outset, "dialectical theology" was a porous concept, open to different ways of interpretation.' Alister McGrath, *Emil Brunner: A Reappraisal* (Chichester: Wiley Blackwell, 2014), p. 24.

45. See Gilland, *Brunner's Earlier Dialectical Theology*, p. 55. See also Chalamet's reading of Barth's early dialectical theology: 'to go all the way with the two trends of thought, not to be either realistic and critically idealist (or employ a mix of the two) but to be both fully realistic and critical'. Chalamet, *Dialectical Theologians*, p. 73.

46. Bruce L. McCormack, *Karl Barth's Critically Realistic Dialectical Theology: Its Genesis and Development 1910–1936* (Oxford: Clarendon Press, 1995), p. 11.

47. Chalamet, *Dialectical Theologians*, p. 11.

Dialectical variety itself is also a facet of the dialectical method, lest the *expectation* of incessant tension become a kind of conceptually static position. However, it is still helpful to categorize the school of dialectical theology as being more antagonistic than resolved in emphasis. This is because the notion of 'synthesis', as found in the prevalent nineteenth-century theologies of divine immanence, was clearly rejected by the dialectical theologians.[48]

In reaction to the ease with which dialectical synthesis had been attained within theological liberalism, the dialectical theologians felt it contingently necessary to refrain from absolutist statements which made no reference to their dialectical other: 'Neither my affirmation nor my denial lays claim to being God's truth…I have never affirmed without denying and never denied without affirming, for neither affirmation nor denial can be final.'[49] Indeed, these critical dialectical theologians felt their situation necessitated the essential 'impossibility' of theology itself, even though theology must remain active in radical openness to God. Indeed, the task of the dialectical theologian was an active grasping for what cannot be *fully* grasped:

> [T]o behave busily, without being straitened by eternity; to be zealous, without noticing that our actions pass to corruption; to be lazy, without the terror of irrevocable time; to be pious, without remembering our essential godliness; to be impious, without a thought of the pre-eminent glory of God.[50]

Such polarized language was typical of the kind of theological tension involved in the navigation between oppositions. This contradictory language was bound up with the sermons that Barth and others preached:

> Precisely this is necessary, that only with human lips we pronounce and with human ears we hear the contradiction – God's wrath and God's mercy, God's dominion and God's help, God's majesty and God's love, God's law and God's gospel. This enigma in the external words of God must ever again overwhelm us and convince us, witness to us that God's goodness and faithfulness are new every morning, lead us to repentance, raise us up, and so prepare us to let God actually speak and listen to Him.[51]

48. Although Barth is more affirmative of synthesis in his 1919 Tambach lecture, this does not come at the expense of temporal tension between thesis and antithesis, but rather becomes the *telos* towards which the yes and no point; ultimately: 'Rest is in God alone.' Barth, 'The Christian's Place in Society', in *The Word of God and the Word of Man*, pp. 311–12. Barth would eventually categorize 'synthesis' as 'the least Christian of all'. Barth, *CD* I/1, p. 176.

49. Barth, 'The Word of God and the Task of Ministry', in *The Word of God and the Word of Man*, , p. 209.

50. Barth, *Romans*, p. 292.

51. Barth and Thurneysen, 'The Eternal Light', in *Come Holy Spirit*, pp. 57–66 [58–9].

Here, dialectics themselves are declared as God's own paradoxical revelation to finite humanity, who are beckoned to hear and live in response to his Word, precisely *in* its apparent contradictions. The tension of Yes-and-No was crucial to dialectical theology, in all its forms. However, overt *emphasis* upon antithetical tension is not the only expression theological dialectic may take. There are numerous ways in which this account can be nuanced, not least because of the complexities to be found in Barth's own 'dialectical' struggles *with* dialectic.

b. *Dialectical Complexity in Barth.*

Despite being the reluctant spearhead of the 'dialectical theology' school, Barth himself had a complex relationship to dialectic. Indeed, even early on he exerted warnings against those who (ironically) sought to glorify 'dialectical theology' as though it somehow sanctified theological speech:

> If one should fancy that it possesses a special pre-eminence, at least in preparing the way for the action of God, let him remember that it and its paradoxes can do no more *to this end* than can a simple direct word of faith and humility.[52]

Barth was reluctant to allow 'dialectical theology' to become its own self-affirming human word, even as it pointed to the denial of the human word. Such warnings, however, came in the midst of Barth also defending and *demonstrating* dialectic. Barth could not allow dialectic to take centre stage for theological speech but nor could he ever reject it entirely. The complexity within Barth's dialectical thought exemplifies just how flexible the term 'dialectic' can become, even with the aforementioned handles that have been suggested thus far, such as 'openness', 'tension', 'restlessness', 'insecurity', 'crisis' or 'negativity'. Barth retains many of these traits in his theological method, but emphasizes them differently at different points. What can be maintained from the outset is that Barth perpetually resisted any outright resolution of polarity tension, as George Hunsinger notes:

> The field of tension...was something to be respected and worked within, not something to be explained away or resolved for the sake of achieving a tidier conceptual outcome. No possible tidier outcome could be achieved except at the expense of hermeneutical adequacy.[53]

It was once widely thought that Barth ceased to be a thoroughgoing dialectical theologian after his 'turn to analogy' following his 1931 book on Anselm. This view was first purported by Hans Urs Von Balthasar,[54] with whom Barth even agreed as a correct reading of his theological trajectory. However many have since

52. Barth, 'Word of God and Task of Ministry', p. 212.

53. George Hunsinger, *How to Read Karl Barth: The Shape of His Theology* (Oxford: Oxford University Press, 1991), p. 107.

54. Hans Urs von Balthasar, *The Theology of Karl Barth*, trans. Edward T. Oakes (San Francisco: Ignatius Press, 1992), pp. 72–86.

argued that Barth maintains this dialectical connection, even within his turn to analogy.[55] What did change for Barth was a move away from overtly emphasizing the paralysing nature of the dialectical *condition*, to emphasizing dialectical theology *in light of* the Gospel. Barth stresses that the 'sum of the Gospel' offers a radical divergence to perpetual theological tension:

> It is not a mixed message of joy and terror, salvation and damnation. Originally and finally it is not dialectical but non-dialectical. It does not proclaim in the same breath both good and evil, both help and destruction, both life and death...
> It does, of course, throw a shadow...The Yes cannot be heard unless the No is also heard. But the No is said for the sake of the Yes and not for its own sake. In substance, therefore, the first and last word is Yes and not No.[56]

The Gospel, for Barth, is not itself dialectical and hence should govern the way theology understands its no-less-dialectical task. Where the earlier dialectical 'school' made a sharp break from divine immanentist theologies by emphasizing theology's necessary brokenness, here the Gospel's pre-eminence becomes the necessary lens through which dialectics are interpreted. Barth still allows 'a place for doubt, for the dialectic of Yes and No, for the attitude of perhaps and perhaps not', but adds the important caveat that dialectic must reside in theology's 'forecourt' of 'possibilities' and should never be the main enterprise.[57] It is the Gospel, he adds, that 'makes it impossible for us to be ceaselessly and therefore hesitantly occupied with these possibilities'.[58] Barth recognized that the potentially 'ceaseless' nature of the dialectical task can easily elevate dialectic to an inappropriate height within theological speech.

Where Barth had once emphasized dialectic as though it was the *only* aspect of revelation, he saw that revelation also reveals dialectic's limitations and the primacy of the 'undialectical' Gospel. The Gospel was not to be seen as an 'equal' to dialectic, but as having determinative value. Barth categorized this divergence *within* revelation as God's 'veiling' and 'unveiling'. Here, like the Reformers' approach to Scripture, any unclarity is viewed *in light of* prior clarity:

> The relationship between veiling and unveiling is not symmetrical equivocal, vacillating or obscure...If we want to describe the relationship between the two

---

55. McCormack notably counters such 'developmental theories which drove a wedge between the early "dialectical" Barth and a later, all-too-positive, "neo-orthodox" Barth'. Bruce L. McCormack, *Orthodox and Modern: Studies in the Theology of Karl Barth* (Grand Rapids: Baker Academic, 2008), p. 113. For a nuanced contestation of this view, see Rustin E. Brian, *Covering Up Luther: How Barth's Christology Challenged the* Deus Absconditus *That Haunts Modernity* (Eugene: Cascade, 2013), pp. 40–56.

56. Barth, *CD* II/2, p. 13.

57. Barth, *CD* IV/3, p. 288.

58. Ibid.

concepts…we must always note that what is involved is an ordered dialectic, and indeed one which is teleologically ordered.[59]

Here, the notion of the 'teleological' dialectic is ultimately what could be called – more broadly – a 'hierarchical' dialectic. The first port-of-call is the 'Yes', which prefigures both the 'No' and, even, the 'Yes-and-No'.[60]

It is in Barth's return to the Gospel's clarity and priority that we see the dialectical complexity in his approach. It would be easy to assume he was no longer concerned with dialectic in emphasizing this 'triumph' of the Yes.[61] However, Barth was *as* 'dialectical' in the 1960s as he was in the 1920s. He knew that dialectics were neither excisable from revelation, nor were they escapable by the theologian or preacher. At all points along the way Barth resists any static norm whereby theology can repose *without* dialectic: 'Nowhere do we find a rule which enables us to grasp [the dialectic] in such a way that we can make organic parts of the distinctions and evade the contradictions as such. We are led now one way, now another.'[62] Barth's return to the 'Yes', then, is by no means a synthesis whereby the antagonistic tension of the Yes-and-No is abolished.[63] Even where the 'Yes' governs the way dialectic is approached within revelation, human speech is still inseparable from 'the contradictions' which remain beyond our grasp, behind the veil. Again, it is apparent that Barth's use of dialectic is not a simple matter of affirming or harmonizing tension, but an ongoing openness to the distinct otherness of God's revelation.[64]

59. Barth, *CD* II/1, p. 236.

60. See also Barth's 'Kierkegaardian' expression of the relationship between time and eternity which permeated many of his earlier 'dialectical' sermons: 'You see, eternity is not time and time is not eternity…these two factors of our existence are not of equal strength. Rather, eternity is in motion toward, nay, into time.' Barth, 'The Freedom of the Word of God', in *Come Holy Spirit*, pp. 216–29 [221].

61. Indeed, a 'triumphant Yes' was always present in Barth's dialectical theology, as Berkouwer says of the *Römerbrief*: 'We must…not see here a strange and peculiar dialectical "balance" between Yes and No, but a conquest of the Yes *in* and *through* the No because the triumph of the Yes becomes manifest exactly at that point where judgement is pronounced over man's *own* righteousness.' G. C. Berkouwer, *The Triumph of Grace in the Theology of Karl Barth* (London: The Paternoster Press, 1956), p. 34.

62. Barth, *CD* I/2, p. 509.

63. Van Vleet, noting the relationship between Barth's and Jacques Ellul's dialectical methods, uses the term 'dialectical inclusion' to speak of how such a method 'seeks to show interconnections and strives towards synthesis.' Jacob E. Van Vleet, *Dialectical Theology and Jacques Ellul: An Introductory Exposition* (Minneapolis: Fortress Press, 2014), p. 21. This, however, misunderstands the fuller scope of what Barth's dialectics actually refer to, particularly in light of Barth's overt critiques of synthesis.

64. It is this openness that has led many commentators to speak of the dynamic nature of Barth's approach: 'Karl Barth's theology is not a static thing: it *happens*, unfolding over time in dynamic ways, often shifting emphasis, sometimes changing, always deepening as

Further to his emphasis on the 'Yes' as governing the 'Yes-and-No', Barth would also speak of dialectic as a consequence of human life itself, an activity of creaturely reality *beyond* the confines of revelation:

> Life involves an unceasing dialectic, in which [humanity] is pushed and rocked backwards and forwards by an alien, irresistible movement, being caught up in a constant change and alternation, in sheer ambiguities, in a relativity and convertibility of all antitheses, which make pointless any will to abide, indeed, any will at all and therefore any consistent action.[65]

Here we find some delineation in Barth's thought between theological and anthropological dialectics. Although dialectical *theology* must be rooted in divine revelation and is inaccessible to humanity by itself, anthropological existence necessitates dialectic because the radical insecurity of *all* human thought and experience. At times, Barth would speak of dialectic as 'our own fatal contribution to the matter' which we should 'refrain from making' in lieu of Gospel proclamation.[66] This appears to demonstrate dialectical method as an 'enemy' to proclamation rather than a necessary element of divine revelation. Indeed, despite maintaining an acute awareness of the Yes-and-No, Barth sometimes speaks as though dialectic were a hindrance to true faith and action, referring to the 'oscillating dialectic of our existence',[67] 'the muffled dialectic of every kind of Yes and No',[68] and the 'idle dialectic' of 'mere deliberations'.[69] For Barth, the anthropological propensity towards obfuscation via dialectical conundrums evaded proper reflection upon (and proclamation of) God's revelation, even as Barth also recognized the necessity of dialectic by eschewing simplistic harmonizations. This creaturely propensity to become engulfed within dialectics is not only seen as sinful but is also deemed a necessary facet of finite human thought:

> Creaturely mind itself does not find itself above but within the dialectic of Yes and No, so that while it would like to prefer the Yes it must also leave some place at least for the No, and can never cling to an unequivocal Yes with the certitude necessary for a life lived in faith.[70]

---

he learns new things, clarifies his thought and responds to fresh questions in his quest to think after God.' Keith L. Johnson, 'A Reappraisal of Karl Barth's Theological Development and his Dialogue with Catholicism', in *International Journal of Systematic Theology* 14:1 (Jan 2012), 3–25 [3].

65. Barth, *CD* IV/3, p. 471.
66. Barth, *CD* IV/2, p. 272.
67. Barth, *CD* IV/3, p. 476.
68. Ibid., p. 821.
69. Barth, *CD* IV/2, p. 540.
70. Barth, *CD* III/1, p. 368.

It is evident, then, that Barth simultaneously regretted and embraced the human propensity towards dialectical thought, since it may obfuscate the clarity of the Gospel via 'mere deliberation' yet is also a necessary condition of creaturely finitude. Barth remains critical of the 'unequivocal Yes' alongside his aforementioned criticism of dialectical indecisiveness, which also hinders the life of faith.

The complexity with which Barth came to view dialectic, then, becomes apparent. We have seen how Barth viewed dialectic as having a number of different starting-points and implications: 1. Dialectic is divinely revealed (in God's veiling); 2. Dialectic is divinely overruled (in God's unveiling); 3. Dialectic is theologically debilitating (in perpetual deliberation); 4. Dialectic is anthropologically innate (in creaturely necessity). As such, Barth could show how dialectical theology was both essential but also dialectically insecure, and must itself remain *in dialogue* with the ongoing task of reflection upon God's unveiling in revelation and the ongoing task of Gospel proclamation.[71] Despite various changes of theological emphasis, the basic problem of human speech in the midst of theological contradiction meant that 'dialectic' would never cease to be a fundamental thrust behind Barth's theology. Although he shifted between different forms and conceptions of theological dialectic, he never ceased to be a 'dialectical' theologian, contemplating the interplay and relationship between opposing polarities of theological truth, in different ways.[72]

The complexity with which Barth's theology embraced (and rejected) dialectical method further evidences the fact that to speak of and use 'dialectic' can never be a straightforward undertaking, and there can be no such thing as an absolute 'dialectical theology' which remains *exclusively* committed to emphasizing theological tension at all times. Approaching theological dialectic conceptually must remain a 'dialectical' process itself. Dialectic must not only be seen as necessary within biblical revelation but must also be called into question itself precisely because of the *locus* of biblical revelation: the Gospel. Yet theological speech can never be so critical of dialectic that it evades theological tension

71. 'The dialectical method itself is not able to proclaim God's Word. This can only happen if God himself intervenes.' Chalamet, *Dialectical Theologians*, p. 208.

72. See Beintker's categories of 'supplementary' and 'complementary' dialectics in Barth's thought. Michael Beintker, *Die Dialektik in 'Der Dialektische Theologie' Karl Barths* (Munich: Kaiser, 1987), p. 38. This distinction between 'supplementary' and 'complementary' dialectics, in fact, precedes Beintker; see Henning Schröer, *Die Denkform der Paradoxität als theologisches Problem* (Göttingen: Vandenhoeck & Ruprecht, 1960), p. 91. McCormack's work leant heavily upon the prior work of Beintker (who in turn had leant upon Schröer's categories). Beintker's identification of four types of dialectic in Barth was, like McCormack's, of landmark importance. However, it has also been more recently critiqued for its inattention to the distinctiveness of paradox within the dialectical schema. Paradox had played the more prominent role in Schröer's earlier categories. See the excursus, 'Rediscovering Henning Schröer's Original Terminology: "*Paradoxie*" and Not "*Dialektik*"' in Brian, *Covering Up Luther*, pp. 40–56.

through false harmonization.[73] What must be maintained is that theological dialectic requires a number of different modes in which it can be observed or used. One of these modes, as will be defined later, is that which poses a further obstacle to dialectic's terminological and functional complexity: 'paradox'.

c. Dialectical Theology and Paradox.

'Dialectics in the theological sense is closely associated with paradox.'[74] Much confusion and fragmentation exists as to the actual difference between dialectic and paradox, with classifications often borrowing from one other's terminology, as in John Macquarrie's definition: 'Paradox is a dialectical conjunction of opposites.'[75] If a paradox is a 'dialectical conjunction', what kind of a conjunction is a dialectic? The following sections will attempt to clear some of this terminological ground, first by noting this terminological tension from within the ranks of the dialectical theologians, before a more specific focus upon what paradox is and how it can be used, theologically.

Paradox played a significant role in the language and methods of dialectical theology. Kierkegaard's varied paradoxical cadence was a key influence,[76] particularly upon the Römerbrief, as were Dostoevsky's 'polyphonies'.[77] McCormack characterizes one of the marks of Barth's early theology as 'the love of paradoxes and dialectic'.[78] Later, Barth would attempt to distance himself not only from the influence of Kierkegaard,[79] but from the use of paradox as a concept: 'It is to be recommended that theology make more sparing use of the term now that it has played its part and also caused all manner of confusion.'[80] Clearly, Barth felt that the overuse and misuse of paradox had become more

---

73. As will be seen, harmonization is not necessarily *un*dialectical per se, so long as it remains 'contingent', existing *alongside* other dialectical possibilities and refraining from abolishing the tension in any absolute sense (see the discussion of dialectical homiletical variety in III.5.i).

74. Bloesch, *A Theology of Word and Spirit*, p. 79.

75. John Macquarrie, *Principles of Christian Theology* (London: SCM, 2003), p. 306.

76. For a helpful overview of Barth's reception of Kierkegaard, see Lee C. Barrett, 'Karl Barth: The Dialectic of Attraction and Repulsion', in Jon Stewart (ed.), *Kierkegaard's Influence on Theology, Tome I: German Protestant Theology* (Farnham: Ashgate, 2012), pp. 1–41. For a specific analysis of Barth's appropriation of Kierkegaard's dialectics, see Peter Oh, 'Complementary Dialectics of Kierkegaard and Barth: Barth's Use of Kierkegaardian Diastasis Reassessed', in *Neue Zeitschrift für Systematicsche Theologie und Religionsphilosophie* 48:4 (2007), pp. 497–512.

77. See Katya Tolstaya, *Kaleidoscope: Dostoevsky and the Early Dialectical Theology*, trans. Anthony Runia (Leiden and Boston: Brill, 2013), pp. 177–340.

78. McCormack, *Barth's Critically Realistic Dialectical Theology*, p. 24.

79. Karl Barth, 'A ThankYou and a Bow – Kierkegaard's Reveille', in *Fragments Grave and Gay*, ed. Martin Rumscheidt, trans. Eric Mosbacher (London: Fontana, 1971), pp. 100–1.

80. Barth, *CD* I/1, p. 166.

trouble than it was worth.[81] Where, in the *Römerbrief*, Barth could state that 'in Jesus revelation is a paradox...He is made known as the Unknown',[82] by the latter stages of the *Church Dogmatics* he declared that ' "Paradox" cannot be our final word in relation to Jesus Christ'.[83] As with dialectic – notably in *precisely* the same way – Barth was unwilling to allow the antithetical nature of theological polarities to undermine or overrule proclamation. Paradox, like dialectic, was not *sufficient* to speak of divine revelation. Although Barth retained the use of dialectic throughout his theology (and distinguished it from paradox), it is clear he also conflates their potentially hindering effects upon faithful theological speech: 'If words like "dialectic" and "paradox" slowly disappeared from Barth's writings at the end of the 1920s...it was because he wished to speak primarily about the good news of Jesus Christ, who is "Yes" and "Amen" and not an ambiguous Yes and No.'[84]

A further complexifying element in assessing the relationship between dialectic and paradox is that many of the 'dialectical theologians' disagreed over precise definitions. As mentioned, dialectical theology necessitates that theological statements are necessarily replete with inner tension and conflict, that all statements involve necessary oppositions and counter-statements. However, what the theologian *does* with this dialectical 'situation' differs widely, as does terminological interpretation. A prime example is Paul Tillich, who had once seen himself 'as a "fellow labourer" with the dialectical theologians'.[85] Tillich's ultimately gaping divergence from Barth is encapsulated in their 'generally polite, but mutually uncomprehending, debate over "paradox" '.[86] His noteworthy essay 'What Is Wrong With the "Dialectic" Theology?' (1935) demonstrates a clear delineation between dialectic and paradox:

A dialectic theology is one in which 'yes' and 'no' belong inseparably together. In the so-called 'dialectic' theology they are irreconcilably separated, and that is why this theology is not dialectic. Rather, it is paradoxical, and therein lies its strength; and it is supernatural, which constitutes its weakness.[87]

---

81. Oddly, Brian argues for Barth's preference for 'paradox' over 'dialectic', in spite of Barth's own comments. See Brian, *Covering Up Luther*, pp. 109–62. This is particularly surprising given his critique of McCormack precisely for overriding Barth's own terminology regarding his 'turn to analogy'.

82. Barth, *Romans*, pp. 97–99.

83. Barth, *CD* IV/2, p. 348.

84. Chalamet, *Dialectical Theologians*, p. 280.

85. John Clayton, 'Tillich, Troeltsch and the Dialectical Theology', in *Modern Theology* 4:4 (1988), pp. 323–44 [325].

86. Clayton, 'Tillich', p. 330.

87. Paul Tillich, 'What Is Wrong with the "Dialectic" Theology', in *The Journal of Religion* 15:2 (1935), pp. 127–45 [127].

Tillich's conception here assumes paradox and dialectic are antithetical: paradox as a separation of opposites, dialectic as an amalgamation of opposites.[88] Tillich's particular distinction appears to be somewhat unusual because 'paradox' is usually defined as a unity of seemingly irreconcilable opposites, and 'dialectic' as the method in which opposites are separated and held in tension. Tillich's definition of a *truly* ' "dialectic" theology' appears to render dialectic as a kind of synthesis ('"yes" and "no" belong inseparably together'), 'a three-dimensional way of thinking'.[89] Here, dialectic is itself a kind of dialogue in which both Yes and No are equally involved in the process towards the final Yes. His criticism of Barth is that the 'supernatural' Yes cancels out the dialogical Yes-and-No, from which the Yes ought to arise. For Tillich, a true dialectic requires resolution to occur from within the sphere of the Yes-and-No rather than inserted 'from above'.

However, it could be said that Tillich's terminological distinction appears to be somewhat arbitrary,[90] since there is no absolutely definitive 'dialectic theology'. As we have seen, the simultaneous emphasis upon the 'yes' alongside the 'no' *and* the 'yes-and-no' does not render something undialectical, but demonstrates the different ways in which dialectic can be used and observed, whether harmonized, antagonized or taxonomically ordered. Conversely, it is also fair to say that Barth is ultimately no closer to helping us distinguish paradox from dialectic due to his multifarious uses of both. Where Tillich's terminological distinction seems obstructively narrow, Barth's appears obstructively vague. Although this demonstrates the complexity of dialectical terminology, it offers no further light on dialectic's relationship to paradox. Thus, we will now attempt a nuanced delineation which grants paradox its proper conceptual place *within* this dialectical complexity.

3. *Paradox*

i. *Defining Paradox*

Paradoxes are baffling. Faced with an apparently impeccable argument that leads to an apparently outrageous conclusion, we are confused and confounded.

88. Later, Tillich would also define paradoxes as those which simultaneously 'reveal and hide' (mirroring Barth's formulation of God's 'veiling and unveiling' in revelation) and as conjunctions of opposites such as 'profane and sublime' or 'demonic and divine'. See Paul Tillich, *Systematic Theology*, vol. 3 (London: SCM Press, 1978), pp. 375–7. Such conjunctions, of course, are not ontological 'unities' as such, but rhetorical formulations. It would be just as appropriate to call them 'dialectics' as 'paradoxes'.

89. Tillich, 'What Is Wrong with the "Dialectic" Theology', p. 145.

90. '[For Barth], disagreement over the meaning of "dialectic" ought not to become the central point of the discussion. He had no stake in the terms "dialectic" or "paradox" with the exception of stressing the radical difference between human and divine and the paradoxical locus of God's word in the human, Jesus Christ.' Uwe Carsten Scharf, *The Paradoxical Breakthrough of Revelation: Interpreting the Divine-Human Interplay in Paul Tillich's Work, 1913–1964* (Berlin: Walter de Gruyter, 1999), p. 88.

On the one hand, the conclusion appears false; on the other hand, it apparently must be true. What appears to be cannot be, we assume.[91]

In spite of the obfuscation of the term 'paradox' in the modern dialectical theology school, it is still possible to see a pattern in the way it has been used throughout the theological tradition. Abstractly, a paradox can be defined as a unified juxtaposition of seemingly incompatible polarities. Paradox is not a 'method' of thinking – it is a concrete *status* of two conjoined entities which appear to be irreconcilable. It is thus necessarily absurd *and* rational: 'Paradox, though chaotic, contains order within it.'[92] This seemingly absurd order relates to being rather than knowing. It is not a way of seeing reality, it *is* a particular reality itself.

Paradox, thus understood, could be exemplified via the ontological status of a marriage, particularly in light of Pauline imagery: '"A man will leave his father and mother and be united to his wife, and the two will become one flesh." This is a profound mystery' (Eph. 5:31–32). The concept of marriage involves two beings as one being while retaining their individual particularity. Evidently, the marriage itself is the paradox – the status. However, to speak about *how* the two marriage partners interact *within* this paradoxical status would be to invoke a type of dialectical method. Because it is impossible to know *how* two people may remain separate individuals within the 'one flesh' union, Paul refers to such a union as a 'profound mystery' (referring simultaneously, of course, to Christ's union with the Church). Such naming can be said to be 'dialectical' because 'mystery' is a way of referring to and interpreting the paradox – but it is not itself the paradox.[93] Understood with this analogy in mind, then, paradox is not the conflating, engaging, conversing or separating of two polarities ('husband' and 'wife'); it is the very status of the two distinct entities in their seemingly impossible unity. Paradox is thus specifically ontological – not methodological – in nature, whereby the multivalent conception of dialectic may connote both ontology *and* method. Paradox refers to a *specific* status of affairs – it is the 'marriage' itself, not the wedding, conversing, divorcing, and the like. Thus, although there may be numerous kinds of dialectic, there is only one form of paradox. Such a definite understanding of paradox might be obfuscated by the 'paradoxes' often found in the form of subversive turns of phrase: 'proverbial paradox', which must be distinguished from what we will call 'ontological paradox'.

91. Doris Olin, *Paradox* (Durham: Acumen, 2003), p. 21.

92. Nathaniel S. Hellerstein, *Diamond: A Paradox Logic* (River Edge: World Scientific Publishing, 2010), p. 23.

93. Some traditions also view 'mystery' in the same light as 'paradox'; both terms refer to the inaccessibility of an ontological truth, usually based upon the creator-creature distinction. See Baugus' definition of theological paradox as 'a particular kind of revealed mystery'. Bruce P. Baugus, 'Paradox and Mystery in Theology', in *The Heythrop Journal* 29:2 (2013), pp. 238–51 [249]. Barth makes a similar point regarding Romans 11:25: 'by mystery Pauls means what we call "paradox"'. Barth, *Romans*, p. 412.

a. *Proverbial Paradox.*

A proverbial paradox is phraseological in nature, with no explicit claim to ontology. Such paradoxical speech usually involves short, ironical axioms in which expected outcomes are subverted. Barth connected such paradoxical language to the concept of 'riddles'.[94] G. K. Chesterton, though a strong advocate of 'ontological paradox', as will be seen, often exemplified the use of such rhetorical riddles. For example: 'Thieves respect property. They only wish to make it their own property that they may more perfectly respect it.'[95] The proverbial paradox is a device used to illuminate or highlight something true through an ironic reversal without making an absolute claim,[96] perhaps unearthing a hypocrisy, offering fresh perspective on a cliché, or highlighting a contradiction in the perceived meaning of a concept (such as the subversion of a thief's attitude to 'property'). Such paradoxical rhetoric often appears throughout the New Testament. Jesus' parables themselves often presented hearers with paradoxical situations,[97] and there are also instances in which he reverses commonly understood concepts within a singular proverbial phrase, such as 'whoever loses his life for my sake will find it' (Matt. 16:25). Superficially, such a statement appears entirely irrational – indeed, 'contradictory' – but its purpose prompts the hearer to think beyond its surface meaning into a reinterpretation of the concept of *losing* and *finding* one's life. Paul, similarly, used phrases of oppositional contrast in order to clarify a pedagogical emphasis: 'God chose what is foolish in the world to shame the wise, God chose what is weak in the world to shame the strong' (1Cor. 1:27). Again, the rhetorical point is to re-evaluate the inherited meanings of 'wisdom' or 'strength'. The setting-up and subverting of oppositions in this way has a rhetorical purpose, not a claim to ontology. Proverbial paradox, then, may be called 'dialectical' in an informal sense but bears no explicit relation to the concerns of dialectical theology as such. As we consider the relationship of paradox *to* dialectic, we will engage with the tenets of the more relevant category, 'ontological paradox'.

b. *Ontological Paradox.*

'Ontological paradox' is the truthful status of a seemingly impossible truth. It is not a witty turn of phrase or an acute use of irony, but a conceptual understanding of apparently contradictory reality as *true* reality. Ontology here necessitates a

---

94. Barth, *CD* III/1, p. 373.

95. G. K. Chesterton, *The Man Who Was Thursday: A Nightmare* (London: Atlantic Books, 2008), p. 37.

96. 'Chesterton's paradox operates by upsetting or inverting our normal assumptions.' David W. Fagerberg, *The Size of Chesterton's Catholicism* (Notre Dame: University of Notre Dame Press, 1998), p. 130. Chesterton himself notes Oscar Wilde's oft-quoted definition of paradox: 'Truth standing on her head to attract attention.' G. K. Chesterton, *The Paradoxes of Mr. Pond* (Kelly Bray: House of Stratus, 2008), p. 41.

97. The etymology of 'parable' means 'putting things side by side', connoting the juxtaposition of two incompatible concepts, as with paradox. See 'Parable', in I. Howard Marshall, et al. (eds.), *New Bible Dictionary* (Nottingham: IVP, 2007), p. 867.

theological interpretation which gives transcendent meaning to such a contradiction (lest the affirmation of contradiction per se render *all* logical formulations redundant). To understand a paradoxical truth as *true* means allowing for the contradiction to exist without logical harmonization or resolution. In observing such a paradox, we see two things at one and the same time that ought *not* exist side-by-side, yet we recognize that they somehow *do* exist side-by-side, and *truthfully* so. Ontological paradox is not a mere axiom in subverting a concept, but a genuine simultaneity of oppositions, and allowing that 'contradiction' can be an inherent aspect of a particular doctrinal truth.

A philosophical concept which emerged in the 1980s ('dialetheism') bears similar – though not identical – connotations to ontological paradox. Dialetheism asserts the possibility that Aristotle's Law of Non-Contradiction (LNC)[98] is not *necessarily* logically binding in all instances: 'The view that the LNC fails, that some contradictions are true, is called *dialetheism*.'[99] Dialetheism is understood as 'para-consistent logic',[100] whereby the allowance of particular contradictions does not lead, consequentially, to logical chaos. Thus, there may be 'true' contradictions alongside 'false' contradictions (which are deemed 'false' precisely *because* of the logical contradiction[101]): 'The dialetheist accepts that some contradictions are true, in which case...the negation of such a (true) contradiction is false and also true. The dialetheist, then, does not reject the LNC but, rather, accepts that it is (logically) true, and also false.'[102] Ontological paradox differs from dialetheism by allowing the possibility that the contradiction is finitely 'apparent' but *in*finitely 'possible' in comprehension; as in Anderson's contrasting account: 'We are not

---

98. 'But since it is impossible that contradiction should be true of the same subject at the same time, it is evident that neither can contraries possibly subsist at the same time in the same subject ...If, therefore, it is impossible at the same time to affirm and deny with truth, it is impossible that also contraries should be inherent in the same subject at the same time; but either both must be inherent partially, or the one partially and the other simply absolutely.' Aristotle, *Metaphysics*, trans. John H. M'Mahon (London: Henry G. Bohn, 1857), p. 106.

99. Graham Priest, 'What's So Bad About Contradictions', in Graham Priest, et al. (eds.), *The Law of Non-Contradiction: New Philosophical Essays* (Oxford: Clarendon Press, 2004), pp. 23–38 [29].

100. Ibid., p. 25.

101. 'The dialetheist accepts that some contradictions are true, in which case...the negation of such a (true) contradiction is false and also true. The dialethetist, then, does not reject the LNC but, rather, accepts that it is (logically) true, and also false.' Bradley Armour-Garb, 'Diagnosing Dialetheism', in *The Law of Non-Contradiction*, pp. 113–25 [114].

102. Within the school of philosophy known as 'logic', paradox usually refers to the 'proverbial' type (noted above), such as 'Zeno's Paradox', the 'Barber Paradox' or the 'Liar Paradox', rather than the ontological. As such, dialetheism appears very similar to ontological paradox. However, this shared philosophical identity is ultimately transformed by the distinctly *theological* element of paradox. To speak of ontological paradox in *Christian* doctrine requires entirely sui generis conceptual categories of revelation which are untranslatable to dialetheism.

positing an exception to the laws of logic, but merely acknowledging an element of imprecision in our systematic comprehension of data.'[103] This means, essentially, that divine transcendence provides the only comprehension of what appears logically impossible. For this reason, ontological paradox is connected to the sibling concept of 'mystery' and may be seen as moving beyond the parameters of non-theistic philosophical logic.

Another point of difference to a purely philosophical notion of contradiction is that ontological paradox, because of these necessarily theological parameters, refers specifically to apparent inconsistencies within Christian doctrine, such as the hypostatic union, in which Jesus Christ is understood to be fully man, fully God and ontologically *one*. Precise demonstration of the logical possibility of this truth is partially inaccessible to the theologian; yet the doctrine is nonetheless acceptable via ontological paradox. The inconsistency is merely 'apparent', or, indeed, there is a way in which it can be accepted as true *despite* the apparent contradiction.[104] Where dialetheism speaks of knowing true truths which *are* contradictory, the theological appeal to ontological paradox does not necessarily admit to ultimate impossibility in the concept itself, but impossibility in our knowledge of *how* it is possible.

Some interpretations of paradox attempt the exact opposite by seeing paradoxes as logically reconcilable. However, this would mean such truths are no longer paradoxes in the *ontological* sense. If a paradox becomes fully explainable, it no longer carries the 'appearance' of contradiction, and only *seems* to be a paradox to those who have not yet encountered its 'explanation'.[105] Ontological paradox cannot allow for comprehensively logical explanation; rather, the paradox is simply expressible as both true and apparently impossible. Although paradox can often be misused to veil logical ineptitude,[106] ontological paradox can be defined as an apparently outright contradiction which is *nonetheless true*. We will now attend

103. See, for example, Anderson's contrasting account: '[With paradox] we are not positing an exception to the laws of logic, but merely acknowledging an element of imprecision in our systematic comprehension of data.' James Anderson, *Paradox in Christian Theology: An Analysis of Its Presence, Character, and Epistemic Status* (London: Paternoster Press, 2007), p. 276.

104. Although it remains difficult to make absolute distinctions between the two, what distinguishes a 'genuine' contradiction (e.g. 2+2=4 and 2+2=5) from a paradox is that a contradiction is *accessibly* contradictory, not just *apparently* contradictory. Reconciling the hypostatic union, for example, is demonstrably inaccessible to human reason, yet it remains possible to affirm its 'trueness' because of the revealed truths of human finitude and divine transcendence; if the essential truth of the hypostatic union is divinely revealed (through Scripture), it is an *inaccessible* contradiction: we know it is impossible to know *how*, but we do not *know* that it is impossible.

105. One nineteenth-century example of this approach suggests theological paradoxes exist only because 'superficial minds' have not *yet* grasped their deeper truth. See J. Bayley, *Scripture Paradoxes: Their True Explanation* (London: Charles P. Alvey, 1868), p. 1.

106. Aristotle saw the appeal to paradox as sophistic, invoked by philosophers only 'when they are unable to solve arguments open to dispute'. Aristotle, *Metaphysics*, p. 108.

to some of the different ways in which ontological paradox has been articulated and used within theological speech, before showing its relationship to dialectic.

ii. 'Paradoxical' Theology

We have seen there is a clear sense in which dialectic has functioned in a uniquely theological method. It could be said, however, that paradox has a far greater legacy in the theological tradition. This is evident even in the creeds, which possess a paradoxical character by pointing to the ontology of acceptable contradiction (particularly regarding the Trinity and Christology). Similarly, the apophatic tradition, by speaking of what ought not – or cannot – be spoken, demonstrates ontological paradox by simultaneously and deliberately breaking the 'law' it asserts, as when Augustine highlights the inherent contradiction of *speaking* of God's ineffability:

> God is not even to be called 'unspeakable', because to say even this is to speak of Him. Thus there arises a curious contradiction of words, because if the unspeakable is what cannot be spoken of, it is not unspeakable if it can be called unspeakable. And this opposition of words is rather to be avoided by silence than to be explained away by speech.[107]

Denys Turner refers to such an apophatic stance as 'an acquired ignorance'.[108] Aquinas, too, despite being renowned for logical exactitude, uses similar apophatic language: 'Man reaches the highest point of his knowledge about God when he knows that he knows him not, inasmuch as he knows that that which is God transcends whatsoever he conceives of him.'[109] Indeed, it has been noted that

Some American Evangelical responses often tend to lean upon Aristotelian logic when rejecting the obfuscating problems of paradoxical usage in modern theology. See, for example, Sproul, who warns against the 'exalted irrationality' of paradoxical claims: 'What is sometimes called *paradox* is nothing more than sloppy thinking.' R. C. Sproul, *Essential Truths of the Christian Faith* (Wheaton: Tyndale House, 1992), pp. 7–8. However, the issue at stake here, ultimately, is whether or not Christian theology is more indebted to Scriptural revelation than to the LNC. Although paradox need not dispense with the LNC as such, to speak of paradox as inherent within revelation is to say that this revelation (even if open to the charge of 'exalted irrationality') must be regarded as being superior to the LNC in our comprehension. As De Lubac aptly puts it, paradoxes 'do not sin against logic, whose laws remain inviolable: but they escape its domain'. Henri De Lubac, *Paradoxes of Faith*, trans. P. Simon, S. Kreilkamp and E. Beaumont (San Francisco: Ignatius Press, 1987), p. 12.

107. Augustine, *On Christian Doctrine*, trans. J. F. Shaw (New York: Christian Literature Publishing Co., 1886), p. 10.

108. Denys Turner, *The Darkness of God: Negativity in Christian Mysticism* (Cambridge: Cambridge University Press, 1998), p. 19.

109. Thomas Aquinas, *De Potentia Dei*, trans. the English Dominican Fathers (Westminster, Maryland: The Newman Press, 1952), q. 7, a. 5, ad. 14.

Aquinas' answer to many questions is 'a simultaneous yes and no', inducing 'the proximity of paradox'.[110] Luther, too, is well known for his embrace of paradoxical theological conceptions: 'From beginning to end his theology of the cross is a theology of paradox, a theology of apparent contradictions that point to a deeper meaning.'[111] It is clear, even in such fleeting samples, that the crossovers between 'dialectic' and 'paradox' are so apparent that they are in danger of becoming synonymous. In the following specific exemplifications of ontological paradox in the theological tradition, then, we will see the distinctiveness of paradox, the way in which dialectical 'method' is used to speak *of* paradox, and the ways in which paradox may be seen as a 'type' of dialectic itself.

a. *Ontological Paradox in Chesterton.*

The Catholic thinker, G. K. Chesterton (1874–1936), known as the 'Prince of Paradox', was certainly one of the most insightful – though eccentric – paradoxical thinkers of the modern era.[112] Although we have noted Chesterton's prominent usage of 'proverbial' paradox, he also holds to the essentiality of ontological paradox.[113] Paradox, for Chesterton, underpins the essential Christological content of Christianity: 'Chesterton places the chief Christological mysteries – the Incarnation and the Atonement – in a mould of paradox which reflects its character.'[114] He articulates this through the juxtaposition of unreconciled, distinct polarities in simultaneity: 'Christ [is] not a being apart from God and man, like an elf, nor yet a being half human and half not, like a centaur, but both things at once and both things thoroughly, very man and very God.'[115] This approach to contradiction is theologically driven, based entirely on the apparent fact that Jesus Christ is (ontologically)

110. Denis R. Janz, 'Syllogism or Paradox: Aquinas and Luther on Theological Method', in *Theological Studies* 59 (1998), pp. 3–21 [15].

111. Ibid., p. 6.

112. Many speak of 'the staggering paradox that animates Chesterton's entire work'. Ralph C. Wood, *Chesterton: The Nightmare Goodness of God* (Waco: Baylor University Press, 2011), p. 221. Chesterton had 'the ability to see how a statement which on the face of it was false or irrational might actually prove to be true or rational'. William Oddie, *Chesterton and the Romance of Orthodoxy: The Making of GKC, 1874–1908* (Oxford: OUP, 2010), p. 188.

113. Kenner has noted the distinction between what he calls 'metaphysical' and 'rhetorical' paradox in Chesterton's thought. Hugh Kenner, *Paradox in Chesterton* (London: Sheed & Ward, 1947), p. 16. Oddie says, however, it is 'misleading to see the distinctions between Kenner's two types as clear-cut'. Oddie, *Chesterton and the Romance of Orthodoxy*, p. 191. For Chesterton, the two were part of the same entity; paradox was engrained in the cosmos, through ontology and – subsequently – through human language.

114. 'Chesterton places the chief Christological mysteries – the Incarnation and the Atonement – in a mould of paradox which reflects its character.' Aidan Nichols, *G. K. Chesterton, Theologian* (Manchester: Darton, Longman and Todd, 2009), p. 99.

115. G. K. Chesterton, *Orthodoxy* (San Francisco: Ignatius, 1995), p. 93.

a paradox. Consequent reflection upon the apparent inconsistency, then, occurs only from the inherited *basis* that this seemingly impossible truth is actually true.[116] The hypostatic union represents two polarities which are simultaneously irreconcilable *and* inseparable. Chesterton argues that such creedal recognition exemplifies a 'pure, *defiant* paradox',[117] unperturbed by its apparent impossibility to the finite mind. To accept such an apparent contradiction as true – with no possible access to its reconciliation – may be seen as a passive response whereby the contradiction is muted *through* its acceptance. However, such paradoxical 'defiance' does not lead Chesterton to a functional resolution between opposing polarities but an insistence that both polarities maintain their total distinctiveness even in their unity. Concepts such as 'dilution', 'balance' or 'synthesis' are inadequate because they lead to a negation of both polarities, where 'neither is present in its full strength or contributes its full colour'.[118] Contrary to the notion of synthesis, Chesterton articulates a resolute conflict between the polarities: 'Christianity got over the difficulty of combining furious opposites, by keeping them both, and keeping them both furious.'[119] These 'furious opposites' are intended not to supersede one another but to maintain a defiant opposition against total resolution *or* separation.

The 'furious opposites' of Christ's dual nature are not 'in tension', but are paradoxically resolved *in* their *unresolved* conjunction. To accept this ontological paradox is to accept that these two opposites *are* 'together', though it remains impossible to see *how*. Indeed, any attempt to demonstrate this would be to exchange this necessary conflict for a static balance, which Chesterton dismisses as fundamentally *un*theological: 'Paganism declared virtue was in a balance. Christianity declared it was in a conflict: the collision of two passions apparently opposite. Of course they were not *really* inconsistent; but they were such that it was hard to hold simultaneously.'[120] Describing an ontological paradox, then, is not a passive solution to contradiction but a continuously active and challenging response to the complexity of revelation, whereby the apparent inconsistency is believed (in faith) to be 'not *really* inconsistent'. Such a theological stance is never fully attainable but can only be demonstrated through the perpetual rearticulation of these opposing polarities as being simultaneously *at war* and *at one*.[121]

116. Milbank defines Chestertonian paradox as 'a truth revealed in and through the contradiction…paradox leads to a moment of recognition beyond the contradictions in which a truth becomes manifest'. Alison Milbank, *Chesterton and Tolkien as Theologians: The Fantasy of the Real* (London: T & T Clark, 2007), p. 88. See, again, the 'transconsistent logic' of dialetheism.

117. G. K. Chesterton, 'Bacon and Beastliness', in *The Speaker* (8 February 1902), p. 532.

118. Chesterton, *Orthodoxy*, p. 95.

119. Ibid., p. 96.

120. Ibid., p. 94.

121. Oddie calls this the 'equipoise of balancing opposites'. Oddie, *Chesterton and the Romance of Orthodoxy*, p. 366. The term 'equipoise' is accurate, though it may be unhelpful to use the term 'balance', which suggests an inadvertent compromise of the full force of each polarity.

The acceptance of dialectical polarities does not mean an acceptance of their compatibility. Each exists side-by-side, neither deleting nor diluting the other.[122]

Evidently, for Chesterton, paradox is not a clever literary escape clause for contradictory logic, picked-up or put-down at one's convenience. He also castigates the affirmation of 'contradiction' as 'the sort of unreason in which only rationalists are allowed to indulge'.[123] Chesterton did not choose paradox as a *preferred* method of thinking; for him, it is ontologically apparent: 'The reason that paradox is continuous and ancient…is that there really is a strand of contradiction running through the universe.'[124] However, he also criticizes the *uncritical* descent into contradictory logic whereby 'paradoxy has become orthodoxy', where 'men repose in a paradox as placidly as in a platitude'.[125] Indeed, he mocks those thinkers 'who maintain that there is something that is both Yes and No. I do not know whether they pronounce it Yo.'[126] It is evident that Chesterton holds logical consistency in high regard and does not accept unjustifiable contradiction: 'It is instantly apparent, even to the child, that there cannot be both affirmation and contradiction.'[127] Such reservations immediately suggest a nuance in his understanding of why the contrariness of particular theological contradictions is apparently acceptable in distinction to any kind of absurdist or radically sceptical philosophical position. As with the dialectical theologians, Chesterton accepts such revealed incongruities on the basis of the finitude of human reason and the transcendence of God, who reveals some *particular* truths 'dialectically' rather than univocally.[128] Reason and logic *remain* essential to the finite mind, while such paradoxes prove to be transcendental exceptions to the equally transcendental rule.

Chesterton's paradoxical focus did not necessarily result in a dialectical 'method'. Although his writings are full of proverbial paradoxical statements, we find no fixation upon the *notion* of theological opposites, on a tension of

122. There is a cadence here with Barth's reflections on the essentiality of acknowledging the 'inconceivability' of the Chalcedonian formula. See Barth, *CD* I/2, 173.

123. G. K. Chesterton, *The Everlasting Man* (Radford: Wilder Publications, 2008), p. 19. See also: 'Though the contradiction may seem to them a paradox, this is the very contrary of the truth.' Ibid., p. 40.

124. Chesterton, 'Bacon and Beastliness', p. 532. Chesterton also connects paradox to the notion of 'common sense', which he saw as an extension of God's revelation: 'Paradox and common sense are…inextricably connected…paradox is an instrument of common sense in a world out of joint.' Oddie, *Chesterton and the Romance of Orthodoxy*, p. 193.

125. G. K. Chesterton, *St. Thomas Aquinas* (New York: Image Books, 1956), p. 144.

126. Ibid., p. 167.

127. Ibid., p. 166.

128. For Chesterton, 'paradox must be of the nature of things because of God's infinity and the limitations of the world and of man's mind. To us limited beings God can express His idea only in fragments. We can bring together apparent contradictions in those fragments whereby a greater truth is suggested.' Maisie Ward, *Gilbert Keith Chesterton* (New York: Sheed & Ward, 1943), p. 155.

Yes-and-No, a radical openness in theological articulation, nor musings upon the inherent questionability of theological speech. Paradox for Chesterton was the necessary category to describe the fundamental tenets of Christian theology, but these oppositional truths are not held in tension, they are merely accepted *as* truths. For this reason, Chesterton differs from the dialectical theologians but is nonetheless 'dialectical' in his consistent awareness and acceptance of ontological paradox. Chesterton's articulation of paradox – where the polarities remain both conflicted *and* married – is helpful in delineating a 'paradoxical dialectic' from other dialectics, as will be seen. We will now see, in Eckhart, a similar conception of paradox which leads to a *different* kind of dialectical articulation, whereby the ongoing paradoxical tension itself is heavily emphasized, particularly regarding preaching.

b. *Ontological Paradox in Eckhart.*

Meister Eckhart (1260–1327), a Christian mystic and preacher, understood all theology through the lens of paradox. Due in part to Eckhart's influence, the term 'paradox' is often misperceived as a way of thinking common or even *exclusive* to theological mysticism. Eckhart's paradoxical theology, however, shares more than a little similarity with dialectical theology. Bernard McGinn has noted that the term 'dialectic' best characterizes Eckhart's theological dynamic,[129] by which he means the back-and-forth cross-examination of all positive or negative statements. Similarly, Cyprian Smith notes that, for Eckhart, paradox is 'the contrast and clash between opposites',[130] while Turner points to Eckhart's 'strategy of *opposing oppositions*'.[131] This antagonistic 'clash' is what we might normally attribute to a dialectical method rather than a static ontological paradox. Although we might disagree with Smith's definition of paradox as a 'clash' (suggesting a *dynamic* tension), this gestures a *type* of dialectic in Eckhart's thought which governs his engagement *with* ontological paradox: 'Eckhart keeps us perpetually swinging from one pole to the other; he will not let us rest in either.'[132] For Eckhart, to remain at one extreme denies the complexity of the truth, which appears as contradiction. Eckhart acknowledges that such truths contain contrary aspects simultaneously, meaning they cannot be engaged in a singular mode but only articulated by reference to their inseparable opposites: 'The one is always in the other: that which embraces is that which is embraced, for it embraces nothing but itself.'[133] This is not merely a dialectical rhetoric, but an expression of ontology. Eckhart affirms the

129. Bernard McGinn, *Meister Eckhart: Teacher and Preacher* (New York: Paulist Press, 1986), p. 26.

130. Cyprian Smith, *The Way of Paradox: Spiritual Life as Taught by Meister Eckhart* (London: Darton, Longman, and Todd, 1988), p. 26.

131. Turner, *The Darkness of God*, p. 209.

132. Smith, *The Way of Paradox*, p. 27.

133. Meister Eckhart, *Sermons & Treatises*, vol. I, trans. M. O'Connell Walshe (Dorset: Element, 1991), p. 121.

simultaneous irreconcilability and inseparability of theological opposites, which – unlike Chesterton – he demonstrates *through* an overtly dialectical utterance.

Eckhart's theological grounding for ontological paradox becomes apparent in his articulation that God is the ultimate unification in which paradox resides: 'These contraries are all contained finally in an all-embracing *unity*; God and man, pleasure and pain, success and failure, are all ultimately one in God.'[134] For Eckhart, it is God's own paradoxical nature that invokes the 'to-and-fro' of interactive dialectical method. This method of theological articulation has a very similar cadence to the early dialectical theology, and also resembles another mystical theologian, Dionysius (c.450–550), who saw paradoxical utterance as the natural medium for theological language, subjected to 'the *twin* pressures of affirmation and negation, of the cataphatic and the apophatic'.[135] This presupposes the impossibility of singularly exclusive statements about God:

> We find people who like the taste of God in one way but not in another, and they want to have God only in one way of contemplation, not in another. I raise no objection, but they are quite wrong. If you want to take God properly, you should take Him equally in all things.[136]

Such an articulation may be questionable with regard to how God might choose to reveal Himself in particular ways for particular purposes, but this is not Eckhart's concern. In his theological conception of paradox he wants to emphasize the paradoxical nature of theological truths via the necessity of *simultaneous* articulation.[137] This occurs through the incessant 'swinging' between the polarities: 'Having made a statement, Eckhart will often go on to deny it; but the truth lies neither in the affirmation nor in the denial, but in the tug-of-war between the two.'[138] For Eckhart, such dialectical tension is necessary because humanity has no access to the simultaneity. Even in the midst of the tug-of-war, this simultaneity can never be finitely expressed: 'God is a word, a word unspoken…who can utter this word? None can do so but he who is this word.'[139] The theologian is left in a precarious position in which they can say nothing concretely and exclusively 'true', articulating only one polarity of God's truth at any one time. Yet Eckhart's incessant stress upon the 'opposite' polarity within each articulation means that *neither* polarity is ever uttered in exclusivity.

Eckhart's dialectical method of engaging ontological paradox, even if helpful in articulating the vitality of paradox within theology itself, highlights the

---

134. Smith, *The Way of Paradox*, p. 26.

135. Turner, *The Darkness of God*, p. 22.

136. Eckhart, *Sermons & Treatises*, p. 112.

137. See again the relation to Dionysius' approach: 'We must both affirm and deny all things of God; and then we must negate the contradiction between the affirmed and the denied.' Turner, *The Darkness of God*, p. 22.

138. Smith, *The Way of Paradox*, p. 27.

139. Eckhart, *Sermons & Treatises*, p. 177.

possible problems such a method might cause for 'decisive' heraldic preaching, due to the perpetual fixation *upon* the paradoxical nature of each theological claim. Nonetheless, this is *how* Eckhart preached. His example points us to the important difference between *contemplating* paradox and *preaching* paradox, whereby the dialectical method itself (unhelpfully) becomes the inescapable lens for *all* proclamatory statements. This also points to the fundamental difference between theological 'explanation' of doctrinal truth and decisive 'proclamation' of doctrinal truth.[140] In Eckhart's grasp of this communicative distinction, we may note a clear difference between 'paradox' and 'dialectic' as concepts. Eckhart bears witness to the paradox of ultimate truth, yet this bearing-witness is not itself 'a paradox', but a dialectical articulation. Eckhart's method is dialectical, reflecting *upon* theological paradox and attempting to preach God's truth *as* ontologically paradoxical. It is clear that his use of paradox coheres with the aforementioned definitions (apparently incompatible oppositions in unity) even as it might be more appropriate to call Eckhart a dialectical theologian and preacher.

As will become clear in the establishing of various dialectical modes, articulating ontological paradox through the overt juxtaposition of incompatible opposites is not the only way theological dialectic may function. Paradoxical articulation itself – as seen in Eckhart's simultaneous clashes and affirmation-denials – bears witness to ontological paradox in one particular way, but becomes limiting if this is the only way the dialectical nature of theology is engaged.

4. *Paradialectical Complexity*

It has been shown that it is possible to define 'paradox' and 'dialectic' as distinct concepts in engaging the problem of variously contradictory polarities. Yet, in order to achieve the terminological clarity required at the outset of this chapter, the full complexity of the interwoven nature of paradox and dialectic must be encountered and reset. The reason for this necessary resetting of the two terms is that – due to the wide and varying uses in the theological and philosophical tradition – many usages overlap between 'concept' and 'method'.[141] We have seen in the dialectical theologians a 'dialectical method' of thinking and speaking *in*

140. 'It is language as *doing* something which the preacher attends to; it is language as *meaning* something which is of principal concern to the teacher. Eckhart the preacher, therefore, can judge with precision what his saying *does*, even while Eckhart the teacher recognizes the possible imprecision of what his saying *says*.' Turner, *The Darkness of God*, p. 149.

141. See, for example, De Lubac: 'Paradox is more charm than dialectics; it is also more realist and more modest, less tense and less hurried; its function is to remind the dialectician when each new stage is reached in the argument, that however necessary this forward movement is no real progress has been made.' De Lubac, *Paradoxes*, pp. 9–10. While he notes something true of paradox here in its 'less hurried' function, he makes the common mistake of conflating dialectic with a simplistic notion of Hegelian synthetic progression.

light of the dialectical problem, as well as a seemingly 'paradoxical method' in Eckhart through the perpetual articulation of polarity tension; these methods are easily conflated and often appear synonymous. We will now see some of the ways this complexity appears most acutely, particularly with Kierkegaard.

i. *Dialectic and Paradox in Kierkegaard*

Søren Kierkegaard (1813–1855) is one thinker who typically complicates the terminological distinctions between paradox and dialectic through his overlapping and various uses of each term. Kierkegaard is a notable figure in the history of dialectic, not only because of his overt and sustained engagement with the dialectical methods of previous thinkers such as Socrates and Hegel, but because his own thought sits somewhat awkwardly in between philosophy and theology. He has been called 'without the smallest doubt the greatest dialectician of modern times',[142] and 'a virtuoso of dialectical dexterity'.[143] A glance at Kierkegaard's various uses of dialectic – knowing also his influence upon subsequent twentieth-century philosophers and theologians – helpfully illustrates the complexity of regarding the different ways dialectic may be used and interpreted. One of the clearest insights emerging from Kierkegaard's multifarious uses of the term is the difference between concept and method. Is dialectic itself 'a contradiction' or do we use dialectic to think *about* contradiction?

Kierkegaard referred to his own philosophical method as having a 'dialectical character', and even a 'dialectical *position*',[144] as though it were the fundamental orientation behind his entire thought-project. David R. Law notes the 'apophatic character' of Kierkegaard's dialectics and highlights their necessity due to the broken insufficiency of human thought and speech.[145] Again, this places Kierkegaard's dialectical rationale in the same line as many of the aforementioned 'dialectical' and 'paradoxical' theologians. Dialectic, for Kierkegaard, is essential to human thought. For Kierkegaard, to deny 'the dialectical' by seeking 'something firm' or 'something magical' (through resolution) is to wilfully evade a necessary human reality: 'Every boundary that wants to exclude the dialectical is *eo ipso* superstition.'[146] The notion of a self-referential 'dialectical position' to his thought also presupposes, of course, that dialectic has a fixed meaning for him

---

142. Haecker, *Kierkegaard*, p. 35.

143. David Cain, 'A Star in the Cross: Getting the Dialectic Right', in Robert L. Perkins (ed.), *International Kierkegaard Commentary*, vol. 21: *For Self-Examination and Judge for Yourself!* (Macon: Mercer University Press, 2002), pp. 315–34 [317].

144. Søren Kierkegaard, *The Point of View for My Work as an Author*, trans. Walter Lowrie (Oxford: Oxford University Press, 1939), pp. 15, 6 (emphasis added).

145. David R. Law, *Kierkegaard as Negative Theologian* (Oxford: Oxford University Press, 1993), pp. 50, 70.

146. Søren Kierkegaard, *Concluding Unscientific Postscript to Philosophical Fragments*, vol. 1, trans. Howard V. Hong and Edna H. Hong (Princeton: Princeton University Press, 1992), p. 44.

(which remains unclear). It has been noted that it may well be impossible that Kierkegaard's dialectics could ever be understood comprehensively.[147] There is, characteristically, a distinct unclarity regarding any familiar dialectical pattern in his work: 'Kierkegaard's dialectics is exceedingly complex and there is a wide range of opinion among Kierkegaard scholars as to its precise nature.'[148] Nonetheless, for Kierkegaard, it can be said that dialectic relates – at the meta-level – to the conflict between oppositional polarities, however the conflict 'occurs'. He refers to 'the criss-cross of dialectics' as though dialectic was a conversational method of back-and-forth interaction without resolution or conclusion,[149] and yet dialectic also appears in many other guises. It may be described as a tension of 'infinite wrestling',[150] but it may also function pejoratively, referring to the human propensity towards 'reflection' over 'action'.[151] Kierkegaard also refers to 'many kinds of dialectic' to separate it from being seen as a purely philosophical concept involving 'logical operations'.[152] Indeed, here Kierkegaard is saying that dialectics are an inherent part of reality itself (they are not imposed *upon* reality by speculative thinking). There also appear to be comical uses of dialectic, including a reference to 'the dialectic of the butter churn',[153] and, even, dialectic as connoting 'battle against wild animals and monsters in the ballads and tales of the Middle Ages'.[154] Evidently, for Kierkegaard, dialectic is 'a kaleidoscopic term',[155] whereby it may also refer non-specifically to *any* relationship between two concepts, subjects or objects.

It is important to note, however, that kaleidoscopic use of a *term* does not necessarily mean an absence of definite meaning. Indeed, despite Kierkegaard's creative uses of the term, he still inherited its philosophical implications from previous thinkers, often referring to Socrates or Hegel whenever discussing dialectic as an idea. It is quite possible, in fact, that Kierkegaard actually had a fairly linear understanding of philosophical dialectics as 'qualitative' (existential) or 'quantitative' (logical).[156] Thus, when dealing with 'quantitative' dialectics, he tends to refer *either* to Socratic dialectic (negation through indirect questioning)

147. Law, *Kierkegaard as Negative Theologian*, p. 36, n. 3.

148. Ibid., p. 35. On Kierkegaard's dialectical variety, see also Stephen. N. Dunning, *Kierkegaard's Dialectic of Inwardness* (Princeton: Princeton University Press, 1985), p. 7.

149. Kierkegaard, *Point of View*, p. 39.

150. Søren Kierkegaard, *Søren Kierkegaard's Journals and Papers* [hereafter, *JP*], vols. 1–6, ed. and trans. Howard V. Hong & Edna H. Hong (Bloomington and London: Indiana University Press, 1967–78), vol. 1, 755, p. 351.

151. Kierkegaard, *The Present Age*, pp. 45–51.

152. Søren Kierkegaard, *Either/Or, Part I*, trans. Howard V. Hong and Edna H. Hong (Princeton: Princeton University Press, 1987), p. 159.

153. Kierkegaard, *Either/Or*, p. 350.

154. Kierkegaard, *JP* 1, 751, p. 350.

155. Mark W. Sinnett, *Restoring the Conversation: Socratic Dialectic in the Authorship of Søren Kierkegaard* (Fife: Theology in Scotland, 1999), p. 8.

156. Kierkegaard, *JP* 1, 759, p. 352.

or to Hegelian dialectic (resolution through sublation). Beyond its more spurious uses, then, dialectic is seen by Kierkegaard as a philosophical 'method' which is applied *to* a set of categories or concepts, but is not necessarily itself indicative *of* those concepts.[157] Although it may not be possible to ascertain any sense of absolute clarity regarding Kierkegaard's conception, it is clear that all dialectics relate to the concept of differing forms of contradiction.[158] Although Kierkegaard may well conceptualize dialectic through an inherited etymological lens, he still *demonstrates* a keen variety in his engagement with dialectical conflicts. But it is the connection between dialectic and 'contradiction' that invokes a further complication in his thought regarding the category of 'paradox'.

Although dialectic is an ever-present lens through which many view Kierkegaard's thought, it is actually the concept of 'paradox' for which he is best known. In Kierkegaard's thought, we are able to see the aforementioned distinction of ontological paradox *from* dialectical method, but we also see how it is impossible to *speak* of paradox without using dialectic, knowing that paradox is itself inseparable from the concepts of 'contradiction' and 'the absurd'.[159] Indeed, despite speaking of the importance of non-contradiction when critiquing Hegel,[160] Kierkegaard happily affirms the 'contradictory' nature of Christian doctrine: 'Christianity itself has such great contradictions that a clear view is hindered, to say the least.'[161] In some cases, then, where Kierkegaard speaks of 'contradiction', we can take this to mean, essentially, 'paradox'.

Kierkegaard's understanding of a paradox is not dissimilar to the aforementioned 'ontological' mode found in both Chesterton and Eckhart. His theological basis for the possibility of ontological paradox is the creator-creature distinction: 'God and man are two qualities separated by an infinite qualitative difference.'[162] This radical distinction between the divine and rational realm necessitates 'dialectical'

157. Sánchez distinguishes between the noun, 'dialectic' ('a process or a philosophical method') and the adjective, 'dialectical' ('the ability to think in dialectical terms or to understand dialectical method'). Alejandro Cavallazzi Sánchez, 'Dialectic', in Steven M. Emmanuel, et al. (eds.), *Kierkegaard's Concepts: Tome II: Classicism to Enthusiasm* (Farnham: Ashgate, 2014), pp. 165–9 [165]. This is a correct distinction between concept and method, although it confuses the categories slightly. Method is, in fact, 'dialectical' (adjective), whereas the process or concept is 'dialectic' (noun). This relates to my own distinction between 'paradox' (concept) and dialectical articulation (method), both of which come underneath the broad schema of 'dialectics' (see II.3).

158. 'One of the characteristics of the dialectical process is precisely its building upon contradictions.' Sánchez, 'Dialectic', p. 166.

159. See Jakub Marek, 'Contradiction', in *Kierkegaard's Concepts*, pp. 73–80 [73, 79].

160. 'Hegelian philosophy has cancelled the principle of contradiction.' Kierkegaard, *Postscript*, pp. 304–5.

161. Kierkegaard, *JP* 5, 5092, p. 23.

162. Søren Kierkegaard, *The Sickness unto Death*, trans. Howard V. Hong and Edna H. Hong (Princeton: Princeton University Press, 1980), p. 126.

thinking (and, hence, paradox). In the divine realm, there is infinite possibility, and hence, a plausible conception for the existence of ontological paradox. As with most progenitors of paradox, Kierkegaard's understanding hinges upon the paradox of the incarnation,[163] which he calls the 'absolute paradox'. The absolute paradox – by its very nature – cannot be explained, resolved or mediated because it will always remain a contradiction *beyond* explanation; it is 'absolute' both because it pertains to the eternal (God) and because it remains paradoxical to *all* intellects (unlike 'relative paradox', which may become accessible to the 'wise' person, and is therefore not truly 'paradoxical').[164]

It is often noted that Kierkegaard's propensity towards paradox emanates from his interpretation of Scripture, as Timothy H. Polk notes: 'Nothing is more essential to Kierkegaard's understanding of the New Testament than is the paradox.'[165] Hugh Pyper also asserts: 'The absurd, the paradox, is of course something that is entirely characteristic of Kierkegaard's thought, and I would argue, of biblical thought.'[166] Indeed, paradox is the central motif in Kierkegaard's well-known interpretation of the Abraham-and-Isaac story, *Fear and Trembling*. It is the impossibility of Abraham's task that invokes the clearest example of paradox: a seemingly impossible situation which (somehow) must not only be contemplated but (crucially) acted-upon.[167] Abraham obeys God despite the fact he cannot access the reasoning behind this seemingly irrational command. This action of faith as an inherently paradoxical event appears numerously through the book; 'faith' and 'paradox' become almost synonymous.[168]

This conflation of paradox and faith is evident in another of Kierkegaard's famously paradox-laden texts, *Philosophical Fragments*:

> Is not Faith as paradoxical as the Paradox? Precisely so; how else could it have the Paradox as its object, and be happy in its relation to the Paradox? Faith is itself a miracle, and all that holds true of the Paradox also holds true of faith.[169]

---

163. Rather than focus on the paradox of the hypostatic union itself, Kierkegaard tends to highlight the paradoxicality of the breech between time and eternity: 'The paradox is primarily that God, the eternal, has entered into time as an individual human being.' Kierkegaard, *Postscript*, p. 596.

164. See Ibid., pp. 218–28.

165. Timothy H. Polk, 'Kierkegaard's Use of the New Testament: Intertextuality, Indirect Communication and Appropriation', in Lee C. Barrett and Jon Stewart (eds.), *Kierkegaard and the Bible, Tome II: The New Testament* (Farnham: Ashgate, 2010), pp. 237–45 [41].

166. Hugh Pyper, *The Joy of Kierkegaard: Essays on Kierkegaard as a Biblical Reader* (Sheffield: Equinox, 2011), p. 6.

167. Søren Kierkegaard, *Fear and Trembling*, trans. Alastair Hannay (London: Penguin, 2005), p. 83.

168. Ibid., pp. 63–4, 81–4.

169. Søren Kierkegaard, *Philosophical Fragments*, trans. David Swenson (Princeton: Princeton University Press, 1967), p. 81.

Such an understanding, however, does not make the paradox any easier to understand, nor does it make the action any more palatable. Abraham's faith, for example, is never resolved; it is bound up in necessary anxiety. Kierkegaard's repeated use of the phrase: 'the fear, the distress, the paradox' in *Fear and Trembling* suggests a grasping-after the meaning of paradox, conflating it with this sense of perpetual uncertainty.[170] As with both Chesterton and Eckhart, it could not be said that Kierkegaard's paradox is an 'escape clause' from rational logic. Paradox is not only rooted in revelation, but it comes at a 'cost': '[Abraham] suffers isolation, ridicule, and the "martyrdom of misunderstanding".'[171] Paradox (with its anxiety-ridden implications) is the very essence of walking in faith: 'The knight of faith is kept awake, for he is under constant trial...otherwise he would be outside the paradox.'[172] To be 'outside the paradox', for Kierkegaard, is to live in ignorance or delusion that paradox does not exist, or is not true. But to accept paradox brings the trials, anxieties, and sleeplessness that characterize Abraham's journey of faith.

This necessary existential uncertainty invoked by paradox connotes the ever-complex relationship between paradox and reason:

> When the Reason says that it cannot get the Paradox into its head, it was not the Reason that made the discovery but the Paradox, which is so paradoxical as to declare the Reason a blockhead and a dunce, capable of saying yes and no to the same thing, which is not good divinity...All that the offended consciousness has to say about the Paradox it has learned from the Paradox.[173]

Evidently, for Kierkegaard, paradox supersedes reason without totally abolishing it; paradox *reveals* itself *to* reason, and reason cannot comprehend it but can only comprehend the fact of its paradoxical *trueness*. Kierkegaard's Shakespearean reference to 'yes and no' being 'not good divinity' evinces his critique of irrational 'contradiction' per se (as also seen in Chesterton). But he is not interested in articulating *how* the two concepts differ as such; paradox exists within its own genre of contemplation as a facet of revelation and has no need of being rationally 'defended'.

However, it is still possible to glean where the limits of such paradoxical thinking could be found in order to locate the parameters of where 'contradiction' may be differentiated. C. Stephen Evans draws a number of helpful insights on this point, arguing that Johannes Climacus (the pseudonymous 'author' of *Fragments* and the *Postscript*) does not advocate paradox as a 'formal contradiction' but employs somewhat 'sloppy and misleading' terminology.[174] Since Climacus' paradox

170. Kierkegaard, *Fear and Trembling*, pp. 74, 76, 78.

171. Timothy Dalrymple, 'Abraham: Framing Fear and Trembling', in Lee C. Barrett and Jon Stewart (eds.), *Kierkegaard and the Bible, Tome I: The Old Testament* (Farnham: Ashgate, 2010), pp. 43–88 [66].

172. Kierkegaard, *Fear and Trembling*, p. 93.

173. Kierkegaard, *Philosophical Fragments*, p. 66.

174. C. Stephen Evans, *Kierkegaard's 'Fragments' and 'Postscript': The Religious Philosophy of Johannes Climacus* (Atlantic Highlands: Humanities Press, 1983), p. 213.

attempts to articulate the 'boundaries or limits to rational understanding',[175] it cannot be equated with a contradiction because the act of *identifying* a formal contradiction 'falls completely within the boundaries of reason's competence'.[176] Given that one's knowledge of ontological paradox is inaccessible, to *verify* a formal contradiction would require comprehensive knowledge of *how* the opposites may not, in fact, be conjoined: 'To know that the "God-man" is a formally contradictory combination, one would have to have a clear understanding of the nature of God and the nature of man'.[177] Evans concludes that Kierkegaard's paradox is not to be understood as a logical contradiction but as 'a logically odd notion that produces contradictory ideas when thought seeks to understand it'.[178] This is helpful not only in helping us see the difference between paradox and contradiction, but also recognizing paradox as being the apparently jarring 'notion' which *induces* dialectical thinking.

In Kierkegaard, it is evident that paradox and dialectic interweave with one another because they both relate, in some way, to contradiction. Kierkegaard asks the question: how are we to engage with irreconcilable contradiction? For Abraham, the answer lies in faithful acceptance rather than dialectical resolution. The absolute paradox, like Abraham's paradoxical command, is divinely revealed and is thus 'the paradox that cannot be mediated'.[179] Even if paradox is reluctantly 'accepted', it still eludes the theologian's grasp. The subject is caught between seemingly contradictory opposites which cannot be mediated but must be (somehow) accepted, in faithful action. In distinction to this, 'dialectic' seems to refer to the activity of *thinking-after* paradox, whether through experiential anxiety[180] or artificial resolution.[181] However, both instances refer to the contradiction inherent in the paradox, since it is the contradiction itself which *invokes* the dialectics (not vice versa). We can see, in Kierkegaard's account, that the dialectical tension (the 'anxiety') is not the paradox itself but the implication of the paradox. Although 'dialectic' is a term used multifariously in Kierkegaard's thought, it may be delineated from paradox if we see dialectic as the way *in which* we engage with paradox (the 'object' of dialectical articulation). The complexity in delineating the two terms *amidst* their interrelatedness can be further emphasized by examining one of Kierkegaard's most important dialectical sources, Hegel, who undoubtedly offers the most comprehensive engagement with contradiction in modern philosophical history. First, however, we will engage with a relatively contemporary discussion of paradox and dialectic in the debate between John Milbank and Slavoj Žižek, over which interpretations of Hegelian dialectic are so influential.

175. Ibid., p. 214.

176. Ibid., p. 217.

177. Ibid.

178. Indeed, paradox 'appears to be, but cannot be known to be, a contradiction'. Ibid., p. 225.

179. Kierkegaard, *Fear and Trembling*, pp. 78, 83.

180. Ibid., pp. 74–8.

181. Ibid. p. 106.

ii. *Paradox* or *Dialectic?: A Conceptual Debate*

The debate between Milbank and Žižek in *The Monstrosity of Christ: Paradox or Dialectic?* (2009) is one of the most overt attempts in recent years to engage with the relationship between paradox and dialectic both philosophically and theologically. It is often a difficult debate to follow, both writers drawing upon a similar pool of 'dialectical' thinkers (including Eckhart, Hegel, Kierkegaard and Chesterton) yet emerging with entirely divergent interpretations. A key driving force behind the debate is a fundamental disagreement over the problem of contradiction.[182] Where Milbank asserts that Žižek 'reduces paradox to dialectic',[183] Žižek argues that he and Milbank have 'two completely different ways of "ontologizing the contradictory"'.[184] These two 'different ways' stem largely from conflicting views over the scope of dialectic, both of which, it will be seen, narrow the dialectical scope.[185]

a. *Milbank: Paradox as 'Misty Conceit'.*

John Milbank's idea of paradox does not move *beyond* contradiction, but accepts it as accessibly inaccessible: 'Paradox affirms the full reality of the impossible and the contradictory, whereas dialectics declares that an existing contradiction, because it is a contradiction, must be destroyed even though it exists.'[186] For Milbank, paradox is 'an outright impossible *coincidence of opposites* that can (somehow, but we know not how) be persisted with'.[187] Here we see a sharp contrast with dialectics, which – in his view – always attempt to 'overcome' the 'impossible contradiction'.[188] For Milbank, dialectic refuses to allow a paradox to *remain* a paradox, seeking only to resolve the polarities via synthesis. Milbank's definition of dialectic thus appears

182. This debate, of course, also involves a number of other important foci beyond dialectical terminological clarification, but such issues will not be engaged here.

183. John Milbank, 'The Double Glory, or Paradox versus Dialectics: On Not Quite Agreeing with Slavoj Žižek', in John Milbank and Slavoj Žižek, *The Monstrosity of Christ: Paradox or Dialectic?* (London: The MIT Press, 2009), p. 188.

184. Slavoj Žižek, 'Dialectical Clarity versus the Misty Conceit of Paradox', in *The Monstrosity of Christ*, p. 252.

185. Indeed, Davis' introduction to the debate belies a notion of dialectic which limits it to the speculative quasi-Hegelian mode, as a 'method', 'removed from the world…a kind of bourgeois academic observer overlooking the world from the safe distance of an armchair, second-order thinker who can only ever think *about* the world'. Creston Davis, 'Introduction', in *The Monstrosity of Christ*, p. 16 (emphasis added). He also notes that, for Žižek, 'method is infused with reality and even constructs reality'. Ibid., p. 16. This widens the dialectical scope, but it does not account for the varieties of dialectical engagement.

186. Milbank, 'The Double Glory', in *The Monstrosity of Christ*, p. 198.

187. Ibid., p. 163.

188. Ibid.

more narrow.[189] Although, as noted earlier, dialectic is generally concerned with negotiating the tension or incongruity between opposites, it may also refer to a contemplation of opposites in unison, just like Milbank's contemplation of paradox. Milbank's definition of paradox disallows the notion of incompatible opposites *and* resolved opposites to exist – it is either/or. This is the problem with framing 'dialectic' and 'paradox' as entirely antithetical, since there are overlaps between both, connoting a varied range of possibilities in facing apparent contradiction. For Milbank, however, dialectic is merely that which nullifies ontological contradiction rather than engaging it as it stands:

> Dialectics is like a civic bureaucrat who says that a bizarre building put up in the town without permission cannot really be there at all because it stands upright without legal warrant, and therefore must be discreetly pulled down at dead of night, to ensure that a bright dawn will reveal that it had only ever appeared to be there, on an earlier day of mist and mirages.[190]

Milbank's response to this intriguingly Kafkaesque expression of dialectic, then, is the conceptualization of paradox as a 'misty conceit', whereby polarities have a heightened distinction despite the lack of delineated clarity between them. The 'mist' metaphor suggests that paradox is visible despite its apparent invisibility: paradox 'at once hides and then reveals'.[191] Oddly, he even uses the term 'dialectical' to speak of the relatedness of the definite and the opaque: 'The univocal and the equivocal are always in a dialectical relationship.'[192] Milbank's paradox-as-mist is not an abandonment of clear logical categories, but more a subtle conflation of the clear and the unclear. The 'mist' reveals the possibility of knowing without an ultimate exactitude behind this knowing. The partial unclarity of Milbank's paradox (as with Eckhart's and Kierkegaard's conceptions of paradox) provokes the theologian to think *beyond* what is before them: 'Without the unclarity of the mist, I would not be inspired to look for things in the mist and so beyond its opacity.'[193] Milbank calls for the 'grander view' beyond logical reconciliation, which contemplates the paradox in its fullness. It could be argued that his conclusion leads to a kind of definiteness in itself which is ultimately no different to dialectical 'harmonization'.

189. In this definition Milbank has in view a conception of Hegelian dialectic as 'thesis-antithesis-synthesis'. Žižek labels this interpretation of Hegel 'cheap "dialectics" according to which a thesis can deploy itself only through overcoming its opposite'. Žižek, 'Dialectical Clarity', in *The Monstrosity of Christ*, p. 240.
190. Ibid., p. 198. It is clear that where I am affirming that there are elements of dialectic and paradox that may cross over despite their distinctiveness, Milbank sees them as entirely incompatible.
191. Milbank, 'The Double Glory', in *The Monstrosity of Christ*, p. 161. Similarly, see Barth's dialectic of veiling and unveiling (II.2.ii.b).
192. Ibid.
193. Ibid., p. 163.

Where Milbank has argued for the clarity within the opacity, this itself could be seen as a staticized form of dialectic. This is because, for all the emphasis upon dialectic as seeking to *resolve* too quickly, Milbank's paradoxical 'misty conceit' is a plea to view the logic of contradiction as a *settled* status, without residual tension. Thus, Milbank's view of paradox has become something akin to a quasi-Hegelian sublation, of which he remains critical. His treatment of paradox as a contradiction to be accepted in and through our logical inaccessibility is, however, another useful insight for encountering apparently contradictory theological concepts.

b. *Žižek: Dialectic as Divine Tension.*

Slavoj Žižek, an atheist, is often seen, alongside some deconstructionist philosophers, as a kind of 'negative theologian' due to his gravitation towards dialectical tensions.[194] Whereas Milbank confines dialectic to the resolving of contradiction, the exact reverse could be said of Žižek's understanding of dialectic, as perpetually *maintaining* contradiction. In Žižek's *The Parallax View* (2006), he asserts that dialectic 'constantly shifts perspective between two points between which no synthesis or mediation is possible'.[195] 'Parallax' (the apparent difference of perspective of the same object when viewed from two separate or opposing angles) is the nuance which best defines Žižek's dialectical method. It is not that 'truth' is simultaneously viewed from separate, fixed angles, as though they were symmetrically balanced polarities; rather, the 'point' is that this perspective remains perpetually dynamic: 'Each dialectical pole remains to an extent a continual component of the other such that they perform a mutually critical correction of each other.'[196] For Žižek, to think *about* these perspectives in motion is impossible because when one views the necessary perspective, it has already shifted. This makes Žižek's method difficult to quantify because there is no allowance for the 'standpoint' of the one negotiating or observing the parallax.

There is clear similarity between Žižek's 'parallaxical' dialectic and Kierkegaard's notion of paradox as inducing dialectical 'anxiety'. For both, there is no 'objective' standpoint for the dialectician, and there is no point *within* the dialectic where one polarity may overcome the other (thus artificially removing the necessary tension). For Žižek, all forms of resolution are falsified approaches to reality, resulting in a 'simplistic Aristotelian middle-of-the-road solution of avoiding two extremes'.[197] Although, for Žižek, this 'middle-of-the-road solution' undermines the logic of paradox, it is actually his greatest point of mutual connection to Kierkegaard: a rejection of mediation.[198]

194. Pound notes that Žižek and Derrida 'dramatize the failure of language, filling their work with paradox, contradiction, hyperbole, and negative images'. Marcus Pound, *Žižek: A (Very) Critical Introduction* (Grand Rapids: Eerdmans, 2008), p. 94.

195. Slavoj Žižek, *The Parallax View* (Cambridge: MIT Press, 2006), p. 4.

196. Pound, *Žižek*, p. 92.

197. Slavoj Žižek, 'The Fear of Four Words', in *The Monstrosity of Christ*, p. 83.

198. This is also true of Milbank, of course, who rejects mediation for the opacity of paradox rather than the parallaxical tension offered by Žižek.

Indeed, Žižek rejects what he calls the 'Chestertonian dialectic' in which God is invoked as the 'unity of opposites', rendering all logical tensions as a merely '*apparent* cacophony' which pays deference to 'the all-encompassing harmony'.[199] For Žižek, the cacophony cannot be simply 'apparent' since it is bound up with the tension of reality itself. If reality itself is understood to be cacophonous, any appeal to some greater harmonious 'Absolute' becomes impossible. Žižek argues that such tension is not resolved in God's humanly inaccessible harmony, but in his intrinsically *dialectical* being: 'Antagonism [is] inscribed into the very heart of God himself.'[200] This theological conception seems to be the founding principle of his dialectic (even if Žižek's own system surely cannot allow for such a notion as a 'founding principle'). Žižek's 'God' is at war with itself, as are all conceptions of logic, necessitating the perpetual antagonism between all (theo)logical concepts and statements.

It is clear that the concept of a 'unity of opposites' (in the 'Chestertonian' sense) challenges Žižek's 'theological' dialectic of God's self-antagonism. To reconcile the challenge of this 'unity' to his own notion of God's 'antagonism', Žižek asserts the total immanence of God. Here, the tensions inherent in human existence become a reflection of those felt within God himself: 'The "unity of opposites" means that in a self-reflexive short circuit, God falls into his own creation.'[201] This appears to be Žižek's theological justification for 'parallaxical' dialectic: truth is observable from perpetually shifting angles because there is no overarching Absolute holding truth together in unity. Thus, the contradictions perceived within dialectical logic are *necessarily* contradictory due to the nature of God and reality itself. It is not simply that they *require* no reconciliation; it is that no reconciliation is ever possible.

Where a truly theological approach to dialectic and paradox are concerned, it is clear that Žižek's immanentist 'theology' differs exceedingly from the emphases of the aforementioned dialectical and paradoxical theologies, particularly because of the absence of the concept of revelation and the creator-creature distinction, which forms the essential (theo)logic underpinning dialectical methods and concepts. Žižek's notion of perpetual self-corrective antagonism, however, may still be mined for its demonstration of what *revelatory* theological tension looks like in practice. Furthermore, it establishes a stark contrast between Milbank's apparently 'static' conception of paradox. We will now conclude this extensive focus upon the relation of paradox to dialectic, by recategorizing paradox as one form of conceptual dialectic.

iii. *Paradox as Dialectic*

We have seen a number of different approaches to theological paradox, with different effects which flow *from* the contemplation of paradox. However, in

---

199. Žižek, 'The Fear of Four Words', in *The Monstrosity of Christ*, p. 49 (emphasis added).
200. Ibid.
201. Ibid., p. 50.

each, there is a consistent thread of what an ontological paradox is, delineating it from general conceptions of dialectics per se, but not necessarily from what might be called 'dialectical modes'. Precisely because paradox is a particular *status* of oppositional unity (not a 'method' of interpreting oppositions) it can still be designated as 'a dialectic'. If all notions of dialectic share the rejection of exclusively one-sided polarities, paradox may be one ontological example of how this works out. Paradoxes are 'static' conjunctions of incompatible polarities because they contain no ongoing movement or tension; they simply exist as irreconcilably true in a kind of obstinate stalemate. However, we can say that paradoxes *become* 'dialectical' as soon as they are observed, formulated or articulated, whereby the dialectic attempts to respond-to or to *speak* the paradox.

Contrary to 'purist' conceptions of dialectic (referring *only* to polar resolution, or *only* to polar tension, etc.), to render something 'dialectical' is merely to state the existence of oppositional polarities, without necessarily specifying *how* these polarities relate. This is why paradox may be seen as one *type* of dialectic, because it exemplifies irreconcilably reconciled polarities in an 'impossible' unity. As with Chesterton's rejection of 'balance' or 'dilution', these polarities exist statically and wholly, without perichoresis, and without slanting, tilting or correcting one another. Such conjoined polarities are simply to be accepted as simultaneously *true* in the midst of their apparent incompatibility. This incompatibility is the problem which induces the dialectical tension. Yet, with a broadened view of what dialectic means, we may see that this 'static' conception of paradox is not antithetical to the concept of dialectic itself. There are, of course, many other dialectical conceptions which are *not* paradoxes, even as they may also appear to negotiate the problem of 'contradictory' antitheses.[202]

We have seen that, for Kierkegaard, dialectics may be *ways* of engaging with contradiction, whereas paradoxes *are* the contradictions themselves. However, given that a paradox is a coming-together of oppositional polarities, we may still refer to it as 'a dialectic' in the broader sense defined earlier because the paradox may *become* a dialectic as soon as one attempts to *articulate* its contradictory nature. Here, dialectic thinks-after paradox in light of the 'wrestling' between the poles. But dialectic also has an ontological status of its own as the very concept of inherent anxiety within the act of faith. It can be seen as both method and yet more-than-method, remaining separated from paradox. Paradox invokes the dialectic of faith, not the other way around.

But where, in Kierkegaard, one might glean something of an order between dialectic and paradox, the Milbank-Žižek debate displays a confusion between their compatibility. This is partly, perhaps, because the debate is framed as 'either/or' from the start, leading Milbank to reject Žižek's 'dialectic' because it appears to be dynamically chaotic, and Žižek to reject Milbank's 'paradox' because it does not reflect the nature of dialectical reality. In fact, both express insights which helpfully

---

202. It is not a paradox, for example, to say that Jesus is divine or that Jesus is human but it *is* a paradox to say that he is *both*. Speaking of any singular polarity may *invoke* the possibility of dialectic indirectly, but it is not itself an articulation *of* a paradox.

contribute to dialectical thought in its broadest sense, even if each thinker's interpretation of one another cannot be 'reconciled'. The primary problem is largely centred on differing interpretations of 'Hegelian' dialectic, which shapes the way their own conceptions of dialectic or paradox are imagined. In both interpretations, we see Hegel fall into one of two general camps: the 'resolution' or the 'antagonism' of opposites. We will now see how we might read Hegel in light of these differences and clarify what Hegel actually means by 'sublating' the opposites.

5. *The Myth of Synthesis*

i. *Nuancing Hegelian Dialectic*

Hegelian dialectic is perhaps the most renowned and complicated approach to the problem of contradiction ever attempted. It has been the cause of much discussion, agreement, disagreement and bafflement: 'Each writer sees in Hegel a version of his own image. To be sure, there are those who contrast their own position with Hegel's so that they can then offer a more trenchant criticism'.[203] As noted earlier, Hegel's dialectic is generally considered to be the benchmark for the reception of dialectic at its modern point of origin. Because of this, it is not only impossible to ignore, it is also essential that it be understood correctly, demonstrating its usefulness in clarifying corollary uses of dialectic in face of contradiction. It will be seen that, in spite of Hegel's many divergent interpreters, his dialectic has more to contribute here than many of his detractors would have us believe.

a. *Interpreting Hegel.*

Many of the prominent 'dialectical' or 'paradoxical' thinkers highlighted thus far have, in one way or another, built their own conceptions of dialectic from – or, in reaction to – Hegelian dialectic. Kierkegaard was one such trenchant objector to Hegel's system for its attempts to over-rationalize the contradictory: 'The Hegelian philosophy assumes there is no justified concealment, no justified incommensurability'.[204] Kierkegaard's notion of the faith-inducing ontological paradox could have no place in Hegel's system, which, for him, had neutered all genuinely oppositional tension: 'Hegelian philosophy has cancelled the principle of contradiction'.[205] Kierkegaard thus saw his own work as entirely antithetical to the Hegelian project. Similarly, Chesterton, despite sharing aspects of Hegel's regard for dialectic as the appropriation of form and content,[206] sought to expose what he saw

---

203. John Burbidge, 'Is Hegel a Christian?', in David Kolb (ed.), *New Perspectives on Hegel's Philosophy of Religion* (New York: State University of New York Press, 1992), pp. 93–108 [94].

204. Kierkegaard, *Fear and Trembling*, p. 98.

205. Kierkegaard, *Postscript*, p. 304.

206. 'The "dialectical" method of Hegel and the "paradoxical" method of Chesterton have more than a little in common – they both saw that reality itself dictated the method'.

as the inherent *ir*rationalism at the heart of Hegelian 'becoming', noting the absurdity 'that a thing can "be" intelligible and not as yet "be" at all'.[207] Where both Kierkegaard and Chesterton would affirm the possibility (and necessity) of ontological paradoxes, Hegel's approach to contradiction appears to nullify the law of non-contradiction itself.

Barth is another notable respondent to Hegelian dialectic. Although he famously admitted to being 'fond of doing a bit of Hegeling',[208] having borrowed a number of Hegelian philosophical categories,[209] Barth was heavily critical of Hegel's method of synthesis as limiting the freedom of the dialectic, playing the role of God,[210] and collapsing the creator-creature distinction.[211] It is notable, however, that Barth had inherited the inadequately simplistic interpretation of Hegelian dialectic as thesis-antithesis-synthesis.[212] This, in fact, has been a common misconception, as though Hegel's dialectic were nothing more than the arbitrary resolution of conflicting ideas into artificial 'third' categories. Significantly, this was not the language Hegel himself used for his dialectic. Although some trace the origins of the summative category ('thesis-antithesis-synthesis') to Fichte, it was made more prominent in Hegel interpretation by Karl Popper,[213] resulting in a simplified obfuscation of Hegelian dialectic.[214] Michael Forster notes that thesis-antithesis-synthesis does, in fact, have its place – it is simply too vague to fully explain Hegel's concerns.[215]

The aforementioned Milbank-Žižek debate over dialectic and paradox interprets Hegelian dialectic as *either* pertaining to 'resolution' or to perpetual 'tension'. Žižek sees Milbank's interpretation of Hegelian dialectic as oversimplistic,[216] while his own formation attempts to shift the notion of polarity reconciliation

Quentin Lauer, *G. K. Chesterton: Philosopher without Portfolio* (New York: Fordham University Press, 2004), p. 48. This overarching principle is clearly visible throughout Hegel's system, even in introductory comments: 'the need to unite the method with the content, the form with the principle'. G. W. F. Hegel, *Science of Logic*, trans. A. V. Miller (Atlantic Highlands: Humanities Press International, 1991), p. 67.

207. Chesterton, *Aquinas*, p. 147.

208. See Eberhard Busch, *Karl Barth: His Life from Letters and Autobiographical Texts*, trans. John Bowden (London: SCM Press, 1976), p. 387.

209. See Jay Wesley Richards, 'Dealing with Barth's Doctrine of God', in *The Untamed God: A Philosophical Exploration of Divine Perfection, Simplicity, and Immutability* (Illinois: IVP, 2003), pp. 129–51 [131].

210. Barth, *CD* I/1, p. 176.

211. Barth, *CD* II/1, p. 270.

212. Graham Ward, 'Barth, Hegel, and the Possibility for Christian Apologetics', in Mike Higton and John C. McDowell (eds.), *Conversing with Barth* (Farnham: Ashgate, 2004), pp. 53–67 [53].

213. See Karl R. Popper, 'What Is Dialectic?', in *Mind* 49:196 (1940), pp. 403–26.

214. Michael Forster, 'Hegel's Dialectical Method', in Frederick C. Beiser (ed.), *The Cambridge Companion to Hegel* (Cambridge: Cambridge University Press, 1993), pp. 130–70 [130].

215. Ibid., p. 131.

216. Žižek, 'Dialectical Clarity', in *The Monstrosity of Christ*, p. 240.

into a dynamic tension.[217] Žižek argues that the very idea of a neat synthesis was something Hegel would have rejected: 'For Hegel, contradiction means tension, conflict, the violence of negativity, i.e., the Hegelian Whole is a Whole kept together by the process of internal antagonisms.'[218] It is difficult to assess Hegel's contribution to dialectic in the midst of so many countervailing interpretations. In order to situate the significance of Hegel in reapproaching contradiction, it will be necessary to articulate more precisely what it is that his dialectic *does* with contradictory polarities. This must begin with the term that is often erroneously understood to mean 'synthesis': *sublation*.

b. 'Sublation'.

The category of 'sublation' (*Aufhebung*) is the concept often interpreted simplistically as thesis-antithesis-synthesis, as noted above. In such a reading, the process of *Aufhebung* destroys any possibility for a residual tension between the polarities, creating a concrete resolution which then becomes a new 'thesis' in the progressive dialectic. This misunderstanding views *Aufhebung* as a kind of intermingling synthesis – a totally new, hybrid category which dissolves the two polarities into one. Sublation, however, has a double meaning: 'partly to annihilate, partly to preserve.'[219] In some sense, this actually verifies Žižek's interpretation of Hegelian dialectic as immanent ontological tension. Indeed, Hegel did not see contradictions in speculative 'isolation' but as part of a wider whole, and thus constantly in motion: 'The truth of the one and the many', he says, 'is to be grasped and expressed only as a becoming, as a process, a repulsion and attraction – not as being, which in a proposition has the character of a stable unity.'[220] It is this connectedness to the overarching system of reality that shows how *Aufhebung* is intended not as an artificial process of diluting the polarities from some imaginary objective standpoint, but as an *observation* of actual reality. This reality exists in a state of permanent 'becoming' as the process of sublation continues ad infinitum. This dialectical 'system' is never fully consummated by the dialectician – it is only realized *within* God (*Geist*) Himself: 'the sum total of all realities'.[221] In the

217. 'What happens in the passage from "antithesis" to "synthesis" is not that another story is added, bringing together the first two (or that we return to the first story, which is now rendered more "rich," provided with its background): all that happens is a purely formal shift by means of which we realize that the "antithesis" is already "synthesis."' Žižek, 'The Fear of Four Words', in *The Monstrosity of Christ*, p. 72.

218. Žižek, 'Dialectical Clarity', in *The Monstrosity of Christ*, p. 252.

219. Justus Hartnack, *An Introduction to Hegel's Logic*, trans. Lars Aagaard-Mogenson (Indianapolis and Cambridge: Hacket Publishing Company, 1998), p. 5. Garrett Green, reinterpreting Barth's use of 'Aufhebung', notes: 'To sublimate something – i.e., to make it sublime – suggests that it will become both higher and better as a result.' Garrett Green, 'Translator's Preface', in Karl Barth, *On Religion: The Revelation of God as the Sublimation of Religion*, trans. Garrett Green (London T & T Clark, 2007), p. ix.

220. Hegel, *Logic*, p. 172.

221. Ibid., p. 442.

finite realm, then, there is only continual contradiction and sublation. Yet it is not that the philosopher assesses that a sublation *ought* to take place to resolve the contradictions; instead, it must be recognized that sublation *continually* occurs in a state of perpetual connectedness and movement. Hegel's principal grounding for sublation is the fact that reality *dictates* thinking-about-reality.

The notion that sublation is a 'static' concept, then, is clearly untenable. In all engagements with contradiction, Hegel seeks to emphasize that concepts or categories cannot be seen in isolation except in their individual 'moments' of interaction.[222] These particular moments occur when one facet of a concept (a particular moment *within* that concept)[223] is faced by its limitations when engaged by its opposite. The moments themselves are all part of the greater system, of which there are many other moments of contradiction and sublation. These sublating moments are a perpetual response to the wider (equally perpetual) problem of contradiction. As with all dialectical methods, apparent contradiction is the driving force. Yet it will be seen that Hegel's notion of contradiction differs widely from the classical Aristotelian concept.

c. 'Contradiction'.

Hegel's notion of contradictory oppositions is far more complicated than is generally perceived.[224] In his *Science of Logic*, the section on 'Contradiction' (*Widersprechen*) states that, in a moment of opposition, there is a positive and a negative pole. These antitheses are distinctly independent: 'Each has an indifferent self-subsistence of its own.'[225] Yet simultaneously, each polarity contains an inherent correlation to what it is *not*: 'It has within itself the relation to its other moment; it is thus the whole, self-contained opposition.'[226] Effectively, then, Hegel conceives of the polarities as having a relatedness from which they cannot escape. Yet this relatedness is also the very thing that separates them from their opposite; they are connected by the fact of their difference, which thus further emphasizes

222. See Ibid., p. 431.

223. An example of such a particularity might be the 'zestiness' of an orange, which will face a different limitation to, say, the 'roundedness' of an orange; and still again, the orange itself will face a different opposition when juxtaposed with an apple or something entirely different, like a person, or an idea. It is the nature of the ultimate connectedness of the system that sees these oppositions and 'moments' as particularities within a greater whole, not as isolated binaries which are summative of ultimate reality in and of themselves.

224. See Priest: 'The arguments for contradiction in Hegel's logic strike the modern reader either as sophistical or else as totally incomprehensible.' Graham Priest, *In Contradiction: A Study of the Transconsistent* (Dordecht: Martinus Nijhoff Publishers, 1987), p. 4. He goes on to say that Hegel was right, that 'our concepts, or some of them anyway, are inconsistent, and produce dialetheias', adding that 'the aim of the enterprise is not to eliminate contradictions but to accommodate them'. Priest, *In Contradiction*, p. 336.

225. Hegel, *Logic*, p. 431.

226. Ibid.

both their separation and their inseparability. This is a concept that bears similarity to an ontological paradox. But for Hegel, the simultaneous relatedness *and* distinctiveness of oppositions is *demonstrably* true, and thus, *not* paradoxical. If it were not demonstrable, it would be an 'apparent' – and therefore, *resolvable* – contradiction (such as what Kierkegaard called a 'relative' rather than 'absolute' paradox); for Hegel, such contradiction is irresolvable precisely because it is *necessary* contradiction. His entire system seeks to demonstrate *how* this is possible.

There is a definite sense in Hegel's system that *both* polarities are fully themselves and – by virtue of the contradiction – fully *not*-themselves at the same time. Each polarity maintains its self-subsistence, and yet it is not totally free to be *itself* in isolation. In its very *being itself*, the polarity points to – and, in some sense, *becomes* – its opposite: '[The] positive and negative...are themselves the positing of themselves, and in this positing each is the sublating of itself and the positing of its opposite.'[227] Here, one sees a further nuance in the use of sublation, as it seems that each polarity is itself already a sublation. Hence, there is no such thing in Hegel as a 'thesis' or an 'antithesis' disconnected from a 'synthesis'. There is, rather, a continual unity between them, since the very moment they posit themselves, they cannot help but make reference to – and thus, *posit* – their opposite. Hegel refers to this continual process of ontological unity as the 'ceaseless vanishing of the opposites.'[228] He declares that, unless it is understood that all polarities (or 'notions') really *do* exist in such a unity, dialectical enquiry is null and void: 'Without this knowledge, not a single step can really be taken in philosophy.'[229] For Hegel, it is not that there is an indeterminable fusion between all oppositions, but rather that it must be taken seriously that the very act of an opposition *being itself* is impossible in total isolation.

We might suggest that Hegel's conception of contradiction is so nuanced with qualifications that it is entirely different from what is usually called a formal contradiction. Where this chapter has so far spoken of the 'problem' of contradiction because it apparently hinders assertive theological speech, this would be alien to Hegel because his notion of contradiction is not 'problematic' at all:

> It is not, so to speak, a blemish, an imperfection or a defect in something if contradiction can be pointed out in it. On the contrary, every determination, every concrete thing, every Notion, is essentially a unity of distinguished and indistinguishable moments, which, by virtue of the determinate, essential difference, pass over into contradictory moments.[230]

The 'contradictory moments' here are the coming-together of oppositions in their own self-subsistence. Again, the self-subsistence of each opposition is not in *stark* opposition, but a kind of related opposition. It is this which lends to Hegel's

227. Ibid., pp. 431–2.
228. Ibid., p. 433.
229. Ibid., p. 438.
230. Ibid., p. 442.

dialectic a semblance of ontological paradox, as the inaccessibly *true* contradiction in the order of being (though, by no means comparable with the static nature of a paradox, as such). Hegel refuses 'the so-called law of the excluded middle' (often rendered as an 'either/or' dilemma). Such a 'law' assumes that there can be no connection between the two oppositions,[231] as though there could be two entirely separate trenches in a battlefield without a 'no-man's-land' in between. Hegel thinks the 'excluded middle' is a misunderstanding of the nuance of oppositions, as though *every* single thing was determinable by stark contrast, which he denies.[232] His suggestion is that there is in fact a *third* which is 'indifferent' to the opposition itself yet still containing elements of each polarity. This would mean that the 'middle' is not related to the one-side-versus-the-other conception, but simply the place in between in which it bears a connectedness to both sides without existing purely for the sake of the either/or dichotomy itself. It is evident, then, that a key part of Hegel's conception of contradiction is a rejection of the either/or binary logic. This may seem obvious, but is a necessary observation in distinguishing Hegel's dialectic from a simplistic model in which the thesis counteracts the antithesis to form a new thesis ad infinitum.

As noted, for Hegel, 'oppositions' have a relational unity and a relational distinctness. Yet they can only be conceived of as opposites in so far as they are in a particular *moment* of contradiction. This is a point Hegel repeatedly returns to as he continually rejects the either/or paradigm. He lists various common oppositions such as 'father and son', 'above and below' and 'right and left' but notes that – although in such configurations we perceive them as opposites – they are not *only* opposites of one another; but they also relate, in varying degrees, to other objects and concepts.[233] We cannot take two concepts and isolate them into a dichotomy without due warrant, as though this was the *only* way to understand them. So he states, for example, that 'the father also has an existence of his own apart from the son-relationship; but then he is not father but simply man'.[234] Yet in rejecting the simplistic idea of contradiction, there is simultaneous admittance that even if the father has a different existence apart from his 'opposition' to the son, he is still recurrently involved in oppositions and limitations to his own self-subsistence – there is always a counterpart, of some sort, and to some extent. We can continually observe in Hegel that *being* cannot be conceived of in isolation, and that *dialectic* is required in order to understand any and every concept as it relates to itself and to everything else. Without accepting the implications of Hegel's entire system,[235] we can certainly see how this idea echoes the

231. This essentially refers to the LNC. See II.3.i.2.

232. Hegel, *Logic*, p. 438.

233. Ibid., p. 441.

234. Ibid.

235. An acute critique of Hegel's system made repeatedly by Kierkegaard is noteworthy here. Hegel appears to have no place for the very act of observing and articulating the contradictory realities within his system. It is as though he, the dialectician, is granted a kind of 'objective' standpoint from which he is able to determine the *whole* of reality *without*

logic of ontological paradox, since Hegel is effectively asserting that the essentiality of truth contains unresolved polar tension, but is nonetheless 'true'.

Hegel's positive conception of contradiction sees oppositional conflict as forming a necessary part of all being: 'Everything is inherently contradictory'.[236] As mentioned, this is rooted in Hegel's sense of the movement and vigour inherent in all forms of reality. A singular polarity (a 'simple immediate') is merely 'dead being'.[237] Contradiction, on the other hand, is what gives reality its essential vitality: 'It is only in so far as something has a contradiction within it that it moves, has an urge and activity'.[238] It is vital, in configuring Hegel's dialectic, that we see his primary concern not as creating static, lifeless resolutions but in *recognizing* the dynamic, continuous motion of reality. Contradiction, for Hegel, is life itself.[239] It occurs because it *must* occur, not because it is conjured up or presupposed by the dialectician: 'The *contradictory* cannot be *imagined* or thought'.[240] Contradiction is the process of being-in-becoming 'a contingency, a kind of abnormality and a passing paroxysm of sickness'.[241] The language of 'paroxysm' (connoting a convulsion or spasm) highlights the fact that contradiction itself is a kind of inappropriate (yet necessarily appropriate) event, and hence cannot be domesticated by a simplistic act of synthesis. Such language is ever-present throughout his articulations of contradiction as he moves through his dialectical process of positing and countering his own argument. All positions and concepts are never simply present in and of themselves; they are 'in a state of collapse'.[242]

ii. *Evaluations*

a. *Systematic Antagonism.*

We have seen that in Hegel's conception of dialectic there is no abstract tranquil resolution, only lingering and persistent tension, inherent within all of

---

that reality impinging upon him. Kierkegaard charges that there is not only no place for ethics in Hegel's system, but that there is no place for *Hegel* in Hegel's system (unless, of course, Hegel *is* the 'Absolute'!): 'But who, then, is this systematic thinker? Well, it is he who himself is outside existence and yet in existence, who in his eternity is forever concluded and yet includes existence within himself – it is God.' Kierkegaard, *Postscript*, p. 119.

236. Hegel, *Logic*, p. 439.

237. Ibid.

238. Ibid.

239. It is here that we see an interesting point of connection to Tillich, whose rejection of Barth's 'dialectical theology' revealed a quasi-Hegelian interest in the perpetual dialectical movement of all reality: 'In push and counterpush, life effects a preliminary balance in all dimensions, but there is no a priori certainty about the outcome of these conflicts. The balance achieved in one moment is destroyed in the next.' Tillich, *Systematic Theology* 3, p. 53.

240. Hegel, *Logic*, p. 439.

241. Ibid., p. 440.

242. Ibid., p. 443.

reality: 'Finite things...in their indifferent multiplicity are simply this, to be contradictory and *disrupted within themselves.*'[243] The inner disruption of all final formulations is, for Hegel, a precondition of thought itself. 'Dialectic' is the way in which Hegel navigates the existence of these conflicts without ever truly escaping them. Despite the fact that Hegel's dialectic forms the inner-workings of his greater system (accounting, purportedly, for 'the Whole'), his notion of contradiction is related entirely to the fact that total resolution is possible only in the Absolute. As with Žižek's dialectical conception of immanent antagonism, Hegel nullifies the creator-creature distinction, whereby 'God' collapses *into* contradictory reality itself. However, while rejecting the overall tenets of Hegelian immanence, it is still possible to take elements from Hegel's dialectical conception of contradiction and incorporate them within a framework of revelatory theology. The incessant tension within the finite realm, as seen in Hegel's dialectic, is an aspect that is shared by many of the aforementioned 'dialectical' thinkers in the theological tradition (including Barth, Chesterton and Kierkegaard), whereby dialectical thought is a *necessary* condition of human finitude. In each of these thinkers, even in the midst of divine revelation, total *resolution* of the opposites is perpetually denied, even as they come into contact through moments of conflict or sublation. All adherence to theological dialectic, at some point, assents to the ongoing necessity of such antagonistic movement, even within a wider dogmatic framework.

Despite the theological faults in Hegel's dialectical system, then, we might yet admit, with Barth: 'Doubtless, theology could and can learn something from Hegel as well.'[244] We have seen, in the previous chapter, that Christian theology and preaching rests upon the authority and clarity of Scripture as the source of revealed theological truth. This truth, as was noted, is canonized within a unity of different perspectives, underlain by a primary message. Canonization is not identical to a system but certainly contains aspects of a system because of the interconnected unity achieved through consolidating the various strands.[245] We have also seen, alongside this unity, the existence of forms of dialectical tension which exist *within* such unity. It is on this point that we may see Hegelian contradiction as a helpful tool

---

243. Ibid.

244. Karl Barth, *Protestant Theology in the Nineteenth Century: Its Background and History*, trans. B. Cozens and J. Bowden (London: SCM Press, 1972), p. 403.

245. 'There is a sense in which the whole had an effect on the parts and played an important role in securing the final form of the canon. This is one element of systematicity that seems present even in the earliest of Christian communities: an awareness of doctrinal comprehensiveness and consistency. Obviously, it does not make the authors of Scripture or the early theologians systematic in the modern sense, since the comprehensiveness is related to the text of Scripture and not a corpus of knowledge external to Scripture. However, it does make them concerned for an appropriate understanding of the witness to the gospel. And this witness seems bound in part to an appropriate rendering of the significance of the texts in Scripture.' Gale Heide, *Timeless Truth in the Hands of History: A Short History of System in Theology* (Cambridge: James Clarke & Co, 2012), p. 14.

by which we can imagine what necessary antagonism may mean when dialectical opposites occur within a unified whole (the canon). As noted, this need not mean an incorporation of Hegelian dialectic itself, since not *all* dialectical oppositions within the canon are 'dialectical' in the same way. Hegelian dialectic, however, offers a lens by which we can see that apparent canonical contradiction (distinguished from the static incompatible compatibility of particular ontological paradoxes) cannot be resolved simplistically but must become engaged in varying moments of polarity interaction. Furthermore, this also establishes that 'contradiction' (in the Hegelian sense) does not come at the *expense* of the system's unity, but actually upholds it. Although canonical dialectical tension is not the primary guarantor of canonical unity,[246] it contributes to the functional engagement *with* the canon in the ongoing 'movement' of engaging with Scriptural multivocity. It is in this sense that Hegel has shown, at least, that dialectical antagonistic tensions, when observed, may be *necessary* within a unified whole.

b. *Dialectical Variety.*

While understanding Hegelian contradiction as systematic antagonism may be a helpful lens for viewing canonical dialectics, it is not readily apparent that Hegel's conception of dialectic helps clarify the differences between different forms of dialectical interaction. Since Hegel's dialectic embodies antagonistic tension through ongoing moments of sublation, it appears that a kind of resolution *and* antagonism is at play simultaneously. However, this is still only one 'type' of dialectical possibility, of which there are many. For example, despite the aforementioned shades of overlap, there is no concept within Hegelian dialectic directly comparable with 'ontological paradox' – Hegel's polarities remain contradictory in dynamic tension, *not* in static incompatibility. Also absent is any notion of a polarity which exhibits priority over another (as, for example, with some of Barth's later dialectical articulations of the 'Yes' triumphing over the 'No'). This lack of dialectical variety in Hegel's thought is, in fact, the very product of his system. Because Hegel has, in Kierkegaard's words, 'cancelled the principle of contradiction',[247] he has also limited the ways in which dialectics can be used (both conceptually and methodologically) because of the inseparability of his particular dialectic *from* his overarching philosophical system.

As has been argued throughout this chapter and confirmed with our analysis of Hegel, dialectic is not (exclusively) the act of resolving *or* maintaining polarity

---

246. It has already been argued, of course, that the Gospel is the overarching 'yardstick' for canonicity. Yet as Childs notes, even this does not exclude the *necessity* of ongoing antagonisms within the canon: 'The canon therefore provided a context for the gospel, but did not attempt a final resolution of its message…It did not establish one doctrinal position, but often balanced several or fixed the limits within which Christians might rightly disagree.' Brevard S. Childs, *The New Testament as Canon: An Introduction* (Philadelphia: Fortress Press, 1984), p. 29.

247. Kierkegaard, *Postscript*, p. 304.

tension, but may correspond to a number of different modes whereby the notion of exclusive 'one-sidedness' is combated variously. Dialectics represent the different ways apparent 'contradictions' or oppositional concepts may be engaged, emphasized and articulated. Before we attempt to apply the 'problem' of dialectics to heraldic preaching (in Chapter III), we must see this broadened scope for what dialectic may encompass in its various modes of possibility.

6. *Distinguishing Primary Dialectical Modes*

As has been argued throughout this chapter, 'dialectic' is not (exclusively) the act of resolving *or* maintaining polarity tension but may correspond to various modes whereby the notion of exclusive 'one-sidedness' is combated in different ways. Dialectics represent the different ways apparent 'contradictions' or oppositional concepts may be engaged, emphasized and articulated We will now establish a set of primary dialectical modes which may be encountered in Scripture (and thus, encountered in the act of expository preaching). It is important to see the aforementioned broadened scope for what dialectic may encompass in its various modes of possibility precisely because of the dialectical variety within the biblical canon. It is appropriate to view *all* interactions between opposing polarities as 'dialectical' even if there are proper designations between dialectical theological tensions in general and ontological paradoxes in particular. Here we will briefly define four *primary* dialectical modes by which oppositional polarities may be engaged: 1. paradoxical dialectics (incompatible polarities in juxtaposition); 2. harmonized dialectics (sublated polarities in synthesis); 3. hierarchical dialectics (ordered polarities in procession); 4. antagonistic dialectics (interactive polarities in tension). There are undoubtedly more than four in 'total' – indeed, there may even be an infinite amount of overlapping variations in combination. However, as seen so far in the approaches of variously dialectical thinkers, what follows are perhaps the most common conceptions found in most theological expressions of either 'paradox' or 'dialectic', and they anticipate the primary oppositional conflicts that will be faced by the preacher in the problematic engagement with inner-canonical diversity. In order for the preacher to speak from or through such dialectics, it is vital to know how such conceptions may be oriented.

The distinctive tenets of each dialectic will now be explicated in their basic abstract form. Although minor exemplification will be given, the specific doctrinal applications will be limited here due to the need for attaining *conceptual* clarity. It will be seen in the following chapter, through the application of these dialectical modes to the 'Paul-James' dialectic, the modes can apply variously to the *same* doctrinal polarities at different times. Thus, although there are some dialectical doctrinal constructs which remain exclusively tied to one particular mode (such as the hypostatic union as an 'ontological paradox') there are other forms in which numerous dialectical combinations may be used to articulate the polarity relationship. In order to help categorize these distinctive dialectics conceptually, 'Yes' and 'No' will be used as a normative trope. Although 'Yes-and-No' has its own cadence within dialectical theology, here it will be used as a tool of theoretical orientation, purely to designate *how* the dialectical polarities relate.

i. *Paradoxical Dialectic (incompatible polarities)*

The first dialectical mode is that of 'incompatible polarities'. It is, principally, an outright apparent 'contradiction', most closely associated with 'ontological paradox'. As noted earlier this is not often perceived as 'a dialectic' because dialectics are sometimes seen (limitedly) to require some kind of interactive polarity relationship. However, although these polarities are outright opposites, it is still possible to speak of them in a *kind* of relatedness because they come together *as* a construct. In the ontological sense, they remain irreconcilably divided: the 'Yes' and the 'No' stand against one another in a static obstinacy, totally unmediated. Simultaneously, they appear as (somehow) *together* in spite of their ontological incompatibility. However, although these polarities are drawn together paradoxically, they do not lose their distinctive oppositional value, remaining precisely what they *are* in their radical difference: 'Yes' (non-'No') and 'No' (non-'Yes'). Thus, one cannot speak of this dialectic as a 'meeting' of the polarities but more as a permanent juxtaposition. Their conceptual unity is that which becomes apparent only upon articulating this unity *as* a 'paradoxical dialectic'. However, this does not involve any movement or oscillation *between* the polarities – each polarity simply posits itself *as* itself in spite of the simultaneous positing of its opposite, which is alongside – but not co-mingled with – itself.

ii. *Harmonized Dialectic (sublated polarities)*

The second dialectical mode contains 'harmonized polarities'. It is most commonly known as a 'synthesis' in which two polarities are merged together to form a newly unified concept. As with the first dialectical mode, this dialectic is static in that the polarities are not involved in an oscillating movement or tension (although their complex unification is based upon a *prior* movement). In this dialectic, the polarities – because they are now conjoined – may be spoken of individually only *apart* from the dialectic, as what they once were *before* their sublation. Within the harmonized dialectic, however, the 'Yes' and 'No' have become a new ontological unity, a 'third' thing not comparable with either 'Yes' or 'No'. (This brings to mind Chesterton's anti-Hegelian quip that such a synthesis might be rendered 'yo'.[248]) Of course, the harmonized dialectic is not, in fact, a fusion of 'Yes' and 'No' *as* 'Yes' and 'No'. Rather, both polarities necessarily lose their essential identity as individual polarities (thus differing from Hegelian sublation, where the polarities retain a semblance of their essence). The polarities have become a new oneness rather than a duality. In this sense, this is a 'weaker' form of dialectic because it has become one-sided, and allows for no necessary *ongoing* sublation once the mediation has

---

248. Chesterton, *Aquinas*, p. 167.

occurred. Despite the *prior* movement of two polarities being infused together, there is no enduring movement since it is now a static harmony, a *new* polarity. The reason such a relationship may still be rendered as 'a dialectic' at all is because we are aware the fusion *has* occurred and we may see particular elements of the formerly separated polarities *within* the sublated 'third'. It is also important to note that polarity harmonization does not *always* entail a 'permanent' synthesis, but it can involve the conceptual bringing-together of polarities for a particular purpose, such as observing the dialectical unity that *might* result through sublation.

iii. *Hierarchical Dialectic (ordered polarities)*

The third notable dialectical mode is that of a hierarchical positioning of the two polarities. Here, each polarity maintains its own ontological unity, yet the polarities are related to one another in a particular way, with a particular ordering. They are not 'equal' partners in the dialectic – one precedes the other, either in the sense of one always being spoken of *first*, or in the sense of one being dependent upon the other.[249] Whereas all dialectics usually involve a conceptual relationship between the two different polarities, this dialectic is not a mutually informing relationship because the 'higher' polarity governs the way in which the two polarities interact.[250] This remains the case even where the two polarities appear as contradictory opposites. If the 'Yes', for example, is deemed (temporarily *or* permanently) to be the 'privileged' polarity in the pair, then the dialectic cannot proceed in a kind of tug-of-war between the two because the freighted 'Yes' must *determine* the way in which the 'Yes-and-No' relate. However, the 'No' must remain essential to the dialectical relationship *as* itself – it cannot become engulfed *by* the 'Yes', sublated *with* the 'Yes', corrective *of* the 'Yes', or statically antithetical *to* the 'Yes'. It remains itself *as* the 'No' but it is always *preceded* by the 'Yes' and dependent upon it. In other forms of this hierarchical dialectic, the 'lower' polarity may emanate or proceed *from* the 'higher', whereby polarity distinctness is maintained but the perpetual order continues to dictate the way in which the dialectic is interpreted.

249. This, for example, could be the case with 'God' and 'creation'; these 'polarities' can be seen within 'a dialectic', but not in the sense of a harmony [ii] or a complete incompatibility [i], nor even as a back-and-forth tension [iv]; rather, they may be called 'dialectical' only in the sense that God and man have some form of relationship, particularly in the event of the incarnation.

250. This inequality between the partners does not mean that the hierarchy is 'fixed' as such; for some dialectical pairs (such as 'God' and 'creation') this ontological hierarchy is indeed permanent; for others, however (such as 'Preacher' and 'Hearer') a non-hierarchical 'taxonomy' could be imagined, whereby the necessary ordering of one polarity over the other does not designate it as 'higher' but designates its differing 'function' within the dialectical construct; thus it appears as *contingently* prior to its opposite but not *ontologically* – nor perpetually – prior.

iv. *Antagonistic Dialectic (interactive polarities)*

The fourth primary dialectical mode is that of an antagonistic tension between the polarities. This echoes the earliest emphases of dialectical theology (whereby 'Yes' and 'No' appear in a state of necessary conflict), and the 'paradoxical preaching' of Eckhart (whereby the impossibility of the 'Yes' and 'No' are pitted against one another). In an antagonistic dialectic, the polarities are ontologically distinct and yet inseparable. They remain their individual selves but are perpetually connected and affective upon one another's movement in the ongoing antagonism. This dialectic is the very opposite of a sublated unity of the polarities because the dialectic is itself engaged in self-corrective conflict. The 'Yes' and the 'No' are mutually necessary to one another despite a particular emphasis in one or other direction at particular times. This self-correctivity, however, never achieves 'balance' per se, and it never strives towards a norm.[251] The dialectical tension may lean one way or the other in a dynamic which partially inflates and partially suppresses each polarity, never to rest in resolution, perpetually wrestling back and forth. This is what is most commonly meant in widespread uses of the term 'dialectic', invoking the problem of uncertainty regarding *decisive* speech in the midst of the ongoing oscillation between the polarities.

7. *Conclusion: Dialectical Bases*

In this chapter we have seen the underlying theological bases for dialectical theological speech and some of the consistent patterns for the dialectical method in a variety of theological contexts. It has been seen that dialectic should not be 'feared' as an enemy to clear theological speech, but embraced as a doctrinally *necessary* reality in light of the Creator-creature distinction. Although it has been noted that dialectic itself can become potentially paralysing for the clear declaration of the Gospel message, this happens only when dialectic itself is privileged in an '*un*dialectical' manner. If dialectic truly opens up thinking against one-sidedness, this also includes the one-sidedness of any exclusive dialectical focus, whereby contingent expressions of either 'Yes' or 'No' are inappropriately excluded in favour of a 'singular' form of dialectical engagement. The goal of delineating various dialectical modes has not been to offer an exhaustive account of every possible dialectical mode or construct, but merely to separate those forms which are most prominent in the task of attending to the dialectical variety within and between theological doctrines. Where the word 'dialectic' is often used synonymously with 'paradox', 'contradiction', or 'relationship', we now have a clearer basis from which to speak of the different ways in which dialectic may function within theological speech.

Having highlighted the four primary dialectical modes, it is important to restate not only that these are only 'primary', but also that to separate them into

251. This concept will be explored in III.5.ii.

distinct camps is not itself without complexity. This is because dialectic crosses between different modes of interaction, as for example, in Hegel's conception of contradiction and sublation, connoting both harmony and antagonism. Where these modes may be said to overlap when used methodologically this will be addressed in the following chapter. It is, in fact, the act of *preaching* which attempts to navigate a way through and beyond these dialectics in the contingent declaration of focused doctrinal truth. Where the different modes of dialectical engagement have shown a variety in what dialectic can mean and how it can be applied, dialectic itself is problematic for the act of heraldic assertions of doctrinal truth wherever those truths are uttered without *some* acknowledgement of their necessary canonical opposites. The following chapter, then, will attempt to place what we have gleaned from theological dialectical theory in step with 'heraldic' preaching, offering a theology *of* heraldic preaching before demonstrating the ways in which the aforementioned dialectical modes may function *within* it.

Chapter III

DIALECTIC, PROCLAMATION, CORRECTIVITY: THE POSSIBILITY OF DIALECTICAL HERALDIC CONFIDENCE

1. *Introduction: Dialectics, Homiletics and Preaching*

Because of the ongoing necessity of preaching in the life of the Church, Scriptural dialectics continue to cause tension *for* preaching. Having highlighted the complexity and theological necessity of theological dialectics, we will now construct a conversation between 'dialectic' and 'proclamation'. This will entail sketching the notion of the 'herald' as a necessary category for understanding what preaching is. Although it is helpful to conceive of the application of preaching in a variety of ways, an overly diverse variety at the conceptual level can sometimes dilute and confuse how we understand preaching's uniqueness in contrast to other forms of verbal communication. Defining preaching as a primarily heraldic activity entails having a message to *proclaim* rather than, for example, 'discuss'. It is the notion of heraldic proclamation which is most problematized by dialectical polarities of theological truth, precisely because of the apparent 'one-sidedness' of the herald's message, which dialectics – at their core – reject.

Given that the concept of 'heraldic' preaching has been significantly critiqued within contemporary homiletics, we will also need to address the primary tenets of the 'New Homiletic', which reacted so strongly against the heraldic motif, preferring the listener-oriented tenets of 'ambiguity' over against the herald's supposed 'certainty'. Here, a more nuanced conception of the herald will be offered which is able to incorporate some of the New Homiletic's concerns theologically without negating the primary importance of the heraldic conception. Upon this foundation, a theology of 'confidence' for heraldic preaching will be given, the foundations of which may be found in God's own speech and God's commission of preachers. This has various theological implications for preaching, including the notion of decisiveness, the elision of sermonic form and content and the understanding of preaching being upheld with paradoxical assurance. Indeed, we will see how the preacher's confidence is grounded in their inability to speak of God in the midst of His commission for them to do so.[1] Having laid this

---

1. See Augustine, *On Christian Doctrine*, trans. J. F. Shaw (New York: Christian Literature Publishing Co., 1886), p. 10.

foundation, we will then reflect upon how such preaching interacts with some of the aforementioned dialectical modes, offering a variety of potential sermonic foci within the 'Paul-James' dialectic (sketched in I.4.ii). These variable dialectical possibilities within the sermon will be evaluated within a conception of preaching as dialectically corrective and contingent, allowing the herald to speak both *from* and *to* Scripture's theological dialectics in particular contextual situations.

First then, since different definitions of preaching significantly alter its relationship to dialectic, we will outline what we mean by 'heraldic proclamation' and why it is a primary reality of the preaching task.

2. *The Necessity of 'Heraldic' Proclamation*

An essential part of proclamation is certainty and from this should spring joy... In large part the power of proclamation to bring certainty seems to have been lost. Most preachers seem to get along without it. Such powerful preaching as there is, is more likely to draw its strength from the compulsion of the religious law than from the liberating urgency of the Gospel.[2]

Although there are many forms of proclamation, it is in apparently 'authoritative' preaching that we see a potential clash with dialectics. If preaching carries a responsibility to be clear, imperative and assured in its theological declarations, it must face up to the inevitable 'other side of the coin' which ensues in dialectical thinking. In spite of this necessary dialectical condition, clear and assured proclamation is still as theologically indispensable as dialectics. As will be seen, contemporary homiletical thought has not engaged sufficiently with this problem, precisely because of a deficient account of the importance of 'confidence' in preaching. Indeed, in much contemporary preaching and homiletics, dialectics have a tendency to engulf the act of preaching, in which no *singular* aspect of truth is proclaimed with confidence for fear of contradicting the other polarity within a particular dialectical construct. Such a condition is theologically insufficient because it silences the polarity of 'proclamation' for the polarity of 'dialectic'. Ironically, this ends up becoming non-dialectical because it cannot allow for the necessary extremity involved in momentarily emphasizing any *particular* text or theme from theological revelation.

There are, of course, dangers with an *overly* certain pulpit voice.[3] The aim here is not to justify theological obscurantism, authoritarianism or quasi-Enlightenment notions of 'certainty'. Yet the opposite side of this problem appears far more

2. Gerhard Ebeling, *Theology and Proclamation: A Discussion with Rudolf Bultmann*, trans. John Riches (London: Collins, 1966), p. 13.

3. See the telling entry for 'pulpit' in Bierce's satirical dictionary of 1911: 'Pulpit: an elevated box, into which the person gets, for fear that people would not otherwise notice his superiority over his congregation.' Ambrose Bierce, *The Devil's Dictionary* (London: Penguin, 1995), p. 256.

prevalent today for various reasons within the current cultural, philosophical and theological climate.[4] Sermons are commonly understood less as the unique moment in which one authoritative voice resounds within the many, but rather as a plurality of dialectical voices, continually shifting back and forth in such a way as to neutralize the notion of divine authority in preaching. The recovery of the theological notion of heraldic proclamation in the face of (and in light of) theological dialectics is essential. This invokes the primary question: what exactly *is* proclamation?

i. *Proclamation as Heraldic*

As we saw in the first chapter, proclamation is not only the very event which gathered the early Church but also the event which 'gathered' the texts of Scripture as they cohered with the message of what was preached. 'Proclamation' can be used to mean a number of different things. The act of preaching in a pulpit on a Sunday morning in front of a gathering of churched people is not the only way proclamation occurs. Broadly, we might define proclamation as the commissioned speech of the people of God whereby the message of the Gospel is delivered and redelivered both within and beyond the confines of the Church.[5] Yet it is not inappropriate to call preaching the *normative* form of proclamation, even if preaching occurs in many formats and contexts. Indeed, Martin Luther contended that 'the office of preaching is second to none in Christendom'.[6] Preaching carries such importance because it is the intentioned, eventful speaking-out of the message of the Gospel. This identifies the core of what proclamation is *for*.[7]

Because of the crucial importance of the role of preaching, it is important to note that when a preacher preaches a sermon, they are not merely speaking words which the congregation might do well to listen to; they are speaking words which come with distinct authority and purpose: 'Preaching is not mere public expression of opinion but an urgent eschatological activity upon which the very

---

4. It would be impossible here, of course, to navigate the complexity of what has *led* to this problem in all its different facets; we might, perhaps, venture to use that overused catch-all term 'postmodernism' as an indicative starting-point to such an enquiry, despite its descriptive insufficiency.

5. 'The story that makes us Christians cannot be known without proclamation.' Stanley Hauerwas, *The Cross-Shattered Church: Reclaiming the Theological Heart of Preaching* (Grand Rapids: Brazos Press, 2009), p. 16.

6. Martin Luther, *The Sermons of Martin Luther*, vol. III, trans. John Nicholas Lenker (Grand Rapids: Baker Book House, 1983), p. 374.

7. 'Without hearing and without preaching there is no salvation. One could not underline the centrality of preaching for the Christian faith more starkly. Since faith comes from hearing, Christian faith is impossible without preaching.' Christophe Schwöbel, 'The Preacher's Art: Preaching Theologically', in Colin E. Gunton (ed.), *Theology Through Preaching: Sermons for Brentwood* (Edinburgh: T & T Clark, 2001), pp. 1–20 [1].

consummation of history depends.'[8] Indeed, the very word 'proclamation' suggests an important message which carries unique significance, rather than a relaxed meandering discussion or playful keynote speech. The Greek term *kerysso* is often used to define the sense of what the act of preaching aims to accomplish, connoting the actions of a 'herald' who proclaims the king's message to the king's subjects. This sense of heralding informs not only the content of preaching but also its form. That is, although *kerysso* is not the only way we can think of preaching – and by no means the only word used for preaching in the New Testament[9] – it encapsulates, theologically, what all preachers do when they attempt to speak on behalf of God.

Another word-form frequently used for preaching in the New Testament is *angello* (derivative of, in many cases, *euangelion*: 'gospel') which connotes the 'announcing' of the message. This also suggests a heightened declaration of important news, not the mere 'portrayal' of a narrative or the 'conveyance' of information. Similarly, a herald is one who has an urgent message which *ought* to be heard by the citizens within (and even beyond) the king's domain. It is in this light that preaching is to be imagined. This does not mean other approaches to what is commonly called preaching are necessarily wrong, but it is often the case that the concept of preaching has been broadened to include various communicative forms which have diluted this *primary* calling of the preaching office.

This dilution of preaching's self-understanding is, of course, exacerbated in light of the social media revolution: 'The time in which church spokesmen communicated like medieval heralds proclaiming their news in front of an astonished audience has passed. "Generation Facebook" likes to *join* the discussions.'[10] To many, it is increasingly inconceivable that singular heraldic

8. David Dunn-Wilson, *A Mirror for the Church: Preaching in the First Five Centuries* (Grand Rapids: Eerdmans, 2005), p. 1.

9. *Kerysso*, used over sixty times in the New Testament, is the most commonly used word for preaching. However, alongside *kerysso*, Greidanus notes there are thirty-three different verb-forms in the New Testament alone for what we simply call 'preaching'. Sidney Greidanus, *The Modern Preacher and the Ancient Text* (Grand Rapids: Eerdmans, 1988), pp. 6–7. 'In their attempt to do justice to their theme, the writers use their homiletic vocabulary very fluidly, discovering new words and creating different combinations of old ones. All that concerns them is that they find the right words to establish the supremacy of Christian preaching over all its rivals.' Dunn-Wilson, *Preaching in the First Five Centuries*, p. 2. Despite such homiletical diversity, it still appears that the concept of *kerysso* is primary for the purpose of what a preacher is actually doing when they stand up to proclaim 'the Word of God'. Although there are different forms of preaching, preachers are always representatives of the kingly message; if they claim to speak what God has revealed they never cease to be 'heralds' whether they are primarily teaching (*didaskein*), evangelizing (*euangelizesthai*) or exhorting (*parakalein*). The heraldic identity of the preacher remains a primary theological foundation of the preacher's office and function.

10. Wilhelm Gräb, 'Practical Theology as a Theory of Lived Religion: Conceptualizing Church Leadership', in *International Journal of Practical Theology* 18:1 (2014), pp. 102–12.

authority could possibly exist in a society of global, viral, digital communication. However, as will be argued, the heraldic identity of the preacher is not merely 'optional' as though it were dependent upon shifting sociological trends. This is because it is a theological – not a missiological – foundation. Indeed, even if other forms of preaching might also be found within the overall category of herald, the primacy of the preacher's heraldic identity must be established at the forefront of any additional facets, however baffling this remains in the digital age.[11]

ii. *Heralds and Dialectics*

The heraldic conception of preaching invokes the starkest homiletical clash with theological dialectics. The connotation of heralding assumes not only an urgent message but an unequivocally *clear* message. Dialectics potentially introduce divergences and pluralities within such a message, threatening to undermine its heraldic clarity. Of course, dialectics need not always be seen as antithetical to preaching, and in many cases they can be welcomed and may even become essential to some particular heraldic messages. However, emphasizing theological dialectics presents significant problems for the preacher whose heraldic message carries an expectation of clarity and univocity. Indeed, because of the perceived authority and subsequent importance of this message ('from the king'), it should not normally find itself entangled in conflicting antagonisms. Unrestrained reflection upon theological dialectical tensions within the moment of preaching can, indeed, hinder the act of heralding (even if dialectical reflection remains essential).

Some preaching situations may require dialectical reflection *for* faithful proclamation, as with sermons based upon a biblical passage overtly emphasizing dialectical tension, such as Paul's rhetorical questioning representing opposing points of view (Rom. 6:1). Such texts may require navigation between opposing viewpoints in a particularly *overt* way in order to be sufficiently 'heralded' in their particularity. There are also instances such as Paul's 'Yes and No' language in 2Cor. 1:17–20, or in the Old Testament's the 'season' dialectics of Ecc. 3:1–8, the dialectical 'balance' of Ecc. 7:18 or the paradoxical juxtaposition of Prov. 26:4–5. Scripture does not *always* present texts with neatly delineated, independent statements of doctrine. Rather, Scripture also contains doctrinal statements which make overt reference to the tension incurred between themselves and a corresponding point of doctrine, or a different viewpoint. Such overt awareness of dialectical tensions

---

11. This is not to say heraldic preaching need be seen as incongruent with social media, by any means. It is not the place here, of course, to examine the possible missiological implications of heraldic preaching upon digital technology, and vice versa, though such connections are important to avoid either diluting the heraldic conception of preaching to gratify the newly formed desires of the digital age, or the equal danger of ossifying the heraldic conception into ill-conceived traditional 'forms' of preaching which lose their missional (and thereby, their truly heraldic) edge.

within the text does not necessarily hinder the heralding of a particular message if that particular message is itself 'dialectical'.

Some of the aforementioned dialectical modes, of course, are less problematic to heraldic preaching than others. 'Hierarchical' dialectics, for example, may offer two messages with one presiding over the other, which may well complement the notion of a clear and heraldic message. 'Harmonized' dialectics, equally, may present two polarities which *become* one as they are fused together within the message itself. These dialectics, in which polarities are *not* presented at odds with one another, do not represent as significant a problem. 'Antagonistic' or 'incompatible' dialectics, however, may offer dialectical problems to the hearers rather than the sense of one authoritative message. These dialectics are theologically *necessary* because Scripture itself contains them, and hence preachers must contend with them in expository heraldic preaching. If preaching as 'heraldic' proclamation is not emphasized from the outset, the difficulties posed by dialectic to preaching become less clear, and ultimately might be more easily ignored. If it is not *necessary* that preaching is seen as an authoritative message which announces truths of great importance and clarity, then dialectics may be incorporated without inducing the same theological dilemma for the preacher.

iii. *Heralds and Homilies*

Many sermonic forms of the wider modern era have produced polished sermons and homilies which do not reflect this *kerysso* imperative of preaching. The classical 'English homily', for example, was a pre-written discourse often crafted to be read as much as spoken. This was particularly the case in the nineteenth century, with the common practice of reading sermons on a Sunday afternoon while sitting in front of the fire or at bedtime.[12] Historically, British preachers ranging from Wesley to Newman to Spurgeon have published their sermons in such tidy collection formats and the practice is continued today by preachers of various denominational and theological backgrounds. In generations in which biblical familiarity and theological literacy within and beyond the Church was significantly greater, these written sermons had considerable impact beyond the preached moment itself. In the era of the Great Awakening, for example, Wesley and Whitefield (among others) sanctioned a 'preach and print' aspect to their ministries whereby the public proclamations could be better remembered in hindsight or even pre-heralded in advance.[13] These printed sermons were seen as supplementary to the preached moment itself, however, which always took precedent.[14]

But beyond these contextually useful reasons for the printing of preaching, the enduring legacy of a predominantly *written* homiletical style today often

12. Hughes Oliphant Old, *The Reading and Preaching of the Scriptures in the Worship of the Christian Church, vol. 6: The Modern Age* (Grand Rapids: Eerdmans, 2006), p. 350.

13. Ian J. Maddock, *Men of One Book: A Comparison of Two Methodist Preachers, John Wesley and George Whitefield* (Cambridge: The Lutterworth Press, 2012), pp. 103–4.

14. See Ibid., pp. 106, 110–11.

results in well-rounded theological orations which neglect the immediacy of the preaching moment. Although such scripted speeches may be extremely astute and theologically nuanced, they risk neutralizing the heraldic emphasis.[15] Such homilies may often be 'well-rounded' because they seek to be theologically balanced, where the preacher may remain in full control of their theological assertions. In one sense they evince a 'high' view of preaching in that the preacher does not want to risk undermining the Word by their own subjectivity; but in another sense they risk eliminating their living heraldic witness. This is an example of both the help and the hindrance of dialectical awareness: ensuring that *both* sides of the proverbial coin are given their due. In well-rehearsed and moderated theological rhetoric, dialectical tensions between biblical passages or doctrines may be discussed at a measured pace without the necessary expectation of a singular, authoritative message in the present moment. To speak of 'heraldic' proclamation, however, means the preacher is not navigating placidly between rhetorical and theological possibilities but is demonstrably assertive in their *particular* message in that particular moment.

The legacy of the rhetorical written homily as a substitute for preaching in the contemporary era has become something of a liturgical artefact of the established Western denominations which have long remained tethered to inherited forms of ecclesial practice. The drastic and irretrievable deterioration of the established churches in the twentieth and twenty-first centuries is the result of a complex matrix of factors, yet it no doubt correlates with the observable loss of assertive confidence in preaching. Simply put, the death of Western Christendom has more than a little to do with the fact that fewer and fewer people can bear to listen to sermons. The pulpit has not been seen as a place where words of life may be found, where they may receive news from on high, because the preachers themselves no longer seemed to believe they had the right to speak from 'on high' at all. Dietrich Bonhoeffer observed this dismal phenomenon even in the 1930s, whereby it seemed the questions of life and death were more likely being met in the cinema than the pulpit.[16] This pervasive loss of confidence, though perhaps susceptible in any era of the Church, becomes its own unique species in modernity.[17] This can be observed in the genealogy of what might be called 'postmodern homiletics' and its consummate assault on the heraldic authority of the preacher.

---

15. 'I believe that the printing and publication of sermons has had a bad effect upon preaching...I would attribute a good deal of the decline in preaching at the present time to those literary effusions which have passed under the name of sermons and of preaching.' D. Martyn Lloyd-Jones, *Preaching and Preachers* (Grand Rapids: Zondervan, 2011), pp. 22–3.

16. See Dietrich Bonhoeffer, 'Ambassadors for Christ', in Isabel Best (ed.), *The Collected Sermons of Dietrich Bonhoeffer* (Minneapolis: Fortress Press, 2013), pp. 87–93.

17. Church decline and loss of confidence in preachers, of course, is also borne of authoritarian abuse whereby preacherly superiority failed to address the lives of its hearers. See Charles Taylor, *A Secular Age* (Cambridge, MA, and London: Harvard University Press, 2007), p. 95. However, as will be argued, a robustly theological account of heraldic preaching does not imply authoritarian abuse and listener neglect when understood in its fullest imaginative scope.

3. *Between Herald and New Homiletic*

i. *A Genealogy of Contemporary Homiletical Thought*

The heraldic notion of preaching has often come under fire within those homiletical circles keen to move beyond monological preaching modes with alternative communicative forms. However, one of the primary problems with the rejection of the heraldic concept is the distinct neglect of a sustained *theological* account of preaching. This is due to a primary fixation within much homiletics today upon the anthropological, the rhetorical and the communicative elements as opposed to the theological foundations which ought to underpin the ways preaching is imagined and, subsequently, practiced. Although homiletical scholarship has been referred to as 'a melting pot of quite different voices',[18] so rife with fragmentation that there is 'no articulated authoritative theory that dominates',[19] it is nonetheless possible to trace many resurfacing trends to the influence of the 'New Homiletic'. This has been undoubtedly the key homiletical movement of the last century, directly shaping the homiletical culture of the 1970s and 1980s, and continuing to influence the ways preaching is conceptualized and practised to this day.[20] Although there were various catalysts behind this innovative movement, one of its primary motivations was responding to the dominance of the 'heraldic' conception of preaching.

a. *Preacher as Herald: Forsyth and Stewart.*

Despite the inevitable variations within the state of preaching before the New Homiletic era, it can be said that, in the first half of the twentieth century, the preacher was predominantly seen in the aforementioned 'heraldic' role. This greatly affected how preaching was envisaged, and influenced not only the way the congregation was perceived, but also the role of sermon construction and preacherly authority. We will focus here, selectively, upon two important adherents of this heraldic notion of preaching, P. T. Forsyth and James Stewart. Both of them rendered the influential *Lyman Beecher Lectures* (Yale) and, in Stewart's case, the *Warrack Lectures* (Edinburgh) – these lectureships were influential in identifying the key homiletical emphases of the time.[21]

Forsyth's influential book *Positive Preaching and the Modern Mind* (1907) has become an enduring benchmark in modern homiletical thought. There, Forsyth

---

18. F. Gerrit Immink, 'Homiletics: The Current Debate', in *International Journal of Practical Theology* 8:1 (2004), pp. 89–121 [89].

19. Lucy-Atkinson Rose, *Sharing the Word: Preaching in the Roundtable Church* (Grand Rapids: Westminster John Knox Press, 1997), p. 8.

20. This is also a reason for what may seem an American-centric approach in this section: 'In recent generations the absolute dominance of American scholarship in matters of homiletic theory means that it forms the backdrop of all serious discussion of the issues.' Chris Burkett, *Homiletics as Mnemonic Practice: Collective Memory and Contemporary Christian Preaching* (unpublished doctoral dissertation, University of Liverpool, 2009), p. 35.

21. See W. P. Stephens 'Scottish Preachers and Preaching', in *The Expository Times* 105 (1994), pp. 330–5; also: Burkett, *Homiletics as Mnemonic Practice*, pp. 33–4.

notably spoke of preaching as 'a living act' through a sacramental lens: 'In true preaching, as in a true sacrament, more is done than said.'[22] Although Forsyth is the best-known modern proponent of this notion, it is similarly echoed by Stewart, who saw the sermon as 'an act of worship, a sacramental showing forth of Christ',[23] and by John Calvin, with whom Forsyth shares much homiletical agreement.[24] For Forsyth, the sacramentality of preaching gave it the status of a sui generis 'event'. This was due to the transcendent nature of the preached Word, which cannot be construed as an ordinary example of human speech: 'The pulpit is another place, and another kind of place, than the platform...The Christian preacher is not the successor of the Greek orator, but of the Hebrew prophet. The orator comes with an inspiration, but the prophet comes with a revelation.'[25] Here, there is no particular emphasis upon the listener or the sermon's form; the preacher's primary responsibility is rather to deliver the divine message. This meant preaching came to be seen as theocentric rather than anthropological in orientation – the listener was not there to have their own situation spoken into, but to be led into the 'situation' of the message: 'Bible preaching...is not leading [people] out of the Bible into subjectivities, fancies, quips, or queries. The Bible has a world and a context of its own. It has an ethos, if not a cosmos, of its own.'[26] Here, the sermonic focus is radically un-anthropological, whereby the Bible stands above the human hearer unchangingly and in complete authority; the hearer can only submit to its authoritative power over the immediate anthropological concerns.[27] Indeed, the question of 'authority' was crucial in this heraldic model of preaching and remains a key homiletical discussion point today. Forsyth declared that 'the pulpit has an authority. If it has not, it is the chair and not the pulpit. It may discourse, but it does not preach...It speaks with authority.'[28]

Stewart also championed the authoritative nature of the preacher's office: 'The very terms describing the preacher's function – herald, ambassador – manifestly connote authority. Far too often the pulpit has been deferential and apologetic when it ought to have been prophetic and trumpet-toned.'[29] Stewart argued that

22. P. T. Forsyth, *Positive Preaching and the Modern Mind: The Lyman Beecher Lectures at Yale University* (London: Hodder & Stoughton, 1907), pp. 81–2.

23. James S. Stewart, *Heralds of God: The Warrack Lectures* (London: Hodder & Stoughton, 1946), p. 37. Although Barth perhaps means something different by the term, he *also* refers to preaching as 'a sacramental act'. Karl Barth, *Homiletics*, trans. Geoffrey W. Bromiley and Donald E. Daniels (Westminster: John Knox Press, 1991), p. 119.

24. See Don Roy Wismar, *A Sacramental View of Preaching: As Seen in the Writings of John Calvin and P. T. Forsyth and Applied to the Mid-Twentieth Century* (unpublished doctoral dissertation, Pacific School of Religion, 1963).

25. Forsyth, *Positive Preaching*, p. 3.

26. Ibid., p. 29.

27. Note here the parallels with the tenor of Barth's 'The Strange New World Within the Bible' (1916), in *The Word of God and the Word of Man*, pp. 28–50.

28. Forsyth, *Positive Preaching*, p. 44.

29. Stewart, *Heralds of God*, p. 211.

the authority of the preacher ought to be evident in both the sermon's theological conception *and* its delivery. Preaching should have 'the note of unabashed, triumphant affirmation – "The mouth of the Lord hath spoken it!" '[30] Such declarations of pulpit authority, which could easily invoke the charge of authoritarian abuse, were often nuanced with a particular designation: 'The authority is not that of the preacher's person; it is not to mere authoritativeness.'[31] The herald-preacher's authority is entirely dependent upon their proclaimed message. Stewart critiqued the preaching of the early twentieth century as lacking this authority, which he saw as essential to the preacher's heraldic identity: 'Christianity sounded in men's ears as good advice rather than good news…There was accordingly an inclination to regard the preacher as the purveyor of religious homilies and ethical uplift, not the herald of the mighty acts of God.'[32] It is evident that in both Forsyth's and Stewart's presentations of preaching there was a polemical necessity to demonstrate who the preacher *is* before designating the particularities of what a preacher should actually *do* in the pulpit.[33]

Given the prevalence of the heraldic image for preaching in the first half of the twentieth century, it is perhaps understandable there would emerge reactionary schools of thought emphasizing its perceived dangers, particularly regarding authoritarianism. In the light of two devastating world wars, tyrannical dictators, totalitarian states, and an inevitably fragmented political and philosophical climate, key intellectual shifts occurred which influenced the ways in which both preacher and listener became sceptical of 'authority' per se.[34] Over a decade before the key homiletical revolutions were to occur, Raymond Browne's influential book titled *The Ministry of the Word* (1958) outlined the state of the culture at that time as 'an age where there is general perplexity and bewilderment about authority'.[35] In Browne's thought, this general suspicion of intentional power meant that preaching should occur in such a way that 'listeners are not conscious of what is being done'.[36]

30. Ibid.

31. Forsyth, *Positive Preaching*, p. 44.

32. Stewart, *Heralds of God*, p. 16.

33. See here another parallel with Barth (III.4.ii.d–e).

34. Numerous philosophers could be cited here as forming part of this grand post-modern chorus (a distinctly 'ironic' chorus, it might be added, given post-modernism's general tendency towards teleological chaos). However, three key voices, Jacques Derrida, Michel Foucault and Jean-François Lyotard, stand out with regards to their pervasive cultural influence upon the suspicion of authority, whether of individual or systemic uses of power (Foucault), ideological texts (Derrida) or conceptual metanarratives (Lyotard). Each of these three primary authorial critiques implicitly seem to condemn the preacher given that the preacher is an individual wielding power as part of a larger informed system (the Church), speaking via the authority of an authoritative text with fixed meanings (Scripture), and proclaiming a message which purports to account for the fate of all human beings for all time (the Gospel).

35. R. E. C. Browne, *The Ministry of the Word* (London: SCM Press, 1976), p. 33.

36. Ibid., p. 89.

In many ways, this prefigured much of what would be seen in the New Homiletic, with a clear movement towards the situation of the listener, who – so it went – was reluctant to be knowingly influenced by the preacher's words.

Indeed, with the rapidly changing social and philosophical climate of the twentieth century, the notion of the heraldic sermon could no longer be proposed without heavy qualification:

> By the early 1970s it was apparent to many that the sermon as a form of communication, was in serious trouble…Dramatic changes in society, church, authority and communication had converged to make preaching look as remote, hopelessly authoritarian and outdated as a swallowtail coat.[37]

When the New Homiletic arrived, it is not merely that the heraldic image of the preacher was 'altered' but, rather, obliterated. The very concept of such monological proclamation was itself called into question: 'The preacher seriously asks whether it is best to continue to serve up a monologue in a dialogical world'.[38] If the preacher was to be considered 'heraldic' under the New Homiletic, it would be so radically different from that articulated by Forsyth and Stewart as to be almost unrecognizable.

b. *Craddock's 'New Homiletic'.*

The New Homiletic is still the most significant reference point for homiletical discourse in recent history. Even five decades beyond its inception it continues to resonate with homileticians and preachers worldwide. The pioneer of this movement was Fred Craddock,[39] whose seminal book *As One without Authority* (1971) has since been hailed as 'the Copernican revolution in North American preaching'.[40] Craddock's New Homiletic was, in part, an attempt to overhaul the previous conception of preaching in relation to the listener. As Stewart asserted, the heraldic preacher sought to overwhelm the complexities of the listener's situation with the sheer force of the Gospel message: 'To confront a bewildered and dishevelled

---

37. Thomas G. Long, 'Out of the Loop: The Changing Practice of Preaching', in Mike Graves and David J. Schlafer (eds.), *What's the Shape of Narrative Preaching?* (Atlanta: Chalice Press, 2008), pp. 115–30 [117].

38. Fred B. Craddock, *As One without Authority* (St. Louis: Chalice Press, 2001), p. 18.

39. Craddock is rightly seen as the beginning point of the movement due to the influence of *As One without Authority* (1971), even though he was not the first to emphasize such radical homiletical reform. See, for example, David Randolph, *The Renewal of Preaching* (Philadelphia: Fortress Press, 1969). Craddock also followed his initial work with *Overhearing the Gospel* (1978) which had similar emphases upon the listener as well as the preacher's methods of communication via the use of narrative and 'indirect' preaching; he grounds much of this in Kierkegaard's concept of 'indirect communication'. See Fred B. Craddock, *Overhearing the Gospel* (Sheffield: Cliff College Publishing, 1995), pp. 79–140.

40. Robin R. Meyers, 'Jazz Me Gene: Narrative Preaching as Encore', in *What's the Shape of Narrative Preaching?*, pp. 131–44 [132].

age with the fact of Christ, to thrust upon its confusion the creative word of the Cross and smite its disenchantment with the glory of the resurrection.'[41] The New Homiletic, however, determined to take more seriously that very 'confusion' and 'disenchantment' that the 'bewildered and dishevelled age' was feeling. It did not seek to speak *into* the confusions of the age from a place of heraldic conviction but to embrace those very ambiguities, highlighting the listener's crucial role within preaching: 'Without question, preaching increases in power when it is dialogical, when speaker and listener share in proclamation of the Word.'[42] Craddock's provocations led to a clear anthropological turn in preaching, where the message could occur from listener *to* preacher, and even, from listener *to* God:

> If a minister takes seriously the role of listeners in preaching, there will be sermons expressing for the whole church, and with God as the primary audience, the faith, the doubt, the fear, the anger, the love, the joy, the gratitude that is in all of us.[43]

In such a conception, the human conditions of which the Gospel had previously been thought the 'cure' had now become a primary component of sermonic expression and content. This emphasis led Craddock to what he called 'inductive' preaching, in which the listener contributes to the meaning of the sermon rather than having that meaning prescribed by the authoritative preacher on God's behalf. Craddock's problem with the earlier sermonic form was that the preacher had inappropriate interpretative authority to force the hearer towards particular conclusions: 'There is no democracy here, no dialogue, no listening by the speaker, no contributing by the hearer.'[44] This opened up the concept of the sermon to various forms and models rather than the traditional propositional mode. The best known of these 'new' forms was narrative preaching, in which the preacher speaks parabolically in the idiom of story, choosing to remain open-ended rather than conclusive.[45] This, again, allows more scope for the listener to 'conclude' for themselves.

It should be noted that this emphasis was not entirely listener-inspired but an attempt to be more faithful to the diverse forms and genres of the biblical texts themselves. The typical expository sermon, such as those of Luther and Calvin (see I.3.iii), came under particular criticism by Craddock: 'Is it possible that a sermon that buries itself in the text, moves through it phrase by phrase, and never comes up for air may prove to be "unbiblical" in the sense that it fails to achieve

---

41. James S. Stewart, *A Faith to Proclaim: The Lyman Beecher Lectures at Yale University* (London: Hodder & Stoughton, 1953), p. 11.

42. Craddock, *As One without Authority*, p. 18.

43. Fred B. Craddock, *Preaching* (Nashville: Abingdon, 1985), pp. 26–7.

44. Craddock, *As One without Authority*, p. 46.

45. Craddock's deliberate emphasis upon sermonic ambiguity has often been criticized for its abdication of interpretative responsibility. See Hughes Oliphant Old, *The Reading and Preaching of the Scriptures in the Worship of the Christian Church*, vol. 7: *Our Own Time* (Grand Rapids: Eerdmans, 2010), p. 19.

what the text achieves?'[46] In the New Homiletic, then, sermons were to follow closely the literary genres of their given text in order to be truly 'expository'. It is the elision of form and content, in fact, that can be seen as another key marker within the movement as a whole: '*how* one preaches is to a large extent *what* one preaches'.[47]

This transition from the traditional sermon form evoked new understandings in the power of language to influence hearers. Again, this could be traced to many of the deconstructive philosophies of language that were infiltrating the academic and cultural consciousness of the time.[48] More particularly, it is often noted that the German theologians Gerhard Ebeling and Ernst Fuchs were the primary influence in the New Homileticians' reinterpretation of linguistic possibilities.[49] It is quite likely, in fact, that the term 'New Homiletic' is a deliberate reflection of Ebeling's 'New Hermeneutic', which had sought to re-evaluate the role of language in biblical interpretation and proclamation. As Dawn Ottoni-Wilhelm notes: 'Ebeling and Fuchs helped American homileticians to recognize that language is inherently powerful. It not only expresses or signifies meaning; it creates it.'[50] Both were students of Rudolf Bultmann, whose theology of preaching as existential 'encounter' (see I.2.iv.a) is evident in their notion of preaching as 'word-event'.[51] The New Homileticians built upon this newfound conception of language as creator of meaning, whereby the preacher did not simply deliver a fixed message with a fixed textual content, but had the task of evoking meaning *in* the listener. This was to occur through the preacher's creative use of language as it arose from the biblical text, which was itself a word-event: 'Related to the performative power of language was a shift in focus from what sermons *say* to what they *do*.'[52] Preaching was opened up to include a wide variety of communicative forms in order to contribute to this sense of 'event'. Yet such an event differed greatly from the heraldic or 'sacramental' notions of preaching seen in previous generations; here, the sermon's eventfulness was focused almost entirely upon the preacher's creative interpretation of the text's language and to the listener's creative interpretation of the sermon. Such emphases continued to gain prominence as the New Homiletic was adopted and applied by other preachers and thinkers.

46. Craddock, *Preaching*, p. 28.

47. Craddock, *As One without Authority*, p. 44.

48. See an overt example of this connection in Phil Snider, *Preaching after God: Derrida, Caputo, and the Language of Postmodern Homiletics* (Eugene: Wipf and Stock, 2012).

49. See Sam Persons-Parkes, ' "The Once and Future Pulpit": Hearing Gerhard Ebeling Again', in *Homiletic* 37:1 (2012), pp. 27–37 [27–9].

50. Dawn Ottoni-Wilhelm, 'New Hermeneutic, New Homiletic, and New Directions: An U.S.–North American Perspective', in *Homiletic* 35:1 (2010), pp. 17–31 [19].

51. Gerhard Ebeling, 'The Word of God and Hermeneutics', in *Word and Faith*, trans. James W. Leitch (London: SCM Press, 1963), pp. 305–32.

52. Ottoni-Wilhelm, 'New Hermeneutic, New Homiletic', p. 19.

c. *Expanding the New Homiletic: Lowry and Buttrick.*

Numerous homileticians, most notably Eugene Lowry and David Buttrick, expanded upon the tenets of the New Homiletic.[53] The genesis of most of these expansive applications can usually be traced in some way to Craddock's primary emphases.[54] Lowry saw the goal of preaching as evoking an *experience* in the listener through narrative strategies.[55] What Lowry attempted to do in applying the revolutionized scope of the sermon was to highlight a sense of 'suspended ambiguity' in preaching. This had similar intentions to Craddock's open-endedness, whereby the unresolved tension in the sermon upsets the 'equilibrium' and expectations of the hearer.[56] Intriguingly, Lowry is also a jazz musician and often speaks of the connections between the ambiguous spontaneity of jazz and the act of preaching.[57] His unique emphasis lies in seeing sermons 'as processes for addressing ambiguity in hearers'.[58] Again, the connections with Craddock's engagement with the situation of the listener are evident, though Lowry's focus on ambiguity is more particularized. Both Lowry and Craddock saw narrative as the appropriate form in which the listener's ambiguity could be reached through the sermon.[59]

Another significant 'second-generation' New Homiletician was Buttrick, whose listener-oriented approach was not explicitly narratival (like Craddock's or Lowry's) but geared towards 'a recovery of rhetoric for preaching'.[60] Much of today's technique-driven approach to homiletics is partly beholden to Buttrick, who stressed the importance of the particular words with which the sermon is communicated: 'Buttrick explores whether preachers should use personal

53. See O. Wesley Allen Jr. (ed.), *The Renewed Homiletic* (Minneapolis: Fortress Press, 2010).

54. It would be fair to say that Craddock's actual preaching practice was far more balanced than the expansive homiletical legacy he helped to shape. When Craddock critiqued expository preachers, for example, he did so as one committed to biblical authority as the primary source of the sermon and without being overly bound up by specific homiletical techniques above the Gospel message itself. In this sense he was more the New Homiletical visionary, but one who birthed a legacy of more theoretical homileticians who brought to birth the implications of his (overstated) critiques of authority.

55. Eugene L. Lowry, *The Sermon: Dancing the Edge of Mystery* (Nashville: Abingdon Press, 1997), p. 37.

56. Eugene L. Lowry, *The Homiletical Plot: The Sermon as Narrative Art Form* (Atlanta: John Knox Press, 1980), pp. 28–46.

57. See Meyers, 'Jazz Me Gene', pp. 131–44.

58. Long, 'The Changing Practice of Preaching', p. 116.

59. See also Richard A. Jensen, *Telling the Story: Variety and Imagination in Preaching* (Minneapolis: Augsburg Press, 1980); William J. Bausch, *Storytelling the Word: Homilies and How to Write Them* (Mystic: Twenty-Third Publications, 1984).

60. David M. Greenshaw, 'The Formation of Consciousness', in Thomas G. Long and Edward Farley (eds.), *Preaching as a Theological Task: Word, Gospel, Scripture: In Honor of David Buttrick* (Louisville: Westminster John Knox Press, 1996), pp. 1–17 [11].

examples, the length of introductions and conclusions, the proper use of alliteration, humour, and doublets, and many other stylistic considerations.'[61] Although Buttrick's approach has been praised for its comprehensive detail in dissecting the act of sermon construction and challenging rhetorical complacency, it has also been criticized for its 'highly technical, even technological rules that are presented as always applicable,'[62] and as 'a quasi-technological monologue in which rhetoric does most of the talking.'[63] It does seem as though Buttrick's attentiveness to rhetorical devices leaves a dearth of genuine theological engagement. Indeed, his magnum opus *Homiletic* (1987) contains only a short ten-page chapter on theology, 'A Brief Theology of Preaching.'[64] It should be noted, of course, that a downplaying of the *theological* nature of preaching is a recurring trait within the New Homiletic in general, since the movement as a whole has held the 'form' of preaching as highest priority.[65]

As with Craddock, Buttrick aimed at reaching the listener's situation through the sermon. His particular method was a heightened attempt to engage the listener's linguistic consciousness. Building upon the language theories of 'consciousness' and 'phenomenology' in Heidegger, Foucault and Ricoeur,[66] Buttrick attempted to show the preaching event as creating a 'communal consciousness' within the congregation through a shared language: 'We do not invent a language out of our secret lives, we inherit a language, in use. When we enter the world we dive into a linguistic pool.'[67] Buttrick was highly critical of those heraldic approaches to preaching which disregarded the significance of this 'linguistic pool' as though existing language were only of marginal concern to the preacher's message. Although Buttrick was equally critical of an *overly* listener-oriented stance in

61. Ibid., p. 11.

62. Ibid., p. 12.

63. Thomas G. Long, 'And How Shall They Hear', in Thomas G. Long and Gail R. O'Day (eds.), *Listening to the Word: Essays in Honor of Fred B. Craddock* (Louisville: Westminster John Knox Press, 1991), p. 183.

64. David Buttrick, *Homiletic: Moves and Structures* (Philadelphia: Fortress Press, 1987), pp. 449–59.

65. Craddock's *Preaching* also has only a short section on theology (pp. 51–65). This trait could lead from the fact that homiletics is often too sharply distinguished from systematic theology as a reflection upon *praxis* rather than an engagement of genuine theological concerns for preaching. Certainly, as Ottoni-Wilhelm states, 'further attention needs to be given to God's role in preaching'. Ottoni-Wilhelm, 'New Hermeneutic, New Homiletic', p. 30. See also Kay's critique, that Craddock 'defines preaching only from "below" as a human task, and not also from "above" as something God is doing'. James F. Kay, *Preaching and Theology* (St. Louis: Chalice Press, 2007), p. 91. Jacobsen also notes that systematic theology has been 'a neglected partner' in homiletical thought. David Schnasa Jacobsen, 'Homiletical Exegesis and Theologies of Revelation: Biblical Preaching from Text to Sermon in an Age of Methodological Pluralism', in *Homiletic* 36:1 (2011), pp. 14–25 [16].

66. See Greenshaw, 'Formation of Consciousness', p. 4.

67. Buttrick, *Homiletic*, p. 179.

which 'therapeutic' or 'narcissistic' preaching dominates,[68] his primary focus is nonetheless the task of relating 'revelation…to human understandings'.[69] One thinker often evoked by Buttrick as entirely antithetical to this correlational approach is Karl Barth.

d. *The New Homiletic and Barth.*

A shared repudiation of Barth's homiletical approach is a significant foundation of the New Homiletic's critique of heraldic preaching. Barth is often evoked as the straw-man who exemplified the kind of heraldic homiletic the New Homileticians were overthrowing. In Buttrick's case, this was particularly acute: 'Buttrick's project has involved an effort to overcome the near stranglehold Karl Barth has had on preaching'.[70] This supposed 'stranglehold' was the perceived impact of Barth's homiletical theology which had – in their eyes – made too radical a break between the human and the divine elements of preaching:

> Barth sought to avoid attention to rhetoric, reference to the self in the sermon, or to specific current events, for these were distractions from the task of proclaiming God's Word. Scholars in homiletics are in general agreement concerning Barth's error. The preacher cannot assume to have a biblically literate or even interested congregation. The effect of Barth's understanding on a generation of preachers… was disastrous.[71]

On the surface, such an impact upon the average pulpit would indeed appear to indicate Barth's abdication of any concern for human language in preaching. But this interpretation of Barth is certainly an exaggeration based primarily on a reading of his *Homiletics*, which should be read alongside his other works rather than in isolation.[72] Nonetheless, Barth continues to be the 'point of contact' with whom the

---

68. David Buttrick, *A Captive Voice: The Liberation of Preaching* (Louisville: Westminster John Knox Press, 1994), p. 14.

69. Buttrick, *Homiletic*, p. 115.

70. Greenshaw, 'Formation of Consciousness', p. 10.

71. Paul Scott Wilson, 'Biblical Studies and Preaching: A Growing Divide?', in *Preaching as a Theological Task*, pp. 137–49 [143].

72. Barth's apparently stringent homiletical emphases were not strictly followed in his own preaching, which demonstrates a more nuanced approach than often comes across in *Homiletics*. See William H. Willimon, *Conversations with Barth on Preaching* (Nashville: Abingdon, 2006), p. 184. It should also be noted that Barth's *Homiletics* was not 'written' by Barth as such, but compiled from students' notes at his homiletics seminars in Bonn in 1932–33. Although certainly attributable to Barth and bearing many consistencies with his overall theological trajectory, these emphases were intended as a particular approach to preaching in response to a particular time period rather than a once-for-all treatise on the practice of preaching. See Angela Dienhart Hancock, *Karl Barth's Emergency Homiletic, 1932–1933: A Summons to Prophetic Witness at the Dawn of the Third Reich* (Grand Rapids: Eerdmans, 2013). This is not to say it is *entirely* different to what Barth says

New Homileticians have chosen to wage war regarding heraldic preaching. Their trenchant critiques have focused not only upon Barth's emphasis on preaching as an objective act, but also an assumed biblicism: 'Preaching became for Barth the reiteration of the biblical text…in which public events are excised from sermons.'[73] However, although Barth discouraged the overuse of current events (using some of his own Safenwil sermons as bad examples),[74] his later preaching referenced such events in almost every sermon.[75] His call for sermons to be solely 'expositions of Scripture'[76] was not, in fact, to ignore the context into which the preacher is to speak, but to provide a grounding for all of the preacher's words in God's Word. This way, the subjective avenues of the sermon might all find their source in the biblical text and not in the subjectivity of the preacher or hearers.

> I have the impression that my sermons reach and 'interest' my audience when I least rely on anything to 'correspond' to the Word of God already 'being there,' when I least rely on the 'possibility' of proclaiming this Word, when I least rely on my ability to 'reach' people by my rhetoric, when on the contrary I allow my language to be formed and shaped and adapted as much as possible by what the text seems to be saying.[77]

The diminishing of 'correspondence' and 'rhetoric' here would certainly not have helped Barth's reputation among the New Homileticians, even if there are plenty of elements here with which they may have been in agreement (such as the text's linguistic content shaping the sermon's content). It is also clear that Barth did, in practice, exhibit a profound concern for his hearers:

> One should…make every effort to ensure that one's sermon is not simply a monologue, magnificent perhaps, but not necessarily helpful to the congregation. Those to whom he is going to speak must constantly be present in the mind of the preacher while he is preparing his sermon. What he knows about them will suggest unexpected ideas and associations which will be with him as he studies his text and will provide the element of actuality, the application of his text to the contemporary situation.[78]

about preaching elsewhere, but merely that the forcefulness of Barth's anti-anthropological concerns here does not mean he neglected the importance of, for example, 'hearer' or 'context' in his understanding of preaching. These homiletical seminars were, in fact, an example of Barth's responsiveness *to* his social and political context.

73. Wilson, 'Biblical Studies and Preaching', p. 143.

74. Barth, *Homiletics*, p. 118.

75. See Karl Barth, *Call for God: New Sermons from Basel Prison*, trans. A. T. Mackay (London: SCM Press, 1967).

76. Barth, *Homiletics*, p. 76.

77. Karl Barth and Emil Brunner, *Natural Theology*, trans. Peter Fraenckel (London: Centenary Press, 1946), p. 127.

78. Karl Barth, *The Preaching of the Gospel*, trans. B. E. Hooke (Philadelphia: Westminster Press, 1963), p. 74.

This appears, even, to suggest a type of 'dialogical' sermonic dimension whereby the 'herald' perceives the situation of the listener as being influential upon their conveying of the heraldic message. Although this by no means demonstrates an alliance between Barth and the New Homiletic, it does show a nuance within the heraldic conception of preaching which was ignored by those who wished to discard it. One imagines, however, that Barth would not have been in support of Craddock's 'inductive' narratives, of Lowry's jazz-like experiments in ambiguity or of Buttrick's rhetorical techniques. In this sense, perhaps the gaping divide between Barth and the New Homiletic is indeed appropriate, even though it is often presented through a skewed lens. Barth remains a key figure in the genealogy of the New Homiletic critique, as a strong theological voice in support of heraldic preaching *from which* the New Homiletic formed its own counter-emphases. Such emphases have continued to influence contemporary homiletical concerns too.

e. *Enduring Emphases of the New Homiletic.*

As noted, despite the variations between different thinkers within the New Homiletic, there are clearly identifiable traits that echo throughout the movement more generally. From what has been seen thus far, it may be possible to identify five of the primary New Homiletic foci as follows:
1. Rejection of traditional conceptions and uses of 'authority'
2. Criticism of the 'herald' image for preaching
3. Accentuation of the homiletical role of the listener
4. Gravitation to dialogical and rhetorical narrative over didactic monologue
5. Emphasis upon the literary genre and performative function of the text.

These concepts are broadly interlinked, since it is evident within the New Homiletic that [1] the concern for authoritarian abuse leads to [2] the rejection of the authoritative heraldic preacher (often connoting 'authoritarianism'). Following this, the rejection of the herald is also a foundation for [3] the primary concern upon the listener, because the focus has shifted from the herald's declaration to the listener interpretation. This concern for the listener is then applied through the use of [4] differing forms of narrative and rhetorical expression in order to 'reach' the listener.[79] These communicative concerns also find a basis in [5] an emphasis upon the existing biblical literary forms, so that the sermon 'performs' the text in its correct genre, embracing the varied listeners by deviating from any singular oratorical mode. Although these primary foci are only general tenets, they summate the most important and influential elements within the New Homiletic. Much of contemporary homiletics is still hugely indebted to these primary emphases. It could even be said that, in many cases, contemporary homiletical debate has a tendency to traverse well-trodden ground whereby a number of these primary emphases are repeated or rephrased while bearing the same essential content.

79. Here, in particular, see Lucy Lind Hogan and Robert Reid, *Connecting with the Congregation: Rhetoric and the Art of Preaching* (Nashville: Abingdon Press, 1999).

The engagement of the role of the listener, for example, is a key feature in Ronald J. Allen's homiletics, which often involves collaborative projects.[80] This 'conversational' approach to homiletics is not a two-way literal conversation mid-sermon but rather a responsibility for the preacher to reflect the thought-patterns of the congregation.[81] Much of this work applies to the varied roles of the listener in different contexts; however, as a foundational homiletical principle it is no different from the earlier affirmations of the role of the listener in Craddock and others. The 'turn to the listener', of course, also correlates in general with the 'turn to the subject' in mid-late twentieth century academia, especially with regard to postmodern epistemological emphases. Other more contemporary homiletical restatements of the turn to the listener can be found in Roger E.Van Harn, who argues for the preacher as 'pioneer listener' to the congregation;[82] in Glenn L. Monson, who sees 'the listener as co-creator of meaning with the preacher during the sermon event';[83] and in Leo Hartshorn, who argues for preaching as a 'multi-voiced collaboration'.[84] Indeed, Hartsorn's notion of dialogical, congregation-led preaching is argued with the precise same reference points as those which had been declared three or four decades earlier:

> Preaching is not simply a one-way monologue from preacher to listener as a herald might announce the news of the kingdom. Monological, one-way preaching, in which the preacher communicates the truth to passive listeners, has been prevalent in the church for centuries. It has been constructed and reinforced in the traditional design of church buildings with the raised pulpit in the front and the pews lined in rows like a theatrical performance with passive audience...Preaching that is located solely with the preacher is missing the congregation as partners in the preaching ministry.[85]

80. See Ronald J. Allen and Joseph R. Jeter, Jr., *One Gospel, Many Ears: Preaching for Different Listeners in the Congregation* (St. Louis: Chalice Press, 2002); Ronald J. Allen and John S. McClure, et al., *Listening to the Listeners: Homiletical Case Studies* (St. Louis: Chalice Press, 2004); Ronald J. Allen, 'Preaching to Listeners: What Listeners Most Value in Sermons', in *Homiletic* 17:5 (2005), pp. 4–17; Ronald J. Allen, et al., *Believing in Preaching: What Listeners Hear in Sermons* (St. Louis: Chalice Press, 2005).

81. Ronald J. Allen, 'Preaching as Mutual Critical Correlation through Conversation', in Jana Childers (ed.), *Purposes of Preaching* (St. Louis: Chalice Press, 2004), pp. 1–23 [2].

82. Roger E. Van Harn, *Preacher, Can You Hear Us Listening?* (Grand Rapids: Eerdmans, 2005), pp. 14–27.

83. Glenn L. Monson, 'A Funny Thing Happened on the Way Through the Sermon', in *Dialog: A Journal of Theology* 43:4 (2004), pp. 304–11 [304].

84. Leo Hartshorn, 'Evaluating Preaching as a Communal and Dialogical Practice', in *Homiletic* 35:2 (2010), pp. 13–24 [22]. See also John S. McClure, *The Roundtable Pulpit: Where Leadership and Preaching Meet* (Nashville: Abingdon Press, 1995), and Doug Pagitt, *Preaching Re-Imagined: The Role of the Sermon in Communities of Faith* (Grand Rapids: Zondervan, 2005).

85. Hartshorn, 'Preaching as Communal and Dialogical Practice', p. 18.

It seems as if such a passage could have been written in precisely the same way at the very dawn of the New Homiletic era in light of the prevalent heraldic image of the preacher. Such overt repetition of these themes emphasizes that many of these concerns remain unapplied. Perhaps it also shows that the New Homiletic – though academically influential – did not actually shape the average church sermon as much as it had shaped the discipline of homiletics itself. After much experimentation with innovative communicative methods, many preachers have found themselves returning to the older form of the monologue in which congregation is spoken *to* by the preacher, even if this is done in a variety of ways. If some forty years of extensive homiletical insight and provocation had not extinguished the shape of the monological heraldic sermon in the average pulpit, it seems it may continue as the normative sermonic form, even with homiletics continuing to regale against it.[86]

Similarly, homiletical engagements with postmodern deconstructive philosophy and reformulations of language are largely beholden to earlier New Homiletic emphases,[87] as are those advocating the aesthetic or narratival approaches to

86. It is important to note that the 'herald' image did not simply disappear throughout the New Homiletic and contemporary era. See John Stott, *I Believe in Preaching* (London: Hodder & Stoughton, 1982); William H. Willimon, *Proclamation and Theology* (Nashville: Abingdon Press, 2005), p. 20; Willimon, *Conversations with Barth on Preaching*, pp. 167–95; Greg Haslam (ed.), *Preach the Word: The Call and Challenge of Preaching Today* (Lancaster: Sovereign World, 2006); and D. A. Carson, J. I. Packer, et al. (eds.), *When God's Voice is Heard: The Power of Preaching* (Nottingham: IVP, 2003). These predominantly Evangelical heraldic emphases continue to influence contemporary preaching – especially in contexts of evangelistic church growth – but are rarely engaged within contemporary academic homiletics, which tends to remain tied to New Homiletic presuppositions and often dismisses such perspectives as being overly concerned with 'certainty'. See Meyers, 'Jazz Me Gene', pp. 135–6. Notably, Lloyd-Jones' hugely influential *Preaching and Preachers* (1971) was published the same year as Craddock's *As One without Authority*, emphasizing much of what Craddock was simultaneously rejecting. Oddly, neither Craddock nor Lloyd-Jones interacted with one other's perspectives.

87. Allen notes the need for preaching to reflect 'the heart of the postmodern mind-set' which is characterized by an 'awareness of the relativity of all human thought and action'. Ronald J. Allen, et al., *Theology for Preaching: Authority, Truth, and Knowledge of God in a Postmodern Ethos* (Nashville: Abingdon, 1997), p. 9. This homiletic remains focused upon the situation of the listener's ambiguities, reminiscent of Craddock and Lowry. For other attempts at incorporating 'postmodern' concerns, see John S. McClure, *Other-wise Preaching: A Postmodern Ethic for Homiletics* (St. Louis: Chalice Press, 2001); and Jeffrey F. Bullock, *Preaching with a Cupped Ear: Hans-Georg Gadamer's Philosophical Hermeneutics as Postmodern Wor[l]d* (New York: Peter Lang, 1999). Some approaches, equally, seek to preach *into* postmodern concerns rather than appropriate them; see Graham Johnston, *Preaching to a Postmodern World: A Guide to Reaching Twenty-First Century Listeners* (Grand Rapids: Baker Books, 2001).

preaching.[88] Many of these argue for the necessity of the performative element of preaching, as opposed to a solitary focus on the material content of the message. Susan Karen Hedahl, for example, stresses 'the role of *imagination* in preaching', in which sermonic meanings can be constructed through creative rhetoric and a connection with the interests and stories of the congregation: 'What of our ethics, our poetry, our prose? Our dreams and delights, our creative justice, as meaning-full ways of proclaiming the good news?'[89] This, again, echoes much of what has been said previously regarding narrative, rhetoric and listener-consciousness.

It is not that all of these contemporary approaches are *merely* repeating the New Homiletic (though some certainly are) but that many remain bound by its fundamental principles. The strong accentuation of appropriate sermonic form, for example, is one the most vital of these inherited principles. As Walter Brueggemann has noted, preachers are to interpret 'not what the text "meant" but what it "means."'[90] Edward F. Farley also warns against neglecting Scripture's 'forms' in preaching, critiquing the much-used 'bridge' paradigm (the sermonic move *from* ancient text *to* present day) which was deemed to be prevalent in the presuppositions of heraldic preaching.[91] As Craddock had done, Farley also attacked the expository sermon for its 'enslavement' to the didactic content of the text, proposing instead to end 'the tyranny of the passage over the sermon' in favour of 'a multivalent use of scripture.'[92] This was an attempt to open the sermon up to the literary and generic diversity within the Bible. Thomas G. Long, similarly, focuses upon the literary forms within Scripture as a model for sermonic forms.[93] Again, these emphases on the technical elision of form and content had long been foundational tenets of New Homiletic thought. Long's thought elsewhere, however, shows a way in which these tenets might be converged *with* heraldic preaching.

88. See Alec Gilmore, *Preaching as Theatre* (London: SCM Press, 1992); Thomas H. Troeger, *Imagining a Sermon* (Nashville: Abingdon Press, 1990); Richard A. Jensen, *Envisioning the Word: The Use of Visual Images in Preaching* (Minneapolis: Fortress Press, 2005); Ruthanna B. Hooke, 'The Personal and Its others in the Performance of Preaching', in Dwayne J. Howell (ed.), *Preaching and the Personal* (Cambridge: The Lutterworth Press, 2014), pp. 19–43.

89. Susan Karen Hedahl, 'All the King's Men: Constructing Homiletical Meaning', in *Preaching as a Theological Task*, pp. 82–90 [86–7].

90. Walter Brueggemann, *The Word Militant: Preaching a Decentring Word* (Minneapolis: Fortress Press, 2007), p. 83.

91. Edward F. Farley, 'Preaching the Bible and Preaching the Gospel', in *Theology Today* 51:1 (1994), pp. 90–103.

92. Edward F. Farley, 'Toward a New Paradigm for Preaching', in *Preaching as a Theological Task*, pp. 165–75 [175]. See *also* Ronald J. Allen, 'Why Preach from Passages in the Bible?', in Ibid., pp. 176–88.

93. Thomas G. Long, *Preaching and the Literary Forms of the Bible* (Philadelphia: Fortress Press, 1989).

f. *Long's Synthesis of Herald and New Homiletic.*

In one sense, Thomas Long's work acts as a bridge between the New Homiletic and the contemporary era.[94] He focuses upon the identity of what preaching *is* in his important book *The Witness of Preaching* (1989), noting three equally valid images of the preacher as 'herald', 'pastor' and 'storyteller'.[95] Unlike many of the New Homileticians, Long does not dispense with the 'herald' image entirely but interprets it as an insufficient category in isolation. He does, however, represent its enduringly contributory aspects: 'Herald preachers…do not strive to create more beautiful and more excellent sermons; they seek to be more faithful to the message they receive in scripture.'[96] This echoes the precise concerns of Forsyth, Stewart and Barth, who had never denied the value of rhetoric entirely but had merely stressed a correctly weighted emphasis upon the message being the *primary* focus (an emphasis subsequently downplayed, post-Craddock). Long notes the refreshingly *theological* orientation of the heraldic image, an emphasis lost among the anthropological emphases of its detractors: 'The main value of the herald image… lies in its insistence upon the transcendent dimension of preaching.'[97] He is simultaneously aware, of course, of the possible neglect of the listener as a result of this approach: 'The herald image fails to take adequate account of the context of preaching. Preaching does not occur in thin air but always happens on a specific occasion and with particular people in a given cultural setting.'[98]

Of all the contemporary homileticians, Long seems the most balanced in his assessment of the varying approaches to preaching. This is because he does not use one image as a reactionary point from which to launch his own image but rather, seeks to utilize them together. His own preferred image of the preacher is 'witness', which is a 'creative blend' of each role.[99] So, in speaking of the importance of the herald, he also juxtaposes it with the 'pastor' image: 'For the herald, the most important dimension of preaching is the message. For the pastor, the crucial dimension is an event, something that happens inside the hearer.'[100] He does the same for the 'storyteller' image: 'The herald seeks to discover the content of the gospel; the storyteller refuses to divorce that content from the rhetorical form

94. Also noteworthy is the influence of Ricoeur's 'kerygmatic' thought upon Long and – subsequently – much contemporary homiletics. See Jacob D. Myers, 'Preaching Philosophy: The Kerygmatic Thrust of Paul Ricoeur's Philosophy and Its Contributions to Homiletics', in *Literature and Theology* 27:2 (2013), pp. 208–26.

95. Thomas G. Long, *The Witness of Preaching* (Westminster: John Knox Press, 1989), pp. 22–41.

96. Ibid., p. 25.

97. Ibid., p. 28.

98. Ibid., p. 29. This concern will be picked up in IV.5 when we relate the heraldic image to the pneumatological 'moment' of preaching, whereby such preaching may retain both its 'transcendent' and 'contextual' dimensions.

99. Ibid., pp. 41–7.

100. Ibid., p. 31.

in which it is found.'[101] Again we see in both the 'storyteller' and the 'pastor' the New Homiletic emphases upon sermonic form and the importance of the listener, yet these are incorporated *alongside* the herald. Although it is helpful to utilize different methods alongside one another in 'creative tension', Long's reading of the herald is ultimately inadequate. This is because it assumes an unnecessary rigidity in the concept, as though the preacher's identifiable heraldic role *necessarily* excludes aspects of form, narrative and the listener. Rather than conflating the 'herald' into a new category, images such as the 'pastor' and 'storyteller' might yet be found *within* the herald image, precisely because the herald is not merely an 'image' but a theological reality.

ii. *Nuancing the Conception of 'Herald'*

It is important that the 'herald' should be seen not as a *function* of the preacher but as a fundamental *identity*. Theologically speaking, although there are many different ways to preach, preachers never cease to be heralds. There is a particular ordering to the conception of preaching whereby the identity of the herald can be *primary* without discounting other aspects of what the herald's 'rival' conceptions emphasize.[102] In this sense, a preacher is not merely a 'part-herald/part-storyteller' because the herald is not a functionally 'equal' partner per se. Rather, the preacher's fundamental heraldic identity informs all their preacherly functions. Even if the conception of what a preacher is may be expressed in different ways, it need not cease to be 'heraldic'. Whereas the notions of the 'storyteller' and 'pastor' may be inferred and should remain important functions of preaching, these are not essential components of the preacher's identity in the preaching event itself. Certainly, the herald should be 'pastoral' too, demonstrating overt concern for the people to whom they are speaking, and they will also use narrative in order to communicate their message effectively as they represent the grand narratives of Scripture and salvation history. But crucially, these functions come *underneath* their primary role as herald. Heralds ought to communicate narratively and pay attention to listener response, but only in so far as these functions make them more faithful to the message they have been entrusted to convey. Where Long places all three images on the same level, the 'pastor' and 'storyteller' actually ought to be seen as *functions* of the preacher, flowing from a pervasive heraldic identity. This allows for a regulative emphasis upon the primary purpose for preaching (conveying the commissioned message) without swinging to other extremes in overemphasizing or de-emphasizing the role of the listener, authority, form or various other homiletical loci.

If a preacher is to be a herald in an appropriate sense, then, they should not be unconcerned with people, context, hearing, situation or style, nor enslaved to any singular rhetorical method or form as though there were only *one* way to be

101. Ibid.

102. See the 'hierarchical dialectic' (II.6.i.3), where various dialectical polarities are differently freighted.

a 'herald'. It is precisely in *being* a responsible herald that one should care about these other aspects of the preacher's task. It seems odd to assume that God would reveal a particular set of 'heraldic' messages to a defined set of exclusive 'herald-preachers', and 'narratival messages' for 'storyteller-preachers'. Rather, there are unique prophetic messages for unique heralds in unique congregations. This is the problem of simply differentiating different *types* of preacher rather than conveying the fact that *all* preaching is heraldic in nature. As has been shown in the New Homiletic, the neglect of this has led to a fixation with particular ways of *doing* preaching rather than the ontological status of what a preacher fundamentally *is*. Having a primary theological category for the preacher does not limit the scope of these different creative methods of preaching. There is, for example, great diversity between the *messages* of the Old Testament prophets and the *methods* by which they convey, present and tailor them.[103] We see Ezekiel called to construct and lay siege to a model of Jerusalem 'as a sign for the house of Israel' (Ezek. 4:1–3); Jeremiah called to wear, bury and unearth a soiled loincloth for a sermon illustration (Jer. 13:1–11); and Jonah called to speak a purely verbal declaration of future judgement (Jon. 3:4). Evidently, God is understood to work differently in *each* act of heralding, seeking response first from his herald, then from the herald's hearers.

This deepens the heraldic concept into considering the realm of sermonic form as well as content, thus addressing many New Homiletic concerns *without* sacrificing the herald as the preacher's primary identity in determining homiletical foci: '[Preaching] is not to be confused with lecturing, nor with diagnosing a situation, nor with providing homiletical advice. Preaching is being a herald because what it proclaims is the word of God which in itself is dynamic.'[104] The reason for emphasizing the herald's priority is that it situates the role of the preacher *theologically*, rather than having it defined by the human communication of a sermon. The anthropological elements of preaching, it could be argued, were overemphasized in the New Homiletic's radical reforms, important though they may have seemed as corrective measures. These anthropological elements should not be neglected but should emanate from a primary emphasis upon the herald as bearer of the prophetic message into the dialectical situation which every text and congregation creates.

iii. *Evaluation: Heraldic Preaching and Dialectics*

It has been necessary to outline the shape of 'heraldic' preaching thus far to provide a platform from which to engage dialectic and preaching most clearly. As we have seen, the New Homiletic legacy has been critical of a theology of heraldic

103. 'The prophets are committed to no single or normative set of images.' Walter Brueggemann, *The Practice of Prophetic Imagination: Preaching an Emancipating Word* (Philadelphia: Fortress Press, 2012), p. 61.

104. D. W. Cleverley Ford, *Ministry of the Word* (Grand Rapids: Eerdmans, 1979), p. 104.

preaching, focusing instead upon anthropologically oriented homiletical aspects such as rhetoric, form and listener collaboration. These emphases often respond *with* the biblical dialectics and uncertainties within the sermon rather than seeking to proclaim any sense of singular authoritative truth. Where heraldic preaching invokes the paradoxical challenge of upholding unambiguous proclamation in the *midst* of theological dialectics, many New Homiletic emphases are interested in what might be done *with* the ambiguities in text or listener.

Another key problem with such emphases has been the absence of homiletical focus upon the biblical text as determinative of the *content* of preaching. Where biblical literary genre is seen as wholly determinative of sermonic form, this limits the notion of a heraldic message to texts in which such a message is appropriate. Given that many biblical texts do not explicitly warrant formal 'heralding' within their genre, this seems to put textual genre in control of one's conception of preaching, thus undervaluing the overtly *theological* foundations which should determine the preaching task. Where heraldic preaching exists alongside the importance of exposition, there is a tendency to ignore the 'problem' of biblical dialectics. Similarly, where theological dialectics or existential ambiguities are taken seriously, this is usually done at the expense of an affirmative notion of heraldic preaching (as with the New Homiletic). Here we are attempting to engage Scriptural theological dialectics with heraldic preaching, positing a *theology* of preaching which is simultaneously attentive to Scripture as primary sermonic content, to Scriptural dialectics and to Spirit-empowered heraldic proclamation. Where some have attempted to account for these elements within preaching, they have not upheld them simultaneously. Thus, dialectics have been affirmed at the expense of heralding, expository preaching has been affirmed at the expense of the creative role of the Spirit in preaching or sermonic form has been affirmed at the expense of sermonic theology.

It is my contention, however, that the loss of confidence in the authority of the heraldic message is a clear example of the hindrances which dialectics can pose to preaching when both are inadequately understood. The act of preaching, because of the potentiality of so many different theological interpretations and standpoints, is commonly perceived as not unlike any general act of communicative oration. The theological heart of preaching has been so neglected that it is no longer expected to denote speaking *for* God anymore,[105] but instead may simply portray the dialectical quandaries with which the preacher is wrestling. As such, there has been a perceived minimizing of the theological uniqueness of preaching, coinciding with the preacher's lack of confidence. As Stanley Hauerwas notes: 'The deepest enemy of truthful preaching in our time is not only the loss of confidence in the words we have been given, but also the lack of trust many who preach have that God will show up in the words we use.'[106]

---

105. For a helpful attempt at reorienting the modern anthropocentric conception of preaching through a distinctly Trinitarian lens, see Mike Pasquarello III, *Christian Preaching: A Trinitarian Theology of Proclamation* (Eugene: Wipf & Stock, 2006), pp. 13–37.

106. Hauerwas, *The Cross-Shattered Church*, p. 18.

If preachers are no longer seen as heralds of a distinctly theological message in which 'God will show up', then preaching may indeed become no different to the public speech of any individual attempting to espouse truths to hearers. The recovery of theology in preaching, then, is essential, as John Stott saw: 'Technique will only make us orators; if we want to be preachers theology is what we need.'[107] Notwithstanding the importance of doctrine *for* preaching, we must focus upon a doctrine *of* preaching before attempting to examine how such preaching might be engaged dialectically.[108]

4. *A Brief Theology of Heraldic Confidence*

We have introduced what heraldic preaching *is* and established the ongoing need for complementary tension between the heraldic message and theological dialectics. We will now identify some theological foundations and implications for understanding heraldic 'confidence' in the face of such dialectics, drawing upon some of the key theological-homiletical voices in the Protestant tradition who have engaged preaching's theological bases. It will be seen that, because of preaching's nature as divine revelation and commission, preacherly confidence may be reclaimed in spite of the necessary 'impossibility' of its paradoxical task. The vital tenet of heraldic humility must not be misapplied to debilitate heraldic confidence. Rather, through faith, God's grace is believed and acted upon to proclaim his Word in spite of its dialectical obstacles. It will be seen that preaching with 'confidence' is possible not because preachers *can* speak for God but precisely because they *cannot*, meaning they must rely upon this divine grace in both the call and fulfilment of their task.

i. *Theological Foundations*

a. *Preaching as Divinely Purposed Revelation.*

Preaching, particularly in the Protestant tradition, has always carried immense significance not simply as an act of Scriptural exposition, but as a unique, revelatory activity. Calvin spoke of such unique significance, even likening preaching to the raising of Lazarus:

> Christ's divine power is all the more evident in that he did not touch [Lazarus] as such, but called him with his voice; meanwhile, in so doing, he has commended to us the secret and astounding efficacy of his Word. How indeed did Christ restore life to the dead except by his Word?[109]

---

107. Stott, *I Believe in Preaching*, p. 92.

108. See III.5.

109. John Calvin, *Commentaries*, trans. Joseph Haroutunian (Philadelphia: Westminster, 1958), p. 395.

It is difficult to imagine the back-and-forth dynamic of theological dialectics in such a conception of what preaching seeks to do. Here, preaching appears to be a unilateral occurrence. It is not entangled in conflicting theological polarities but happens directly, forcefully and with particular purpose. The preacher is designated the authority to say 'Lazarus, come forth!' as a clear and efficacious 'message' in rousing the hearer from the dead. This same power is what Calvin believes accompanies the act of proclamation.

Although preaching consists of theological oration, it is not theological oration alone. It is a *heralded* theological message which – in form and content – is both dynamic and assured. Its assurance is based upon its decreed message, which has the distinct intention of being *heard* and *received*: 'and how are they to hear without someone preaching?' (Rom. 10:14). Thus, preaching is not itself a presentation *of* theological dialectics; it is a purposeful declaration with the strong intention of clarity and powerful transformation. Even if the message has a number of facets, elements and dimensions to it, it seeks to be univocal in this purpose. This means that the message the preacher brings is to be held with confidence, which should not only be present in the preacher but also be efficacious in the hearer as they are assured of God's power *through* the sermon: '[Preachers] are commanded to lift up the minds of the faithful with the confidence of the Lord's coming.'[110] This confidence, as with the preacher's confidence in the clarity of Scripture,[111] is centred upon the inherent assuredness of the Gospel message, apprehended in faith.

It is theologically appropriate to locate preacherly confidence not only in the efficacy or assuredness of the Gospel message, but in God himself: 'Behind the concept of the act of preaching there lies a doctrine of God, a conviction about his being, his action and his purpose. The kind of God we believe in determines the kind of sermons we preach.'[112] An important conviction about preaching is that a preacher is attempting to speak for a God who desires to be revealed: 'Preaching is a theological act, our attempt to do business with a God who speaks.'[113] If God is light (1John 1:5) in the sense of a 'revelation', then he desires in the preaching of his Word to *reveal* truth (i.e. Himself). This affects the way in which we view the act of preaching, knowing from the outset that its purpose is to speak a revelation. Preaching is 'light' shining into 'darkness'; it does not seek to offer a *suggestion* to darkness; it seeks to reveal light, and thereby to *eradicate* darkness. This is one of God's primary purposes of revealing Himself through preaching.

Of course, as noted,[114] theological dialectics stem from our conception of God's veiled hiddenness. God's self-revelatory light is yet to be revealed to finite humanity in *all* its fullness. However, though divine hiddenness remains a simultaneous reality, it is important that preaching is not grounded upon this, but upon the

110. Ibid., p. 398.
111. See I.3.
112. Stott, *I Believe in Preaching*, p. 93.
113. Willimon, *Proclamation and Theology*, p. 2.
114. See II.2–3.

imperative promise that God has chosen to reveal His light through his Word (Ps. 119:130). If this theological presupposition can be grasped as a foundation for preaching, then the preacher can speak with a theologically curtailed confidence in their preaching. The very fact that God speaks is the foundational pardon for all preacherly confidence: 'We should never presume to occupy a pulpit unless we believe in this God. How dare we speak, if God has not spoken?'[115] Indeed, God's own speaking is the first movement towards another foundation for confidence: divine commission.

b. *Preaching as Divinely Commissioned Event.*

Not only does preaching rest upon God's self-revelation but also in His authorizing commission of the preacher's message. As Dietrich Bonhoeffer asserts: 'We preach because we are called and sent by Christ; it is Christ who gives us the mission of delivering his message.'[116] It is this conviction of the preacher as 'sent' that ultimately validates their authority. This is what leads Bonhoeffer to speak of preaching as – in similar terms to Barth – an utterly unique and divinely inspired event:

> This is what makes a sermon something unique in all the world, so completely different from any other kind of speech. When a preacher opens the Bible and interprets the word of God, a mystery takes place, a miracle: the grace of God, who comes down from heaven into our midst…[117]

The 'miraculous' nature of preaching, then, means it cannot be regarded as a normal human speech-act, even though it may occur through the medium of normal human words. Even within human agency, it should never be overlooked that *God* is expected to speak in preaching. Confidence (for both preacher and hearer) is located in the knowledge that the preacher is not alone in their proclamation, as Paul well knew: 'when you received the word of God, which you heard from us, you accepted it not as the word of men but as what it really is, the word of God, which is at work in you believers' (1Thess. 2:13). God is not only self-revelatory in general but self-revelatory in a particular *way* through preaching. Indeed, preaching is an especially chosen avenue for God's self-revelation.

The language of 'event', for some, is problematic. Richard Lischer noted, with a criticism of Barth, that 'Protestants must rethink the metaphor of *event* with which they have long described the nature of preaching.'[118] This critique stems from the perceived dangers of the preacher as a 'virtuoso', divorced from congregational receptivity, and leading to 'inattention to the church'.[119] However,

115. Stott, *I Believe in Preaching*, p. 96.

116. Bonhoeffer, 'Ambassadors for Christ', p. 90.

117. Ibid.

118. Richard Lischer, *A Theology of Preaching: The Dynamics of the Gospel* (Eugene: Wipf & Stock, 2001), p. 83.

119. Ibid., p. 85.

this is to misunderstand what constitutes the event. The sermon is not (as might be assumed) a theatrical event centred upon a singular performer, despite the individual preacher's 'otherworldly' commission.[120] The sermon is an event in which the Church as a body is formed and edified, even via the singular preacher's heraldic witness. If the 'event' language is open to misuse via the idolizing of individual sermons, this is simply to misunderstand the theological freight of the event. A subsequent repealing of such language would certainly not ensure that preaching is understood as divinely and congregationally transformative. Preaching (in whole and in parts) *is* eventful because it is distinct from all other communicative operations in human life; it is this ongoing event in which the expected Word calls, forms and sustains the Church.

These two very briefly sketched founding theological principles necessitate important theological implications for our understanding of the preaching task in light of dialectics.

ii. *Theological Implications*

a. *Preaching as Dialectically Decisive.*

To conceive of the sermon as revelatory miracle paves the way for the 'decisiveness' of preaching as an inherent component of preacherly confidence. Preachers, as 'sent' heralds, proclaim a distinct and decisive message. Even though preaching maintains biblical revelation as its primary sermonic content (I.1), it need not offer a comprehensive biblical theology within each sermon. For this reason, the sermon as 'event' allows for an *eventfully decisive* emphasis. This was a noticeable quality of Luther's 'distinctly existential' preaching:

> One feels that through it God is speaking directly to His people...It was this factor that ensured Luther's preaching should always be decisive. There was nothing vague or cloudy about it. It was clear-cut and definite. A sense of reality prevailed. Luther was no mystic. Christ and Antichrist, God and the devil – these were objective personalities to him, and this awareness gave a peculiar urgency to his preaching.[121]

Such preaching is possible only with the undergirded confidence that one has the derived authority to preach in such decisive terms.[122] Luther often preached using strong conceptual antitheses. Such apparently simplistic contrasts are better understood under the rubric of the aforementioned 'eventfulness' of the sermon: 'He preached as if the sermon were not a classroom but a battleground!

120. G. Campbell Morgan, *Preaching* (Edinburgh: Marshall, Morgan & Scott, Ltd., 1937), p. 29

121. A. Skevington Wood, *Captive to the Word: Martin Luther, Doctor of Sacred Scripture* (Exeter: The Paternoster Press, 1969), pp. 90–1.

122. On pneumatology and decisiveness, see IV.3–4.

Every sermon was a battle for the souls of the people, an apocalyptic event that set the doors of heaven and hell in motion.'[123] Bonhoeffer, who was influenced by Luther's conception of preaching, stressed the importance of decisiveness not only in the preacher but in the congregational response to the Word: 'Toward Jesus Christ, there can only be an absolute Yes or an absolute No.'[124] Again, it is this sense of 'antithesis' in Bonhoeffer's and Luther's preaching that encapsulates the importance of preacherly confidence. Of course, preaching can easily become inappropriately or artificially antithetical, presenting excluded middles as a 'form' in itself. Yet it is important to retain the place of such starkly extreme preaching against mere rhetorical dialectical speeches whereby the heraldic reality of preaching may be undermined.

Decisiveness is closely linked to the colloquial sense of the word 'dogmatic', suggesting a singularity of focus, harbouring demonstrative (even forceful) clarity which cannot be found in the midst of a dialectical 'conversation' per se. Such forcefulness does not mean manipulating the hearer (a charge often brought against heraldic preaching) but connotes a declarative power, akin to Calvin's aforementioned notion of preaching as 'raising the dead'. Christ's call to Lazarus is 'forceful', not indecisive or hesitant. Such singularity of intent denotes an apparent resoluteness which most dialectics appear incapable of allowing. This is why such 'dogmatic' preaching appears so alien to the realm of dialectics. Preaching cannot vanquish – nor be vanquished by – dialectics; but it must remain open to the singularity of decisive declaration over dialectical ambiguity. As noted, God's self-revelation – made most explicit in Jesus Christ (Heb. 1:1–3) – necessitates the prioritization of the *singular* message: 'Living faith knows nothing of an undogmatic Christ. An undogmatic Christ is the advertisement of a dying faith. Christ's permanent relation to the world is dependent on something that can only be dogmatically expressed.'[125] To express something 'dogmatically', then, is to speak *as if* it were the only truth available in that particular moment. Such dogmatic confidence must also be nuanced as being contingent rather than absolute, lest dialectics be ignored completely (as has often been a danger within heraldic preaching).[126] For the preacher to speak dogmatically is not to deny dialectics but to remove them from the immediate foreground of the message.

b. *Preaching as Content-led Form.*

A preacher's grasp of such 'dogmatic' confidence is not rooted in their own superior grasp of the truth, but in the revelation of God and in his commissioning

123. Fred W. Meuser, 'Luther as Preacher of the Word of God', in Donald K. McKim (ed.), *The Cambridge Companion to Martin Luther* (Cambridge: Cambridge University Press, 2003), p. 137.

124. Bonhoeffer, 'Turning Back', in *Collected Sermons*, pp. 95–100 [99].

125. P. T. Forsyth, *The Person and Place of Jesus Christ* (London: Independent Press, 1955), p. 324.

126. See III.5.ii.

of preachers as His heralds, proclaiming His word, not their own. This affects not only one's theology *of* preaching but also the way a sermon may be conveyed, *as if* it were God's message: 'whoever speaks, as one who speaks oracles of God' (1Pet. 4:11). The heraldic preacher speaks *for* God, expecting God to speak *through* their own words. Although many different sermonic forms might encapsulate this notion, the 'heraldic' nature of preaching implies there ought to be a demonstrable conviction in the way the preacher holds and proclaims their message. They need not speak with particular vocal volume nor with particular gesticulations or rhetorical flourishes, but in whichever way is contextually appropriate they are to preach *as if* their message is clear, true and – crucially – *important*.

If a sermon is seen as incomparably important (worthy of significant human attention), the preacher has a duty to convey this importance to their hearers. This should not dictate the form of the sermon in any artificial sense, of course, but it might *inform* aspects of its composition and delivery. The sermon, as heraldic proclamation, should not only be *understood* as a divinely commissioned event, but *preached* as such. Indeed, although homiletical fixation upon sermonic form is not essential (and can often be detrimental) to heraldic preaching, it is not irrelevant. Sermonic form is the appointed vehicle to its presiding theological content, and it is necessary insofar as the commissioned Word is to be stewarded with diligence. This connotes what Hauerwas has called 'the inexplicably dramatic character of the sermon'.[127] Even if the 'drama' is primarily dependent upon a God who speaks rather than a preacher who gesticulates, it is rare in the history of the Church that the form of impactful heraldic preaching has not conveyed some sense of the existential drama that ought to accompany an existentially dramatic message,[128] even if it has done so in highly variable ways.

George Whitefield (1714–1770), a key figure of the 'Great Awakening', exemplified content-led sermonic form more than most. Whitefield's preaching was renowned not only for its Scriptural content and unusual settings (open-air sermons at that time having been frowned-upon in many ecclesiastical quarters), but for its dramatic, quasi-theatrical urgency.[129] Although the many tens of thousands converted through his ministry were responding to a definitive message, it was Whitefield's sermonic delivery that was most memorable. While the message itself was of primary importance, such delivery was inseparable *from* the message. Indeed, when the idea of printing Whitefield's sermons was first considered, he is reported to have said: 'You may put them into print but you will not capture the thunder and lightning.'[130] He could say this not because he himself

127. Stanley Hauerwas, 'Introduction', in Stanley Hauerwas and William H. Willimon, *Preaching to Strangers: Evangelism in Today's World* (Louisville: WJK Press, 1992), pp. 1–16 [2].

128. See IV.4.

129. John Pollock, *George Whitefield and the Great Awakening* (Oxford: Lion Publishing, 1972), pp. 147, 196.

130. See Lloyd-Jones, *Preaching and Preachers*, p. 58.

was merely *adding* this performative element to the fixed content of the message, but because this was intrinsic *to* the message. Its importance meant it could not be adequately conveyed as mere information on a page; it required imperative and impassioned proclamation: 'Always there was an urgency in what he had to say; an urgency none the less sincere for being dramatically expressed.'[131] Although all may not preach like Whitefield, a widely applicable principle is present in his emphasis upon sermonic delivery as signifying the importance of its message.

Indeed, the wedding of content to form without allowing form to supersede content remains one of Whitefield's most illuminating contributions to homiletical practice. Whitefield's existential urgency in preaching was not a calculated technique to render the content more aesthetically engaging as a spectacle; it was related to his belief that the nature of the heraldic Word demands an appropriate form.[132] If it is worthy of attention, it should be proclaimed as such: 'Gospel-ministers in general are commanded to "cry aloud, and spare not, and to lift up their voices like trumpets [2 Chr. 15:14]." '[133] The directness and confidence of the preacher should flow from the content of their proclamation as well as the divine commission, even if, as Barth cautions, 'Preaching is not an art that some can master because they are good speakers.'[134] Preaching is theologically – not methodologically – oriented. Yet its theological content is not itself devoid of appropriate form, particularly since preachers are indeed 'sent' in order to herald the Word of God. They are sent because this heraldic Word must be 'earthed' in the midst of life. In this light, then, something as apparently 'technical' as a sermon illustration may take on theological significance. Sermons do not require illustration as though the content was colourless and otherwise devoid of life without them; rather, their illustratedness is a proper conveying of what the Word *is* and what it is meant to *do* in infiltrating the world with salt and light (cf. Matt. 5:13–16). In this sense, we might even recognize such illustrative forms as partial envoys of the coming kingdom itself.

The connection between form and content in the sermon is not exclusive or innate to a preacher like Whitefield alone, of course (though he did demonstrate it

131. James Downey, *The Eighteenth Century Pulpit: A Study of the Sermons of Butler, Berkeley, Secker, Sterne, Whitefield and Wesley* (Oxford: Clarendon Press, 1969), p. 156.

132. Whitefield sought to lead the hearer away from their aesthetic concerns into eternal concerns by virtue of a distinctly aestheticized form. This has been interpreted more cynically as 'the contradiction at the centre of his oratorical practice'. Emma Salgård Cunha, 'Whitefield and Literary Affect', in Geordan Hammond and David Ceri Jones (eds.), *George Whitefield: Life, Context, and Legacy* (Oxford: Oxford University Press, 2016), pp. 190–206 [205]. However, with reference to the categories of the previous chapter, we might instead see this practice as 'paradoxical' in that the content requires the form even as it supersedes it; the two must exist alongside one another in a related though superficially 'incompatible' sense.

133. George Whitefield, *The Works of George Whitefield*, vol. 4, ed. John Gillies (Edinburgh: Kincaid & Bell, 1771), pp. 338–40, quoted in Maddock, *Men of One Book*, p. 75.

134. Barth, *Homiletics*, p. 119.

in a particularly overt way). It is noteworthy that Calvin, who is not renowned for such 'dramatic' preaching, nonetheless preached in such a way as to portray the importance of his divinely decreed message: 'Sometimes Calvin paints dramatic scenes with his words to capture the imagination of his audience and convey urgency to them.'[135] We see again how one with as high a theology of the Word as Calvin has does not thereby assume a necessary aridity in its proclamation. Such attention to dramatic form again conveys a heraldic confidence which appears to be at odds with any sustained attentiveness to dialectical tensions. If the preacher is dramatically urgent, their message cannot merely navigate between countervailing doctrinal emphases but retains an intentional contingent singularity to its message. Such 'dogmatic' preaching, of course, is not without its accompanying theological parameters.

c. *Preaching as Impossibility.*

It has been argued that preachers are called to speak as though they themselves are *bringing* the Word of God, speaking *for* God in the midst of their hearers: 'Preaching is not only talk about God but miraculous talk by God.'[136] Because of this, preachers 'risk everything to speak because they are confident that God has spoken to them.'[137] Although preacherly confidence is a vital outworking of this, its counterpoint – preacherly humility – is equally essential to this authoritative commission. Preachers cannot assume that each time they speak from the pulpit they automatically speak with the same divine authority. Proclamation always remains an act of divine grace. This is the very thing that makes preaching miraculous: preachers speak confidently *for* God despite being utterly unable to do so. Preaching can and should *expect* this divine authority, but it cannot assume an entitlement or possession of it. The preacher submits to the God who promises that He will graciously speak through His Word, commissioning and empowering the preacher to speak it.

Barth, reflecting upon this precise problem as a full-time preacher in Safenwil, highlighted the sheer 'impossibility' of the preaching task: 'Moses and Isaiah, Jeremiah and Jonah knew of a certainty why they did *not* want to enter into the preacher's situation...There can be no such thing as a minister. Who dares, who can, preach knowing what preaching is?'[138] The close examination of this impossible task revolved around the finitude and sinfulness of humanity, which cannot possibly carry (let alone 'herald') the Word of God. Preaching cannot be entered into lightly, as though any preacher were in and of themselves capable of being such a herald apart from divine grace. Indeed, preachers must do what they know to be inherently counter-intuitive: 'The Word of God on the lips of man

135. Scott M. Manetsch, *Calvin's Company of Pastors: Pastoral Care and the Emerging Reformed Church, 1536–1609* (Oxford: Oxford University Press, 2013), p. 163.

136. Willimon, *Proclamation and Theology*, p. 56.

137. Ibid., p. 23.

138. Karl Barth, 'The Need and Promise of Christian Preaching', in *The Word of God and the Word of Man*, trans. Douglas Horton (London: Hodder & Stoughton, 1928), p. 126.

is an impossibility; it does not happen: no one will ever accomplish it or see it accomplished.'[139] Preachers are locked in the tension of this paradoxical call. They are made restless by it because they must continue to enact this impossible act.

Søren Kierkegaard, who was a significant influence upon Barth's dialectical conceptions, spoke of the innate reverence that accompanies preaching:

> It is a risk to preach, for as I go up into that holy place – whether the church is packed or as good as empty, whether I myself am aware of it or not, I have one listener more than can be seen, an invisible listener, God in heaven...This listener, he pays close attention to whether what I am saying is true, whether it is true in me...he looks to see whether my life expresses what I am saying...Truly it is a risk to preach![140]

Here, the 'risk' of preaching is grounded on the lived life of the preacher corresponding to their words. But this risk is not simply rooted in the preacher's subjective application of their sermons. It relates also to the *theological* nature of preaching: the preacher is not merely speaking human words before a human audience, but divine words before God Himself, who is his primary 'hearer' (even as the simultaneous 'speaker'). Kierkegaard is highlighting the important point that not all so-called preaching is, in fact, preaching. The preacher must remain in a state of humility and confession before God, who stands in judgement over these words. This humility is essential even with the knowledge of a preacher's divine commission to speak God's Word, lest this assumption somehow validate their own idolatrous speech or hypocrisy. This guards not only the preacher's content ('whether what I am saying is true'), but its truthful efficacy ('whether it is true in me'). What is most clear in Kierkegaard's conception here is the awareness of God's watchful eye over the preacher as they attempt to speak. Precisely because it is *not* a merely human act, precisely because God not only commissions but also surveys the act of preaching, preachers have great cause for trepidation in the pulpit. However, such a conception in isolation might nullify our reflection upon the simultaneous reality of God's gracious empowerment *within* this 'risky' trepidation.

d. *Preaching as Paradoxical Possibility.*

It is important to acknowledge, as was evident with Barth's dialectical complexity,[141] there is a divine Yes as well as a divine No to preaching: 'Our possibility of knowing God's Word is the possibility of a clear and certain knowledge, not equal but at least similar to the clarity and certainty with which God knows Himself in His Word.'[142] Such a conception of the 'possibility' of preaching is not, however,

---

139. Ibid., p. 125.
140. Søren Kierkegaard, *Practice in Christianity*, trans. Howard V. Hong and Edna H. Hong (Princeton: Princeton University Press, 1992), p. 235.
141. See II.2.ii.b.
142. Barth, *CD* I/1, p. 240.

at the expense of understanding the simultaneous 'impossibility' of preaching. This paradoxical possibility means, precisely, that we *cannot* speak for God, and nevertheless that we *must* speak for God with 'a clear and certain knowledge' of his Word. Barth's shift in emphasis from overtly highlighting preacherly impossibility to highlighting possibility demonstrates how an awareness of theological dialectics can become untenable in the midst of concrete ecclesial realities. Despite its inherent risks, preaching cannot be forever caught reflecting upon its own 'illegitimacy' before God. Whenever this happens, God's commissioning of the preacher and God's own *willingness* to speak through the preacher is undermined by a human preoccupation with dialectics. Attention to the dialectical condition and the need to emphasize humility is essential but not to the extent that it could undermine the paradoxical confidence that preaching simultaneously requires. The dialectical condition 'does not permit [preachers] to be faint-hearted, as though in their humanity they were not able to speak the Word of God, but only their own human words'.[143] The genuine (paradoxical) possibility of the Word of God in preaching remains crucial.

Even though Barth continues to operate within theological dialectics here, this is a marked change from his earlier *restlessness* between the dialectical polarities. He is here acknowledging the dialectical condition, yet alongside an emphatic affirmation of the Church's call to preach:

> It is true that to think we can do this is always a venture for which without God's own action we necessarily lack the authority, insight and courage. It is true that God alone can speak about God. Only it is not to be forgotten that all these considerations can only be qualifications and elucidations of the positive affirmation that God gives the Church the task of speaking about Him, and that in so far as the Church fulfils this task God Himself is in its midst to proclaim His revelations and testimonies.[144]

The fact of the Church's commission to preach is of greater weight within the aforementioned dialectic of possibility and impossibility.[145] So, although the dialectical condition of the impossibility of preaching remains, the greater emphasis weighs upon the confessional condition that God has indeed promised the stewardship of this task to the Church. We must presuppose the impossibility of preaching in our fallibility, but we must also pre-pre-suppose that the Church *is* – not maybe, but *definitely* – gifted with this task. For Barth, this positive confession became the new starting-point for understanding preaching:

> We must begin with the affirmation that, by the grace of revelation and its witness, God commits Himself with His eternal Word to the preaching of the

143. Barth, *CD* I/2, pp. 746–7.
144. Ibid., p. 757.
145. See the 'hierarchical dialectic' (II.6.iii).

Christian Church in such a way that this preaching is not merely a proclamation
of human ideas and convictions, but…it is God's own proclamation.[146]

Preaching begins not in a state of apophatic paralysis, but in the *reality* of
proclamation as divinely authorized, commissioned and accompanied: 'The
Church rests, not on the presupposition, but very definitely on the recollection and
the expectation that God in fact has spoken and will speak the Word to us in the
Bible.'[147] This expectation in the midst of preaching's simultaneous 'impossibility'
leads to a vital tension between confident faith and non-assumptive humility.

e. *Preaching as Dialectic of Faith and Humility.*

The preacher's orientation towards the promised commissioning of preaching is
grounded upon faith: that God truly has spoken and truly does speak through human
preaching. This is crucial to seeing preaching as paradoxical possibility. As noted
in the previous chapter, faith is linked very closely with the notion of paradox.[148]
Indeed, ontological paradox (which was defined as an 'incompatible' dialectic which
appears and remains unresolved to the finite mind)[149] is directly applicable to the
definition of faith in Heb. 11:1: 'the assurance of things hoped for, the conviction
of things not seen'. The paradox of how a preacher may speak of God even as they
cannot speak of God is conceptually inaccessible except by faith. For Barth, such
faith is displayed through the very activity of preaching, doing so as if one really
will proclaim the Word of God: 'The proof of faith consists in the proclamation of
faith. The proof of the knowability of the Word consists in confessing it. In faith and
confession the Word of God becomes a human thought and a human word.'[150] Thus,
the possibility of preaching is grounded in the concrete activity of proclamation,
holding fast to God's promise to speak. Any hesitant presupposition over 'impossibility', then – if not accompanied by this paradox – lacks this vital element of faith.

Faith, of course, could potentially imply fideism, as though such subjective
faith were all that was required in each case, potentially leading to abusive or
misplaced confidence in the preacher. Faith, though essential, does not remove the
importance of theological reflection upon the dialectical condition. Barth was keen
to hold to both, even if he ultimately stressed the faith polarity more emphatically.
Because of the reality of theological dialectics, preachers find themselves torn
between polarities of various doctrines, unsure which to preach or how to do so
with conviction. To this anxiety, Barth grounds the words of the preacher in their
authoritative divine source:

> [Preaching] does not cling to its own humanity – either in arrogance or
> diffidence – but to the task imposed upon it in its humanity. And as it does so,

146. Barth, *CD* I/2, pp. 746-7.
147. Barth, *CD* I/1, pp. 254-5.
148. We find this connection, particularly, in Kierkegaard (see II.4.i.b).
149. See II.3.i.b.
150. Barth, *CD* I/1, p. 241.

it can confess, but with a final certainty, that as it speaks about God in human words, it proclaims God's own Word. But doing this, how can it fall into arrogance or indolence? It can do so only if it is uncertain in this confession. And it will be uncertain in this confession only if it allows itself to look elsewhere than to Jesus Christ.[151]

Thus, both arrogance and reticence in preaching are countered by embracing the paradox of grace that is Church proclamation. An overtly apophatic stance in face of dialectics, then, renders preaching powerless by *remaining* paralysed by the dialectical condition rather than empowered by God's grace. Such preacherly paralysis, for Barth, reveals the preacher has not *truly* understood their condition before God. Indeed, preachers must see their powerlessness as the very ground of their paradoxical confidence. Preachers are indeed *absolutely* powerless to preach, and it is precisely because of this that God may allow them to preach in *his* power. As Lance B. Pape affirms: 'The shadow of the cross falls so heavily upon the preaching situation that the event of proclamation recapitulates its paradoxical power.'[152] In spite of the preacher's finitude, God makes the impossible possible through the paradoxical enablement of preaching. To deny this reality under the supposedly modest rubric of 'humility' could quite possibly be *more* arrogant, by imagining one could deny God the freedom of his gift of grace to the preacher.[153]

This dialectic of faith and humility,[154] then, grounds the proper theological justification for preaching. Faith must supersede the dialectical condition of preaching's 'impossibility'. Although such preaching can never be done in a whimsical 'spirit of self-assertion',[155] it can nonetheless be confident because its assurance is set upon God's own promise in his Word: '[The preacher] is not sure of himself but of the Word of God, and he is not sure of the Word of God in and of himself but in and of the Word.'[156] Faith is the mode through which the preacher may grasp the grace which is offered them to speak – paradoxically – as God's herald. Thus, there can be no confidence whatsoever in a preacher's own ability or worthiness to preach; they should, in fact, remain in fear-and-trembling in the pulpit. Yet, by faith in this gracious commission, they may also believe the promise that God *chooses* to speak through preaching, counteracting both extremities of arrogance or inactivity:

151. Barth, *CD* I/2, pp. 757–8.

152. Lance B. Pape, *The Scandal of Having Something to Say: Ricoeur and the Possibility of Postliberal Preaching* (Waco: Baylor University Press, 2012), p. 6.

153. Indeed, Barth calls such a diversion 'scepticism in the guise of piety'. *CD* I/2, p. 758.

154. This dialectic may as easily be referred to as 'paradoxical', connoting the first dialectical mode (II.6.i).

155. Barth, *CD* I/2, p. 765.

156. Barth, *CD*, I/1, p. 224.

There is no possible place for idleness, indifference or lukewarmness. No appeal can be made to human imperfection where the claim is directed to the very man whose incapacity and unworthiness for this ministry is known and admitted even when he is charged with it, without altering the fact that he really is charged with it. If there is no escape in arrogance, there is no escape in pusillanimity or indolence.[157]

We see here a rigorous outworking of the confidence-humility paradox. A true preacher of the Gospel is to be as confident (*more* confident, even) than the most arrogant, self-serving preacher, because such confidence is grounded in humility and dialectical awareness. Where the idolatrous preacher may attempt to short-circuit their way to confidence by *avoiding* the dialectical condition, such confidence is illegitimate because it does not reflect the true confidence involved in speaking for *this* God, who reveals dialectics and *nevertheless* enables heraldic proclamation. Indeed, preaching may be confident because God's calling of the Church to the task of proclamation is *real*. We may conclude that preacherly confidence must take precedence over any homiletical or theological emphasis upon dialectical uncertainty. Indeed, preachers may be confident not because they *can* speak for God, but precisely because they *cannot*, by which they may only rely on God's gracious commission and intention to do so.

Having argued for the appropriate theological grounding for heraldic preaching in the midst of dialectics, it remains to be established *how* dialectics might be brought to bear upon heraldic confidence in *particular* preaching moments. While preaching one specific passage or doctrine, could the awareness of its theological antithesis threaten to negate this act of heralding?

5. *Between Herald and Dialectician*

Given that varied dialectical tension exists within the canon, even as the comprehension of this tension may be filtered through the lens of the Gospel,[158] the preacher is bound not only by their given text(s) in a sermon, but by those other texts or truths which appear to be in conflict with their given text(s). As discussed in the previous chapter, 'dialectic' cannot be understood solely as a tension between two conflicting theological truths, but as taking many different forms in which two theological polarities exist in juxtaposition or interaction.[159] As such, the sermon is subject to various potential conflicts or divergences from within the canon itself. There are many texts which, even if not outright contradicting other texts, appear to make it difficult to speak of one truth without stating its relationship to a different truth. But there are many variations in which such a

157. Barth, *CD* I/2, p. 757.
158. See I.2.iii.
159. See II.6.

dialectical situation might occur within a particular sermon. Here we will evaluate some of the different ways of establishing and relating dialectical relationships within Scripture on the basis of the previously outlined dialectical modes.[160]

Having introduced this basic concept of different sermonic and dialectical possibilities, we will outline several possible sermonic foci in which these variable dialectical approaches might be applied to the aforementioned Paul-James dynamic. Each sermonic 'focus' expresses at least one of these forms of dialectical engagement. We will then attempt to distinguish and relate these dialectical sermonic foci in light of the dialectical modes. It will be noted where contradiction or correlation between certain foci may appear, whereby there arises a necessity that each preaching moment emphasizes something specifically rather than attempting to represent all dialectical possibilities at all times. This introduces the concept of preaching as a contingent – rather than necessarily systematic – act. This particularized understanding of preaching's function allows for variable dialectical foci to the extent that one sermon within a given context may appear to 'contradict' another. This is due not only to the nature of variable dialectics but also to the nature of preaching as emphasizing a particular doctrinal facet at a particular time.[161]

i. *Dialectical Modes and Sermonic Variety in Paul-James*

It has been argued that every Scriptural emphasis that could be preached in a sermon could – in theory – be related or opposed by another (or several other) Scriptural emphases. The ways in which such dialectical oppositions or relations function is not found in any one singular 'dialectic' but in variable modes of dialectic. Here, we will attempt to evaluate the sermonic possibilities that could be faced when one of these dialectics is encountered in preaching. Here we will focus, in particular, upon the Paul-James dialectic outlined in I.4.ii. Within this conjunction, as was noted by way of illustration, a number of different theological foci might be preached when dealing with various aspects of the relationship of grace and works when viewed as different 'polarities'. In the last chapter, four primary modes of interpreting dialectical polarities were considered: 1. Paradox (incompatible polarities); 2. Harmony (sublated polarities); 3. Hierarchy (ordered polarities); 4. Antagonism (interactive polarities). If we apply these different modes to specific sermon *foci* (i.e. what the sermon is primarily or exclusively focused upon in its theological content), we can identify many different ways in which a sermon considering this Grace–Works dialectic might be oriented.[162]

160. II.6.i.

161. This will also provide the groundwork for the concept of preaching as 'pneumatological moment' in the final chapter (IV.6).

162. It should be stressed that these foci are merely illustrative of the theological parameters one *may* confront when attempting to preach different dialectical possibilities within the same doctrinal theme or passage. Their purpose here is to move one step beyond

Each sermonic focus noted here involves an *exclusive* emphasis upon a particular element within the dialectic, notwithstanding the fact that a variety of these sermonic foci might be used by the same preacher in different sermons. With due note of their relationship to the aforementioned dialectical modes, these varying sermonic foci can be identified as follows:

[a] (i) '*Grace*' – emphasizing the necessity of grace (Singular polarity I)

[a] (ii) '*Works*' – emphasizing the necessity of works (Singular polarity II)

[b] '*Grace–Works*' – emphasizing the simultaneous necessity of Grace and Works (mode 2: Harmony)

[c] '*Grace/Works*' – emphasizing the radical incompatibility of Grace and Works (mode 1: Paradox)

[d] '*Grace > Works*' – emphasizing the hierarchical importance of Grace over Works (mode 3: Hierarchy I)

[e] '*Works > Grace*' – emphasizing the hierarchical importance of Works over Grace (mode 3: Hierarchy II)

[f] '*Grace > < Works*' – emphasizing the relational tension between Grace and Works *as* they interact (mode 4: Antagonism)

[g] '*Grace+Works*' – highlighting each of the dialectical combinations simultaneously, or a select variation of dialectical combinations (modes 1–4)

We will now evaluate and distinguish these sermonic possibilities in light of the various dialectical modes and in light of the uniquely *contingent* function of preaching, which renders such variations homiletically possible. To understand preaching as 'contingent' is not to say that preaching is necessarily *un*systematic in nature, but that it is not-necessarily-systematic.[163] Although a 'balanced' perspective (of sorts) is often helpful, such balance is never fully attainable and is itself perpetually questionable. It is important that 'balance' does not become hierarchically decisive for *all* preaching. Other dialectical constructs must be allowed for, even if at times they clash with one another. The explication of the aforementioned sermonic foci, then, show different ways in which preaching might engage with the same two illustrative biblical emphases ('Grace' and 'Works').

a. *Singular Polarity ([i] 'Grace') ([ii] 'Works').*

Sermon focus [a] presents Grace and Works as extreme polarities in isolation. Within either of these sermons there may be a passing reference to the *other* polarity, or a suggestion that such another polarity exists, but for the most part, the

the purely conceptual to see what the varied dialectical dynamic might look like within the concretized Grace–Works dialectic, which was introduced in the first chapter. It is not that a preacher ought to think in these categories in advance, but the categories do allow us to consider some of the concrete possibilities within this particular dialectical schema, which may also be applicable to other biblical dialectical constructs.

163. See the difference between 'preaching' and 'teaching' (IV.4.i.a).

intention of such a sermon would be to declare as strongly as possibly *either* that justification is by grace alone, *or* that faith in justification *without* works is utterly hopeless and impossible. In such sermons, no paradox is presented, nor is there even a sense of dialectical tension (though, of course such tension may arise in the minds of the hearers who are aware of the other polarity). There is a polemical necessity with these sermon types in which the dialectic is left un-explicated. Rather, one side of the dialectic is deliberately and contingently silenced. This is a perfectly acceptable doctrinal expression because some biblical texts themselves appear to express extreme polar positions which rest upon an assumed knowledge of their opposite. James, for example, feels no need to offer an antithesis to his own strong thesis that 'a person is justified by works and not by faith alone' (2:24). He merely declares the thesis in the strongest possible sense, allowing for the force of the contradiction. Within the wider scope of the other texts and theological positions within the canon, such an apparently 'exclusive' polarity need not be seen as an *actual* contradiction, but it may be seen as a *contingent* contradiction, whereby, in the moment of preaching itself, the dialectical opposite is entirely muted so that the other may be heard in its fullness.

Of course, such a sermonic approach can become problematic if such extreme positions are repeated without *any* dialectical awareness, or if they *never* seek to offer the voice of the opposite. Such polarized preaching can easily become dangerous and manipulative under the guise of the preacher's own preference to retain the exclusively singular polarity. Furthermore, such an approach, if used exclusively, would neglect the 'whole counsel of God' (Acts 20:27) reflected in the other texts of the canon. However, such polarized preaching can be effective in isolation when subsequently combined with other forms of dialectical preaching. In this way, the force of a singular polarity – as with James – can be momentarily decisive and effective when preached within the 'safety' of an implied knowledge of its relatedness to the whole of biblical revelation. In such a situation, the force of the doctrine remains uninhibited by the propensity to harmonize its acuteness too quickly with the other voices in the canon. However, the effectiveness and doctrinal faithfulness of such singularly focused sermons depends upon a panoptic canonical focus in other preaching moments lest the fuller scope of Scripture become obscured.

b. *Harmony ('Grace–Works').*

Sermon focus [b] may present a synthesis which shows how grace and works are inseparable. Such a sermon need not say *how* these two apparently antithetical doctrines are compatible, but it may declare that the Bible presents both and that we are not to see these as contradictory. It may speak of the extremities of James or Galatians as instances which demonstrate the fact that these polarities are *not* incompatible, and that Grace and Works are equally biblical, and equally important. Such a sermon might involve combinations of [a] by presenting both sides of the dialectic, before resolving the apparent tension in articulating a 'third' polarity in which Grace and Works are complexly interwoven without a particular stress on either one in isolation.

c. *Paradox ('Grace/Works').*

Sermon focus [c] may present a dichotomy which is presented as a paradox, whereby Grace and Works are portrayed as extremely incompatible polarities but are juxtaposed side by side. This would present both Grace and Works as isolated polarities within the same sermon. Such a sermon would preach *both* grace *and* works simultaneously (or in sequence) without connecting the two together in a synthesis. Such a sermon is, in a sense, a different kind of combination of the singular polarities [a] but not an amalgamation such as the harmony [b]. Rather, it simply presents the two concepts as though two sermons were being preached one after the other or side by side. However, this should still be understood as a singular sermon focus in spite of the two antithetical polarities. Such a conjunction of opposites could be framed as 'one' sermon by referring to the antithesis itself as a paradox, which could be interpreted as an essential facet of divine revelation. In this way, the presentation of this apparent contradiction in itself emphasizes the important point about the inexplicability of certain dialectical elements of Christian doctrine. Despite its radical difference from the aforementioned sermonic foci, [c] could also be a valid homiletical expression of how Scripture presents these two concepts, even though a preacher may seem to contradict [b] by preaching [c].[164]

d. *Hierarchy I ('Grace > Works').*

Sermon focus [d] could present a hierarchical dialectic whereby Grace and Works are seen as proceeding in a particular order. This bears resemblance to [b] in showing the inseparability of the two concepts, where [c] had maintained their incompatibility. However, showing their mere connectedness is not its *main* purpose, which is rather is to show the significance of *how* these two are related; namely, that it is necessary to see their particular dialectical order. They are to be seen not as equal partners, but hierarchically ordered. Such a sermon would communicate that Grace *must* precede Works (even while understanding that faith without works is impossible), emphasizing that Works cannot precede Grace, and thus, that Grace is the 'stronger' polarity in the dialectic, as the generator of its other. This sets the dichotomy in an entirely different light than saying the two merely 'belong together' (which has validity in its own right in a different sermon, perhaps). This sermonic focus would state that Grace ought to be a *primary* focus of the Gospel even given its necessary counterpart, Works. Again, this could be demonstrated as an entirely 'biblical' way of preaching on these two concepts, in spite of its difference to the aforementioned foci.

e. *Hierarchy II ('Works > Grace').*

Sermon focus [e] shows an opposite hierarchy which puts Works *first* in the order as a corrective to an overdependence upon a previously expressed hierarchy. Here, Works is contingently declared to be the primary point of contact for understanding

---

164. In this sense it becomes a form of what Kierkegaard called 'indirect communication' (which is closely linked to paradox) because the preacher – by not resolving the paradox – communicates something beyond their stated words.

the act of divine Grace in the Gospel.[165] This demonstrates the need both to *represent* an order, but also to not-*only*-represent this order. It does this by ensuring that such an order does not become manipulative to the expression of the other polarity. So, to declare Grace *above* Works ([d]) should not undermine the importance of Works, but provides the appropriate preliminary focus in how we conceive of the Gospel. However, although this ordering is unchanging,[166] it is still possible to say, contingently, that Works should be *emphasized* before Grace in a particular moment or season. For example, if a congregation is attempting to justify an absence of Works by citing the order of 'Grace > Works' as a hierarchy where Grace has *consumed* Works, it becomes contingently *necessary* to declare that Works are seen as more important than *mere* faith in Grace. This remains the case even as one knows and upholds that the hierarchical order of 'Grace > Works' must be maintained as fixed and irreversible. Again, this finds biblical precedent in James' polemical exhortation: 'Show me your faith apart from your works and I will show you my faith by my works' (2:19). Here, James – who is, effectively, *preaching* – appears to present an opposite ordering in which Works is the 'stronger' polarity in the pair. This is, most likely, because he is speaking to a contextual situation in which a certain polemical belief in the triumph of Grace had resulted in an inappropriate conception of the Gospel's influence upon their actions.[167]

f. *Antagonism* ('Grace > < Works').

Sermon focus [f] could present these two polarities as opposing but relating to one another antagonistically. In the same way, for example, as tricep and bicep muscles in the arm perform simultaneously opposing actions of extension and flexion in order to create movement, neither polarity performs the same action at the same

---

165. The polemical attitude of Kierkegaard might be an example of such preaching, in opposition to Luther, who stressed the opposite hierarchy of Grace > Works. See III.5.iii.

166. It would be an inappropriate doctrinal contradiction (differing from a theological paradox in which an appeal to divine mystery and revelation could be made) to *also* present the *exact* opposite of the 'Grace > Works' hierarchy by saying that Grace is *always* before Works *and* that Works is *always* before Grace as the prior polarity. Again, this highlights the importance of distinguishing between preaching and teaching, since preaching aims to focus upon a particular position or doctrinal locus, but not to explicate it in its entirety. It is in this way that a preacher may *appear* to be contradicting themselves in their corrective polemical expression of a particular doctrine without this necessarily being the case; indeed, they may be merely declaring a facet within a wider doctrinal schema. It is the role of preaching not only to *present* doctrine, but to *declare* that which is doctrinally necessary to the particular moment.

167. Although such an example seems to equate a biblical 'text' with a 'sermon', this is less problematic with James since this epistle is often understood as itself a homily (see I.2.iv.e). When we speak of dialectical 'polarities' within Scripture more generally, however, we are still saying that where a sermon seeks to *declare* the theological content of a particular biblical text as a particular sermonic polarity, the various biblical texts within the canon are already polarities themselves since they advocate, defend, oppose or declare a particular position which is then explicated by the preacher within a sermon.

time, but both actions complement one another's primary goal. With Grace and Works, such a dialectical focus would declare – like [b] the 'Grace/Works' synthesis – that *both* Grace and Works are necessary. But this sermon focus would differ from [b] by explicating *how* this is possible, theologically, by virtue of the fact that neither polarity allows the other to become overly dominant, via a constant back-and-forth tension. Here, the importance of both Grace and Works are declared in the same sermon. They are declared as distinct (unlike [b], which presents a synthesized 'third' polarity) and they are declared as dynamically interactive (unlike [d], which presents a static paradox). Such a sermon could also declare the necessity of dialectical tension itself as a theological principle, with Grace and Works used merely illustratively. In this sermonic focus, the two polarities are shown to be *inseparable* because of their complementarity; they are also wholly *distinct* because of their oppositionality, and dynamically *related* in perpetual tension. This tension need not be ontological, but may relate to a theological tension in the hearer's own dialectical grasp of these two doctrines as they meet in opposition. The key distinguishing factor of this construct is the interactive movement between the polarities, whereby no singular position is ever held without being counter-challenged by another position, providing a perpetual back-and-forth interaction.

g. *Combination ('Grace + Works').*

Sermon focus [g] could highlight each of the dialectical combinations simultaneously, or a select variation of dialectical combinations. Thus, such a sermon might preach both hierarchies of 'Grace > Works' [d] and 'Works > Grace' [e] in order to show the essential harmony [b], the essential paradox [c] or the essential antagonism [f] between them. Equally, many other combinations could lead to an entirely different approach to the Grace–Works dialectic in which each dialectical mode is utilized as a process for making a larger substantial point. Thus, Grace and Works might be shown as paradoxically incompatible [c], antagonistically incompatible [f], or harmonically compatible [b], all in order to construct a primary point that these are indeed hierarchically compatible [d/e]. Thus, these dialectical modes might be used communicatively as well as ontologically by demonstrating markers on the way towards a particular emphasis or primary sermonic focus. Highlighting the fact that these dialectical sermonic foci can be amalgamated is important not only because this is often the case in the *practice* of preaching itself, but also because it restricts us from viewing the Grace–Works dialectic too narrowly. In attempting to understand the relationship of dialectic to preaching we must not assume that one can use only *one* dialectical mode or *one* sermonic focus at any given time. This is not to say that such combinations are always helpful, but merely to say that they must be allowed for in a theological approach to the complexity of the dialectical preaching task.

ii. *Evaluation: Preaching as Contingent Dialectical Corrective*

The aforementioned sermonic modes are not intended to be exclusive and certainly allow for additional variations, but they do highlight the most prevalent dialectical combinations which may occur when a preacher might consider these two doctrinal foci simultaneously. It should be noted that, with a conception of the sermon as contingent 'event',[168] the sermon's aim is not to exhaust every explorative doctrinal possibility within a passage but to declare that which is most significant and relevant in that particular moment. This perpetually contingent element of preaching means that a sermon which might focus upon the 'paradox' of Grace and Works [c] is not necessarily contradicted by a sermon on another occasion which emphasizes the 'harmony' of Grace and Works [b]. This is because the sermon itself is never the final word, but the *fitting* word. Preaching remains faithful to Scripture not only by accurately representing its content but also by considering what *cannot* be communicated at that time.[169] The apparent contradiction between sermon foci [b] and [c] highlights the importance of the conception of preaching as a contingent act rather than one part of a 'whole'.

Although a more 'systematic' preaching practice should not be discouraged, preaching cannot be restricted to aspirations of inter-sermonic harmony lest they neglect the true purpose of sermons themselves as declaring the Word of God. So long as sermons remain 'expository',[170] they need have no binding responsibility to be reconciled *with* one other, as though a body of sermons could form a composite and consistent whole. Indeed, it is possible that some sermons may even appear to contradict one another. However, this possibility of contingent contradiction may never become fully concretized into a static ontological contradiction because of the necessary ongoing openness to *other* dialectical possibilities (which bring perpetual challenge to any sense of modal singularity). Referring this to the aforementioned Paul-James dynamics, if one sermon emphasizes that Grace and Works are paradoxically incompatible [c], such an expression could act as a communicative stepping-stone in highlighting the significance of each polarity's distinctness before proceeding to communicate the ways in which one *can* understand these two emphases working together in harmony [b] or antagonism [f]. Of course, if preaching is truly 'open' to various dialectics, this also necessitates that, in certain contexts, it may well be *in*appropriate to emphasize the incompatibility of Grace and Works if the context does not warrant this. There may even be contexts in which it might *never* be helpful (or faithful) to emphasize 'incompatibility', or even 'harmony'.[171] And in yet another context, one might preach a sermon in which the doctrinal unity within the canon could be highlighted via a wholly different dialectical formulation (harmony).

168. See III.4.i.b.

169. See 'moment' (IV.6).

170. See I.1

171. This is because particular texts (such as James 2:14–26) emphasize a particular focus upon *one* truth (works) rather than an existing harmony between *two* truths, even as this particular focus connotes the other polarity within the discussion without overtly declaring its importance.

Preaching, then, is not an activity which requires *necessary* coherence between sermons. That is not to say that sermons should *never* cohere with one another, nor even that they should only occasionally cohere. Sermonic contradiction should not be pursued deliberately, and sermonic coherence will in many cases be the most edifying and faithful way to preach. But it is important to note that the function of a sermon is not *necessarily* to offer one successive part of a theological system on the basis of previous, current or future sermons. Indeed, certain theological emphases which occur in preaching may require various dialectical foci in order to be faithful to both Scriptural theological content and to the unique preaching context. Given that dialectics are present within Scripture itself it becomes necessary to assert that preaching cannot assume its task as wholly systematic in the sense of merely *representing* the coherence of Christian doctrine. As such, preaching must respond to Scripture's content in such a way as to be equally aware of the context into which this Scriptural content is spoken.[172] Given this contextual necessity for the activity of preaching, then, it is appropriate to see preaching as what could be termed *contingent dialectical correctivity*.

The 'contingent' element in preaching means there is no fixed point at which one's context can be said to be perfectly 'prepared' for *any* given message of Scripture.[173] For each sermon the preacher must interpret and consider their context as they interpret and consider Scripture rather than assuming that *any* Scriptural emphasis is *always* heraldically appropriate for the context. This is not to limit each sermon to a narrow selection of texts or foci but merely to state that the context into which one preaches is *as important* to the task of homiletical preparation as expositing the text itself, precisely because such an emphasis demonstrates faithfulness to the intentions of the text *as* Scripture.[174] By emphasizing 'context', of course, this does not mean a preoccupation with contemporary events or anthropological concerns in the sermon itself,[175] but rather an awareness of what this context *needs* (note: not 'wants') at a particular time. This contextual awareness determines the way in which preaching can be seen as dialectically corrective. Here, Scriptural dialectical foci

172. This 'context' for the sermon is influenced by the very preaching itself. Indeed, in regular ecclesial preaching in which a congregation is fairly consistent in attendance week upon week, the previous sermon lays the ground for the subsequent sermon. This remains the case even if two sequential sermons do not necessarily 'cohere' in the sense of a demonstrable harmonious connection; the previous sermon 'lays the ground' because it shapes and contributes to the conditions and context into which the subsequent sermon will be preached. Such a context would assume, of course, a relatively 'fixed' congregation each week. Although such a situation is increasingly less reliable in a post-Christendom, digital, and globally transient age, this should not mean a departure from the theological understanding of genuine ecclesial formation under the Word, whatever form it takes.

173. See IV.6.ii.

174. See IV.2.iv.

175. Such a danger is evident in so-called confrontational hermeneutics whereby preachers are encouraged towards active 'resistance to the canon' in order to reject texts which have (or could) cause social oppression. See Valerie Bridgeman, ' "It Ain't Necessarily

are emphasized selectively in light of the particular situation. An exemplification of this dialectical awareness in preaching can be seen in Kierkegaard's corrective approach to Luther's doctrine of justification by faith alone.

iii. *Exemplification: Kierkegaard and Luther*

Kierkegaard's 'corrective' attitude towards Luther illustrates the importance of varying Scriptural emphases in different historical contexts.[176] It also involves the very Scriptural dialectic illustrated earlier: grace and works. As noted in the previous chapter, Kierkegaard's conception of dialectics is helpful in that it allows for a number of dialectical possibilities in polarity conjunctions.[177] Indeed, he did not seek to address the prevalent 'polarities' of his time with any singular dialectical formulation, but remained open to a variety of dialectical responses. Although his corrective to Luther exemplifies the notion of theological corrective in a *general* doctrinal sense (which need not be exclusive to preaching per se), the aim here is to illuminate the *concept* of how dialectical correctivity might work, which will point towards its particular function within heraldic preaching.[178]

Kierkegaard saw his own role as a dialectically corrective thinker to the overemphases within Danish Christendom, which had largely abused its inherited conception of Lutheran justification, where the call of 'by grace alone' had begun to resemble a spiritless and secularized domestication of faithful Christianity:

> Luther's emphasis is a corrective – but a corrective made into the normative, into the sum total, is *eo ipso* confusing in another generation (where that for which it was a corrective does not exist)…[T]he end result is that this corrective, which has independently established itself, produces characteristics exactly the opposite of the original.[179]

So": Resistance Preaching and Womanist Thought', in *Preaching and the Personal*, pp. 71–9 [74]. Such a naïvely ideological perspective seems to want to correct abuses of the biblical text by literally condemning – or, we might say, 'oppressing' – the text itself. The question is not about deciding which texts we personally disagree with (remembering that even Luther accepted – and preached – the Epistle of James), but rather which texts are necessary for particular moments of emphasis. A dialectical corrective should never be seen as 'resisting' the canon as such but working *particularly* within its overarching confines.

176. According to Tilley, a Kierkegaardian corrective contains three necessary tenets: 'it must aim at reforming the established order, be expertly one-sided, and it must not become normative'. J. Michael Tilley, 'Corrective', in *Kierkegaard's Concepts*, pp. 81–6 [86].

177. See II.4.i.a.

178. See also IV.3.

179. Kierkegaard, *JP* 1, 711, p. 333. See also: 'The tragedy of Christendom is clearly that we have removed the dialectical element from Luther's doctrine of faith… We completely forget that Luther urged faith in contrast to a fantastically exaggerated asceticism.' Kierkegaard, *JP* 3, 2484, p. 70.

Where Luther had overemphasized 'grace' in his own context, Kierkegaard felt he must equally overemphasize 'works' in order that grace not be taken 'in vain'.[180] Grace would be misapplied and misunderstood, he felt, if it led to an *absence* of works in the Christian life.

Importantly, Kierkegaard emphasized 'works' in his own context not because of any *dis*belief in justification by grace alone: 'The error from which Luther turned was an exaggeration with regard to works. And he was entirely right; he did not make a mistake – a person is justified solely and only by faith.'[181] Far from denying the 'Lutheran' doctrine, then, Kierkegaard felt that justification by grace alone could no longer be *heard* in that particular context. This context needed to be 'prepared' once more to hear the significance of that important truth: 'Times are different and different times have different requirements.'[182] Indeed, the context not only 'required' a knowledge *of* grace (which it already had) but also its subjective appropriation in the hearers' lives. Kierkegaard draws on James' emphasis in order to declare his new corrective:

> The Apostle James must be drawn forward a little, not for works *against* faith…
> but for faith, in order, if possible, to cause the need for *grace* to be felt deeply…
> to prevent *grace*, faith and grace as the only redemption and salvation, from
> being taken totally in vain, from becoming a camouflage even for a refined
> worldliness.[183]

Kierkegaard did not uphold works, then, in order to emphasize that justification is, in fact, *by* works, but rather to emphasize that a true reception of grace in such a context *necessitates* the outward display of works as revealing the true nature of one's reception of grace.

By highlighting James' emphasis as a 'singular polarity', Kierkegaard hoped to bring back the emphasis which Luther himself had before he had realized the significance of justification by grace alone as the *triumphant* polarity. Luther, as Kierkegaard notes, strove to justify himself by works for twenty years in a monastery, and as a result, 'suffered an exceedingly anguished conscience and needed a cure'.[184] Yet this presupposition was non-existent in Danish Christendom, thus rendering Luther's singular polarity of 'grace' not only meaningless, but dangerously wayward of the Christian Gospel. The problem with Danish Christendom's reception and declaration of 'grace' was that it had not *experienced* the 'impossibility' of

---

180. Søren Kierkegaard, *For Self-Examination* and *Judge for Yourself!*, trans. Howard V. Hong and Edna H. Hong (Princeton: Princeton University Press), p. 24.

181. Ibid., p. 193. It should be noted that where Kierkegaard uses the term 'faith' here, this is a virtual synonym for 'justification by grace alone through faith alone', which may be referred to variously as 'grace', 'faith', 'the Lutheran conclusion' or 'the Lutheran corrective'.

182. Ibid., p. 15.

183. Ibid., p. 24.

184. Kierkegaard, *JP* 3, 2550, p. 101.

justification by works, as Luther's generation had. Kierkegaard's generation could not hear grace sufficiently because they had not experienced grace as a true 'cure' to their failed condition.[185] The grace–works dialectic required a new *emphasis* in a new context.

We have seen, then, that Kierkegaard sought to correct Luther with an opposing singular polarity. Yet it is important that Kierkegaard's corrective approach is not viewed as narrow or simplistic. By communicating a new singular polarity (works), it is not that he merely wanted to show a harmonized dialectic (II.6.ii) in which the two polarities become a *new* polarity. Rather, he wanted to express a *particular* communication within the dialectic in which the context could truly hear the significance of *both*, even if this meant hearing only one at a particular time. The 'singular polarity' of works, in fact, is not *entirely* singular; it is not totally divorced from grace but exists to guarantee a true reception of grace. Elsewhere, even, Kierkegaard speaks of a kind of hierarchical dialectic (II.6.iii) in which he distinguishes the 'major premise' (grace) and the 'minor premise' (works) within Lutheran doctrine:

> Not that the minor premise should now be made the major premise, not that faith and grace should be abolished or disparaged – God forbid – no, it is precisely for the sake of the major premise...[that] it certainly becomes most proper to pay more attention to the minor premise.[186]

Here we see a hierarchical dialectic in which the two polarities are related in a particular order (major and minor), in addition to Kierkegaard's aforementioned 'singular polarity' focus. In addition, Kierkegaard also expresses this grace–works dynamic as a paradoxical dialectic (II.6.i).[187] We can see that Kierkegaard is able to correct differently in various modes of expression in different moments, without suppressing either polarity entirely.

We may also learn something helpful about dialectical correctivity by correcting Kierkegaard's own perception of his corrective. Kierkegaard not only attacks Danish Lutheranism's *interpretation* of Luther but also Luther himself: 'On the whole Luther struck too hard. He should have done everything to remove self-righteousness from such works and then otherwise have left them standing.'[188] It is not entirely clear, therefore, whether the problem for Kierkegaard is in the subsequent generation's lack of understanding of Luther's context, or in Luther's polemical expression. This seems to highlight a slight deficiency in Kierkegaard's

185. Ibid.

186. Kierkegaard, *For Self-Examination*, p. 24.

187. '...works and nevertheless grace'. Ibid., p. 17.

188. Kierkegaard, *JP* 3, 2522, p. 84. Barth launches a similar critique: 'Out of his great knowledge Luther believed that he had to say again and again the one thing that motivated him. He ignored whole complexes of biblical concepts, e.g., that of law and reward, because he knew only too well what justification by faith is.' Barth, *Homiletics*, p. 78

conception of dialectic since he assumes that Luther was 'undialectical' precisely because he offered a singular polarity:

> Ah, but Luther was not a dialectician; he did not see the enormous danger involved in making something else supreme, something which relates to and presupposes a first... He did not understand that he had provided the corrective and that he ought to turn off the tap with extreme caution lest people automatically make him into a paradigm.[189]

This criticism fails to recognize that Luther was indeed emphasizing a singular polarity in a particular context for a particular purpose. Where, elsewhere, Kierkegaard seems to affirm and demonstrate such a contextual approach, here he criticizes its irresponsibility as devoid of truly 'dialectical' thought. Not only does this appear to limit dialectic to an *overt* emphasis upon both polarities (which Kierkegaard himself did not exhibit) but it neglects the fact that it need not necessarily be the corrector's responsibility to 'turn off the tap' through self-corrective correctivity. The corrective task is often essentially polemical, not necessarily envisaging where future misinterpretations might occur.

   Notably, although Kierkegaard assumes 'Luther was no dialectician' because 'he always saw only one side of the matter',[190] Luther evidently believed that preaching *required* antithetical awareness: 'Luther's only advice [to preachers] was to employ tensions, conflict, paradox: law/gospel, sin/grace, God/Satan, free will/bound will, and to use dialogue, at which he was a master. One finds dialogue in a high proportion of his sermons.'[191] Luther's dialectical preaching held deliberate contrasts in order to emphasize the clarity of the point he was making, often juxtaposed with the dialectical opposite within a doctrine: '[Luther] never proclaimed God's great Yes, his acceptance of man in the gospel, without at the same time proclaiming his No, his rejection of all man's presumption and pretence.'[192] It is also worth noting that Luther's sermons actually demonstrate a clear understanding of works as 'tributary' to faith in Grace.[193] Luther even admonished his congregation for their lack of 'works' in response to his own preaching, once warning his Wittenberg congregation 'that he would stop preaching unless he saw more fruit of the gospel among them'.[194] Luther's sermons, then, do not relinquish the tension between grace and works as entirely as Kierkegaard thought. Polemical emphasis does not necessitate an absence of dialectical awareness.

   It is evident, however, that Luther actually presented grace and works mainly as a 'hierarchical' dialectic, rather than conveying dialectical variations within it

189. Kierkegaard, *JP* 3, 2521, p. 83.
190. Ibid., 2541, p. 92.
191. Meuser 'Luther as Preacher', p. 143.
192. Wood, *Captive to the Word*, p. 91.
193. Luther, *Sermons* VIII, p. 225.
194. Meuser, 'Luther as Preacher', p. 146.

(works being 'tributary' to grace, not vice versa). He faced similar critiques of his supposed overemphasis on grace in his own time – his response further reveals this hierarchical dialectic:

> Today, Papists, Anabaptists and other sects make outcry: 'What mean you by preaching so much about faith and Christ? Are the people thereby made better? Surely works are essential.' Arguments of this character have indeed a semblance of merit, but, when examined by the light of truth, are mere empty, worthless twaddle.[195]

The admittance of a 'semblance of merit' shows Luther's dialectical awareness of the other polarity, and its importance, as evidenced above in his desire for congregational 'fruit'. However, his concession does not alter the fact that he could render the argument's substance as entirely meaningless if it did not situate grace at the head of the dialectical order. Luther was happy to speak about the importance of works, but not in competition with declaring grace *before* works – and separated *from* works – in the first instance: 'Absolute, then, is the conclusion that Law and works are powerless to justify before God; for how can a doctrine proclaiming only sin, death and condemnation justify and save?'[196]

Kierkegaard's partial misconception assumes that Luther preaches only a singular polarity rather than a hierarchical dialectic.[197] In Luther's own time, in fact, his narrower dialectical focus is not necessarily inappropriate. Indeed, it would be incorrect to assume that a simultaneity and variety of dialectical modes *ought* to be present and overtly portrayed at *any* given time. Luther's relentless declaration of grace over works (but not *excluding* works) can also be seen as a valuable and faithful expression of the biblical dialectic of grace and works in his own context.[198] Similarly, Kierkegaard's multivocal dialectical approach (with a *heightened* awareness of works) could be seen as biblically faithful in *his* time. Despite Kierkegaard's partial misunderstanding of Luther, his dialectical reflections prove invaluable as a demonstration of the complexity of contingent dialectical correctivity. We will now see, in conclusion, how this concept relates to the aforementioned notion of heraldic 'confidence'.

195. Luther, *Sermons* III, p. 240.

196. Ibid., p. 245.

197. Indeed, 'Luther's postils not only regularly censure pre-Gospel Pelagian self-righteousness with the full merit of the Gospel won by Christ but also regularly censure post-Gospel antinomianism with a dialectical rigour often missed by Luther's inheritors'. David L. Coe, 'Kierkegaard's Forking for Extracts from Extracts of Luther's Sermons: Reviewing Kierkegaard's Laud and Lance of Luther', in *Kierkegaard Studies Yearbook* 1 (2011), pp. 3–18 [16].

198. For a nuanced account of Luther's contextual development and variation within his Law/Gospel dialectic, see Robert Kolb, *Martin Luther and the Enduring Word of God: The Wittenberg School and Its Scripture-Centred Proclamation* (Grand Rapids: Baker, 2016), pp. 119–25.

6. Conclusion: The Contingently Confident Herald

We have seen the value of a nuanced conception of heraldic preaching and its potentially problematic clash with dialectics. Heraldic preaching, in any and every moment, is faced with the task of responding to biblical-theological dialectics, which continually challenge the possibility of any *total* emphasis. Preaching can only declare the element or mode of the dialectic which is necessary in the particular contextual moment.[199] This notion of preaching arises out of a faithful reading of the biblical texts themselves. Indeed, Scripture speaks both 'confidently' *and* 'dialectically' into particular situations. One cannot maintain a fully systematic grasp of Scriptural emphases in preaching without contingent correctivity.[200] As argued, there are complex and varied ways in which dialectical correctives may function within a sermon. Faithful preaching must be attentive *to* Scripture's multifaceted dialectics as well as to preaching's necessary function *as* multifaceted corrective. Homiletical correctivity is 'multifaceted' because it is more complex than the supposed swinging of a pendulum from one extreme to the other. Even if 'pendulum-swinging' may indeed become contingently necessary, we have seen this is not the only way correctivity might function, which contains various complexities.[201] Preaching's task is to bring the *required* corrective to the foreground.

Alongside this necessary dialectical attentiveness, heraldic preaching must also remain an act of *true* heralding rather than a mere harmonizing or balancing of dialectical possibilities, as though the sermon were simply a dialectical discussion itself. The herald must bring a *particular* declaration, even as this message has been pre-emptively filtered through a nuanced consideration of Scriptural dialectical foci. Whether the herald proclaims a challenge, comfort, consolation or exhortation, their method is *always* 'corrective'. This does not mean such preaching must be inherently 'critical', nor even, 'reactionary'; indeed, preaching as 'corrective' here simply refers to the necessary shifts within the contextual apprehending of biblical dialectics. The herald 'corrects' merely by proclaiming that which is necessary to the particular time. This is not because the context is to dictate the doctrine or the message, but rather that a faithful homiletical declaration *assumes* a contextual appropriateness to the heraldic message. This is the case even if the dialectical emphasis is a singular polarity which *appears* 'undialectical' (as with Luther's 'grace'), though this is actually a particular expression of *dialectical* heralding.

199. See IV.6.

200. Correctivity 'should not take the form of diminishing one tendency in order to bring it down to the level of the other. Rather, the point is to heighten both tendencies, as well as the theoretical tension between them. Each must be emphasised strongly in order to prevent the other from taking a theoretical hold, and it is precisely in emphasising their mutual theoretical incompatibility that we create room for their practical correlative unity.' Daniel H. Weiss, *Paradox and the Prophets: Hermann Cohen and the Indirect Communication of Religion* (Oxford: Oxford University Press, 2012), p. 179.

201. See III.5.i.

It is evident, then, that heraldic preaching must be attentive to biblical dialectics and contextually considerate of which dialectical corrective is contingently required. It is also clear that such dialectical heralding must not be overly ruled by this dialectical attentiveness to the extent that it ceases to truly 'herald' its particular message. Preaching must not lose its voice in the navigation between dialectical polarities and thus fail to fulfil its *specific* proclamation. However, truly heraldic preaching cannot remain perpetually univocal. Such preaching must itself be open to further corrective lest it echo Kierkegaard's Danish Christendom, which had failed to correct a skewed polarity of 'grace'. Where dialectical ambiguities could catalyse the rejection of heraldic confidence altogether – as seen, partially, with the New Homiletic – we have seen that dialectics should be maintained and engaged because preaching's heraldic reality is entirely compatible with dialectical variety. The herald proclaims particular emphases to contingently various contexts, attempting to offer dialectical correctives based upon Scripture's dialectical representations.

The herald may indeed harbour a sense of contingent confidence in their proclamation not only because they are a dialectically corrective voice to a particular context but because such correctives fall under the divine commission and purpose of preaching.[202] This confidence does not preclude an appropriate use of authority in the pulpit, even as – paradoxically – the authority used to say *one* thing could be challenged by its Scriptural dialectical *other*. Preaching's paradoxical confidence in the 'impossible possibility' of their task enables them to speak *for* God – and indeed *for* Scripture – despite dialectical complications. This paradox occurs whenever *one* Scriptural voice is spoken while others remain simultaneously (and necessarily) *un*spoken. Preaching is not preoccupied with 'balancing' the dialectical polarities per se, but with speaking the biblical Word that is contingently necessary. However, this paradoxical confidence in preaching requires more than a theological awareness of both 'dialectic' and 'heralding'. It requires the power of the Spirit for both interpretative guidance and sermonic decisiveness. It is the notion of the sermon as 'pneumatologically prophetic' that gives the preacher a distinctly *theological* framework for the task of contingent dialectical correctivity. A theological account of dialectical discernment in relation to the pneumatological nature of preaching, then, will be the focus of the final chapter.

---

202. III.4.i

Chapter IV

DIALECTIC, PROPHECY, DECISIVENESS: A PNEUMATOLOGY OF DIALECTICAL HERALDIC PROCLAMATION

1. *Introduction: Correctivity and Decisiveness*

The previous chapter concluded by noting the need for contingent dialectical correctivity in heraldic proclamation. We saw how various dialectical emphases are available to the preacher when interpreting a biblical text, each of which may be deemed legitimate. However, this awareness does not eradicate the preacher's ongoing dilemma over the *choice* between dialectical sermonic foci. Why might one emphasis be proclaimed and another ignored? How do we comprehend such decisions theologically, especially where the 'right' corrective seems less obvious? This chapter will explore the preacher's unique, decisive authority in the midst of preaching's dialectically corrective task. Preaching can only be understood as both multifariously 'dialectical' *and* multifariously 'heraldic' (as this book has argued) through the simultaneously essential role of the Spirit in speaking *through* and sometimes *beyond* the dialectics.[1]

Preaching, though an exegetical activity, is fundamentally prophetic in nature. This does not necessarily mean it causes dramatic social upheaval or reacts to a pressing issue of the *Zeitgeist*; it means that the Spirit acts *uniquely* to bring specific revelation, insight and decisiveness *through* human proclamation of the Word. In this way, the problem of dialectic and preaching is encountered and, to some extent, overcome. This does not mean that Scriptural dialectics are thereby discarded, but it ensures they are retained precisely *as* dialectics rather than new polarities, and without diluting heraldic authority into sermonic ambiguity. This also means that any singular dialectical mode (such as a 'harmony') is not unnecessarily privileged over other dialectics (whereby no polarity would ever

---

1. Where the 'heraldic' conception of preaching was heavily emphasized in the previous chapter, this chapter will expand upon this motif in specific areas; thus, where preaching is described as 'pneumatologically prophetic' (IV.2), 'expository' (IV.2–3), 'dialectically decisive' (IV.3), 'sacramental' (IV.4) and 'kairotic' (IV.5), these are not to be seen as competitive with the heraldic concept but as particular features *of* it.

be heard in its fullness). An understanding of preaching as pneumatologically prophetic allows not only for different kinds of dialectical emphasis, but even for singular polarities of emphasis in particular moments. Pneumatologically prophetic preaching is the theological key by which we might understand the possibility of decisive, heraldic proclamation with a full awareness of the dialectical possibilities in Scripture.

Given that this conception needs some unpacking both conceptually and theologically, it is worth stating the sequential process this chapter will take as we move towards an overall conclusion. We will begin by defining prophecy as a category of divine speech through a human agent, which serves to inform a nuanced notion of 'prophetic preaching' (IV.2.i–iii). Having established the prophetic office of preaching, this will be counterbalanced with preaching's 'expository' dimension, whereby prophetic heraldry remains undivorced from Scripture's content and purpose (IV.2.iv). The prophetic nature of preaching will then be connected to the problem of dialectical decisiveness specifically: the preacher's engagement with the Word necessitates an engagement with Scriptural dialectics (IV.3). However, the inseparability of Word and Spirit means preaching may not be stifled by the ambiguity of dialectical indecisiveness, but decisively empowered (IV.3.i). We will see how the Spirit works in Scriptural interpretation through prophetic illumination (IV.3.ii), which provides the first marker towards preacherly decisiveness, *discerned* in faith by both preacher and congregation (IV.3.iii). It will be argued that, although the preacher's dialectical restlessness cannot be entirely extinguished, an interpretative peace in the midst of proclamation is necessary, apprehended in faith alongside the Spirit's work of assurance (IV.3.iv). The chapter's final two sections will then offer a lens through which to view such pneumatological decisiveness through two specific activities of the Spirit in preaching: 'encounter' (IV.4.i) and 'manifestation' (IV.4.ii); both of these find consummation in the context of the 'pneumatological moment' (IV.5). Each of these distinctive tenets reflects a different way in which the Spirit's work in preaching instantiates a unique way of comprehending theological dialectics. It will be argued that, if preaching is fundamentally purposed as an 'encounter' with God through the 'manifestation' of the Spirit in a unique pneumatological 'moment', this allows the preacher to address the dialectical problem in a different light, whereby the prophetic word is *the* word for the moment in time rather than one of many possible messages. The notion of preaching as a moment *in time* will then be related back to the opening concern of this thesis: preaching's inseparable relationship to canonicity (see I.1–2). Here, it will be argued that the changing 'timeliness' of momentary preaching cannot be separated from a nuanced understanding of the unchanging 'timelessness' of Scripture (IV.5.iii). It will be seen that Scripture is not proclaimed *anew* in each moment but proclaimed *afresh* in the power of the Spirit, remaining tethered to canonical content. This tetheredness to the clear-but-dialectical Word ensures that preaching may be understood as expository, heraldic, prophetic *and* dialectical.

2. *Preaching as Pneumatologically Prophetic*

Following the argument of Chapter III, preaching has a unique way of encountering Scriptural dialectics because it is divinely commissioned heraldic speech.[2] This heraldic speech will now be pneumatologically grounded by outlining the concept of 'prophetic' preaching (an implication of the heraldic office). In relating heraldic decisiveness to dialectic, it is vital that proclamation be understood as a fundamentally prophetic activity. This means we must first establish what is meant by 'prophecy' – the larger category within which 'prophetic preaching' resides. Prophecy may take various forms and may manifest itself in different ways within preaching, but should not be *equated* with it. Prophecy, rather, provides a category through which we might understand how God speaks *through* preaching.

i. *Defining Prophecy*

Prophecy is often defined as an act in which God speaks uniquely. The prophet is not always a 'preacher' as such, but can be a member of the believing community who is spiritually gifted to speak timely prophetic messages to God's people: 'Prophets are those who have unusual gifts of discernment into the purposes of God and who are unusually bold in bringing those purposes to speech.'[3] The New Testament conception of the prophetic gift roots the prophetic word *within* the community:

> A Christian who functions within the church, occasionally or regularly, as a divinely called and divinely inspired speaker who receives intelligible and authoritative revelations or messages which he is impelled to deliver publicly, in oral or written form, to Christian individuals and/or the Christian community.[4]

These 'authoritative revelations or messages' in and *to* the life of the Church are unique situations which are differentiated from the conveying of doctrine or the recounting of God's acts in history. In preaching, of course, these 'doctrinal' and 'prophetic' activities become comingled, so that prophecy may be seen as something more complex than a detached revelation about a current or future event pertinent to the ecclesia.[5] Beyond the apostolic period, of course, ongoing prophetic revelation is not 'new' in the sense of delivering previously unknown truths which may alter fundamental Christian belief – prophecy is merely illuminative upon what has already been revealed, with particular directedness and implication for the present moment. Barth maintains that 'prophetic does not

---

2. III.2–4.

3. William H. Willimon, *Proclamation and Theology* (Nashville: Abingdon, 2005), p. 22.

4. David Hill, *New Testament Prophecy* (London: Marshall, Morgan, and Scott, 1979), pp. 8–9.

5. See IV.4.i.a on 'preaching' and 'teaching'.

mean ecstatic, enthusiastic or violent' as is often imagined.[6] He defines prophecy more normatively as that which exhibits a 'new clarity' and affirmation of divine revelation:

> Prophecy rests on a special apprehension and consists in a special declaration of the Word of God that is continually spoken in His work...God does not replace, amplify nor supersede what He has said... [but] He does repeat and confirm it at a given time with a new clarity and in a way which demands new attention and obedience.[7]

Prophetic revelation should acquiesce with what has already been known and revealed by God. What distinguishes prophecy from 'doctrine' per se is its vital freshness of insight into previous revelation *for* a specific time.[8] Nonetheless, the 'freshness' of prophetic revelation means that it is not simply the reordering or reapplying of previously known theological knowledge, but it is true revelation from God which was otherwise beyond human comprehension; as Aquinas notes, 'The object of prophecy is something known by God and surpassing the faculty of man.'[9] Prophecy is a distinct act of the Spirit, who makes use of the prophet in order to convey his message: 'In prophetic revelation the prophet's mind is moved by the Holy Ghost, as an instrument that is deficient in regard to the principal agent.'[10] In defining prophecy as an ongoing activity of the Church today, then, we maintain that prophetic revelations are communicated within the bounds of who God is already understood to *be*. Furthermore, in such prophetic utterance, human faculties – incapable of prophecy in any 'natural' sense – are empowered and authorized by *this* God to speak the appropriate message. Indeed, it is the *spokeness* of prophecy which connects it so closely with preaching, whereby God is said to speak uniquely *through* the preacher's words in this same sense. However, there is often a difficulty in ascertaining what is meant today by 'prophetic preaching', which can obscure its important function within the life and witness of the Church.

ii. *Defining Prophetic Preaching*

Prophetic preaching is a corollary facet of what it means for preaching to be an act of heralding (III.2). Adding 'prophetic' to 'heraldic' brings a heightened sense of immediacy, whereby the pneumatological activity is more overtly apparent.[11]

---

6. Barth, *CD* IV/3, p. 898.

7. Ibid., p. 896.

8. See 'pneumatological moment' (IV.6).

9. Thomas Aquinas, *Summa Theologica* 2:2, trans. Fathers of the English Dominican Province (New York: Benziger Bros., 1947), q. 174, a. 1.

10. Ibid., q. 173, a. 4.

11. See 'pneumatological moment' (IV.6).

However, 'prophetic preaching' is often difficult to define because it is commonly used and understood in an overly broad sense which empties its particularity as Spirit-inspired human speech. Many homiletical and cultural understandings of 'prophetic preaching' equate the term with *any* form of public speech (religious or secular) which bears significant cultural or socio-political impact in any present moment. Indeed, the adjective 'prophetic' often categorizes a stirring message from a public orator on a timely subject touching the pulse of the *Zeitgeist*, often inspiring some form of significant change. Contextual theologies often use 'prophetic' terminology when describing significant cultural shifts which occur as a result of an outspoken voice regaling against an established norm or status quo.[12] These cultural shifts, it is often thought, provide evidence of the definite need or relevance of such a message, since it evoked such radical response in the contemporary moment. Predominantly, this conception of the prophetic usually bears the hallmarks of anti-establishment political leanings. It is not to say that such preaching is *not* prophetic (by any means), but merely that what *makes* it prophetic – if it is – is not the radical social change itself but the distinct pneumatological activity in the moment and aftermath of the proclamation. Indeed, prophetic verification is not always within the interpretative reach of the would-be prophet; it is divinely instigated.

Walter Brueggemann is one homiletician who accentuates the correlation between the task of contemporary preaching and that of the Israelite prophets' vis-à-vis the critiquing of dominant societal norms. An equivalent 'established norm' today, he argues, is 'a homogenous, white, male-dominated, straight society'.[13] It is such social power structures, Brueggemann says, which the likes of Jeremiah, Amos and Isaiah would find themselves counteracting today. This sets up the purpose of preaching as predominantly social in its orientation, rather than fundamentally theological. In such 'prophetic' witness, socio-political issues drive the agenda for what preaching *is*. This leads to the danger of reading contemporary philosophical categories of thought back into the prophetic ministries of the Old Testament and then reapplying them today, somewhat anachronistically. Thus, 'YHWH' becomes labelled as 'an awkward misfit who does not accommodate the ancient regime'.[14] Such charged predications loosely connote and reflect the general 'postmodern' rejection of authority and structure. This is not to say that such critiques cannot necessarily be called prophetic but merely that it appears potentially dubious to say they are emanating primarily from Scripture when they also happen to reflect the equally dominant radical sociological agendas of Western intellectual culture.

---

12. Figures such as Martin Luther King Jr., Oscar Romero or Nelson Mandela might be invoked as examples of such people, whose words were pertinent to the cultural moment and led to significant social transformation.

13. Walter Brueggemann, *The Practice of Prophetic Imagination: Preaching an Emancipating Word* (Philadelphia: Fortress Press, 2012), p. 145.

14. Ibid., p. 23.

Similar approaches appear in so-called dialogical conceptions of prophetic preaching in which 'prophetic' denotes that which is conversant with the contemporary culture, as in David Schnasa Jacobsen's approach:

> When we preach prophetically...we do so in ways that publicly must take account of our 'being-disestablished' in a pluralistic world. What this invites, to my mind, is a public, prophetic articulation of the gospel that not so much thunders an ethical-monotheistic 'thus says the Lord' to the monarch and his minions, but humbly and prophetically 'names God into the world' in a way that makes connections with others – whether Christian, non-Christian religious, or even 'free thinkers' – for the sake of the world God so loves.[15]

In seeking to provide a kind of middle-ground for cultural and religious pluralism, such an approach demonstrates a desire to see prophecy as inherently dialogical, and one in which the presiding cultural norms may even begin the conversation and formulate the content of pulpit proclamation. This seems widely divergent from the notion of prophecy as God speaking through the anointed and commissioned herald (even if God may well address the concerns of the cultural consciousness within prophetic speech). Jacobsen's approach here renders the prophetic activity as referring almost exclusively to the preacher's creative use of rhetoric to 'name' God into unspecified secular and religious cultures. This may well be an important accompanying tenet of prophetic preaching and one which the preacher should aspire to undertake,[16] but it does not delineate the theological parameters under which the notion of prophecy should be guided. Instead, 'prophetic' here merely means speaking *into* culture, without offering a clear enough caveat regarding the source *from which* this occurs. This is primarily why such accounts of preaching tend to overemphasize social issues as the earmark of prophetic speech.

Although Brueggemann concedes the dangers of 'liberal prophetic preaching that is often preoccupied with advocacy for specific issues',[17] his own notion of the prophetic is also rooted in the preacher's creative rhetoric to 're-imagine' the dominant cultural narrative. This narrative is inherently socio-political in its landscape, rendering prophetic preaching primarily as a voice for political and cultural activism. Again, such a conception places the preacher's heraldic activity more firmly in their own hands rather than in a divinely appointed message through the enabling power of the Spirit. Such imaginative, politically confrontational elements are indeed corollary activities of the prophetic preacher. There is also the essential role of the preacher to 'embody' their prophetic preaching, as Jacques Ellul warned, countering the problem of 'mere' preaching which lacks concrete concern for the cultural plight:

15. David Schnasa Jacobsen, '*Schola Prophetarum*: Prophetic Preaching Toward a Public, Prophetic Church', in *Homiletic* 34:1 (2009), pp. 12–21 [19].

16. See Acts 2:14–15; 17:22–28.

17. Brueggemann, *The Practice of Prophetic Imagination*, p. 60.

When we have truly taken seriously the concrete situation of the men and women of our day, when we have heard their cry of anguish and understood why they have no desire for our disembodied gospel, when we have participated in their physical and spiritual suffering, in their despair and hopelessness, when we have entered into solidarity with our fellow citizens and our universal church... then our voice will be able to proclaim the Word of God. But not before![18]

However, as important as such traits are, they do not actually address the core theological foundation of what prophetic preaching is. This is because they do not account for God's *specific* role in the midst of the sermon.

Although it is important not to discount voices which speak of radical and necessary social change, it is nonetheless necessary to differentiate such conceptions from what we mean by prophetic preaching – not because such voices are not 'prophetic' but because the criteria by which such preaching is *deemed* prophetic proves insufficient. This is because it loses the vital connection between prophecy, Scriptural exposition and pneumatological empowerment (as will be explored below). It is important, then, to distinguish the aforementioned cultural prophetic speech from what will be termed 'pneumatological prophetic preaching', referring to the Spirit's unique role in illuminating, inspiring, applying and – ultimately – *speaking* through the preacher's Scriptural words.

iii. *Pneumatology and Preaching*

Identifying preaching as 'pneumatologically prophetic' highlights it as an activity in which a unique Word from God is declared to the hearers. Within this theological schema, the problem of dialectical decisiveness must be approached differently than if preaching were a rudimentary human speech-act. Indeed, the preacher is not called primarily to be a dialectician but to be a commissioned herald who carries a specific message for a specific congregation.[19] Such divinely appointed heraldic speech does not occur abstractly but in concrete situations and contexts, necessitating a wide variety of prophetic possibilities. Fundamentally, however, the preacher must be seen not only as an 'orator' but as a prophet, as Luther proclaimed: 'God, the creator of heaven and earth, speaks with you through his preachers...These are the words not of Plato or Aristotle. It is God Himself who speaks.'[20]

Such a high preacherly calling does not diminish the human elements which preaching may necessarily require, such as diligent exegesis, sermonic structure, rhetorical delivery or illustrative applications. These, however, must be seen as subservient to the primary content of the prophetic message; that is, the *appointed*

18. Jacques Ellul, *Presence in the Modern World*, trans. Lisa Richmond (Eugene: Cascade, 2016), pp. 93–4.

19. See III.4.i–ii.a.

20. Martin Luther, *Luther's Works*, in 55 Volumes, ed. Jaroslav J. Pelikan and Helmut T. Lehmann (Philadelphia and St. Louis: Concordia Publishing House, 1955–1986), 53, p. 68.

message for the specific context or congregation. For preaching to be understood as 'heraldic' in the sense of a preacher speaking *for* God,[21] exegesis alone cannot determine the preacher's interpretative and homiletical decisions over Scriptural dialectics. Rather, they are to speak with the kind of derivative authority that allows David to say: 'The Spirit of the LORD speaks by me; his word is on my tongue' (2Sam. 23:2). Even if we must differentiate the level of authority for contemporary (trans-canonical) prophecy, this sense of theocentric heralding must remain the primary definition of prophetic preaching, regardless of whether it speaks *for* or *against* particular social norms, establishments or powers, or whether it ignores them completely. Although heraldic awareness of context is essential,[22] human interpretations of contextual 'timeliness' must not supersede the notion of prophecy as trans-contextual divine speech, intended to convey the divine message at the divinely appointed time. This means that a preacher's primary task is to speak for God *wherever* such speech may lead them. *How* this happens is unpredictable and might only be understood through the catalysing role of the Spirit in preacherly speech: 'One of the earliest and most widely attested properties of the Spirit is that he spoke through the prophets. As soon as he acts, words are spoken. There is no effective word of salvation other than with the Spirit.'[23]

It is well-noted that preaching is an activity of the Church in which the Spirit works in a unique and specific way.[24] In the New Testament, preaching is distinguished from other forms of public speech or rhetoric: 'my speech and my message', Paul declares, 'were not in plausible words of wisdom, but in demonstration of the Spirit and of power' (1Cor. 2:4). This conception of prophetic preaching also distinguishes the activity of the Spirit from other ways in which the Spirit works in the life of the Church. There is, seemingly, a 'special' work of the Spirit which accompanies the preached Word. Indeed, referring to the unique, prophetic work of the Spirit in the contemporary announcement of the Gospel, Peter speaks of 'the things that have now been announced to you through those who preached the good news by the Holy Spirit sent from heaven' (1Pet. 1:12).[25] The heraldic preacher cannot 'announce' anything in God's name unless the Spirit allows and enables them. This relates not only to the sermon's content, but also the sermon's context: 'And they went through the region of Phrygia and Galatia, having been forbidden by the Holy Spirit to speak the word in Asia' (Acts 16:6). The Spirit operates in many different ways through preaching, ranging from the location of the sermon, the actual words spoken, the manner in which they are

---

21. See III.2–3.

22. See III.5.ii–iii.

23. Yves Congar, *The Word and the Spirit*, trans. David Smith (London: Harper & Row, 1986), pp. 18–19.

24. See Ibid., p. 23.

25. Where this referred initially to the first announcements of the good news by the apostles in the first century, this may still be said to refer to the contemporary announcement of the Gospel, and to all truly Christian preaching.

spoken, and the manner in which they are heard, received and applied in the midst of the community.[26]

Pneumatology, then, is central to and inescapable from any conception of preaching. There is an expectation in the preaching event that God will speak by his Holy Spirit through the words of the preacher:

> The person who preaches the gospel makes a statement about the Holy Spirit just by entering the pulpit. Even before the first word is uttered, presuppositions and definitions from across the centuries speak volumes about the Spirit-led event to be experienced by the preacher and the community of worshippers. The preaching event itself – without reference to specific texts and themes – is a living, breathing, flesh-and-blood expression of the theology of the Holy Spirit.[27]

Although this is not always how preaching is imagined today, this unique pneumatological expectation was evident in a vast majority of conceptions of preaching throughout Church history across a broad range of interpreters. For Origen, 'preaching is a supernatural exercise',[28] while Gregory the Great declares that 'unless the Holy Ghost fill the hearts of the hearers, in vain does the voice of the teacher resound in the ears of the body'.[29] Similarly, Calvin asserts that 'outward preaching is vain and useless unless the Spirit himself acts as the teacher',[30] and even Aquinas speaks of preaching as a mode of speech in which 'the Holy Ghost makes use of the human tongue as of an instrument'.[31] There is a discernible thread in such notions that speech *for* God is deemed impossible without this divine verbal accompaniment. This does not mean that such words cease to be human words but that they become the means by which the Spirit communicates prophetically:

> Even as by a miracle God sometimes works in a more excellent way those things which nature also can work, so too the Holy Ghost effects more excellently by the grace of words that which art can effect in a less efficient manner.[32]

This means that all preaching is dependent upon the Holy Spirit for its prophetic efficacy. But this occurs not merely in a vague sense of instrumentality; there is a

---

26. See the notion of 'hearing' (IV.3.iii).

27. James Forbes, *The Holy Spirit and Preaching* (Nashville: Abingdon Press, 1989), p. 19.

28. David Dunn-Wilson, *A Mirror for the Church: Preaching in the First Five Centuries* (Grand Rapids: Eerdmans, 2005), p. 36.

29. Gregory the Great, 'Homily 30', in *Forty Gospel Homilies*, trans. David Hurst (Piscataway: Gorgias Press, 2009), pp. 236–48.

30. John Calvin, *Commentaries*, trans. Joseph Haroutunian (Philadelphia: Westminster, 1958), p. 397.

31. Aquinas, *Summa* 2:2, q. 177, a. 1.

32. Ibid.

uniqueness to the Spirit's work in preaching since it is the 'moment' in which the Word is consummated as divine *speech*.[33]

There are obviously times in which preaching may *appear* to occur 'without' the Spirit (thus, it could not be said that every time a preacher speaks words from a pulpit they are authoritatively 'heraldic' in the aforementioned sense), but this would simply mean such speaking is not truly heraldic preaching. Although we cannot always know the difference between 'truly' or 'falsely' prophetic preaching – and the many shades in between – preachers should *expect* the Spirit in faith whenever they preach. We may say, with Yves Congar, that all preaching should be 'preceded and accompanied by an invocation of the Spirit'[34] or, with C. H. Spurgeon, that all preachers should 'tarry at Jerusalem till power is given'.[35] Such pneumatological expectancy affirms the inseparable dependence of preaching upon the Spirit, recognizing that a sermon cannot be truly preached unless the Spirit is present, not simply in the general sense of *being present* in the sermon's midst, but in *actively speaking* through it. It is the Spirit's *speaking* in the sermon that makes preaching 'prophetic'.

It is important to note that this prophetic function is a necessary part of what preaching *is* rather than an optional addition with which to aid the efficacy of one's sermon.[36] If a sermon is 'heraldic', the Spirit must speak. Preaching, at its core, is an act of prophetic communication: 'It is true that human words, as the signs by which Christian preaching points to the self-disclosure and self-testimony of the Word of God, only become operative when they are inspired and used by God Himself by the Holy Spirit.'[37] Homiletical agency is paradoxically necessary as the means through which the Spirit speaks, even though it is the 'prophetic' dimension which is essential, as Augustine declares:

[The preacher] does all he can to be heard with intelligence, with pleasure, and with obedience; and he need not doubt that if he succeed in this object, and so far as he succeeds, he will succeed more by piety in prayer than by gifts of oratory... he ought, before he opens his mouth, to lift up his thirsty soul to God,

33. See IV.5.ii.d.

34. Congar, *Word and Spirit*, p. 23.

35. C. H. Spurgeon, *Lectures to My Students* (London: Passmore and Alabastar, 1875), p. 89.

36. Some accounts of prophetic preaching almost seem to categorize it as one type (or even, 'style') of preaching, among many others. See Lee Roy Martin, 'Fire in the Bones: Pentecostal Prophetic Preaching', in Lee Roy Martin (ed.), *Toward a Pentecostal Theology of Preaching* (Cleveland: CPT Press, 2015), pp. 34–63. Again, this runs the risk of stripping away the *theological* foundation for preaching as being pneumatologically prophetic in itself, whether it occurs with lively or sober language, whether it occurs in a Pentecostal *or* a Presbyterian Church. Indeed, there are ecclesial traditions where 'prophecy' may even be rejected as an ongoing possibility, and yet even this does not diminish God's use of the faithful preaching of His Word to speak prophetically into the life of the ecclesia.

37. Barth, *CD* I/2, p. 757.

to drink in what he is about to pour forth, and to be himself filled with what he is about to distribute.[38]

Preaching is not merely theological public speech; it is a unique event in which the Spirit speaks through the words of the preacher. As will be seen, this prophetic eventfulness is crucial to one's understanding of interpreting and emphasizing dialectical modes in preaching because it offers an overarching lens through which preaching is conceived. Preaching is not *merely* the product of human dialectical interpretation; it is fundamentally an act of the Spirit communicating the Word. 'Prophetic' preaching, of course, should not be seen as competitive with 'expository' preaching. Before making the connection between Scriptural dialectic and Spirit-illumined decisiveness (IV.3), we will highlight this vital relationship between 'prophetic' and 'Scriptural' sermonic content.

iv. *Prophecy and Scripture*

The content of the prophetic sermon is not divorced from but emanates from the theological content of the biblical text. The aforementioned prophetic dimension of preaching ensures it cannot be understood as 'mere' exegesis,[39] even though its exegetical content ensures that all prophetic preaching is grounded upon the biblical Word: 'Preaching is that sort of public speaking that strives never to be original. Preaching is Christian only when it is biblical, when it is obviously derivative of, submissive to, and controlled by the biblical word.'[40] Indeed, Scripture is the genesis of preaching because it is the very deposit of God's Word, as divinely inspired in an entirely unique way from other forms of divine speech.

As this unique deposit of God's Word, then, Scripture is the place *from which* God's Word is continually proclaimed. This means that 'prophetic' preaching is authoritative only insofar as it maintains a *biblical* message. Preachers rest upon this Word in the faith that preaching speaks on the shoulders of Scripture's own unique authority by its divine inspiration.[41] Prophecy and exegesis are interwoven because the Spirit may inspire both (albeit distinctly). In preaching, the Spirit works *through* the inspired text *with* the inspired proclamation, thus amplifying Scripture's own distinct voice: 'Apart from the power of the Holy Spirit, Scripture lies dumb at best, or is used in a misleading way at worst.'[42] The concept of prophetic

---

38. Augustine, *On Christian Doctrine*, trans. J. F. Shaw (New York: Christian Literature Publishing Co., 1886), p. 86.

39. For the Spirit's work *in* exegesis ('illumination'), see IV.3.ii.

40. Willimon, *Proclamation and Theology*, pp. 33–4.

41. 'The sermon is not the preacher's word; it is God's Word.' Sinclair B. Ferguson, 'Exegesis', in Samuel T. Logan Jr. (ed.), *The Preacher and Preaching: Reviving the Art* (Phillipsburg: Presbyterian and Reformed Publishing Company, 2011), pp. 192–211 [192].

42. Paul J. Achtemeier, *Inspiration and Authority: Nature and Function of Christian Scripture* (Peabody: Hendrickson Publishers, 1999), p. 147.

preaching, then, distinguishes it from *mere* exegesis (even as exegesis remains its essential foundation).

It is noteworthy that one of the most important early homiletics treatises in English, written by William Perkins, was aptly titled *The Arte of Prophesying* (1606).[43] Puritan preachers, though not ignorant of the complexity of debating preaching's place amidst other pastoral and leadership roles within the Church,[44] saw themselves almost in the guise of the Hebrew prophets, disturbing and comforting their congregations with a fresh word from God.[45] Such words were not necessarily understood as ultimately 'original' but, with Calvin, these words spoke to 'the immediate need of the people'.[46] This conception opens the sermon's scope to speak not only *from* the text of Scripture, but *into* the situation of the day. It is important, of course, to distinguish the revelatory authority of an Old Testament prophet and a contemporary preacher: 'Today's preachers are neither prophets nor apostles, for we are not the recipients of any fresh, direct revelation.'[47] However helpful this may be as a distinction between canonical and ecclesial authority, this does not account for a full understanding of preaching as revelatory 'event'.[48] The contemporary preacher will often be led into interpreting the Scriptural text in such a way that the Spirit speaks *uniquely* even as the sermon remains 'expository'.

Indeed, it is possible to affirm the unique authority of both the written Word of God *and* the unique authority of the preaching event, through which the Spirit becomes presently active: 'Though you may go into the pulpit with what you regard as an almost perfect sermon, you never know what is going to happen to it when you start preaching.'[49] It is in the very moment of preaching that the Spirit

---

43. James Thomas Ford, 'Preaching in the Reformed Tradition' in Larissa Taylor (ed.), *Preachers and People in the Reformations and Early Modern Period* (Leiden: Brill, 2001), pp. 65–88[76].

44. See Chad B. Van Dixhoorn, *A Puritan Theology of Preaching* (London: St. Antholin's Lectureship Charity Lecture, 2005), pp. 8–11.

45. On the relationship of preaching to the five-fold ministries of Eph. 4:11, see Morgan, who notes that 'preaching' is involved in all the roles of apostle, prophet, evangelist, pastor and teacher. G. Campbell Morgan, *Preaching* (Edinburgh: Marshall, Morgan & Scott, Ltd., 1937), pp. 11–12. This need not mean, of course, that the general 'prophetic' category is not applicable to all preaching, even with the specific gifting for Eph. 4 'prophets' which is not applicable to all preachers. This highlights one of the many complexities when it comes to specifying New Testament categories within specific ministerial contexts. See Jonathan I. Griffiths, *Preaching in the New Testament: An Exegetical and Biblical-Theological Study* (Downers Grove: Apollos, 2017), pp. 121–34.

46. Calvin, *Commentaries*, p. 82.

47. John Stott, *I Believe in Preaching* (London: Hodder & Stoughton, 1982), p. 113.

48. See III.4.i.

49. D. Martyn Lloyd-Jones, *Preaching and Preachers* (Grand Rapids: Zondervan, 2011), p. 90.

can elevate the sermon to genuine divine proclamation, while its content remains entirely Scriptural:

> [Preaching] is based upon exposition, but it is this exposition turned or moulded into a *message*...The message has come to the prophet as a *burden*, it has come to him as an entire message, and he delivers this. That is something...which is never true of an essay or of a lecture, and indeed is not true of a mere series of comments upon a number of verses.[50]

Although the idea of a 'prophetic burden' can be misused or abused,[51] this concept still plays a pivotal role in all genuinely prophetic preaching. The preacher is to feel a sense of gravitational pull towards a particular text or truth for the purposes of contextual proclamation. Many preachers have identified with Jeremiah's burning fire shut up in his bones that he cannot hold in (Jer. 20:9), or Paul's sense of 'necessity' or 'obligation' laid upon him to preach the Gospel (1Cor. 9:16). But the preacher cannot simply preach out of this subjective burden alone; they are to bring this revelatory message *through* the exposition of the text.

As noted, this prophetic dimension of preaching is not antithetical to biblical exposition but functions out of Scripture's very intentionality. The nature of the Bible itself is aimed towards prophetic proclamation; it is inspired for the very purpose of being spoken, as God's *Word*:

> In taking the Bible into the pulpit...we are not doing something inherently problematic, something alien to its nature. It belongs there. We open it before a congregation with a similar concern to the one which motivated its own authors, a concern with people encountering God.[52]

Prophetic preaching, then, is not 'optional' but an essential component of the preaching task: *proclaiming* Scriptural truth. Even if prophetic preaching is not the only way in which Scripture is 'active' in the life of the Church, it is bound up in the

50. Ibid., p. 83.

51. 'Of course, there is a danger that one may desire to take possession of the opened door and quickly to identify preaching with the voice of the Lord. This is the great and ominous misunderstanding with respect to all preaching, that the "is" of the confession and the authority of preaching is loosened from its context of the test and responsibility.' G. C. Berkouwer, *Holy Scripture* (Grand Rapids: Eerdmans, 1975), p. 337.

52. John Goldingay, 'The Spirituality of Preaching', in *The Expository Times* 98 (1987), pp. 197–203 [197]. See also: 'When we preach from the Scriptures, to the congregation, the Bible is living in its natural habitat. It is functioning as it was intended.' Willimon, *Proclamation and Theology*, p. 34; 'Scripture...does not merely tolerate interpretation and proclamation; by its very nature it demands them, in order that the inspiring power of the Spirit may continue to work through the traditions.' Achtemeier, *Inspiration and Authority*, p. 129.

very ontology of Scripture itself, which bears an impulsion towards proclamation. Scripture is not merely objectively true in an abstract sense; it is objectively true for the distinct purpose of subjective illumination by the power of the Spirit,[53] to speak not merely its own *repeating* word, but a *renewing* word to its hearers. Indeed, Scripture is 'living and active' (Heb. 4:12), 'useful for teaching, reproof, correction, and training' (2Tim. 3:16), and 'a lamp unto our feet' (Ps. 119:105) precisely by its inseparability from the Spirit who breathed it: 'Behind the written word is the living word and the written word is meant to become alive again by being spoken. It is here that preaching has its place.'[54] In the Spirit's re-breathing of the Word in the event of preaching, it does not move *beyond* Scripture, it simply embodies what Scripture is designed to *do*: speak into the lives of its hearers, prophetically.

This 're-breathing', of course, must be differentiated from the initial *breathing* that takes place in the original 'event' of Scriptural inspiration (2Tim. 3:16) in order to differentiate the authority of the preacher's fallible words and the Bible's infallibly authoritative words: 'Proclamation is not a substitute for, or an addition to, Scripture. It is also clear that the inspiration of the sermon is subordinate to the inspiration of Scripture.'[55] However, the very Spirit who first breathed the Word breathed it for the particular purpose of speaking it out *again*. This restrains the unhelpful assumption that the Spirit, having breathed Scripture in a once-and-for-all fashion, leaves it as a separate entity from Himself. Because Word and Spirit are intrinsically connected, the Spirit is active not only in the initial inspiration of Scripture but also in its ongoing interpretation and proclamation.

Mere homiletical exegesis, though essential, is not a fully faithful rendering of the biblical text. The Spirit's activity in preaching *consummates* the faithful reading of Scripture, speaking both from and *through* the text in its truest form.[56] It is in this way that preachers are authorized to speak 'as those who utter oracles of God' (1Pet. 4:11) precisely because they *are* uttering oracles of God (if, indeed, they remain faithful to the biblical text).[57] When we come to Scripture in the event of preaching with the expectation that God will speak powerfully and uniquely, we

53. See IV.3.ii.

54. Christophe Schwöbel, 'The Preacher's Art: Preaching Theologically', in Colin E. Gunton, *Theology Through Preaching: Sermons for Brentwood* (Edinburgh: T & T Clark, 2001), p. 4.

55. Achtemeier, *Inspiration and Authority*, p. 129.

56. 'The Bible is not what God "said". By the Holy Spirit it becomes what God "says". The Bible when used by God becomes "prophetic word" once again just as it was "prophetic word" in its origins.' Michael Eaton, *The Gift of Prophetic Preaching* (Chichester: New Wine Press, 2008), p. 29; 'the sermon recapitulates the biblical text and explicitly wrestles with its displayed world, bringing its implications sharply into focus for the ecclesial gathering'. Lance B. Pape, *The Scandal of Having Something to Say: Ricoeur and the Possibility of Postliberal Preaching* (Waco: Baylor University Press, 2012), p. 123.

57. 'Expository preaching ought to be as momentous an event as the giving of an oracle of God (1Peter 4.11). That it so often isn't is the fault not of preaching *per se* but of low expectations on the part of the preacher.' Ian Stackhouse, 'Charismatic Utterance: Preaching

affirm that this expectation of hearing God in this way is an inherent part of our faithfulness to Scripture.[58] Having demonstrated the conjunction of 'prophetic' and 'expository' preaching, then, we will now relate this notion of preaching to dialectical decisiveness.

3. *Attaining Dialectical Decisiveness*

Having encountered the problem of biblical dialectics in the approach to proclamation, the preacher has a further problem of 'decision'. Although the preacher must remain responsive to theological dialectics, they must ensure these dialectics do not necessarily overshadow or neutralize their singular message. This means that a number of decisions will be made in which particular truths are emphasized over others; these are decisions for which the preacher must be accountable, lest they merely *prefer* one aspect of biblical revelation at the expense of another. For proclamation to be consummated, it will require decisive action regarding *which* contingent dialectically corrective emphasis to affirm.[59] This is where we see the Spirit functioning in a specifically decisive way in preaching. After restating the essential dialectical problem for heraldic proclamation (IV.3.i) the attaining of preacherly decisiveness will be mapped out through the concepts of 'illumination' (IV.3.ii), 'discernment' (IV.3.iii) and 'faith' (IV.3.iv).

i. *Word, Dialectic, Spirit*

For the preacher, a primary engagement with Scripture necessitates a primary engagement with Scriptural dialectics.[60] Dialectics are inevitably encountered in preaching not necessarily because of preacherly indecisiveness but because Scripture itself does not *always* present fully reconciled oppositions of truth.[61] Because of this expository reality, preaching is prone to the potential stumbling block of inescapable ambiguity.[62] However, precisely because preaching is

as Prophecy', in Geoffrey Stevenson (ed.), *The Future of Preaching* (London: SCM Press, 2010), pp. 42–6 [43].

58. 'Preaching…fails to be faithful to Scripture if it follows Scripture's *content* without also seeking to be the re-enactment of the *purpose* for which that content was given.' Timothy Ward, *Words of Life: Scripture as the Living and Active Word of God* (Downers Grove: IVP, 2009), p. 163.

59. See III.5.ii.

60. See I.4.

61. For example, Scripture presents such ontological paradoxes as the injunction to both speak-to and not-speak-to fools (Prov. 26:4–5), human responsibility and divine sovereignty (Gen. 3:16–19; Eph. 1:4–5), and Satan as *under* God's ultimate authority while being an oppositional power to be resisted (Job 1–2; 1Peter 5:8–9).

62. See II.1–2.

more than an interpretative navigation through biblical dialectics, preacherly decisiveness is not only possible but essential. The inseparable connection between Word and Spirit means that Scriptural dialectics are not interpretable in isolation and do not instantiate perpetual ambiguity.[63] Indeed, the aforementioned prophetic conception of preaching ensures the decisiveness of preaching; as Paul declares: 'Our gospel came to you not only in word, but also in power and in the Holy Spirit and with full conviction' (1 Thess. 1:5). The Spirit carries the proclamation *through* the Word – thus, through the corollary dialectical problem which the Word 'creates' – to homiletical *conviction*.[64] The preacher cannot rest in the dialectical condition alone, but must pursue the activity of the Spirit so that their message will not merely restate the dialectical condition, but will declare (with conviction) the prophetic message at the prompting of the Spirit. Preacherly conviction is not merely to be pursued but is fundamental to what preaching *is*.[65]

It is the prophetic dimension of preaching that enables the preacher to emerge through the dialectical process of Scriptural interpretation with a clear, decisive, Spirit-illumined message. No methodological practice for this can be prescribed in advance because there are a variety of ways in which the manifestation of the Spirit occurs in different preachers and sermons.[66] Indeed, any decisive response to dialectics must also account for various dialectical modes and variably 'decisive' sermonic foci.[67] The preacher's dialectical decisiveness must resist any

63. 'Today theology needs to recover the paradoxical unity of Word and Spirit, for only on the basis of this unity can Scripture be made to come alive and be a transforming leaven in the life of the church.' Donald G. Bloesch, *Holy Scripture: Revelation, Inspiration and Interpretation* (Carlisle: The Paternoster Press, 1994), p. 25; 'But the truth is that without the good sense we receive from the Spirit, it helps us little or nothing to have the Word of God in our hands; for its meaning is bound to escape us…we are fit to judge only when we receive discretion from the Spirit and are guided by him.' Calvin, *Commentaries*, p. 87.

64. Although 'Word' may also refer to Christ (cf. John. 1:1), its predominant use in this chapter refers to the complex of God's revelatory content in both Scripture and preaching; that is, God's sanctified communicative message(s) – both personal and universal – to humanity. See Barth's important caveat that the three forms of the Word (written, preached and revealed) remain inseparable, though distinct – even as Scripture and preaching proceed *from* revelation (Christ). Barth, *CD* I/1, pp. 135–40.

65. See III.2.i.

66. It is for this reason that Proctor's intriguing use of the simplistic 'Hegelian' dialectical trope is not fully faithful to a dialectical approach to preaching because it remains tethered to a singular methodology for practice rather than approaching the dialectical issue theologically through the multifaceted lens of Scripture. See Samuel D. Proctor, *The Certain Sound of the Trumpet: Crafting a Sermon of Authority* (Valley Forge: Judson Press, 1994), pp. 29–31. For a more authentically theological (and rhetorical) attempt at combining dialectics and homiletics at the doctrinal level, and with an ear for the Scriptural cadence, see Timothy Matthew Slemmons, *Groans of the Spirit: Homiletical Dialectics in an Age of Confusion* (Eugene: Pickwick, 2010), pp. 78–111.

67. See II.6; III.5.i.

default to one or two particular modes, lest it impose a dialectical preference *upon* Scripture's dialectical variety.[68] In the last chapter we applied the four dialectical modes ('paradoxical', 'harmonious', 'hierarchical' and 'antagonistic') to a particular Scriptural dialectic, finding a number of ways in which 'decisiveness' could be manifest. A strong emphasis, for example, on 'grace' may appear with *conviction* in a number of modes while remaining emphatically heraldic rather than ambiguous.

The Spirit's work in such decisiveness does not remove dialectics from the sermon entirely, since this would effectively subordinate the holistic witness of the canon for singularly extreme polarities in isolated texts. Although 'extreme' emphases may well function within some instances,[69] the Spirit brings conviction *through* the dialectical process, engaging with the emphasis of the text *as* it stands alongside its dialectical counter-emphases in the canon. The Spirit brings a sense of clarity *to* what is being proclaimed and will ensure the prevalence of varying dialectical possibilities does not override the prophetic conviction by which the message becomes demonstrably 'heraldic'.[70] Where heraldic proclamation may appear to limit dialectical decisiveness to *one* particular decisive mode in Scriptural interpretation, the perpetual emphasis upon dialectical variety allows us to see such decisiveness with the full range of Scriptural possibilities.[71]

The prophetic dimension of preaching disables the otherwise unavoidable captivity to navigating the dialectical 'other' in Scripture, enabling the preacher to proclaim 'the whole counsel of God' without declaring *all* of it simultaneously. The Spirit-enabled preacher may be decisive in interpretation and proclamation, ensuring the sermon is not necessarily bound by the ambiguities of perpetual counterbalance (unless such an overtly 'dialectical' emphasis is itself essential to the particular message). If one started and ended merely with the pneumatological prophetic aspect of preaching, one might avoid the problem artificially via a 'short-cut'. Yet, because Scripture is the generator of the dialectical problem, dialectics

---

68. This notion of Scripture's 'unreconciled' dialectics is not to controvert the primary hierarchical dialectic inherent within the 'clarity' of Scripture: the Gospel, by which all dialectical constructs must be measured. See I.2.iii–v.

69. See III.5.iii.

70. See III.4.i–ii.b.

71. Bos connotes this dialectical exegetical awareness, albeit with an unspecified commitment to the category of 'balance' (which can only remain a perpetually shifting reality): 'To reduce the variety of witnesses of Scripture to a single "core witness" in the center and to remove other voices to the periphery runs the risk of opening the door to all kinds of religious legitimized extremism and fanaticism…Both poles of every ellipsis keep each other in balance and prevent possible radical opinions that center the attention in one focus only'. Rein Bos, 'Surely There is a God Who Judges on Earth: Divine Retribution in Homiletical Theology and the Practice of Preaching', in David Schnasa Jacobsen (ed.), *Homiletical Theology in Action: The Unfinished Theological Task of Preaching*, Volume 2: The Promise of Homiletical Theology (Eugene: Cascade, 2015), pp. 147–71 [171].

may not be pneumatologically circumnavigated but are drawn into the prophetic process. The Spirit does not allow the preacher to avoid the ever-complex difficulty of engaging with biblical dialectics, but enables the preacher to be both dialectically astute and prophetically decisive in their proclamation. It will now be explored *how* this contingent 'solution' of the prophetic dialectical emphasis may work within Scriptural interpretation itself.

ii. *Scriptural Illumination*

Divine illumination is one important way the Spirit acts to manifest homiletical conviction and overcome the dialectical problem for expository preaching. The Spirit sheds light upon particular truths or passages of Scripture which might remain partially obscure without such interpretative assistance or guidance.[72] This process is a consummation of the inseparability of Word and Spirit: 'Scripture speaks for itself, beyond our interpretation, sometimes despite our interpretation, through the enlivening, empowering of the Holy Spirit.'[73] Various evocations of this are found in Ps. 119: 'Open my eyes, that I may behold wondrous things out of your law'; 'The unfolding of your words gives light; it imparts understanding to the simple'; 'give me understanding according to your word!' (Ps. 119:18, 130, 169). Such prayers demonstrate and prescribe the necessary attitude of utter dependence upon the Spirit for biblical interpretation, as a precursor to proclamation. The Spirit sheds light in a number of ways: opening the preacher's eyes that they may 'see' the words (119:18), unfolding the 'closed' words themselves that they may become visible (119:130), and bestowing the gracious gift of 'understanding' that the opened eyes may *comprehend* the opened words (119:169). These functions of the Spirit point to the utter inability of the interpreting preacher to attain decisiveness *without* such illumination. As argued in Chapter I, the clarity of Scripture offers the lens *through which* Scriptural dialectics should be interpreted.[74] This prevents dialectical ambiguity or 'unclarity' *leading* one's approach to Scripture. However, as also noted, clarity does not discount the need for human interpretation,[75] which cannot properly occur without prophetic illumination.[76]

When applying biblical interpretation to preaching, divine illumination could be virtually synonymous with the idea of prophetic *revelation*, in which the Spirit gives the preacher a particular burden, emphasis or application of truth that is

---

72. See Zwingli's notion of Scriptural clarity (I.3.ii.b).

73. Willimon, *Proclamation and Theology*, p. 34.

74. I.3.

75. I.3.ii.

76. 'The texts are *perspicuous*: by the Spirit's inspiration and promised presence to the reader, Scripture is not an obscure and indefinite word but the place where illuminated intelligence may discover the knowledge of God clearly set forth.' John Webster, 'Illumination', in *The Domain of the Word: Scripture and Theological Reason* (Edinburgh: T & T Clark, 2013), pp. 50–64 [60].

not the product of mere study (though not necessarily *unrelated* to study).[77] If Scripture contains a whole variety of truths in unison in various forms of dialectical interaction, a preacher may only act *decisively* upon any *particular* aspect through illuminating guidance from the Spirit. For the mind to be illumined towards the apprehension of a particular truth, something must be revealed *to* it: 'I will pour out my spirit to you; I will make my words known to you' (Prov. 1:23). In illumination, God's words are 'made known' not in the sense of an Old Testament prophet or New Testament apostle hearing 'new' doctrines, but in these words *becoming known* to the preacher in a particular way. A dialectical incongruity in the unenlightened eyes of the preacher may become – via the Spirit – a contingently *decisive* apprehension of a particular aspect of God's Word. If, indeed, 'the purpose of illumination is that the words of God's inspired ambassadors may be understood rightly',[78] understanding 'rightly' is not simply understanding what the words *say* (because Scriptural illumination is non-exhaustive), but understanding what is imperative *in* these words at a particular time. Indeed, illumination relates not only to what *has* been said by God *in* the text but also what God would say now *from* the text.[79]

Such illumination relates immediately to the problem of *what* to preach, denoting choice of text, emphases *within* the text and their importance within the sermon. The many dialectical options that lie before the preacher must become decisively discerned and filtered whereby some of these options are contingently affirmed and others are contingently ignored. Such decisions are the fruit of divine illumination. As noted previously, contingent dialectical correctivity in the sermon excludes any singularly 'static' corridor of homiletical interpretation.[80] Yet such correctivity is not a perpetually reactionary 'pendulum-swing' through various dialectical emphases; it points rather to trusting the Spirit's promptings in accordance with the Word.[81]

To speak of revelation within prophetic expository preaching is not to say that a preacher gains some extra-biblical doctrinal revelation. The preacher's illumined

---

77. 'Holy Scripture is a text, and its sense is *made* over time, not infused in a moment; and the making of sense is an exercise of studiousness in the form of exegetical practices.' Webster, 'Illumination', p. 62; 'To confess Holy Scripture and its authority is to be aware of the command to understand and to interpret it.' Berkouwer, *Holy Scripture*, p. 137.

78. Webster, 'Illumination', p. 64.

79. This notion of 'imperative' Scriptural emphasis prefigures preaching as 'pneumatological moment' (IV.5).

80. III.5.

81. Trusting the Spirit's freedom need not mean abandoning all parameters for *how* we might expect the Spirit to move based upon God's previously normative acts in history: 'The Spirit blows where he will…God is free to intervene *ubi et quando* – where and when he pleases. We cannot, however, make that freedom the formula of our ecclesiology without denying the existence of the historical interventions by means of which God has revealed and carried out his plan.' Congar, *Word and Spirit*, p. 58.

revelation emanates *from* Scripture even if this 'fresh' revelation is something they have previously known.[82] Aquinas helpfully offers a broader understanding of different layers and types of prophetic revelation: 'Prophetic revelation is conveyed sometimes by the mere infusion of light, sometimes by imprinting species anew, or by a new coordination of species.'[83] This guards against an overly narrow corridor for one's conception of prophetic preaching, lest the kind of clarity espoused in such prophetic exhortations beginning 'Thus Saith the Lord...' be regarded as normative for *all* acts of prophetic utterance. It is important to maintain shades of prophetic revelatory illumination which the preacher may receive in varying degrees and forms. Such revelation may be an entirely 'new species' or may be based upon something naturally garnered in the human mind through studious observation which is *taken up* by the Spirit.[84]

It is clear, then, that the Spirit's activity in illumination can be seen as a guide for the ordering and relaying either of new revelation or previous revelation. This remains the case regardless of how such revelation is attained, whether *directly* (in the form of a supernatural vision, dream or prophetic intuition) or *indirectly* (through the learning of a particular doctrinal, social or ecclesial condition requiring attention). If the prophetic revelation relates to something pertinent within the congregation or popular culture, the issue's importance may be impressed upon the preacher by the Spirit's guidance, which illuminates how the biblical witness relates to such circumstances. If an unusual cultural or ecclesial condition arises, the Spirit may imbue the preacher with a sense of urgency for imminently addressing a particular situation,[85] through a *freshly applied* proclamation of a particular Scriptural emphasis. Illuminative revelation is beyond mere cultural awareness; it remains a function of the Spirit, as God's continual provision. Since illumination remains *God's* gift to bestow, this means that – like the Israelites' inability to retain the daily manna – homiletical illumination cannot be 'stored' for repetitive future use (unless otherwise prompted). The preacher's decisiveness over biblical dialectics prior to proclamation remains bound by this unceasing dependency upon the Spirit to 'unfold' the word, 'open' their eyes and 'give' understanding (Ps. 119), all of which are beyond their own natural capacity. Although this activity remains *God's*, this does not dissolve human reception of divine illumination through

82. See IV.2.iv.

83. Aquinas, *Summa* 2:2, q. 173, a. 2.

84. Illumination should not be seen as competitive with human intellect. Through illumination, intellect becomes a properly coordinated and empowered agent: 'Divine illumination sets created intellect in motion, arousing the exercise of the powers which God bestows.' Webster, 'Illumination', p. 57.

85. This could be evidenced in the sense of immediacy many preachers may feel as they seek to proclaim their prophetic burden: 'I don't know how to explain it, but I have a sense of urgency every time I teach. I really do believe my message is from God, and it is something that he's revealed to me.' Francis Chan, 'The Basis of Prophetic Preaching', in Craig Brian Larsen (ed.), *Prophetic Preaching* (Peabody: Hendrickson, 2012), pp. 11–18 [14].

prophetic 'discernment', to which we now turn. Discernment is the receptive point at which dialectics in preaching may be interpreted and decided upon.

iii. *Prophetic Discernment*

How can we can be sure that the preacher's 'prophetic word' is truly prophetic? Given that there are numerous examples in Church history of illegitimate claims to authority and abuses of the pulpit, it is not immediately clear how the preacher or hearer can attain such decisive conviction in their proclaiming or hearing of the sermon as a unique Word from God.[86] Some have emphasized the 'criteria' of those who do not avoid Scriptural dialectics: 'False prophets, whose interpretation of life is always neat and tidy, will not wrestle with the ambiguities of this paradoxical word and so they tear apart its two halves and become soothsayers of unmitigated doom or purveyors of unalloyed bliss.'[87] One might question whether this categorization is itself a little too 'neat and tidy' for its own good, though it certainly does signify an important aspect of the necessary wrestling with dialectics in any true rendering of the Word, whatever its final form. Where such analysis fails, perhaps, is in overlooking the possibility of a prophetically contingent 'one-sided' emphasis.

It is in the midst of such ambiguities and contingencies that we see the need for the Spirit's work in overcoming the problem of dialectical discernment via the creation and upbuilding of faith. Faith is essential for both preacher and hearer if the prophetic word of preaching is to complete its work. Faith provides the 'fertile soil' onto which the seed of the Word may be scattered (Matt. 13:23), enabling the Word to be proclaimed and heard with genuine decisiveness. Prophetic discernment encompasses what is often called 'hearing the Word', whereby the Spirit acts in correspondence with the hearer to attain prophetic decisiveness that what they hear truly *is* the Spirit. This process occurs both in the preacher's initial hearing of the Word and in the congregation's own hearing of the sermon.

a. *Preacherly Discernment.*

There are various ways in which one could imagine a preacher increasing the sharpness, clarity and authenticity of their prophetic witness. Various biblical injunctions might be incited such as keeping 'in step with the Spirit' (Gal. 5:25) over against the 'works of the flesh' (Gal. 5:19–21), remaining steadfast in prayer (1Thess. 5:17), maintaining diligent and continual study of Scripture (2Tim. 3:14–16) or having a general posture of humility rather than selfish ambition (Phil. 2:3–4). These are essential aspects of the preacher's prophetic witness if the Word is to be heard, delivered and received correctly: 'The humility, the admission of emptiness and need, and the expectant attentiveness that are the disciplines of prayer are also the disciplines of sermon preparation.'[88]

---

86. See Berkouwer, *Holy Scripture*, p. 337.

87. Colin Morris, *The Word and the Words: The Voigt Lectures on Preaching* (London: Epworth Press, 1975), p. 70.

88. Willimon, *Proclamation and Theology*, p. 21.

The preacher's piety in this regard, though by no means acting as guarantor of the validity of prophecy, should at least be seen as foundational for faithful prophetic preaching.

However, it is not in these things alone that 'decisive' prophetic discernment is located. It is through *faith* that the preacher may attain the 'assurance of things hoped for, the conviction of things not seen' (Heb. 11:1). With faith in the Spirit-illumined Word, the preacher may trust that the Spirit is speaking rather than their own consciousness alone: 'What guards the preacher from arrogance, and from the blasphemous claim that his own words are the words of God when they are not, is the constant reminder that every aspect of the act of preaching is enabled only by the activity of the Holy Spirit.'[89] It is clear that in many cases, as noted above, prophetic revelation cannot always be separated from 'natural' signs or thought-processes; thus, the intuitions of the prayerful preacher may themselves become instantiations of definitive prophetic revelation.

There are, of course, different *kinds* of discernible revelation. Again, Aquinas makes a distinction between an 'express revelation' and 'a most mysterious instinct'; one may have the 'greatest certitude' about the former but remains perpetually uncertain about the latter: 'He is unable to distinguish fully whether his thoughts are conceived of Divine instinct or of his own spirit.'[90] In one sense, this is a helpful distinction that differentiates between two contrasting modes of hearing a 'prophetic word' because we cannot assume all prophetic revelation arrives in the same form. In another sense, however, the designation of 'certitude' to one and 'uncertainty' to the other is not necessarily the case. In prophetic expository preaching, the preacher's dialectically decisive *emphasis* upon a theological truth or application is likely to arrive through this secondary, more 'uncertain' prophetic mode rather than an 'express revelation' of a visionary or theophanous experience. However, this should not mean that 'great certitude' should be thought of as unavailable to the preacher who is without such an immediate or incontrovertible revelation, especially if we are to ascertain that the Spirit's illumination is truly efficacious. It may be true that all prophecy lies in a tension between uncertainty and faith, in believing that the apparent prophetic instinct truly *is* prophetic. This is because prophecy does not arrive in a perfect form to a perfect herald. Indeed, Aquinas himself also says,

> When the prophet's mind is moved to think or apprehend a thing, sometimes he is led merely to apprehend that thing, and sometimes he is further led to know that it is divinely revealed to him...Nevertheless it must be observed that since the prophet's mind is a defective instrument...even true prophets know not all that the Holy Ghost means by the things they see, or speak, or even do.[91]

89. Ward, *Words of Life*, p. 159.
90. Aquinas, *Summa* 2:2, q. 171, a. 5.
91. Ibid., q. 173, a. 4.

The Spirit acts in ways beyond the prophet's own comprehension or knowledge, even when such a prophetic word was merely an instinctive or intuitive act on the part of the preacher, who acts 'in faith'. Although ways of correctly and faithfully *hearing* the prophetic word may be linked to some of the preacher's own spiritual habits, it does not rest upon any one act in particular. But unlike Aquinas' earlier distinction, faith – as a gracious act of Spirit-empowerment – is not devoid of a *contingent* form of certitude which may actually resemble the 'great certitude' of an unambiguous revelation. In this realm of prophetic instinct, then, the preacher's indwelling witness of the Spirit may direct as to what should be apprehended for proclamation. The preacher is to speak the discerned Word in faith not only that God *has* spoken it, but in faith that God will empower its proclamation through the Spirit.

b. *Congregational Discernment.*

Beyond the preacher's own faith, it is also important to note the role of the believing community, which has accepted the preacher's commission as 'anointed' by God for the preaching task. They do this not necessarily 'officially' but simply by virtue of their choosing to hear the preacher speak *as* a preacher of God's Word, not their own.[92] The congregation's acceptance and wilful submission to the authority of the preaching office is an act of faith even before the preacher has spoken: 'Under the guidance of the Holy Spirit the church has the authority to call the preacher, recognizing that the Spirit will work and speak prophetically through him.'[93] This is what might be called the communal responsibility of preaching.[94] This does not locate the authority in the preacher, nor in the congregation per se, but in the Word to which the community is bound. With this Word comes the definite *anticipation* that the Spirit will speak in the moment of preaching: 'The Church rests, not on the presupposition, but very definitely on the recollection and the expectation that God in fact has spoken and will speak the Word to us in the Bible.'[95]

In the actual hearing of the sermon itself, faith is required to correctly hear and correctly apply the sermon towards decisive personal response, whether this happens merely by catalysing a deliberate shift in thinking or perhaps instituting some decisive action. Such response also applies to the corporate congregation, who listen not only as individual members but as one body (1 Cor. 12:12). However, such faith is not the responsibility of the hearers alone and is impossible without the creative activity of the Holy Spirit, who enables the community to interpret prophecy, in faith. It is in this way that the Church is rightly called 'the

92. 'It is the word of God the congregation gathers to hear, but it is the preacher the congregation trusts to proclaim rightly that Word by carefully and faithfully engaging the biblical witness.' Pape, *The Scandal of Having Something to Say*, p. 122.

93. Ward, *Words of Life*, p. 167.

94. See James Hayes, 'Listen to My Sighing', in Gregory Heille (ed.), *Theology of Preaching: Essays on Vision and Mission in the Pulpit* (London: Melisende, 2001), pp. 55–68.

95. Barth, *CD* I/1, pp. 254–5.

illuminate of the Holy Spirit.[96] Through the prophetic declaration of the Word, the Spirit may birth, renew and enliven faith in the believer that they may hear, receive and obey the Word.

There will, no doubt, be variations within the frequency and gravity of preacherly prophecy, which may correlate with any obstinacy, lukewarmness or unpreparedness – in preacher or congregation – to receive the Word. Determining when and whether pulpit-speech is *not* 'prophetic' requires the faith and wisdom of testing (1Thess. 5:21). But primarily the congregation's faithfulness in hearing should begin with the expectation that God *will* speak as the Word is declared to them, rather than beginning with outright suspicion: 'Do not quench the Spirit. Do not despise prophecies' (1Thess. 5:19–20).[97] The prophetic word may be sifted or filtered through the hearers' own engagement of faith in what they have heard. Again, this does not place the authority of the prophetic word in the listeners themselves, but in the Word being enlivened by the prophetic activity of the Spirit. Scripture itself also acts as guarantor here,[98] by which a prophetic word might be measured: 'If anyone thinks that he is a prophet, or spiritual, he should acknowledge that the things I am writing to you are a command of the Lord. If anyone does not recognise this, he is not recognised' (1Cor. 14:37–8). This highlights that a self-imposed 'prophet' who contradicts the message of Scripture with a supposedly 'prophetic' word should immediately come under suspicion:

> God gives no one his Spirit or grace, unless by or with a previous external word. That is our safeguard against the enthusiasts...those spirits who delude themselves that they possess the Spirit independently of the word...and who accordingly judge, interpret and hear Scripture or the spoken word as they wish.[99]

This act of interpreting the prophetic word requires hearers' faith to trust the preaching witness, as they 'test the spirits to see whether they are from God' (1John

96. Webster, 'On the Clarity of Holy Scripture', p. 39.

97. Here, as in 1Cor. 14, 'prophecy' appears as something separate to preaching. However, prophecy should not be distinguished too sharply from Spirit-infused proclamation (cf. Acts 10:44), even if the gift of prophecy extends to a unique gift of 'foretelling' (cf. Acts 11:27–8) which is differentiated from Scriptural proclamation (cf. 2Tim. 4:2).

98. In addition, Scripture is a guarantor by the need to self-correct each dialectical emphasis with other biblical emphases. Article 20 of the *Thirty-Nine Articles* demonstrates an awareness of the dialectical condition by warning that the Church may not 'so expound one place of Scripture that it become repugnant to another'. *The Thirty-Nine Articles of the Church of England*, vol. 2, ed. Edgar C. S. Gibson (London: Meuthen, 1897), p. 511. Although this does not help a prophetic decision to be made between *two* opposing biblical emphases it is a helpful guiding principle if preacher and congregation are to discern how a biblical dialectic may be interpreted, since it is possible to *sound* 'biblical' by perpetually emphasizing only *one* side of a biblical dialectic without *fully* representing Scripture.

99. Congar, *Word and Spirit*, p. 31.

4:1). Although such biblical parameters usually relate to the clear distinction between 'true' and 'false' teaching, they can also be applied to varying levels of prophetic discernment as the congregation inclines their ear to hear the Word of God in the sermon. Here, Scripture's clarity is truly consummated by the Spirit's kindling of subjective faith: 'The clarity of Scripture…is not simply a linguistic or semantic property of the biblical text, perceptible *remote deo*; clarity is that which Scripture acquires by virtue of the presence and action of God, and that which is seen as it makes itself visible to faith.'[100] The believer's indwelling witness of the Spirit can be trusted for discerning the prophetic word alongside the biblical witness. Indeed, because the sheep hear *His* voice (John 10:27), they have the Spirit-empowered ability to hear the Word correctly and ignore the voice of the stranger.

The fruit of such discernment for dialectical decisiveness, as will now be seen, is a distinct sense of decisive peace. The faithful hearing of both preacher and congregation promotes a responsible expectation that God will speak through the sermon, by which the issue of dialectical decisiveness is significantly counteracted. This is not because the dialectics themselves are annihilated or smoothed-over,[101] but because the dialectical problem is superseded by the imminence of the prophetic word.

iv. *Decisive Peace and Decisive Faith*

It is important that the faithful acceptance of the prophetic message is not excessively burdened by the existence of biblical dialectics, even as the preacher seeks to navigate their right interpretation. There should not only be a wrestling with the biblical dialectics but also a peaceful acceptance of the prophetic, illumined Word. Calvin speaks of the necessity of peace in counteracting such restlessness: 'All who try to provide their own security will always be turning anxiously in all directions, and can have no peace of mind…[and] we shall find quiet nowhere except in faith.'[102] This could be applied more specifically to the preacher's interpretative dialectical situation, in which the 'anxiety' of Scriptural tensions threatens to engulf the sermon. It is faith that may apprehend such peace through hearing the sermon's prophetic emphasis. Attending to Scripture's dialectical 'restlessness', therefore, does not represent the *whole* truth of Scripture's message. There is also a propensity in the biblical message towards peace (Phil. 4:7) which comes via faith. This means that dialectics alone are never allowed to be the final word. Through the Spirit, there is a biblical injunction towards peace – attained by faith – which should be reflected in prophetic preaching. Such peace does not mean an overarching calmness or quietude, but a decisive interpretative and sermonic assurance. This peace secures the preacher's decisive actions

---

100. Webster, 'On the Clarity of Holy Scripture', p. 38.

101. As noted, dialectics remain part of the prophetic process (IV.3.i).

102. Calvin, *Commentaries*, p. 223.

regarding how they have engaged with the biblical dialectics in navigating and proclaiming the message.

The role of faith is crucial in the hearing, declaring and receiving of the prophetic word in preaching. The prophetic word, though itself an activity of the Holy Spirit, is not the *only* activity of the Spirit in preaching. This prophetic *speaking* must be consummated, as we have seen, through the *hearing* of the Word by both preacher and congregation, as Calvin says: 'God therefore teaches in two ways. He makes us hear his voice through the words of men, and inwardly he constrains us by his Spirit. These two occur together or separately, as God sees fit.'[103] This second activity of the Spirit ('constraining') is the upbuilding and cultivation of faith in the midst of preaching, which relates to the interpretation and testing of prophecy as well as the decisive proclamation itself. This must occur in accordance with Scripture's own witness and should correlate with the believer's inner witness of the Spirit, which amplifies the Word.

The faithful hearing of preacher and congregation means that – even where particular dialectics have been amplified or muted in particular preaching moments – there is a possibility of contingent prophetic assurance. This same Spirit who inspired Scriptural dialectics also inspires the reading, hearing, declaring and applying of the Word. These activities are apprehended only in faith through the Spirit's empowerment: 'The Scripture itself is a product of the Spirit, and when the Spirit works in the preacher and in the hearers, the words of God are mediated and bear fruit in the lives of those who hear.'[104] Although we may ascertain some normative parameters by which we might measure or 'discern' the activities of the Spirit through what has already been revealed, this does not constitute a holistic apprehension (or even comprehension) of how the Spirit may be working through the illumination, proclamation and hearing of the Word. There can be 'no method of scriptural exegesis which is truly pneumatic', and 'no method of living, rousing proclamation that truly comes home to the hearers in an ultimate sense'.[105] It must be maintained that preacherly decisiveness is contingent upon the power of the Spirit to speak both *from* and *through* the words of Scripture and preacher to bear the Word's fruitful purpose (Is. 55:11). Such decisiveness is located entirely in God's prophetic movement, not in any particular style of human interpretation, proclamation or reception, even as subjective faith is the necessary receptive mode in which decisiveness arrives.

Faith, as we have seen, is a theological key to understanding the possibility of dialectical decisiveness in prophetic heraldic proclamation. However, faith and discernment could also apply to many other kinds of hearing and speech. What makes 'preaching' itself a legitimate arena in which such decisively prophetic faith may be exercised? We return, in these final two sections, to a more specified

103. Ibid., p. 397.

104. Peter Adam, *Speaking God's Words: A Practical Theology of Preaching* (Vancouver: Regent College Publishing, 2004), p. 118.

105. Barth *CD* I/1, p. 183.

account of the unique nature of preaching in regards to pneumatology, through its distinct purposes as divine 'encounter' and 'manifestation' (IV.4), and in its essence as a 'momentary' act of revelatory speech (IV.5).

4. *Distinctive Purposes of Pneumatological Prophetic Preaching*

Although preaching has been defined as 'heraldic' and thereby 'pneumatologically prophetic' in the midst of biblical dialectics, it is also necessary to highlight two important overlapping 'purposes' which lie behind pneumatological prophetic preaching: pneumatological 'encounter' and pneumatological 'manifestation'. These factors position preaching as a *specifically* pneumatological event, differentiating it from other activities of ecclesial speech or other activities of the Spirit. To understand preaching as both a divine encounter and a manifestation of the Spirit's presence changes the way we view the dialectical problem for preaching. Were preaching merely an activity in which the words of Scripture were understood cognitively without recourse to the Spirit's unique activity, the dialectical problem would be potentially insurmountable. However, if preaching is seen as pneumatological in these distinct ways, it is not that Scriptural dialectics cease to be problematic but that they are superseded by grasping the primary *purpose* of preaching: to *encounter* the hearer with the Word through the *manifestation* of the Spirit. This sets the ground for the primary conception of pneumatological prophetic preaching in the final section, where these purposes of 'encounter' and 'manifestation' will be understood within the instantiation of a unique pneumatological 'moment'. The 'moment' further differentiates preaching's eventfulness and its propensity towards confident heraldic speech *over* the potential paralysis of dialectical uncertainties.

i. *Preaching as Pneumatological Encounter*

a. *Preaching and Teaching.*

Distinguishing preaching as a pneumatological encounter is one unique way of overcoming the problem of theological dialectics. Broadly speaking, 'encounter' refers to the sermon as the event in which God makes Himself present in the *hearing* of the Word: 'By proclaiming God's name, the sermon is, by God's will, his presence itself.'[106] When speaking of various dialectical problems within the text or sermon, conceiving of preaching as 'encounter' illuminates the reality that preaching has an altogether sui generis intention from that of the merely di-dactic delivery of informative content (which may be referred to, in contrast, as 'teaching'). As will be seen, the distinction between preaching and teaching is not entirely antithetical, and is easily overstated, but it is visible enough to be able to speak of them as separate entities, even with various overlaps between them. As

---

106. Oswald Bayer, 'Preaching the Word', in Virgil Thompson (ed.), *Justification Is for Preaching* (Eugene: Pickwick Publications, 2012), pp. 196–216 [207].

was argued in the previous chapter, 'preaching' is a unique event in which the herald, in some sense, speaks *for* God.[107] Given that this event is 'pneumatologically prophetic' in the ways identified in this chapter,[108] it is appropriate that preaching is strongly distinguished from 'teaching'.[109]

The idea of encounter in proclamation was emphasized heavily by Emil Brunner. The notion of the 'Word of God' (which we may take in this instance to mean 'preaching', despite its concomitant forms) is framed by Brunner as something different in kind from the relaying of doctrinal information: 'In his Word, God does not deliver to me a course of lectures in dogmatic theology, he does not submit to me or interpret for me the content of a confession of faith, but he makes himself accessible to me.'[110] If it truly *is* the case that preaching exhibits such a radically different purpose to 'teaching',[111] then preaching may be somewhat exempt from the *necessary* task of communicating holistic biblical coherence per se either within or between sermons. Even if sustained, long-term

107. III.4.ii.

108. IV.2.iii.

109. This distinction cannot be examined exhaustively here. However, see the following broadly indicative (though slightly hyperbolized) definition: 'When the preacher becomes an educator, he no longer preaches – he lectures. He talks about many things and gives out many facts. He changes no lives, he provides no answers, he redeems no hearts. Somehow he does not go deep enough to get at the root of the trouble…The preacher does not stand aloof and talk about life objectively. He is committed to a Way and to a Person. He is not after casual consideration, but commitment. He is a propagandist, and he drives toward a decision. He deals with facts, but only to find their meanings for human destiny. He never assumes that knowledge alone will solve the human problem. His task, in a word, is to introduce men to the unsearchable riches of Christ.' Gerald Kennedy, 'Using Preaching as Teaching', in *Religious Education* 44:4 (1949), pp. 229–32 [229].

110. Emil Brunner, *Truth as Encounter*, trans. David Cairns (London: SCM Press, 1964), p. 114.

111. Much confusion abounds in how preaching is understood precisely because it is conceived, practiced and received so differently within various expressions and denominations of the Church, especially within Protestantism. For many, the average Sunday sermon may well effectively *be* teaching in how it is anticipated and expressed, but happens to be called 'preaching', and vice versa. It is difficult to abstract preaching from the liturgical practices of church worship because our ecclesial experience so often feeds our theological imagination. This is especially the case given that sermons themselves have shaped (and continue to shape) concrete ecclesial realities. See William K. Kay, 'The Ecclesial Dimension of Preaching', in Lee Roy Martin (ed.), *Toward a Pentecostal Theology of Preaching* (Cleveland: CPT Press, 2015), pp. 200–15 [15]. This is not to say a theology of preaching for the whole Church is impossible, but that the predominant source of confusion needs to be acknowledged as arising from ecclesial liturgical variety. To understand preaching *as* a doctrine frees it from the moorings of individual ecclesial expressions which have allowed a particular form of public address to impinge upon the doctrinal imperative of what proclamation fundamentally *is*.

preaching to the same congregation should seek to 'proclaim the whole counsel of God' (Acts 20:27) through a roughly holistic coverage of the canon, this series of preaching events cannot be equated with the discipline of systematic theology, which bears a more overt responsibility to convey the interconnected coherence of theological doctrine as derived from those same canonical texts.[112]

If preaching may be granted this special dispensation as a truly unique communicative event, it is necessary to provide an account of what actually occurs there, especially regarding how the Spirit works *specifically* within it. As argued, the Spirit acts in various ways between preacher and congregation as the decision-making guarantor for the sermon's acutely preferential emphases amidst the dialectics.[113] But, as also noted, the Spirit is active not only in *what* words are spoken but also *how* these words are spoken, and – subsequently – how they are received and applied.[114] Thus, the activity of the Spirit renders the act of preaching as a moment in which human utterance and human reception are transformed by the divine-human encounter.[115] Preaching as pneumatological encounter means that what occurs there evokes a supernatural conviction in the human heart for those who subjectively receive the objective Word in faith.

b. *Objectivity and Subjectivity.*

In preaching, pneumatological encounter occurs through the 'objectivity' of the Word meeting the 'subjectivity' of the hearer.[116] By 'Word', in this particular sense,

112. See also III.5.ii.

113. IV.3.iii–iv.

114. See here Augustine on the role of human rhetoric: 'If the hearers need teaching, the matter treated of must be made fully known by means of narrative. On the other hand, to clear up points that are doubtful requires reasoning and the exhibition of proofs. If, however, the hearers require to be roused rather than instructed, in order that they may be diligent to do what they already know, and to bring their feelings into harmony with the truths they admit, greater vigour of speech is needed. Here entreaties and reproaches, exhortations and upbraidings, and all the other means of rousing the emotions, are necessary.' Augustine, *On Christian Doctrine*, p. 73. Homiletical rhetorical eloquence is to be pursued not to ascertain or contribute to the meaning, but to present the meaning.

115. 'We can hear Christian sermons and ask what really happens as they take place. What does actually correspond to all these words?…We can even hear Holy Scripture and simply hear words, human words, which we either understand or do not understand but along with which there is for us no corresponding event. But if so, then neither in proclamation nor Holy Scripture has it been the Word of God that we have heard. If it had been the Word of God, not for a moment could we have looked about for God's acts. The Word of God itself would then have been the act. The Word of God does not need to be supplemented by an act. The Word of God is itself the act of God.' Barth, *CD* I/1, p. 143.

116. Objectivity and subjectivity are much-used and much-debated concepts in modern theology. No extensive account of their theological use can be offered here beyond a brief explication. For a helpful account of the complexity of the modern subject-object relationship regarding 'encounter' in particular, see James Brown, *Kierkegaard, Heidegger, Buber and*

is not meant 'the Bible' or a particular passage of Scripture,[117] but the prophetic emphasis of the preached message. Even as this message is indeed inseparable from Scripture, it is not the mere spoken words of Scripture which comprise 'the Word', but the prophetic speaking of God *through* the inspired and proclaimed words of Scripture. As Scripture is initially *heard* by the preacher, this 'Word' becomes a definitive proclamation within the preaching event. It does not meet the congregational hearer with the same dialectical struggle which the preacher experiences with the dialectics of the text. Rather, it arrives as a clearly heraldic *message* through which the Spirit *encounters* the hearer as the Word is received; as Barth argues:

> Encounter with the Word of God is genuine, irrevocable encounter, i.e., encounter that can never be dissolved in union. The Word of God always tells us something fresh that we had never heard before from anyone. The rock of a Thou which never becomes an I is thrown in our path here. This otherness which is yet related to us and made known to us, though only in this way, stamps it fundamentally and comprehensively as the Word of God, the Word of the Lord, compared to which all other words, however profound or new or arresting, are not words of the Lord.[118]

The objectivity of the Word, then, meets the subjectivity of the hearer, whose reception of the Word consummates the overall event of proclamation.[119] If, indeed, the Spirit's intention through proclamation is to encounter the hearer, this means any proclamation *without* such encounter remains unfulfilled in its task.[120] Such an understanding ensures that heraldic proclamation cannot be conceived of

117. For a discussion of the objective-subjective dynamic in relation to texts and sermons, see Charles L. Aaron, 'Reflections on Objectivity and Subjectivity in Moving from Text to Sermon', in Dwayne J. Howell (ed.), *Preaching and the Personal* (Cambridge: The Lutterworth Press, 2014), pp. 104–120.

118. Barth, *CD* I/1, p. 141.

119. Human reception is vital to this process, even if we must maintain that the Spirit remains the catalysing and consummating *agent* within this encounter. 'Christian faith and speech are essentially response and not essentially source. God produces faith, not vice versa.' Trevor Hart, *Regarding Karl Barth: Toward a Reading of His Theology* (Downers Groves: IVP, 1999), p. 8; 'In revelation the human being is encountered by an eschatological reality; something really new has happened.' Hans Vium Mikkelsen, *Reconciled Humanity: Karl Barth in Dialogue* (Grand Rapids: Eerdmans, 2010), p. 52.

120. 'The objective and the subjective understanding of revelation must not be seen as two exclusive alternatives...[but] as two moments in one and the same movement.' Mikkelsen, *Reconciled Humanity*, p. 44.

in a vacuum, divorced from the contextual realities of the hearer, whose reception and application of the Word is the very *purpose* of preaching.[121]

However, this does not mean that the Word is 'objective' in the sense of being a piece of mere doctrinal information transported from God (objectivity) to hearer (subjectivity). This would mean that preaching relied merely upon the retrieval of this information from the objective source followed by the passive transfer of this information to the subject. In fact, in prophetic preaching, this 'encounter' means that the objective *meets* the subjective in the sense that the two become contingently connected. Of course, this does not relegate the objective *to* the subjective in any sense, nor does it collapse the creator-creature distinction.[122] What it does mean is that the subject becomes a recipient not only of a cognitive proposition derived from the preached message but they become a recipient of the objective *source* itself: they encounter God *in* his Word by the activity of the Spirit.[123]

This notion of preaching as the objective-subjective encounter is crucial in avoiding the collapse of preaching into teaching, whereby the conveyance of informative content may be imparted from the objective to the subjective realm, without any actual connection between the two. In such a scenario, the Word of God is imagined as an isolated gift, delivered *from* God *to* the hearer, dispassionately divorced from the giver Himself. Brunner's distinction between 'proclamation' and 'doctrine' is helpful here (even if overly antithetical): 'Genuine proclamation always has a prophetic character – even if we preachers are no prophets; pure doctrine, on the other hand, has a didactic character.'[124] Despite this important distinction, it is nonetheless important to note that the prophetic word which is received and then proclaimed by the preacher is not divorced from didactic content. 'Doctrine' remains the primary content of what is proclaimed, even as

121. See, for example, Augustine's existential-congregational use of Scripture in sermons. Peter T. Sanlon, *Augustine's Theology of Preaching* (Minneapolis: Fortress Press, 2014), pp. 71–91.

122. Many notions of 'encounter' invoke perichoretic connotations which, if used here, would unnecessarily complexify the notion of pneumatological encounter in preaching. For example, Buber: 'Relation is reciprocity. My You acts on me as I act on it. Our students teach us, our works form us...Inscrutably involved, we live in the currents of universal reciprocity.' Martin Buber, *I and Thou*, trans. Walter Kaufmann (Edinburgh: T & T Clark, 1970), p. 67. What is important to establish in this section is not the dynamics of 'encounter' itself (as Buber conceives it) but the fact that preaching *instantiates* an encounter between God and humanity in the meeting of the hearer with the Word of God. Such an encounter does not conflate God and humanity; it is a 'hierarchical dialectic' (II.6.iii) in which God *confronts* the hearer in the 'moment' of the sermon (IV.5.ii.c).

123. 'The concept of truth determined by the object-subject antithesis which deals with "something true" is indeed foreign to what is ultimately the concern of faith...[I]n faith we are dealing, not with truths, not even with divinely revealed truths, but with God, with Jesus Christ, with the Holy Spirit.' Brunner, *Truth as Encounter*, p. 134.

124. Ibid., p. 178.

the Spirit encounters the hearer through the *reception* of that doctrinal content.[125] However, pneumatologically, this doctrinal content is proclaimed and received as being more than *mere* information. Again, Brunner stresses, in preaching, '[God] does not communicate "something" to me, but "himself."'[126] Indeed, to *hear* the Word of God truly is to be encountered *by* God *in* the preaching event.

This encounter, in turn, occurs *through* the preacher's own words, the content of which is already filtered by Scripture. Thus, Scripture once again becomes a 'prophetic word' when proclaimed in the power of the Spirit: 'The truth of which the Bible speaks is always a happening, and indeed the happening of the meeting between God and man, an act of God that must be received by an act of man.'[127] God is not absent from proclamation; he is pneumatologically present in the proclaimed words. Here, both preacher and hearer receive not merely the functional 'product' of the Spirit's work, but the Spirit Himself. Preaching, then, cannot be imagined as static propositional content (even though sermons nonetheless relate propositional truths). It is truly 'living and active' as *God's* Word rather than a human word. Thus, it remains connected *to* Him in its declaration and reception. Both Barth and Brunner stress this emphasis upon humanity being unable to dispassionately 'possess' the Word of God; rather, the proclaimed Word 'possesses' us.[128] Preaching remains a primarily pneumatological activity, transcending any notion of a purely cognitive event. Regarding dialectics, this

---

125. Doctrine is the derived and interpreted theological *content* of Holy Scripture. As such, its explication provides a framework which guards and guides preaching. It provides, as Barth says, 'self-examination' for Church proclamation. Barth, *CD* I/1, pp. 74–7. Similarly, Gerhard Forde defines doctrine as 'rules for proclamation'. Gerhard O. Forde, *The Preached God: Proclamation in Word and Sacrament* (Grand Rapids: Eerdmans, 2007), pp. 250–3. The relationship between 'doctrine' and 'preaching' is not simplistically antithetical. An initial distinction arises with the impetus of preaching as catalysing the 'encounter' between Word and hearer. Contrastingly, doctrinal teaching aims to *supplement* preaching with an adequate biblical framework, lest preaching become separated from the holistic Scriptural witness. Forde also makes a further nuanced distinction: 'A sermon does indeed include explaining, exegeting, and informing, but ultimately it must get around to and aim at a doing, an actual pronouncing, declaring, giving of the gift…We must learn to speak a word that not only explains but does something'. Gerhard O. Forde, *Theology Is for Proclamation* (Minneapolis: Augsburg Press, 1990), pp. 149–50. It is this 'doing' that connotes the aforementioned 'pneumatological encounter' of preaching; it is not that *preachers* 'do something', but that the Spirit does something *through* their words.

126. Brunner, *Truth as Encounter*, p. 114.

127. Ibid., p. 199.

128. 'This truth cannot be *held*, or possessed. Its nature is, rather, such that it takes possession of us…The truth with which faith is concerned can only be received'. Ibid., p. 28; 'If a man, the Church, Church proclamation and dogmatics think they can handle the Word and faith like capital at their disposal, they simply prove thereby that they have neither the Word nor faith. When we have them, we do not regard them as a possession but strain after them, hungering and thirsting…' Barth, *CD* I/1, p. 225.

means the preacher cannot merely understand preaching as the act of interpreting and delivering Scriptural content; the preacher brings a message *through which* the Spirit instantiates this unique divine-human encounter. The dialectics of the Word further contribute to this encounter as the divinely purposed stumbling block which ensures the necessary 'instability' of preaching and, thus, its dependence upon God's manifest presence.

ii. *Preaching as Pneumatological Manifestation*

To identify preaching as 'encounter' highlights – at a meta-level – what it means to speak of preaching as pneumatological 'event'. The way in which this encounter occurs will vary; it cannot be restricted to any singular expression or tradition. However, one significant way of observing the 'how' of this divine-human encounter involves the 'unction' of the Spirit: the unique experience of the Spirit's manifest presence in the sermon. This demonstrates another avenue for conceptualizing preaching as sui generis from a purely didactic decision-making process over dialectical emphases. The notion of unction exemplifies one way in which the aforementioned 'encounter' may occur. Although unction can be spoken of as a special anointing of the Spirit in other areas of ministry too (such as healing), it is often applied directly to proclamation, differentiating it from other moves of the Spirit which may accompany ecclesial activities. It is not always clear *how* such unction occurs, but it is important to highlight this important facet of preaching, even as its corollaries remain somewhat mysterious. It is this element of 'mystery' – surrounding the tangible experience of the Spirit's presence – which links unction to notions of 'sacramental' preaching. This connection will be explored briefly before addressing unction and preaching more specifically. This illustrative account of these more experiential aspects of preaching further clarifies the aforementioned preaching-teaching distinction, and further nuances the discussion of the homiletical 'problem' of dialectics.

a. *Sacramentality.*

As noted previously, there is a traditional propensity to employ 'sacramental' language to help understand the presence of Word and Spirit in preaching.[129] In this sense, preaching becomes a kind of 'real presence' of God, not simply a set of words to be cognitively understood:

> The Word of God, whether written or preached, seems also to have a sacramental condition or structure. It is meaningful and effective beyond the material nature of the written or spoken words. In the case of the written Word, Scripture is actually there, rather like the Eucharist. There is, in other words, a 'real presence' of the Word. Like the Eucharist too, it calls for a 'spiritual eating' involving the [Spirit's] intervention.[130]

129. III.3.i.a.
130. Congar, *Word and Spirit*, p. 25.

This kind of language does not *equate* preaching with the sacraments as such, but rather points to them analogously in showing the connection between the materiality of the spoken words and the spiritual encounter which occurs in preaching. The early Barth referred to preaching as primarily sacramental in its truest sense: 'The *verbum visible*, the objectively clarified preaching of the Word, is the only sacrament left to us. The Reformers sternly took from us everything but the Bible.'[131] Brunner also employs sacramental language to speak of what this encounter means for sermonic speech: 'As God himself is present with us in the bread and wine of the Lord's Supper, in these tokens, so the Word of God wills to be present with us in words.'[132] Sermonic speech is sacramentally elevated to speak beyond the confines of the elements (words) themselves. The preacher's words are not supernatural in themselves, but they are mysteriously indwelt by the Spirit for the distinct *purpose* of divine encounter.

To speak of 'anointed' preaching, however, suggests a more specific manifestation of the Spirit which the concept of 'sacramental preaching' does not necessarily imply. 'Sacramental' preaching alludes to the Spirit but does not emphasize the Spirit's work *explicitly*. Pneumatological 'unction' may be seen as one branch of this sacramental conception of preaching. Through unction, the divine-human 'encounter' is overtly evident, whereby the hearers of the Word are met *by* God in the Word, *through* the power of the Spirit.[133] In this way, the Spirit enables dialectical decisiveness in both preacher and hearer.

b. *Unction.*

Although the manifestation of 'unction' is often associated with Protestant charismatic preaching, Catholic theology has long understood preaching as requiring a 'special charism' whereby, like the Eucharist, 'the Christian sermon is a supernatural action':[134]

> [The Preacher] acts not on his own initiative, but as moved by God, whose envoy he is. His mission includes not simply his original designation, but the divine afflatus which is upon him when he speaks. Thus the prophet is an instrument – a living, conscious, rational instrument – of God, who speaks in and through him.[135]

This 'divine afflatus' is virtually synonymous with the notion of 'pneumatological unction': the demonstrable divine accompaniment to the preacher's words in the preaching event. This conception is not without biblical precedent, especially

131. Karl Barth, 'The Need and Promise of Christian Preaching', in *The Word of God and the Word of Man*, trans. Douglas Horton (London: Hodder & Stoughton, 1928), p. 114.

132. Brunner, *Truth as Encounter*, p. 133.

133. See IV.4.i.b.

134. Avery Dulles, 'Protestant Preaching and the Prophetic Mission', in *Theological Studies* 21:4 (1960), pp. 544–80 [549].

135. Ibid., p. 545.

when compared with the experiences of preaching in Acts, such as Peter's sermon at Cornelius' house: 'While Peter was still saying these things, the Holy Spirit fell on all who heard the word' (Acts 10:44–5). It is evident that this move of the Spirit occurs by virtue of the *preached* Word, upon those who *heard* it. This is not an isolated manifestation of the Spirit but a manifestation intrinsically connected to the preaching and hearing of the Word.

As noted, it is difficult to ascertain with exactitude what pneumatological unction *is* as a *unique* mode of the Spirit's working. The prominent twentieth-century preacher Martyn Lloyd-Jones spoke of this manifestation with particular significance. His definition and general thought regarding unction is noteworthy as an example of understanding preaching through this particular lens of pneumatological manifestation:

> [Unction] is the Holy Spirit falling upon the preacher in a special manner...It is God's giving power, and enabling, through the Spirit, to the preacher in order that he may do this work in a manner that lifts it up beyond the efforts and endeavours of man to a position in which the preacher is being used by the Spirit and becomes the channel through whom the Spirit works.[136]

It is true that *all* preaching could be understood, theologically, as the Spirit 'lifting up' the efforts of the human speaker – but it is important to differentiate this unique mode of spiritual 'encounter' from simply *any* mode of the Spirit's activity. With pneumatological unction, the atmosphere of the preaching and hearing is said to be demonstrably 'special' in a somewhat tangible way; this is the aforementioned 'divine afflatus' that is also evoked in Catholic notions of pneumatological preaching. Lloyd-Jones also references a wide variety of preachers in the history of Protestantism between the sixteenth and twentieth centuries who could testify to such experiences of unction accompanying their preaching.[137] This demonstrates that such anointing is not the experience of a certain 'type' of person or indeed a certain 'type' of tradition or theological background, it is a particular mode in which the Spirit can be said to create the pneumatological encounter in preaching. It should also be noted that such extraordinary power in one's preaching ministry is not permanent, and should not be thought of as normative, even if preachers are – somewhat paradoxically – to 'seek' such extraordinary pneumatological power with *every* sermon.[138]

It is important to differentiate between unique manifestations of the Spirit and the normative work of the Spirit in preaching. We may not necessitate that preaching must – in any and every case – result in the same kinds of outwardly demonstrative manifestation. This would unhelpfully restrict the Spirit's work to certain modes of visible operation in human actions. However, it should be

---

136. Lloyd-Jones, *Preaching and Preachers*, p. 322.

137. Ibid., pp. 331–9.

138. Ibid., pp. 339–41.

understood that the Spirit often moves *discernibly* in such preaching, so that it could be possible to know that the Spirit may 'fall' on hearers in a unique way (as with Peter's hearers in Acts 10). Here, the aforementioned category of prophetic discernment may guide understanding in receiving the Spirit's work *as* the Spirit work.

Although such unction cannot be verified phenomenologically – since the Spirit may manifest in varieties of experiential encounter – Lloyd-Jones suggests there are discernible traits in the preacher's own experience which *may* demonstrate such anointing. His own account of such discernment is intriguing:

> How does one know it? It gives clarity of thought, clarity of speech, ease of utterance, a great sense of authority and confidence as you are preaching, an awareness of a power not your own thrilling through the whole of your being, and an indescribable sense of joy. You are a man 'possessed', you are taken hold of, taken up…I know nothing on earth that is comparable to this feeling – that when this happens you have a feeling that you are not actually doing the preaching, you are looking on. You are looking on at yourself in amazement as this is happening. It is not your effort; you are just the instrument, the channel, the vehicle: and the Spirit is using you, and you are looking on in great enjoyment and astonishment.[139]

It is evident here that Lloyd-Jones is attempting to grasp for some sense of articulation regarding the occurrence of unction. He is not attempting to parameter such an experience within a set of strictures, but rather pointing to experiential tenets which tend to manifest within such 'anointed' preaching. The most notable of these discernible traits is the suggestion that such unction gives the preacher a sense of 'clarity', 'confidence', 'assurance' and 'authority'. Clearly such assurance comes not because the preacher believes in their *own* ability or authority – it is a confidence which they are able to 'observe' *as* they preach; they are 'looking on' and marvelling that such confidence is possible.[140] Even if such traits can be abused by a preacher with a misplaced sense of authority or clarity (a charge often legitimately brought against such preaching), this should not discount the preacherly experiences where such a discernible manifestation of the Spirit harbours the direct *consequence* of authoritative decisiveness.

The observable experience of such pneumatological decisiveness in preaching is another instance in which dialectics cease to become *as* problematic for the preacher. As argued in the previous chapter, heraldic decisiveness in no way signals an abolition of dialectical engagement. Indeed, such decisive preaching – if

139. Ibid.

140. Another preacher's account notices a similar trait: 'I, the speaker, felt myself at one with the crowd. While I was speaking the words, it was as if I was more one of the audience than the one addressing them.' Michael Raiter, 'The Holy Hush: Biblical and Theological Reflections on Preaching with Unction', in Paul A. Barker, et al. (eds.), *Serving God's Words: Windows on Preaching and Ministry* (Nottingham: IVP, 2001), pp. 161–79 [162].

biblically expository – cannot possibly avoid dialectics. The primary point regarding such decisive unction is that the preacher becomes aware that whatever is proclaimed is indeed the very thing which *ought* to be proclaimed there and then. This is because the preacher's decisiveness is not self-generated; they 'observe' its Spirit-enabled occurrence even as they simultaneously enact it. Such experience, of course, may be vulnerable to deception and must remain connected to the symbiosis of Word and Spirit.

iii. *Experience, Word and Spirit*

It is vital that the important connection between Word and Spirit is not obscured by overemphasizing the experiential tenets of unction. Any such experience should not occur isolated from the preached message but should emanate from it. This specifies it is not the kind of Spirit manifestation which could occur at any time in *any* activity. To speak of anointed *preaching* means that any manifestation of the Spirit in the event should be a consequence of the decisively preached message itself. This brings 'expository' preaching and 'pneumatologically prophetic' preaching together in that the prophetic word *consummates* the purpose of the biblical text.[141] If Scripture is meant to *encounter* its hearers in the moment of proclamation, pneumatological unction is one way in which Scripture truly becomes 'living and active' in the here-and-now, ensuring unction is not an ecstatic experience which overpowers or deviates from the preached Word. Barth cautions against any definition of prophetic preaching anchored in such subjective experience alone:

> True preaching from the Holy Spirit of Pentecost, will not consist in pointing to our own or other men's seizure, but in pointing to the divine seizing, and therefore once again to Christ Himself...Christian proclamation does not lead the listener to experiences. All the experiences to which it might lead are at best ambiguous. It leads them right back through all experiences to the source of all true and proper experience, i.e., to Jesus Christ...It is Christ, the Word of God, brought to the hearing of man by the outpouring of the Holy Spirit, who is man's possibility of being the recipient of divine revelation.[142]

Here, Barth helpfully reminds us that the manifest experience of the Spirit in preaching (which he downplays as a 'necessity' but does not deny as a 'possibility') should *always* lead us back to the Gospel and, therefore, to Christ. Concurrently, this also means that such experiences of 'decisiveness' through pneumatological unction are immediately called back to the Word as the anchor for all such decisiveness, since Christ is Himself the Word to whom Scripture perpetually points (John 5:39). This is not to cancel out the significance of pneumatological unction as a way in which the Spirit manifests in preaching;

141. See IV.2.iv.
142. Barth, *CD* I/2, p. 249.

it merely acts as a counterfoil lest the subjective 'encounter' becomes divorced from the objective Word.[143]

Pneumatological unction remains an important example in the history of preaching in which dialectical ambiguities within the text(s) may be overcome through the decisive action of the Spirit. The Spirit empowers the chosen words of the preacher to consummate the divine proclamation. This unique and mysterious 'experience' within preaching stands on the cusp of the conceptions of 'encounter' (IV.4.i) and 'manifestation' (IV.4.ii), illustrating how we might see the encounter in practice. In turn, this leads onto the conception of preaching as 'pneumatological moment', whereby the Sprit's uniquely manifest presence *initiates* the aforementioned divine-human encounter. Here, the hearers' hearts are extraordinarily convicted by the spoken words; consequently, these words will contain a sense of contingently decisive efficacy. This 'pneumatological moment' – in which dialectical decisiveness finds its proper grounding – will now be defined and explored.

5. *Pneumatological Prophetic Preaching as 'Moment'*

We have seen how preaching is a unique event through which the Spirit works. Pneumatological 'encounter' and pneumatological 'manifestation' were connected because the demonstrative manifestation of the Spirit's presence in the act of preaching is itself a demonstration of the *purpose* of preaching: a divine-human 'encounter'. Having highlighted these two purposes, it is now important to render these activities of the Spirit into a conceptual framework of what this preaching *event* actually is: a 'moment'. The aforementioned divine-human encounter which occurs through the activity of the Spirit happens in and through a unique and unrepeatable instance. This concept of 'moment' refers to the timely uniqueness of the 'encounter' and 'manifestation' of the Spirit *within* a specific sermonic context. This momentary encounter is prepared and consummated by the Spirit, and highlights the importance of the urgent uniqueness of each preaching event, which further influences dialectical decisiveness.

The notion of the sermon as 'moment' might recatalyse Richard Lischer's aforementioned criticisms of individual sermonic events.[144] Even if it is true that, for the congregation, preaching could be seen as 'formative-over-time rather than persuasive-in-an-instant',[145] the rejection of the instantaneous 'encounter' in favour of the steadfast 'journey' of the Word could well be a false dichotomy. Are not all journeys full of encounters which radically shape the multiple directions, contours and diversions of the journey? This is especially so given that journeys of faith (both individual and congregational) are rarely of a straightforwardly linear

143. See IV.4.i.b.

144. See III.4.i.b.

145. Richard Lischer, *A Theology of Preaching: The Dynamics of the Gospel* (Eugene: Wipf & Stock, 2001), p. 90.

nature. We must certainly resist the notion of disembodied sermons which appear in a vacuum and remain disconnected from the holistic life of the Church, but this must not come at the expense of the existential importance of each present moment, which remains of perennial importance in Jesus' exhortations (cf. Matt. 6:34) and remains an essential aspect of the Spirit's prophetic sermonic address. That the Gospel demands a hearing *presently* and *uniquely* is part of what forms the very essence of preaching's heraldic nature.

i. Kairos *and* Augenblick

The concept of the 'moment' has often been conceived through the lens of the Greek word 'kairos' ('time'). This occurs in the New Testament to convey the notion of a 'timely' moment rather than a chronological moment (*chronos*). For example, the use of *kairos* as 'the *time* is at hand' (Rom. 13:11), 'the *time* is near' (Rev. 1:3) or 'signs of the *times*' (Matt. 16:3) aptly conveys its intended meaning as a moment of definitive significance. This differs from *chronos*, which usually conveys periodic moments, such as: 'for a long *time*' (Luke 8:27), 'spending some *time* there' (Acts 18:23) or 'the *time* that is past' (1Peter 4:3; emphases added). It is important to distinguish the concept of *kairos* here because it catches precisely what is meant by preaching as 'prophetic event'. It is not merely *any* moment but 'the conception of a special temporal position',[146] 'a seizing of a time which is "opportune" ".[147]

Kairos is also the word for which the notion of time has often been conceived theologically. Tillich uses *kairos* to convey the idea of a momentary event, even as he remains reluctant to pin down its meaning too tightly: 'In the English word "timing," something of the qualitative character of time is expressed, and if one would speak of God's "timing" in his providential activity, this term would come near to the meaning of *kairos*'.[148] It is the 'timeliness' of *kairos* that is so applicable to pneumatological prophetic preaching, as will be seen. Barth's definition is similar: 'the *kairos*, the particular "command of the hour" ',[149] again connoting a gravitationto the immediate. However, this does not necessarily mean captivity to the contemporary or anthropological. Rather, *kairos* is understood to be *God's* 'activity' (Tillich) and *God's* 'command' (Barth) *for* the purposes of speaking and acting *within* the contemporary moment.[150] It is in this theological sense that the

---

146. John E. Smith, 'Time and Qualitative Time', in James S. Baumlin and Phillip Sipiora (eds.), *Rhetoric and Kairos: Essays in History, Theory, and Praxis* (Albany: SUNY Press, 2002), pp. 46–57 [47].

147. Ibid., p. 54.

148. Paul Tillich, *Systematic Theology*, vol. 3 (London: SCM Press, 1978), p. 369.

149. Barth, *CD* III/4, p. 15.

150. It is clear that Tillich also developed an extension of *kairos* which collapses the finite within the infinite in ways Barth could not have envisaged. Seeing their *general* definitions of the concept, however, at this broad level both relate *kairos* to the *theological* rather than the anthropological.

connection between *kairos* and pneumatologically prophetic preaching is evident. 'Kairotic' preaching means God's special revelation intersecting with *specific* human realities. This allows the work of the herald to form one part of God's wider redemptive purposes in history. The sermon, then, can be seen as one medium of the many *kairoi* in and through which God acts in history; yet the sermon bears a unique and distinct purpose as the 'moment' of the *preached* Word rather than simply *any* kind of 'timely' moment.

The *kairos* of preaching is the Spirit's speaking something *afresh* to a new situation.[151] This elevates the status of each and every genuinely heraldic sermon as a significant and unrepeatable momentary event. This echoes Bultmann, who imagines preaching as the instance in which Scripture becomes personal kairotic 'address' to the hearers in the immediate contemporary situation: 'The Bible is transmitted through the church as a word addressing us.'[152] Although Bultmann's application of *kairos* connotes, perhaps, too much of a 'dynamic' nature of Scriptural truth, it highlights the importance of the sermon as the mode in which Scripture does indeed speak *afresh* to the contemporary hearer in a way that differentiates it from any other moment of address.[153] This is not necessarily because something doctrinally 'new' is spoken but because the situation *in which* it is spoken is utterly unique and unrepeatable. In spite of the contemporary ways in which sermons may be 'repeated' through various technological media, each preaching moment remains unrepeatable because the time in which it is preached is the *one* time that *this* particular message is preached in *this* particular way by *this* particular preacher to *this* particular people in *this* particular place. As Luke A. Powery notes, 'Sermons are always new because every day is new.'[154] The rootedness of each sermon to each *kairos* is inescapable.[155]

Kairos also bears connection with the German word *Augenblick*, which – in modern theology and philosophy – often refers to a 'decisive' moment:

---

151. See IV.2.iii.

152. Rudolf Bultmann, *Jesus Christ and Mythology* (New York: Scribner, 1958), pp. 78–9.

153. See Spurgeon's exegetically pneumatological advice to preachers: 'Get your message fresh from God. Even manna stinks if you keep it beyond its time; therefore, get it fresh from Heaven, and then it will have a celestial relish.' C. H. Spurgeon, *An All-Round Ministry: Addresses to Ministers and Students* (London: Banner of Truth, 1960), p. 336.

154. Luke A. Powery, 'Nobody Knows the Trouble I See: A Spirit(ual) Approach to the Interpretive Task of Homiletical Theology', in Jacobsen, *Homiletical Theology in Action*, pp. 85–107 [95].

155. 'This unique Augenblick…resists any repetition or iteration.' Heidrun Friese, 'Augen-Blicke', in Heidrun Friese (ed.), *Moment: Time and Rupture in Modern Thought* (Liverpool: Liverpool University Press, 2001), pp. 73–90 [74]. More could be explored regarding *kairos* in the 're-hearing' of sermons, as often occurs via downloadable sermons today. These re-hearings could, perhaps, be understood as 'secondary' *kairoi*. However, it is important to distinguish the importance of the primary *kairos* in the sermon's initial time-and-space proclamation. This should not limit the pneumatological possibilities inherent in re-hearing sermons, but it should distinguish these from the unique moment of a 'live'

Augenblick describes an experience of a fleeting but momentous event, an occurrence usually accompanied by an altered perception of time, either as condensed and swiftly passing or slow and drawn out. At its extreme, we might experience something like an arresting of time itself; an experience seems to stand out from time, though in actuality time moves on taking these moments with it. This itself is necessary to the moment: that it must pass.[156]

Augenblick could be conflated with *kairos*, though it differs in its specificity. Where *kairos* could connote an extensive and widely related 'timeliness' in the event(s), *Augenblick* has the character of a sharp interjection as the *genesis* of such an event. It is a 'disruptive force', an 'intense presence' and the 'opening of the moment'.[157] In connecting 'the moment' to preaching, both *Augenblick* and *kairos* could be used to speak of the potentially 'disruptive' activity of the Spirit in proclamation. A sermon – or a moment *within* a sermon – could be understood as one of the aforementioned 'time-arresting' moments in actuality, where the encounter of the Word is *realized* within the hearer.[158] The preaching event itself, then, is an 'elevated' moment bearing a distinguished significance, even though it is a *mere* moment which 'must pass'.[159] In this sense, preaching is also a 'relegated' moment, playing merely one small role in the wider network of God's providential activities in *all* moments, which are tethered to God's ultimate revelation of Himself in Christ.[160] But, as will be seen, the *preaching* moment is that which interjects theological dialectics most acutely.

To understand how this moment actually occurs *in* time, a pointer may be found in Kierkegaard's category of 'the instant', often translated 'the moment' (Danish: *øjeblik*; derived from *Augenblick*). This notion conceptualizes the intersection of time and eternity as the 'creation' of the *Augenblick*: 'The moment is that ambiguity in which time and eternity touch each other, and with this the concept of *temporality* is posited, whereby time constantly intersects eternity and eternity constantly pervades time.'[161] There is a complexity to this concept which

hearing, lest the initial proclamation become divorced from the gathered ecclesia, as with the more individualistic relationship to the downloaded sermon.

156. Koral Ward, *Augenblick: The Concept of the 'Decisive Moment' in 19th and 20th Century Western Philosophy* (Farnham: Ashgate, 2009), p. 12.

157. Friese, 'Augen-Blicke', p. 74.

158. See IV.4.i.

159. Ward, *Augenblick*, p. 12.

160. Barth links all *kairoi* – and all preaching – to the 'fulfilled kairos' of Jesus' life on earth: 'For when Jesus taught in His here and now and to-day, as He saw it His presence was not one moment of time among and after and before many others, but fulfilled *kairos* – the moment of the event, the Word, to which every past word or event can only move, just as every future word or event can only move to the revelation of its actual scope.' Barth, *CD* IV/2, p. 200.

161. Søren Kierkegaard, *The Concept of Anxiety*, trans. Reidar Thomte (Princeton: Princeton University Press, 1980), p. 89.

need not be expounded fully here.[162] However, Kierkegaard's conception (which also influenced both Barth and Tillich) offers a clear way to think about what this moment actually *is* and how it is differentiated from other conceptions of time:

> The moment is not a determination of time, because the determination of time is that it 'passes by'. For this reason time, if it is to be defined by any of the determinations revealed in time itself, is time past. If, on the contrary, time and eternity touch each other, then it must be in time, and now we have come to the moment.[163]

If 'the moment' is the instance in which time and eternity *meet* (without becoming conflated), we can see a way in which the pneumatological activity (derived from 'eternity') enacts something unique in the otherwise ordinary sermon (derived from 'time'). This is why Kierkegaard also speaks of the moment as that in which time is intersected by an activity from *beyond* time (eternity): 'The moment is not properly an atom of time but an atom of eternity. It is the first reflection of eternity in time, its first attempt, as it were, at stopping time.'[164] The 'moment' is not something which occurs *from below* in the realm of time itself; it is interjected *from above* and finds its ontological basis *as* a moment which can come into being only when eternity and time meet in this unique way. It is for this reason that this 'moment' cannot be relentlessly *pursued* as though it could be generated by human activity alone.[165] One can only 'lay hold' of it upon *receiving* it, as with the objective-subjective 'encounter'.[166] Applying this pneumatologically, the Spirit 'creates' the new moment *in* time. By thus *invading* time, the Spirit 'stops' time in order to prepare the way for the moment of the Word.[167]

162. This apparent pervasiveness between time-and-eternity in the above quotation suggests a kind of perichoresis which is difficult to reconcile with other Kierkegaardian leanings, such as his oft-quoted 'infinite qualitative distinction'. See Søren Kierkegaard, *Practice in Christianity*, trans. Howard V. Hong and Edna H. Hong (Princeton: Princeton University Press, 1992), pp. 28–9.

163. Kierkegaard, *Concept of Anxiety*, p. 87.

164. Ibid., p. 88.

165. Kierkegaard criticized this misguided pursuit of the 'timely' moment as one of the chief misunderstandings of his age: 'Instead of learning…how to lay hold of the eternal, we only learn how to drive ourselves, our neighbours, and the moment to death – in the pursuit of the moment…never reaching it.' Ibid., p. 105. This is now a common reflection in subsequent philosophical reflections upon *kairos*; see: 'Only the present moment then remains, which inexorably escapes us every time we try to seize it.' Giacomo Marramao, *Kairós: Towards an Ontology of Due Time* (Aurora: The Davies Group Publishers, 2006), p. 92.

166. See IV.4.i.b.

167. 'The right moment not only cuts into the flow of time, but it is the end of time.' Geoffrey Bennington, 'Is It Time?', in Friese, *Moment*, pp. 17–32 [20]. This moment>time intersection will be further explicated in IV.5.ii.d.

By relating *Augenblick* and *kairos* to a pneumatology of preaching, the Spirit is understood as the enabling and sustaining generator of the time-arresting moment. In such a moment, God speaks in a pronounced and definitive way *for* that time. Divine revelation in preaching is catalysed by the Spirit's blessing *of* the preaching. Concurrently, the sermon may be conceived as the vessel in which this time-arresting, decisively *kairotic* moment arrives, without rendering the sermon infallible in itself.[168] It is only *through* the pneumatologically kairotic sermon that dialectics may be interjected or emphasized with adequate authority. It is now necessary to specify some different ways this kairotic moment could actually be conceived.

ii. *What Kind of 'Moment'?*

Preaching as 'moment' means that it bears a unique responsibility to address its contextual situation. However, this responsibility may be conceived in a number of 'momental' types: a. *'congregational moment'*; b. *'cultural moment'*; c. *'sermonic moment'* and d. *'pneumatological moment'*.[169] It will be seen that the 'pneumatological moment' [d] most aptly captures the specific activity of the Spirit in preaching, highlighting – most effectively – that the sermon's message is a unique *kairos* itself, not a form of speech which communicates *from* or *to* a *kairos*. The pneumatological moment will be seen to encompass the emphases of these other types ('congregational', 'cultural', 'sermonic'), and so becomes pivotal to the question of dialectical decisiveness. Through the pneumatological moment, the Spirit draws together each of these more contextual moments, creating a 'new' *kairos* by the very proclamation of the Word of God, which interjects the dialectics. First, then, some of the indicative possibilities for understanding the 'moment' in preaching should be identified.

a. *'Congregational Moment'.*

The 'congregational moment' refers to the various subjective particularities which exist within the sermon's given setting. This is less a theological than an anthropological category of moment, relating to the subjective situations of the hearers rather

168. Although the *kairos* application elevates the importance of each sermonic event, understanding the *kairos* of preaching within God's wider providential activity should simultaneously curtail any overinflated sermonic importance, lest preaching be given 'a burden which it is unable to bear'. Adams, *Practical Theology of Preaching*, p. 72. Preaching merely forms *one* element of God's greater communicative purposes within human history. Indeed, preaching is not significant in and of itself (as though preaching were the fundamental bringer and bearer of providential activity) but by virtue of preaching's inseparable relationship *to* God, through the perpetual enabling and re-enabling of each kairotic sermon by the Spirit.

169. This is not an exhaustive list, but is indicative of the possible varieties of 'moment' in preaching.

than the Spirit's encountering *of* them, as such.[170] Such congregational particularities, of course, cannot possibly be 'normative' for all sermons. Each particular
sermon is a different moment due to its occurrence in a truly unique scenario, even
when preached to the same people.[171] These ever-changing subjective factors will
affect both the delivery and reception of the preaching, and include a wide range
of possibilities such as: differing existential moods; important events occurring in
hearers' lives; accompanying liturgical activities within the ecclesial gathering or
the cumulative impact of the previously preached sermons to the same congregation.[172] It is even possible that architectural or seating arrangements could play
some role in the subjectivity of the preacher or hearer, and thus influence the ways
in which the sermon is proclaimed, received and applied in its context.

Clearly, an exhaustive account of each contingent possibility for the sermon's
congregational setting is unnecessary. What is noteworthy is that sermons
never occur *apart* from these unique scenarios, each of which could bear
unique existential, liturgical and even architectural influence upon the sermon's
proclamation and reception. Although such contextual factors cannot be assumed
to *provide* anything of the content of the prophetic word in preaching, they cannot
be discounted from being *means* through which the Spirit catalyses the message
and accommodates it to the hearers. In addition, such factors will also influence
the hearers' reception of the dialectical emphasis, since they may already be
leaning towards a particular polarity or dialectical 'mode' at that particular time
which could be confronted by the decisive Word of the sermon.

b. *'Cultural Moment'*.

The 'cultural moment' is closely linked to the 'congregational moment', relating to
the pertinent cultural events occurring at the time of the sermon. These will often
be *outside* the Church, in the local, international, political and social sphere, potentially further influencing the consciousness or mood of the hearing congregation
(or the preacher) at any given time. The connection between *kairos* and preaching
is often seen as this cultural moment, as though 'kairotic preaching' were a particular 'form' of preaching where a topical sermon is applied to a thematic concern
pertinent to a cultural *kairos* (rather than the *kairos* being the proclaimed Word
itself). In such a notion, preaching is conceived as kairotic only when it speaks

---

170. As noted in III.3.i.e, emphasizing such congregational elements as *primarily*
important is a recurring focus within contemporary homiletics. See Allen and Jeter, Jr., *One
Gospel, Many Ears: Preaching for Different Listeners in the Congregation* (2002).

171. 'The church is the *scene*: that historically and liturgically contains the acts and
agencies of our individual sermons.' Lischer, *Theology of Preaching*, p. 88.

172. 'Methods for crisis preaching cannot be developed in isolation from the liturgical
context in which most preaching occurs. The word is proclaimed within a larger framework
of praise, lament, prayer, sacrament, and other corporate ritual acts.' Carol M. Norén, 'Crisis
Preaching and Corporate Worship', in *Liturgy* 27:1 (2012), pp. 44–53 [44].

into something, circumventing a recent event or crisis in Church or society.[173] This misunderstanding echoes the aforementioned notion of 'prophetic preaching' as meaning that which reflects the cultural norm or enacts significant cultural change, rather than being a discernibly unique activity of Word-and-Spirit.[174]

A contemporary example of such an approach can be found in Jacobsen's *Kairos Preaching* (2009) in which he reflects upon the situational aspects of what is happening in and *to* the congregation as *informing* the sermon (such as a pertinent public issue, financial crisis or congregational bereavement). 'Kairos preaching', then, is invoked as a kind of emergency homiletical schema which relates the sermon *to* such moments, to 'those occasions, those *situations*, when the planets don't align…those situational moments that require more than programs, lectionaries and denominational emphases can provide'.[175] In one sense, this is true – preaching should address such situations, but this in itself does not constitute a theological grounding for what 'kairotic preaching' means. The error here is the assumption that there is such a thing as 'kairotic' and 'non-kairotic' preaching.[176] If preaching is to be heraldic (and thus, pneumatologically prophetic) then it must *always* be 'kairotic'. This is not because it references or addresses specific events in culture or the hearers' everyday lives, but because it addresses the hearers *in* the *kairos* of the sermon itself, as the *encounter* with God through the *pneuma*. All sermons must speak to the *now* because all sermons are situated in time and space with the express purpose of God speaking *to* a specific people with a specific word for a specific time, even as such specificities are derivative of God's 'timeless' words of Scripture.[177] The primary problem with the 'cultural moment' approach is that it deviates from the essentiality of Scriptural exposition as informing the primary content of the message, in which the issue of the day *leads* the content of the sermon.[178] The Spirit can, of course, guide the preacher as to what may be of relevance from cultural *kairoi* for use within the sermon, but such homiletical application is not the *kairos* of preaching itself.

173. The concept of 'crisis' in regards to preaching bears much similarity to both *kairos* and *Augenblick*: 'an unstable or crucial time in a state of affairs, a decisive moment that may come unexpectedly'. Ibid., p. 44.

174. See IV.2.ii.

175. David Schnasa Jacobsen, *Kairos Preaching: Speaking Gospel to the Situation* (Minneapolis: Fortress Press, 2009), p. 2.

176. This may, in fact, stem from a misunderstanding of the distinction between preaching and teaching, whereby the communication of doctrinal information is conflated with the activity of heraldic proclamation with the two merely seen as different 'types' of preaching (see IV.4.i.a).

177. See IV.5.iii below.

178. Barth laments former occasions in which his own preaching allowed the *kairos* of the day to shape the sermon rather than Scripture itself: 'We do not always have to bring in the latest and most sensational events. For instance, if a fire broke out in the community last week, and church members are still suffering under its awful impact, we should be on

c. 'Sermonic Moment'.

The 'sermonic moment' relates to the different 'decisive' moments *within* a sermon. To speak of the 'momentariness' of a sermon does not necessarily equate the entirety of the sermon as being one unbroken stream of decisive significance, but it may involve a number of decisive or less decisive moments which occur in various instances. Hearers and preachers may often speak of key moments in which the Spirit seemed to be present which differentiate those sub-moments from other sub-moments within the larger 'moment' of the sermon.[179] Any account of *kairos* in preaching must consider the kairotic variety *within* the sermon for different hearers lest the notion of *kairos* become too generalized.

Dale L. Sullivan asserts that 'proclamation is a kairotic rhetoric' in itself,[180] rendering the speech of the sermon as being 'pregnant' with potentially kairotic efficacy. Indeed, certain words, passages, illustrations or flourishes within a sermon may have an acutely profound impact upon the hearer, whether such impact was intentional or not. In many cases, these smaller *kairoi* form different access points for the reception of the Word, without being divorced from the sermon's overall Scriptural message.[181] It is not that these smaller rhetorical moments of the sermon are somehow 'magical', but simply that the Spirit directs their use in particular ways as the Word is taken-up by the Spirit to be heard in faith by the listener.[182] This means that *within* the sermon there may be a number of invoked 'experiences' as a result of the kairotic Word:

guard against even hinting at this theme in the sermon. It belongs to everyday life, but now it is Sunday, and people do not want to remain stuck in everyday problems. They want to go beyond them and rise above them. In my parish work in Switzerland I often fell into this danger of misunderstanding how preaching is to be congregational. In 1912, when the sinking of the Titanic shocked the world, the next Sunday I had to make this disaster the main theme of my sermon, and a monster of a full-scale Titanic sermon resulted...I had disgracefully forgotten the importance of submission to the text.' Karl Barth, *Homiletics*, trans. Geoffrey W. Bromiley and Donald E. Daniels (Westminster: John Knox Press, 1991), p. 118.

179. This relates to the efficacy of Scripture as inherently transformative, as noted earlier (IV.2.iv). See also this account of the power of spoken Scripture in specific decisive 'moments' in the lives of Antony of Egypt, Augustine and Girolamo Savoranola: Gerald O' Collins, 'The Inspiring Power of Scripture: Three Case Studies', in *Irish Theological Quarterly* 79:3 (2014), pp. 265–73.

180. Dale L. Sullivan, 'Kairos and the Rhetoric of Belief', in *Quarterly Journal of Speech* 78:3 (1992), pp. 317–32 [317].

181. On the relationship between prophetic 'hearing' and the text of Scripture in preaching, see IV.2.iv and IV.4.ii.c. This connection ensures that the subjective *experience* of a prophetic sermonic 'moment' is not divorced from the actual content of the proclamation; rather, what is heard *in* such a moment is, in fact, the message of Scripture itself, rendered *afresh* to the hearer.

182. See IV.3.iii on faith and discernment.

Proclamation [is] a non-rational or supra-rational rhetoric bound up with the concept of *kairos*. When successful, such rhetoric produces what is called a kairotic experience, which presents a single alternative, filling the entire consciousness of the auditor, producing belief when the auditor says 'yes' instead of 'no.'[183]

These 'supra-rational' moments of decision could be understood as *specific* times in which the Spirit highlights or illuminates something within the text or sermon (either for preacher or congregation) whereby this 'kairotic experience' is received and faithfully responded to through decisive action.[184]

As noted in the last chapter,[185] the New Homiletic's emphasis upon the sermon's form can lend itself – if mishandled – to an overly technical approach whereby these 'sermonic moments' could be manufactured through mere rhetorical devices.[186] In such an approach, preaching could be no different to *any* stirring oratorical act – irrespective of theme or content – so long as parts of the oration were sufficiently dramatic, poignant or captivating. If we are to maintain that the Spirit is the primary instigator of the preaching *kairos*, then even if the Spirit may *use* preacherly rhetorical devices, the Spirit's speaking must be understood as beyond the *control* of such strategies.[187] It can be assumed, then, that there are different instances of kairotic rhetoric *within* the sermon where the Spirit convicts or impresses Himself upon the hearer in a particular way. Any sermon event will almost certainly contain various 'moments' in which the spoken words have different effects and are heard in different ways. This includes, of course, momentary dialectical emphases, especially when particular dialectics are engaged which involve a dual emphasis within the same sermon.[188] However, the category of 'sermonic moment' still does not encapsulate what it means to understand 'kairotic' preaching theologically. Preaching as pneumatological *kairos* must be understood in the broader sense of the Spirit empowering the proclamation of Scripture before, during and after the sermon.

183. Sullivan, 'Kairos and Rhetoric', p. 317.
184. See IV.3.iii–iv.
185. See III.3.i.e.
186. This could occur, for example, via Buttrick's linguistic emphasis to create the necessary rhetorical 'effect' upon the listener, or with Lowry's notion of deliberate 'suspended ambiguity' whereby the listener is engaged *within* their own situation by the narratival plot of the sermon (see III.3.i.c). Of course, such homiletical approaches do not *necessarily* lead to an overemphasis on technique for crafting the 'sermonic moments', but they certainly lend themselves to this potentiality due to the lack of an overt focus upon the Spirit's work in *instantiating* the sermonic *kairos* (see IV.5.ii.d).
187. Thus, it is not necessarily more 'probable' that the Spirit will convince the hearers of a particular truth or encounter them with his presence *because* of the preacher's use of a dramatic pause or illustration, though the Spirit may choose to speak *through* such agencies.
188. See III.5.i.b–f.

d. *'Pneumatological Moment'*.

The distinct 'pneumatological moment' is the most helpful way to conceptualize preaching as kairotic, attending to and encapsulating the three aforementioned concepts of moment. The pneumatological moment may address the events of the day or the existential situations of the hearers, but is not bound *to* these connotations in order to *be* 'kairotic'. The 'pneumatological moment' in preaching is itself something different to – and transcendent of – these minor *kairoi*; it is something entirely 'new' as the creation of a moment *into which* the hearers are drawn rather than being a moment which *interjects* the pressing anthropological *kairoi* of the present time: 'The *kairos* is always another time appearing in *the present* time.'[189] This new moment into which the hearer and preacher are drawn occurs as the Spirit indwells the words of the preacher and acts to guarantee the appropriate hearing of these words, bringing efficacious transformation to the hearts of these hearers. As such, the 'pneumatological moment' may refer to the entirety of the workings of the Sprit in the midst of the sermon's preparation, delivery and hearing: 'It is not just that the Spirit is at work in the actual delivery of a sermon. He has also *gone before* the preacher...The sermon is preached in a Spirit-formed and Spirit-infused situation.'[190]

Since the Spirit is at work on multiple levels before, during and after the preaching event itself, the pneumatological moment can be said to speak *into* and to shape the 'congregational', 'cultural' and 'sermonic' moments. The pneumatological moment is itself *above* these subsidiary conceptions of moment as an overarching concept reflecting the Spirit's instantiating presence governing the preaching and hearing of the Word. For this reason, the 'pneumatological moment' is very closely related to 'encounter' and 'manifestation'.[191] It relates to these other pneumatological functions as the unique, situated activity of the Spirit that brings about the pneumatological relationship between Word and hearer. Thus, it can be said that this moment *creates* and *upholds* the unique situation in which the aforementioned demonstrative *effects* of the Spirit's presence in preaching – such as unction – may occur.[192]

The concept of the pneumatological moment further differentiates the kairotic nature of preaching from other oratorical events, or indeed, from becoming conflated with any contextually kairotic speech-act.[193] If kairotic preaching was

189. Bennington, 'Is It Time?', p. 22.
190. Ward, *Words of Life*, p. 161.
191. See IV.4.
192. See IV.4.ii.b.
193. Here, philosophical approaches to the moment are less helpful since they would not consider 'preaching' as having any special pre-eminence compared with other kairotic speech-acts: 'Whatever I talk about, I implicitly claim that it is the right moment to talk about it – any speech act, however mistakenly or apologetically, lays claim...to its own timeliness.' Bennington, 'Is It Time?', p. 18. Although this is true in one sense, the kairotic speech-act of preaching is of a different order to the 'timeliness' of any other speech-act.

merely understood to speak acutely *into* its context, it would be difficult to argue for the difference between a kairotic biblical sermon and a kairotic political speech. The important point is not that the timely contextual eccentricities shape the prophetic word of preaching but that the prophetic word speaks *into* these eccentricities by having them 'taken up' into this *new* Spirit-formed moment. Here, a genuinely new *kairos* is declared, announcing a new reality into which the hearers are invited. When preaching is truly pneumatologically prophetic, the hearers do not *remain* in their current 'context' entirely. They are, as it were, moved to a *different* context – the new *kairos* – in which the Word addresses them *as* a word from God, and in which they receive this prophetic word subjectively. Such a pneumatological event will not happen in exactly the same way for any given hearer (for some, it may not occur at all), but this event – wherever it occurs – should be understood as the instantiation of the Spirit who empowers and consummates the declaring and hearing of the Word.

It is also important to note the counterpoint to this focus upon sermonic context. Many sermons could be preached almost identically in vastly different settings without much change or adaptation whatsoever. This, however, cannot be seen as somehow *avoiding* the contextual specificity of each and every sermon, even where differentiation is not apparent in the sermon's form (as with itinerant ministries in which sermons may be repeated in a number of different contexts). However, if the sermon forms part of a wider 'pneumatological moment', a sermon is never actually 'repeated' as such, even if it bears an identical form to other moments in which the same doctrinal content is preached. If a sermon *could* be repeated in every conceivable sense, this would mean preaching is no different to teaching (*contra* IV.4.i.a) because it would rely on a particular, planned series of doctrinal or exegetical words which are spoken for merely cognitive reception alone. But, if preaching bears the *pneumatological* moment, this means the Spirit does something *particular* in different settings according to the 'cultural moment', the 'congregational moment' and the 'sermonic moment', in which the Spirit has created the appropriate setting for the hearing of the Word. Indeed, although the pneumatological moment is *beyond* time (as Kierkegaard partially saw), preaching itself remains spatially and temporally limited. The purpose of preaching is not to speak a word (or series of words) which will be perpetually remembered; rather, preaching perpetually *speaks* prophetic words as God continues to communicate and 'encounter' his people *by* his Word *through* his Spirit.

This sense of preaching's timeliness is vital for our understanding of dialectical correctivity,[194] which correlates somewhat with Tillich's kairotic emphasis: 'Not everything is possible at every time, not everything is true at every time, nor is everything demanded at every moment.'[195] Notwithstanding the perennially Tillichian dangers of relativism here (regarding what is 'true'), this concept urges consideration over which Scriptural emphases may be efficaciously true *for* the

194. See III.5.ii.
195. Paul Tillich, 'Kairos', in *The Protestant Era*, trans. James Luther Adams (Chicago: University of Chicago Press, 1948) pp. 32–51 [33].

moment, as the Spirit prompts.[196] This informs how one may engage or emphasize the dialectical possibilities in Scripture. Preaching speaks to the *hic et nunc* with the decisive force of a prophetic word, not with the perpetually corrective concern of a 'system' (which, by definition, attempts to smooth out the rougher edges of conflicting polarities or emphases).[197] Hence, dialectics are never fully abolished, antagonized, harmonized or separated because preaching does not attempt to account for them all at once but to draw *from* them as led by the Spirit. Preaching, then, is a prophetic splicing into the dialectical Word, which becomes proclaimed as the decisive *prophetic* Word.

iii. *Timely Moment and 'Timeless' Scripture*

It is important, in this final section, to tie the emphasis upon the primacy of 'moment' back to the emphasis upon the primacy of Scripture.[198] It has been argued that preaching speaks into specific, contextual situations by creating a unique pneumatological moment into which all subsidiary moments may be drawn. This moment is 'timely' not because of any necessary connection to a *Zeitgeist* or momentary cultural theme but because the Spirit enacts a new *kairos* in the midst of the proclamation event. However, this pneumatological moment does not occur *beyond* the uniquely panoptic standpoint of the biblical canon. Proclamation is simultaneously rooted to its pneumatological moment, the text of Scripture and

196. Even with the highest possible view of the eternally fixed truth of Scripture, all preachers choose to privilege some aspects of Scripture as more pertinently true to some moments than others. In doing so, they are not implying that what is not emphasized is not true (an extension with which Tillich perhaps flirts) but they are saying what is functionally true *for that moment*.

197. This contrasts Lloyd-Jones' important cautions over such *specific* textual emphasis in preaching, which he saw as dangerously deviating from the constraints of systematic theology: 'To me there is nothing more important in a preacher than that he should have a systematic theology, that he should know it and be well grounded in it. This systematic theology, this body of truth which is derived from Scripture, should always be present as a background and as a controlling influence in his preaching. Each message, which arises out of a particular text or statement of the Scripture, must always be a part or an aspect of this total body of truth. It is never something in isolation, never something separate or apart. The doctrine in a particular text, we must always remember, is a part of this greater whole – the Truth or the Faith. That is the meaning of the phrase "comparing Scripture with Scripture". We must not deal with any text in isolation; all our preparation of a sermon should be controlled by this background of systematic theology.' Lloyd-Jones, *Preaching and Preachers*, p. 77. Although this rings true, it was not *entirely* consistent with Lloyd-Jones' actual practice in preaching particular emphases, and perhaps highlights the perpetual tension between preaching and system, both of which require one another for their coherence, though never in static resolution.

198. See I.1; IV.2.iv.

the Gospel in which Scripture's unity is founded.[199] In preaching, an element of the panoptic narrative of Scripture is angled in a specific way towards the particular context in which the unique proclamation event occurs. This maintains the connected relationship between Word and Spirit, as the Spirit-breathed Word is Spirit-breathed afresh through proclamation. Barth calls this the 'contingent contemporaneity' of Christian proclamation, since 'it has the character of an act, an event'.[200] This event is both Scriptural and (concomitantly) Christological:

> In the relation between Holy Scripture and proclamation there is always a contingent *illic et tunc* from the standpoint of the speaking God and a contingent *hic et nunc* from the standpoint of hearing man...The problem of God's Word is that this specific revelation of God is granted to this specific man to-day through the proclamation of this other specific man by means of this specific biblical text, so that a specific *illic et tunc* becomes a specific *hic et nunc*.[201]

Although it is right to speak of preaching as being tethered to revealed Christian doctrine through Scripture, there is an extent to which the act of proclamation 'reveals' this Scriptural revelation anew to the hearers. In the pneumatological moment, God speaks *through* His Word to *this* people in the here-and-now.

It is evident, then, that proclamation must be rooted both to Scripture *and* to 'moment' if it is to remain faithful to its purposes. Admittedly, any approach arguing for the 'momentariness' of preaching runs the inevitable risk of over-correlation *to* the *Zeitgeist* in the misguided attempt to 'render' the content of Scripture relevant to its hearers. Barth points out the incessant danger of the Church's captivity to the *Zeitgeist* in its witness if placed under the rubric of *kairos* alone:

> Alienation takes place when [the Church] allows itself to be radically determined and established and engaged and committed and imprisoned...by the adoption of a particular philosophy or outlook as the norm of its understanding of the Word of God...by the commandment of a specific tradition or historical *kairos*...by a distinctive ideology or by the most respectable or novel or simply the strongest of current political and economic forces...by allowing itself to be determined by what seems to be the most urgent and sacred need in its Own particular environment.[202]

The notion of the 'most urgent and sacred need' should not be what defines pneumatologically prophetic preaching, even if such terminology could easily be used to argue for the Church's reactionary activity to various cultural *kairoi*. As argued above, kairotic preaching should speak *into* these needs and should not

---

199. See I.2.i–iii.
200. Barth, *CD* I/1, p. 149.
201. Ibid.
202. Barth, *CD* IV/2, p. 667.

neglect them, but these needs are not the essence of the true *kairos* itself, which is God's pneumatological action in the declaration and reception of his Word. Such an event may indeed *address* the cultural *kairoi*, but it lifts the hearers *from* these momentary situations into a new moment, instantiated by the Spirit in the proclamation of the Word. Preaching gets its 'eventfulness' not from its ability to reference the cultural *kairos* but by its actuality as the Word of God speaking revelation to its hearers. Such preaching will indeed speak-of and speak-to the *Zeitgeist*; but this is not its primary purpose. The *Zeitgeist* – or, 'cultural moment' – is not itself the Word of God, it is merely the 'soil' in which the Word of God is planted and 'realized' within each instantiation of its proclamation.

To avoid the 'alienation' of which Barth spoke (between the Church's proclamation and the true Word of God), the commitment to both 'Scripture' and 'pneumatological moment' must be maintained. To speak of Scripture as the ground from which this pneumatological moment is drawn emphasizes that there is no moment of genuine proclamation which is *not* kairotic. This is due to Scripture's injunction *towards* the kairotic in its initial composition and in its eschatological purpose in speaking the same message *afresh* to successive generations. The prophetic preaching of the Old Testament reflects this same need within contemporary preaching: 'Those oracles of the prophets were always of immediate relevance to the situation in which they were spoken. There was apparently for the prophets no "timeless" word of God. There was only the word directly relevant to a specific situation.'[203] This notion of the Word's 'timefulness' correlates with the aforementioned idea of preaching as 'moment'. Yet this also evokes one of the foundations underpinning this book's overall thesis: canonicity.[204]

If the biblical canon provides the foundation for expository prophetic preaching, there is a true sense in which this canonical foundation may be seen as simultaneously 'timeless'. This is not to say it is *wholly* timeless, since it was conceived and written *in time* in particular historical contexts from which it should not be excised. But to speak of the canon's 'timeless' nature refers to the fact that it has fixed parameters: 'Forever, O Lord, you word is firmly fixed in the heavens' (Ps. 119:89).[205] Indeed, insofar as the canon speaks to the Church *today*, it is not

---

203. Achtemeier, *Inspiration and Authority*, p. 157.

204. See I.1–2.

205. It is this 'fixed' conception of Scripture that makes postmodern homileticians most uncomfortable: 'should we not see the canon as closed with a comma instead of a period, listen for God "still speaking," and redact scriptural passages as needed to speak the gospel instead of simply applying that passage as "fixed"?' O. Wesley Allen, Jr., Doing Bible: When the Unfinished Task of Historical Theology Pushes the Envelope of Canonical Authority', in David Schnasa Jacobsen (ed.), *Homiletical Theology in Action: The Unfinished Theological Task of Preaching*, Volume 2: The Promise of Homiletical Theology (Eugene: Cascade, 2015), p. 139. This imagines the (common) false dichotomy between 'preaching the Bible' and 'preaching the Gospel'. A fixed canon does not negate the ongoing activity of a God who still speaks *through* that fixed canon.

rooted to a single historical moment; rather, *as* canon it stands above *all* moments that it may speak *to* them. Because the canon is free from total captivity to specific moments, this is also the very reason it is not *entirely* 'timeless', because it cannot speak in the abstract but must speak *to* each moment as the 'objective' addressing the 'subjective' realm:[206] '*Kairos* signals the need to bring universal ideas and principles to bear in historical time and situations.'[207] This 'timely' element to the use of Scripture in preaching echoes the initial intentions of the texts themselves as they spoke to their own *kairoi*, thus informing how Scripture might speak to ongoing *kairoi* today:

> God's word in the biblical traditions continually comes to specific situations, addressed to the community of faith in the midst of its historical existence. It is this very vitality in the nature of Scripture and its inspiration which demands that it be newly interpreted for new historical situations.[208]

Although the notion of 'new' interpretation for 'new situations' is a little too open to misuse (as with Bultmann's approach to the 'dynamic' nature of Scripture or Tillich's conception of 'truth'), this echoes an important need within proclamation for the Bible to speak afresh as it was initially spoken afresh.

However, although we rightly understand Scripture as historically rooted and historically pointed in the original purposes of the canonical texts, we also recognize that it is nonetheless the *canon* by and through which we speak today. This means there *is* a kind of 'timelessness' to our use of Scripture for the purposes of preaching. For Protestants, at least, it is *this* canon – and not some other collection of texts – which provides the content for preaching in each and every *kairos*, without exception. Even where different texts are emphasized differently in different epochs,[209] these are still emphases which emanate from *within* the same canon. Expository and pneumatologically prophetic preaching cannot merely speak in a *wholly* 'new' or 'kairotic' way in each and every moment; it is appropriately constrained by the yardstick of Scripture as guardian and guarantor. For preaching to be truly expository and truly kairotic, it must hold these two key tenets in its own hierarchical dialectic,[210] where Scripture is the anchor to which each pneumatological moment is tied. Otherwise *canon* no longer acts as the 'measuring rod' to prophetic proclamation, and the cultural *kairoi* may indeed hold the Church's preaching in captivity in the ways Barth both warned against and witnessed in his own time.[211]

206. See IV.4.i.b.

207. Smith, 'Time and Qualitative Time', p. 56.

208. Achtemeier, *Inspiration and Authority*, p. 128.

209. See, for example, the differing canonical and doctrinal emphases of Luther and Kierkegaard (III.5.iii).

210. See II.6.iii.

211. See Hancock, *Barth's Emergency Homiletic*, pp. 112–38.

Where Scripture and kairotic proclamation meet, the work of the Spirit brings the objective 'timelessness' of the canonical witness into contact with the subjective 'timeliness' of the *kairos*.[212] This renders Scriptural 'timelessness' as being only a *contingent* timelessness. Although its parameters remain fixed (thus, Scripture is not open to 'kairotic' alteration or correction), Scripture always intends to speak a timely word rather than a merely repetitive word.[213] Barth succinctly speaks of this conjunction of Scripture and preaching as the interaction of the past and present moment: 'The fact that takes place in God's Word...consists especially in its coming to us, in its contingent contemporaneity as revelation, Holy Scripture and Church proclamation. *Illic et tunc* becomes *hic et nunc*.'[214] It is the arrival of the given Word in the present moment that renders the *illic et tunc* Word an efficacious *hic et nunc* Word, thus consummating its distinctly pneumatological purposes as eventful encounter with the hearer, whatever that encounter entails. The pneumatological decisiveness in the moment of this event occurs in the midst of – and sometimes in spite of – the inescapable dialectical content of the Word.

6. *Conclusion: Dialectical Heraldic Proclamation*

This chapter has outlined the nuances of what it means to speak of preaching as 'pneumatologically prophetic' and 'kairotic', which are interconnected implications of preaching's fundamentally 'heraldic' nature.[215] The meaning of preaching as pneumatologically prophetic has been differentiated from culture-centric notions of the 'prophetic',[216] and it was argued that the crucial decision-making process regarding potential sermonic contradictions between divergent Scriptural emphases[217] should not undermine the aforementioned heraldic confidence in preaching.[218] This confidence does not spring from the preacher's own sense of certainty, but a contingent certainty held through spiritual discernment, and apprehended through faith.[219] Dialectically decisive preaching involves a *specific* work of the Spirit in the proclamation event which renders such decisiveness efficacious and appropriate.[220] Further to this, it has been explored what is meant

212. See the objective-subjective 'encounter' (IV.4.i.b).

213. It is in this sense that we speak of Scripture as both 'God-breathed' in respect of its authoritative inspiration and 'useful' in respect of its ongoing functionality in different 'moments' of life (2Tim. 3:16–17), even as it is to be preached both 'in season and out of season' (2Tim. 4:2).

214. Barth, *CD* I/1, pp. 205–6.

215. See III.2.

216. IV.2.i–iii.

217. IV.3.i.

218. See III.4.

219. See IV.3.

220. IV.3.ii–iii.

by speaking of the Spirit's work in preaching as 'encounter' and 'manifestation'.[221] These distinct purposes for preaching occur in the midst of the primary essence of such preaching: the pneumatological 'moment'.[222] This moment is created by the Spirit *within* the midst of time, clarifying and amplifying the prophetic message in the sermon. In emphasizing this sui generis event, the dialectical problems inherent in preacherly decisiveness are illuminated and overturned by the new *kairos*, which bears prophetic priority. However, this notion does not give preachers a license for unaccountable independence within the sermon, but this moment must be understood as inseparable from the connection between preaching and Scripture via Word and Spirit.[223] Precisely because preaching must be uniquely pneumatological *and* uniquely Scriptural in content, the preacher may remain contingently and legitimately decisive in the face of theological dialectics.

The thematic purpose of this chapter's exploration – in connecting preaching to pneumatology *alongside* Scripture – is suitably summated by Bonhoeffer, speaking of how the preacher ought to conceive of their task:

> The preacher needs to approach the sermon with the utmost certainty. The word of Scripture is certain, clear, and plain. The preacher should be assured that Christ enters the congregation through those words which he proclaims from the Scripture...The sermon should not leave the preacher despairing and perplexed, but rather it should make him joyful and certain.[224]

Such a statement does not make mention of the dialectical obfuscations which might 'perplex' the preacher but has arrived at a revitalized understanding of the possibility of 'certainty'. This is held in faith, allowing the Word to be approached *as* the clear Word from God when proclaimed in the power of the Spirit. The preacher's choice to *prefer* one dialectical emphasis over another is not *merely* a human decision. This means that, in preaching, dialectics must be conceived in a wholly unique way than in other modes of theological discourse. This pneumatologically prophetic element does not entirely remove the problem of dialectical tension for the preacher, since the human decision is still required in faith, and is one with which the preacher must continually struggle in prayer, interpretation and consideration. What the prophetic conception of preaching does, however, is give the Spirit-filled preacher a kind of license – in the pneumatological moment – to make their emphasis truly decisive, and an expectation that the dialectical possibilities (which may otherwise lead to perpetual uncertainty) are not the *final* word in preaching:

---

221. IV.4.

222. IV.5.

223. IV.3.i.

224. Dietrich Bonhoeffer, *Worldly Preaching: Lectures on Homiletics*, ed. and trans. Clyde E. Fant (Nashville and New York: Thomas Nelson, 1975), p. 130.

The prophets and apostles do not squint away from but look steadily at the one thing which it always repays us to consider. They do not engage in the uneasy movements of those who try to hear one thing with one ear and another with the other, and would try to hear a thousand things if they had a thousand ears. They listen quietly because the one thing which they hear is enough.[225]

It should be maintained that the Spirit has a *particular* message to proclaim through the preacher, not merely a dialectical negotiation to articulate (as tempting as such an enterprise will be in an age which prises the perpetual expression of hermeneutical vulnerability). This message may arrive in a variety of surprising forms but never deviates from the Word from which the message is birthed. This does not mean a sermon should never be overtly dialectical if that is in fact the appropriate prophetic message for the moment, but it means that the primacy of a *decisive* message should be upheld if proclamation can be seen as truly heraldic.

225. Barth, *CD* IV/3, p. 92.

CONCLUSION

This book has argued for the conjunction of biblical-theological dialectics and heraldic proclamation through the lens of the pneumatological moment. It has been seen that expository preaching is possible because of the clarity and unity of the biblical text, which is ultimately grounded in the preaching of the Gospel, which underpins canonicity.[1] However, despite this important starting framework, expository preaching is problematized by the apparently contradictory polarities of doctrinal truth which *remain* canonical.[2] It was then outlined that there are various ways in which theological dialectics are conceived and different modes in which they occur.[3] Significant dialectical varieties were established, culminating in at least four different ways of framing dialectical relationships.[4] With the dialectical problem for preaching still prevalent – though more carefully defined – this was applied to heraldic preaching, which first required a nuanced articulation of what heraldic preaching is[5] and a theological account of heraldic confidence.[6] The various dialectical modes previously established were then applied to one biblical dialectical emphasis in particular by way of illustration.[7] Having demonstrated different ways in which heraldic preaching encounters the same dialectical construct in different ways, the notion of 'contingent dialectical correctivity' was established as one of preaching's primary functions.[8]

Upon the aforementioned outline of dialectical heraldic proclamation, the contingent confidence required for this corrective task was given an explicitly theological grounding via the role of the Spirit.[9] This approach highlighted the nuances of the 'prophetic' aspect of preaching,[10] detailing the practical aspects of

1. I.1–3.
2. I.4.
3. II.1–5.
4. II.6.
5. III.1–3.
6. III.4.
7. III.5.i.
8. III.5.ii.
9. IV.1.
10. IV.2.

the preacher's own discernment and decisive dialectical emphasis, and the hearer's role in faithfully discerning the Word of God in the decisive proclamation.[11] To buttress the framework for dialectical decisiveness, some important pneumatological 'purposes' of preaching were then highlighted to differentiate preaching from teaching, emphasizing that the Spirit *encounters* the hearer with the Word through His *manifest* presence.[12] These 'purposes' were said to occur through the unique pneumatological 'moment',[13] in which the hearer is drawn *into* and encountered *by* the decisive prophetic message.

In essence, this book has been a systematic theological reflection upon the nature of preaching as both dialectical and heraldic. With a proper theological grounding for both, a preacher may know why they can think dialectically without losing their heraldic confidence, and speak heraldically without losing their dialectical awareness. Although the preacher cannot escape the dialectical problem of attending to Scripture's multivocity, their role as herald necessitates that 'dialectic' itself is not an equal partner within this dialectic, but is ordered beneath the priority of the (dialectically nuanced) heraldic message. This is because proclamation is not merely an exercise in biblical exegesis but a unique act in which the Spirit speaks both in and *to* the moment with the dialectically corrective Word. In spite of the ambiguous possibilities that may threaten to engulf the preacher's decisiveness, this message may be discerned, received and proclaimed by the preacher with genuine theological confidence. This allows us to reinterpret Scripture's dialectical complexity as being a vital element of proclamation, since it forms the backdrop to the preacher's reliance upon both Word and Spirit. We *need* dialectics in precisely the same way that we *need* preaching.

This book serves not only as a new theological approach to preaching, but also a new homiletical approach to theological dialectics. Much confusion and vagueness still surrounds theology's dialectical task and many laud the word 'dialectic' hastily without due consideration of its meaning or implications within different contexts. Although this thesis has not sought to attain *total* clarity in this regard, it is hoped that some of dialectic's terminological confusions have been elucidated, offering further light on what is at stake when attending to theological dialectic. For interpreting Scriptural dialectics specifically, the possibility of a variety of approaches was outlined through the various dialectical modes,[14] and the prevalence of Scriptural clarity as a vital presupposition to the dialectical task. Some hyper-critical approaches attempt to 'go for the jugular' and reject biblical unity and clarity *because* of the dialectical tensions within the canon. Here, however, a more genuinely *dialectical* approach was offered whereby it should be seen that Scripture is clear, unified *and* dialectical, but that its clarity and unity frame the discussion in which dialectical questions may be ventured.

11. IV.3.
12. IV.4.
13. IV.5.
14. II.6.

Another original aspect of this contribution is the attempt to articulate a *theology* of preaching in relation to dialectic, rather than a straightforward 'homiletic'. Thus, this book has not attempted to argue *how* one ought to preach or *how* one's communicative rhetoric may be improved, but it has attempted to better understand the heraldic nature of preaching itself and show how that understanding benefits both preacher and theologian in their inevitable dialectical interactions. By providing the pneumatological account of preaching while retaining Scripture as the anchor of prophetic preaching, this brought two homiletical approaches together which have not usually been conjoined (especially when concerning 'dialectic'). Furthermore, pointing to the issues of 'hearing', 'discernment', 'faith' and 'decisiveness' in relation to dialectic,[15] I have also sought to gesture towards some of the practical implications of this approach *without* losing the primarily conceptual theological emphasis. Where other theological approaches to preaching have occasionally been ventured, they are not normally concerned with providing such accounts of how a theology of heraldic preaching can be understood in praxis *alongside* the principal doctrinal emphasis.

Having outlined the distinctive aspects of dialectic and pneumatologically prophetic heraldic preaching, it has been established that the necessary Scriptural dialectics with which the preacher is faced do not negate the possibility of preacherly decisiveness. This is not because of the preacher's self-confidence but because of the divine imperative in the commissioned and empowered task of proclamation. In this book I have articulated a theological *reclaiming* of the preacher's confidence both in and through dialectical method. As such, it is not only a theological reflection upon preaching but a homiletical reflection upon dialectical theology. Hopefully, this will be of benefit not only to the systematic theologian who has neglected the task and the place of preaching within theology, but also to the preacher who finds themselves, as Barth did, bewildered by the 'riddles' of the very Bible they are commissioned to proclaim.[16] It is hoped that preachers may speak as confident heralds in spite of the inherent 'impossibility' of this paradoxical task, despite – and, indeed, by virtue of – the variously dialectical nature of Scriptural theology.

This book highlights much which could not be considered fully but stimulates further enquiry. Indeed, the conjunction of theological dialectics and heraldic preaching could be expounded and applied in a number of ways. The varied implications of this thesis could be seen in four distinct camps: 1. Theology, 2. Homiletics, 3. Preaching and 4. Dialectics.

For theology, further reflection is needed upon how preaching may be considered more seriously *within* the process of doctrinal frameworks rather than as an application of doctrinal reflection or as mere 'practice'. Preaching is significant not merely as an act of disseminating doctrine to a congregation, but requires its

---

15. IV.3.

16. Karl Barth, The Need and Promise of Christian Preaching', in *The Word of God and the Word of Man*, trans. Douglas Horton (London: Hodder & Stoughton, 1928), p. 100.

own doctrinal account. Indeed, preaching perhaps ought to lead the charge in one's approach to the very task of dogmatic or systematic theology. Not that all theology ought to revolve directly around preaching but that one's conception of preaching ought to have some bearing upon the conceptual relationships between other doctrinal loci. As such, preaching ought to play a significant role within one's doctrinal schema itself and not simply be a practical terminus of doctrinal outworking.

Correspondingly, for homiletics, further reflection is needed upon how theology may be considered more seriously *within* the process of sermon construction and rhetorical reflection. Many homiletical approaches – though not devoid of theology entirely – can become imbalanced by a central focus upon the linguistic, communicative, sociological or anthropological sphere. A better approach would be to work from the basis of theological reflection on *God's* role in catalysing, commissioning, maintaining and empowering the preaching task. Insights regarding communicative norms and practices, of course, certainly have due warrant, especially given much of the preaching that wrongly prevails under an obscurantist 'heraldic' rubric. However, where much homiletics seeks to improve the ways we imagine sermonic form and delivery, such endeavours might be better nourished with the theological implications placed at the forefront rather than prefaced, footnoted or 'appendixed'.

For preaching itself, this thesis aims to simultaneously 'tear down' and 'build up' the preacher's confidence in their own conceptions of both Scripture and preaching. Further practical questions could be posed, therefore, ensuring that sermons do not evoke tired repetitions of a 'heraldic style', which would remain just as form-focused as those attempts to move away from the heraldic motif. To provide a robust theological grounding for heraldic preaching – as this book purports – necessitates that preaching must not swear by any *one* particular format. So long as the herald speaks *as* a herald (with all its noteworthy implications), they may embrace all kinds of creative ways in which the heraldic Word may be proclaimed. However, if such creative forms obscure the impetus and efficacy of the pneumatological heraldic event, such instruments may become a hindrance to preaching rather than a help.

A further evocative question could be posed regarding dialectic and systematic theology. As argued, dialectic – although varied in method, type and scope – is an inherent aspect of Christian theology, even in light of the unifying Gospel message. Given this precedent, to what extent can one articulate an entirely 'coherent' body of Christian truth which remains unproblematized by theological dialectics? Where this book articulated a way out of the dialectical 'problem' through a reassessment of the nature and purpose of heraldic preaching, systematic theology does not harbour these same caveats. Instead, it seeks to communicate the interrelated Scriptural truths in light of the theological tradition and the contemporary era. The role of dialectic *within* a theological system, then, would be a fascinating area to explore further. As a catalyst to this discussion, it could be gestured that systematic theology also has a dialectically 'corrective' task even though it does not share preaching's immediately 'momentary' traits. The dialectical problem does, however, point to the limitations of a *wholly* systematic theology, without negating the importance of the wider systematic task of demonstrating the conceptual and functional coherence of Christian belief.

What can be affirmed from the work of this book is that Scripture's various dialectics remain both a help and hindrance to authentic Christian preaching. To this extent they are concomitant: dialectics beget preaching, and preaching begets dialectics. Because dialectics are multifarious, they may be employed in different ways within the preaching event. Approaching and interpreting them is not a quest to neutralize their complexifying effect but to respond to them as *revealed* within the overarching unity of Scripture. These dialectics are rendered paradoxically compatible with authoritative heraldic preaching due to the Spirit's role in guiding and empowering the expository *and* prophetic task of preacherly decisiveness, which occurs in the genuine creativity of the pneumatological moment.

BIBLIOGRAPHY

Aaron, Charles L., 'Reflections on Objectivity and Subjectivity in Moving from Text
   to Sermon' (pp. 104–20), in Dwayne J. Howell (ed.), *Preaching and the Personal*
   (Cambridge: The Lutterworth Press, 2014).

Achtemeier, Paul J., *Inspiration and Authority: Nature and Function of Christian Scripture*
   (Peabody: Hendrickson Publishers, 1999).

Adam, Karl, 'Die Theologie der Krisis', in *Hochland* 23 (1926): pp. 271–86.

Adam, Peter, *Speaking God's Words: A Practical Theology of Preaching* (Vancouver: Regent
   College Publishing, 2004).

Adorno, Theodor W., *Negative Dialectics*, trans. E. B. Ashton (London: Routlege, 1996).

Allen, Jr., O. Wesley, 'Doing Bible: When the Unfinished Task of Historical Theology
   Pushes the Envelope of Canonical Authority' (pp. 131–46), in David Schnasa Jacobsen
   (ed.), *Homiletical Theology in Action: The Unfinished Theological Task of Preaching*,
   Volume 2: The Promise of Homiletical Theology (Eugene: Cascade, 2015).

Allen, Jr., O. Wesley (ed.), *The Renewed Homiletic* (Minneapolis: Fortress Press, 2010).

Allen, Ronald J., 'Preaching as Mutual Critical Correlation through Conversation' (pp. 1–
   23), in Jana Childers (ed.), *Purposes of Preaching* (St. Louis: Chalice Press, 2004).

Allen, Ronald J., 'Preaching to Listeners: What Listeners Most Value in Sermons', in
   Homiletic 17:5 (2005): pp. 4–17.

Allen, Ronald J., 'Why Preach from Passages in the Bible?' (pp. 176–88), in Thomas
   G. Long and Edward Farley (eds.), *Preaching as a Theological Task: Word, Gospel,
   Scripture: In Honor of David Buttrick* (Louisville: Westminster John Knox Press, 1996).

Allen, Ronald J. and Jeter, Jr., Joseph R., *One Gospel, Many Ears: Preaching for Different
   Listeners in the Congregation* (St. Louis: Chalice Press, 2002).

Allen, Ronald J. and McClure, John S., et al., *Listening to the Listeners: Homiletical Case
   Studies* (St. Louis: Chalice Press, 2004).

Allen, Ronald J., et al., *Believing in Preaching: What Listeners Hear in Sermons* (St. Louis:
   Chalice Press, 2005).

Allen, Ronald J., et al., *Theology for Preaching: Authority, Truth, and Knowledge of God in a
   Postmodern Ethos* (Nashville: Abingdon, 1997).

Anderson, James, *Paradox in Christian Theology: An Analysis of Its Presence, Character,
   and Epistemic Status* (London: Paternoster Press, 2007).

Aquinas, Thomas, *De Potentia Dei*, trans. Fathers of the English Dominican Province
   (Westminster, Maryland: The Newman Press, 1952).

Aquinas, Thomas, *Summa Theologica* 2:2, trans. Fathers of the English Dominican
   Province (New York: Benziger Bros., 1947).

Aristotle, *Metaphysics*, trans. John H. M'Mahon (London: Henry G. Bohn, 1857).

Armour-Garb, Bradley, 'Diagnosing Dialetheism' (pp. 113–125), in Graham Priest, et al.
   (eds.), *The Law of Non-Contradiction: New Philosophical Essays* (Oxford: Clarendon
   Press, 2004).

Augustine, *On Christian Doctrine*, trans. J. F. Shaw (New York: Christian Literature
   Publishing Co., 1886).

Barker, Paul A., et al. (eds.), *Serving God's Words: Windows on Preaching and Ministry* (Nottingham: IVP, 2001).

Barrett, Lee C., 'Karl Barth: The Dialectic of Attraction and Repulsion' (pp. 1–41), in Jon Stewart (ed.), *Kierkegaard's Influence on Theology, Tome I: German Protestant Theology* (Farnham: Ashgate, 2012).

Barrett, Lee C. and Stewart, Jon (eds.), *Kierkegaard and the Bible, Tome I: The Old Testament* (Farnham: Ashgate, 2010).

Barrett, Lee C. and Stewart, Jon (eds.), *Kierkegaard and the Bible, Tome II: The New Testament* (Farnham: Ashgate, 2010).

Barth, Karl, 'A ThankYou and a Bow – Kierkegaard's Reveille' (pp. 95–101), in Martin Rumscheidt (ed.), *Fragments Grave and Gay*, trans. Eric Mosbacher (London: Fontana, 1971).

Barth, Karl, 'Barth to Thurneysen, 11 November 1918', in *Revolutionary Theology in the Making: Barth-Thurneysen Correspondence, 1914–1925*, trans. James D. Smart (Richmond: John Knox Press, 1964).

Barth, Karl, 'The Strange New World Within the Bible' (pp. 28–50), 'Biblical Questions, Insights, and Vistas' (pp. 51–96), 'The Need and Promise of Christian Preaching' (pp. 97–135), 'The Word of God and the Task of Ministry' (pp. 183–217), and 'The Christian's Place in Society' (pp. 272–327), in *The Word of God and the Word of Man*, trans. Douglas Horton (London: Hodder & Stoughton, 1928).

Barth, Karl, *Call for God: New Sermons from Basel Prison*, trans. A. T. Mackay (London: SCM Press, 1967).

Barth, Karl, *Church Dogmatics*, 4 Volumes in 13 Parts, ed. and trans. G. W. Bromiley and T. F. Torrance (Edinburgh: T & T Clark, 1956–75).

Barth, Karl, *Homiletics*, trans. Geoffrey W. Bromiley and Donald E. Daniels (Westminster: John Knox Press, 1991).

Barth, Karl, *On Religion: The Revelation of God as the Sublimation of Religion*, trans. Garrett Green (London: T & T Clark, 2007).

Barth, Karl, *Protestant Theology in the Nineteenth Century: Its Background and History*, trans. B. Cozens and J. Bowden (London: SCM Press, 1972).

Barth, Karl, *The Epistle to the Romans*, trans. E. C. Hoskyns (London: Oxford University Press, 1933).

Barth, Karl, *The Preaching of the Gospel*, trans. B. E. Hooke (Philadelphia: Westminster Press, 1963).

Barth, Karl, *The Word of God and Theology*, trans. Amy Marga (London: T & T Clark, 2011).

Barth, Karl and Brunner, Emil, *Natural Theology*, trans. Peter Fraenckel (London: Centenary Press, 1946).

Barth, Karl and Thurneysen, Eduard, 'The Great "But"' (pp. 13–23), 'The Eternal Light' (pp. 57–66), and 'The Freedom of the Word of God' (pp. 216–29), in *Come Holy Spirit*, trans. George W. Richards, et al. (Edinburgh: T & T Clark, 1934).

Barth, Karl and Thurneysen, Eduard, *Revolutionary Theology in the Making: Barth-Thurneysen Correspondence, 1914–1925*, trans. James D. Smart (Richmond: John Knox Press, 1964).

Barton, John, *The Spirit and the Letter: Studies in the Biblical Canon* (London: SPCK, 1997).

Bauckham, Richard, 'Reading Scripture as a Coherent Story' (pp. 38–53), in Ellen F. Davis and Richard B. Hays (eds.), *The Art of Reading Scripture* (Michigan: Eerdmans, 2003).

Baugus, Bruce P., 'Paradox and Mystery in Theology', in *The Heythrop Journal* 29:2 (2013): pp. 238–51.

Baumlin, James S. and Sipiora, Phillip (eds.), *Rhetoric and Kairos: Essays in History, Theory, and Praxis* (Albany: SUNY Press, 2002).

Baur, F. C., *Paul, the Apostle of Jesus Christ*, 2 Volumes, trans. Allen Menzies and Eduard Zeller (London: Williams and Norgate, 1873; 1875).

Bausch, William J., *Storytelling the Word: Homilies and How to Write Them* (Mystic: Twenty-Third Publications, 1984).

Bayer, Oswald, 'Preaching the Word' (pp. 196–216), in Virgil Thompson (ed.), *Justification Is for Preaching* (Eugene: Pickwick Publications, 2012).

Bayley, J., *Scripture Paradoxes: Their True Explanation* (London: Charles P. Alvey, 1868).

Beintker, Michael, *Die Dialektik in 'Der Dialektische Theologie' Karl Barths* (Munich: Kaiser, 1987).

Beiser, Frederick C. (ed.), *The Cambridge Companion to Hegel* (Cambridge: Cambridge University Press, 1993).

Bennett, Jonathan, *Kant's Dialectic* (Cambridge: Cambridge University Press).

Bennett Brown, Cynthia, *Believing Thinking, Bounded Theology: The Theological Methodology of Emil Brunner* (Cambridge: James Clarke & Co., 2015).

Berkouwer, G. C., *Holy Scripture* (Grand Rapids: Eerdmans, 1975).

Berkouwer, G. C., *The Triumph of Grace in the Theology of Karl Barth* (London: The Paternoster Press, 1956).

Best, Ernest, *From Text to Sermon: Responsible Use of the New Testament in Preaching* (Atlanta: John Knox Press, 1978).

Best, Isabel (ed.), *The Collected Sermons of Dietrich Bonhoeffer* (Minneapolis: Fortress Press, 2013).

Bierce, Ambrose, *The Devil's Dictionary* (London: Penguin, 1995).

Bloesch, Donald G., *A Theology of Word and Spirit: Authority and Method in Theology* (Illinois: IVP, 1992).

Bloesch, Donald G., *Holy Scripture: Revelation, Inspiration and Interpretation* (Carlisle: The Paternoster Press, 1994).

Bonhoeffer, Dietrich, 'Ambassadors for Christ' (pp. 87–93) and 'Turning Back' (pp. 95–100), in Isabel Best (ed.), *The Collected Sermons of Dietrich Bonhoeffer* (Minneapolis: Fortress Press, 2013).

Bonhoeffer, Dietrich, *Worldly Preaching: Lectures on Homiletics*, ed. and trans. Clyde E. Fant (New York: Crossroad, 1991).

Bos, Rein, 'Surely There Is a God Who Judges on Earth: Divine Retribution in Homiletical Theology and the Practice of Preaching' (pp. 147–71), in David Schnasa Jacobsen (ed.), *Homiletical Theology in Action: The Unfinished Theological Task of Preaching*, Volume 2: The Promise of Homiletical Theology (Eugene: Cascade, 2015).

Brazier, Paul, 'Barth's First Commentary on Romans (1919): An Exercise in Apophatic Theology?' in *International Journal of Systematic Theology* 6:4 (2004): pp. 387–403.

Brazier, P. H., *Dostoevsky: A Theological Engagement* (Eugene: Pickwick, 2016).

Brian, Rustin E., *Covering Up Luther: How Barth's Christology Challenged the Deus Absconditus That Haunts Modernity* (Eugene: Cascade, 2013).

Bridgeman, Valerie, ' "It Ain't Necessarily So": Resistance Preaching and Womanist Thought' (pp. 71–79), in Dwayne J. Howell (ed.), *Preaching and the Personal* (Cambridge: The Lutterworth Press, 2014).

Brown, Colin, *Karl Barth and the Christian Message* (London: Tyndale, 1967).

Brown, James, *Kierkegaard, Heidegger, Buber and Barth: A Study of Subjectivity and Objectivity in Existentialist Thought* (New York: Collier, 1967).

Browne, R. E. C., *The Ministry of the Word* (London: SCM Press, 1976).

Bruce, F. F., *The Canon of Scripture* (Downers Grove: IVP, 1988).

Brueggemann, Walter, *The Practice of Prophetic Imagination: Preaching an Emancipating Word* (Philadelphia: Fortress Press, 2012).

Brueggemann, Walter, *The Word Militant: Preaching a Decentring Word* (Minneapolis: Fortress Press, 2007).

Brunner, Emil, *Truth as Encounter*, trans. David Cairns (London: SCM Press, 1964).

Buber, Martin, *I and Thou*, trans. Walter Kaufmann (Edinburgh: T & T Clark, 1970).

Bullock, Jeffrey F., *Preaching with a Cupped Ear: Hans-Georg Gadamer's Philosophical Hermeneutics as Postmodern Wor[l]d* (New York: Peter Lang, 1999).

Bultmann, Rudolf, *Jesus Christ and Mythology* (New York: Scribner, 1958).

Bultmann, Rudolf, *Theology of the New Testament*, Volume 2, trans. Kendrick Grobel (London: SCM, 1955).

Burbidge, John, 'Is Hegel a Christian?' (pp. 93–108), in David Kolb (ed.), *New Perspectives on Hegel's Philosophy of Religion* (New York: State University of New York Press, 1992).

Burkett, Chris, *Homiletics as Mnemonic Practice: Collective Memory and Contemporary Christian Preaching* (unpublished doctoral dissertation, University of Liverpool, 2009).

Busch, Eberhard, *Karl Barth: His Life from Letters and Autobiographical Texts*, trans. John Bowden (London: SCM Press, 1976).

Buttrick, David, *A Captive Voice: The Liberation of Preaching* (Louisville: Westminster John Knox Press, 1994).

Buttrick, David, *Homiletic: Moves and Structures* (Philadelphia: Fortress Press, 1987).

Cain, David, 'A Star in the Cross: Getting the Dialectic Right' (pp. 315–34), in Robert L. Perkins (ed.), *International Kierkegaard Commentary*, Volume 21: *For Self-Examination and Judge for Yourself!* (Macon: Mercer University Press, 2002).

Calvin, John, *Commentaries*, trans. Joseph Haroutunian (Philadelphia: Westminster, 1958).

Calvin, John, *Institutes of the Christian Religion*, Volume 1, ed. John T. McNeill (Louisville: Westminster John Knox Press, 1960).

Calvin, John, *Sermons on the Epistle to the Ephesians*, trans. Arthur Golding (Edinburgh: Banner of Truth Trust, 1973).

Campbell Morgan, G., *Preaching* (Edinburgh: Marshall, Morgan & Scott, Ltd., 1937).

Carson, D. A., *Collected Writings on Scripture* (Nottingham: IVP, 2010).

Carson, D. A., 'Unity and Diversity in the New Testament: The Possibility of Systematic Theology' (pp. 65–95), in D. A. Carson and John D. Woodbridge (eds.), *Scripture and Truth* (Grand Rapids: Baker Books, 1995).

Carson, D. A. and Packer, J. I., et al. (eds.), *When God's Voice Is Heard: The Power of Preaching* (Nottingham: IVP, 2003).

Carson, D. A. and Woodbridge, John D. (eds.), *Scripture and Truth* (Grand Rapids: Baker Books, 1995).

Chalamet, Christophe, *Dialectical Theologians: Wilhelm Herrmann, Karl Barth and Rudolf Bultmann* (Zürich: TVZ, 2005).

Chan, Francis, 'The Basis of Prophetic Preaching' (pp. 11–18), in Craig Brian Larsen (ed.), *Prophetic Preaching* (Peabody: Hendrickson, 2012).

Chesterton, G. K., 'Bacon and Beastliness', in *The Speaker* (8 Feb 1902).

Chesterton, G. K., *Orthodoxy* (San Francisco: Ignatius, 1995).

Chesterton, G. K., *St. Thomas Aquinas* (New York: Image Books, 1956).

Chesterton, G. K., *The Everlasting Man* (Radford: Wilder Publications, 2008).

Chesterton, G. K., *The Man Who Was Thursday: A Nightmare* (London: Atlantic Books, 2008).

Chesterton, G. K., *The Paradoxes of Mr. Pond* (Kelly Bray: House of Stratus, 2008).

Childers, Jana, *Purposes of Preaching* (St. Louis: Chalice, 2004).

Childs, Brevard S., *Biblical Theology of the Old and New Testaments: Theological Reflection on the Christian Bible* (Minneapolis: Fortress Press, 1993).

Childs, Brevard S., *The New Testament as Canon: An Introduction* (Philadelphia: Fortress Press, 1984).

Clayton, John, 'Tillich, Troeltsch and the Dialectical Theology', in *Modern Theology* 4:4 (1988): pp. 323–44.

Cochrane, Arthur C. (ed.), *Reformed Confessions of the 16th Century* (London: SCM, 1966).

Coe, David L., 'Kierkegaard's Forking for Extracts from Extracts of Luther's Sermons: Reviewing Kierkegaard's Laud and Lance of Luther', in *Kierkegaard Studies Yearbook* 1 (2011): pp. 3–18.

Congar, Yves, *The Word and the Spirit*, trans. David Smith (London: Harper & Row, 1986).

Congdon, David W., 'Dialectical Theology as Theology of Mission: Investigating the Origins of Karl Barth's Break with Liberalism', in *International Journal of Systematic Theology* 16:4 (Oct 2014): pp. 390–413.

Craddock, Fred B., *As One without Authority* (St. Louis: Chalice Press, 2001).

Craddock, Fred B., *Overhearing the Gospel* (Sheffield: Cliff College Publishing, 1995).

Craddock, Fred B., *Preaching* (Nashville: Abingdon, 1985).

Cunha, Emma Salgård, 'Whitefield and Literary Affect' (pp. 190–206), in Geordan Hammond and David Ceri Jones (eds.), *George Whitefield: Life, Context, and Legacy* (Oxford: Oxford University Press, 2016).

Dalrymple, Timothy, 'Abraham: Framing Fear and Trembling' (pp. 43–88), in Lee C. Barrett and Jon Stewart (eds.), *Kierkegaard and the Bible, Tome I: The Old Testament* (Farnham: Ashgate, 2010).

Davis, Creston, 'Introduction', in John Milbank and Slavoj Žižek, *The Monstrosity of Christ: Paradox or Dialectic?* (London: The MIT Press, 2009).

Davis, Ellen F., 'Critical Traditioning: Seeking an Inner Biblical Hermeneutic' (pp. 163–180), in Ellen F. Davis and Richard B. Hays (eds.), *The Art of Reading Scripture* (Michigan: Eerdmans, 2003).

Davis, Ellen F. and Hays, Richard B. (eds.), *The Art of Reading Scripture* (Michigan: Eerdmans, 2003).

De Lubac, Henri, *Paradoxes of Faith*, trans. P. Simon, S. Kreilkamp, and E. Beaumont (San Francisco: Ignatius Press, 1987).

DeVries, Dawn, 'Calvin's preaching' (pp. 106–24), in Donald K. McKim (ed.), *The Cambridge Companion to John Calvin* (Cambridge: Cambridge University Press, 2004).

Diem, Hermann, *Kierkegaard's Dialectic of Existence* (Westport: Greenwood Press, 1978).

Dillenberger, John, *John Calvin: Selections from His Writings* (Atlanta: Scholars Press, 1975).

Dodd, C. H., *The Apostolic Preaching and Its Developments* (London: Hodder & Stoughton, 1936).

Dorrien, Gary, *The Barthian Revolt in Modern Theology: Theology without Weapons* (Louisville: Westminster John Knox Press, 2000).

Downey, James, *The Eighteenth Century Pulpit: A Study of the Sermons of Butler, Berkeley, Secker, Sterne, Whitefield and Wesley* (Oxford: Clarendon Press, 1969).

Dulles, Avery, 'Protestant Preaching and the Prophetic Mission', in *Theological Studies* 21:4 (1960): pp. 544–80.

Dunn, James D. G., *Unity and Diversity in the New Testament: An Inquiry into the Character of Earliest Christianity* (London: SCM, 1977).

Dunning, Stephen N., *Kierkegaard's Dialectic of Inwardness* (Princeton: Princeton University Press, 1985).

Dunn-Wilson, David, *A Mirror for the Church: Preaching in the First Five Centuries* (Grand Rapids: Eerdmans, 2005).

Eaton, Michael, *The Gift of Prophetic Preaching* (Chichester: New Wine Press, 2008)

Ebeling, Gerhard, 'The Word of God and Hermeneutics' (pp. 305–32), in *Word and Faith*, trans. James W. Leitch (London: SCM Press, 1963).

Ebeling, Gerhard, *Theology and Proclamation: A Discussion with Rudolf Bultmann*, trans. John Riches (London: Collins, 1966).

Eckhart, Meister, *Sermons & Treatises*, Volume I, trans. M. O'Connell Walshe (Dorset: Element, 1991).

Edwards, Aaron, 'Life in Kierkegaard's Imaginary Rural Parish: Preaching, Correctivity, and the Gospel', in *Toronto Journal of Theology* 30:2 (Fall 2014): pp. 235–46.

Edwards, Aaron, 'Preacher as Balanced Extremist: Biblical Dialectics and Sermonic Certainty', in *The Expository Times* 126:9 (June 2015): pp. 425–35.

Edwards, Aaron, 'The Paradox of Dialectic: Clarifying the Use and Scope of Dialectics in Theology', in *International Journal of Philosophy and Theology* 77:4–5 (November 2016): pp. 273–306.

Edwards, Aaron, 'The Strange New World of Confidence: Barth's Dialectical Exhortation to Fearful Preachers', in *Scottish Bulletin of Evangelical Theology* 32:2 (Autumn 2014): pp. 195–206

Edwards, Aaron, 'Thus Saith the Word: The Theological Relationship between Biblical Exposition and Prophetic Utterance in Preaching', in *The Expository Times* 125:11 (August 2014): pp. 521–30.

Edwards, Richard, *Scriptural Perspicuity in the Early English Reformation in Historical Theology* (New York: Peter Lang, 2008).

Ellul, Jacques, *Presence in the Modern World*, trans. Lisa Richmond (Eugene: Cascade, 2016).

Emmanuel, Steven M., et al. (eds.), *Kierkegaard's Concepts: Tome II: Classicism to Enthusiasm* (Farnham: Ashgate, 2014).

Evans, C. Stephen, 'Canonicity, Apostolicity, and Biblical Authority: Some Kierkegaardian Reflections' (pp. 146–66), in Craig G. Bartholomew and Anthony C. Thiselton (eds.), *Canon and Biblical Interpretation* (Milton Keynes: Paternoster Press, 2006).

Evans, C. Stephen, *Kierkegaard's 'Fragments' and 'Postscript': The Religious Philosophy of Johannes Climacus* (Atlantic Highlands: Humanities Press, 1983).

Fagerberg, David W., *The Size of Chesterton's Catholicism* (Notre Dame: University of Notre Dame Press, 1998).

Farley, Edward F., 'Preaching the Bible and Preaching the Gospel', in *Theology Today* 51:1 (1994): pp. 90–103.

Farley, Edward F., 'Toward a New Paradigm for Preaching' (pp. 165–75), in Thomas G. Long and Edward Farley (eds.), *Preaching as a Theological Task: Word, Gospel, Scripture: In Honor of David Buttrick* (Louisville: Westminster John Knox Press, 1996).

Ferguson, Sinclair B., 'Exegesis' (pp. 192–211), in Samuel T. Logan, Jr. (ed.), *The Preacher and Preaching: Reviving the Art* (Phillipsburg: Presbyterian and Reformed Publishing Company, 2011).

Forbes, James, *The Holy Spirit and Preaching* (Nashville: Abingdon Press, 1989).

Ford, D. W., Cleverley, *Ministry of the Word* (Grand Rapids: Eerdmans, 1979).

Ford, James Thomas, 'Preaching in the Reformed Tradition', in Larissa Taylor (ed.), *Preachers and People in the Reformations and Early Modern Period* (Leiden: Brill, 2001), pp. 65–88.

Forde, Gerhard O., *The Preached God: Proclamation in Word and Sacrament* (Grand Rapids: Eerdmans, 2007).

Forde, Gerhard O., *Theology Is for Proclamation* (Minneapolis: Augsburg Press, 1990).

Forster, Michael, 'Hegel's Dialectical Method' (pp. 130–70), in Frederick C. Beiser (ed.), *The Cambridge Companion to Hegel* (Cambridge: Cambridge University Press, 1993).

Forsyth, P. T., *Positive Preaching and the Modern Mind* (New York: Armstrong, 1907).

Forsyth, P. T., *The Person and Place of Jesus Christ* (London: Independent Press, 1955).

Friese, Heidrun (ed.), *Moment: Time and Rupture in Modern Thought* (Liverpool: Liverpool University Press, 2001).

Friese, Heidrun, 'Augen-Blicke' (pp. 73–90), in Heidrun Friese (ed.), *Moment: Time and Rupture in Modern Thought* (Liverpool: Liverpool University Press, 2001).

Fuller, Daniel P., 'Biblical Theology and the Analogy of Faith' (pp. 195–213), in Robert A. Guelich (ed.), *Unity and Diversity in New Testament Theology: Essays in Honor of George E. Ladd* (Grand Rapids: Eerdmans, 1978).

Gamble, Harry H., *The New Testament Canon: Its Making and Meaning* (Philadelphia: Fortress Press, 1985).

Gibson, Edgar C. S. (ed.), *The Thirty-Nine Articles of the Church of England*, Volume 2 (London: Meuthen, 1897).

Gilland, David Andrew, *Law and Gospel in Emil Brunner's Earlier Dialectical Theology* (London: T&T Clark, 2015).

Gilmore, Alec, *Preaching as Theatre* (London: SCM Press, 1992).

Goldingay, John, 'The Spirituality of Preaching', in *The Expository Times* 98 (1987): pp. 197–203.

Graves, Mike and Schlafer, David J. (eds.), *What's the Shape of Narrative Preaching?* (Atlanta: Chalice Press, 2008).

Green, Garrett, 'Translator's Preface', in Karl Barth, *On Religion: The Revelation of God as the Sublimation of Religion*, trans. Garrett Green (London: T & T Clark, 2007).

Greenshaw, David M., 'The Formation of Consciousness' (pp. 1–17), in Thomas G. Long and Edward Farley (eds.), *Preaching as a Theological Task: Word, Gospel, Scripture: In Honor of David Buttrick* (Louisville: Westminster John Knox Press, 1996).

Gregory the Great, 'Homily 30' (pp. 236–48), in *Forty Gospel Homilies*, trans. David Hurst (Piscataway: Gorgias Press, 2009).

Greidanus, Sidney, *The Modern Preacher and the Ancient Text* (Grand Rapids: Eerdmans, 1988).

Griffiths, Jonathan I., *Preaching in the New Testament: An Exegetical and Biblical-Theological Study* (Downers Grove: Apollos, 2017).

Guelich, Robert A. (ed.), *Unity and Diversity in New Testament Theology: Essays in Honor of George E. Ladd* (Grand Rapids: Eerdmans, 1978).

Gunton, Colin E., *Theology Through Preaching: Sermons for Brentwood* (Edinburgh: T & T Clark, 2001).

Haecker, Theodor, *Søren Kierkegaard*, trans. Alexander Dru (London: Oxford University Press, 1937).

Hammond, Geordan and Ceri Jones, David (eds.), *George Whitefield: Life, Context, and Legacy* (Oxford: Oxford University Press, 2016).

Hancock, Angela Dienhart, *Karl Barth's Emergency Homiletic, 1932–1933: A Summons to Prophetic Witness at the Dawn of the Third Reich* (Grand Rapids: Eerdmans, 2013).

Hanson, Paul D., *The Diversity of Scripture: A Theological Interpretation* (Fortress Press: Philadelphia, 1982).

Hart, Trevor, *Regarding Karl Barth: Toward a Reading of His Theology* (Downers Grove: IVP, 1999).

Hartnack, Justus, *An Introduction to Hegel's Logic*, trans. Lars Aagaard-Mogenson (Indianapolis and Cambridge: Hacket Publishing Company, 1998).

Hartshorn, Leo, 'Evaluating Preaching as a Communal and Dialogical Practice', in *Homiletic* 35:2 (2010): pp. 13–24.

Haslam, Greg (ed.), *Preach the Word: The Call and Challenge of Preaching Today* (Lancaster: Sovereign World, 2006).

Hauerwas, Stanley, *The Cross-Shattered Church: Reclaiming the Theological Heart of Preaching* (Grand Rapids: Brazos Press, 2009).

Hauerwas, Stanley and Willimon, William H., *Preaching to Strangers: Evangelism in Today's World* (Louisville: WJK Press, 1992).

Hayes, James, 'Listen to My Sighing' (pp. 55–68), in Gregory Heille (ed.), *Theology of Preaching: Essays on Vision and Mission in the Pulpit* (London: Melisende, 2001).

Hedahl, Susan Karen, 'All the King's Men: Constructing Homiletical Meaning' (pp. 82–90), in Thomas G. Long and Edward Farley (eds.), *Preaching as a Theological Task: Word, Gospel, Scripture: In Honor of David Buttrick* (Louisville: Westminster John Knox Press, 1996).

Hegel, G. W. F., *Science of Logic*, trans. A. V. Miller (Atlantic Highlands: Humanities Press International, 1991).

Heide, Gale, *Timeless Truth in the Hands of History: A Short History of System in Theology* (Cambridge: James Clarke & Co., 2012).

Heille, Gregory (ed.), *Theology of Preaching: Essays on Vision and Mission in the Pulpit* (London: Melisende, 2001).

Hellerstein, Nathaniel S., *Diamond: A Paradox Logic* (River Edge: World Scientific Publishing, 2010).

Heppe, Heinrich, *Reformed Dogmatics*, trans. G. T. Thomson (Eugene: Wipf and Stock, 2007).

Higton, Mike and McDowell, John C. (eds.), *Conversing with Barth* (Farnham: Ashgate, 2004).

Hill, David, *New Testament Prophecy* (London: Marshall, Morgan, and Scott, 1979).

Hobbs, Thomas S., *Dialectic and Narrative in Aquinas: An Interpretation of the* Summa contra gentiles (Notre Dame: University of Notre Dame Press, 1995).

Hogan, Lucy Lind and Reid, Robert, *Connecting with the Congregation: Rhetoric and the Art of Preaching* (Nashville: Abingdon Press, 1999).

Hooke, Ruthanna B., 'The Personal and Its others in the Performance of Preaching' (pp. 19–43.), in Dwayne J. Howell (ed.), *Preaching and the Personal* (Cambridge: The Lutterworth Press, 2014).

Howell, Dwayne J. (ed.), *Preaching and the Personal* (Cambridge: The Lutterworth Press, 2014).

Hunsinger, George, *How to Read Karl Barth: The Shape of His Theology* (Oxford: Oxford University Press, 1991).

Immink, F. Gerrit, 'Homiletics: The Current Debate', in *International Journal of Practical Theology* 8:1 (2004): pp. 89–121.

Jacobsen, David Schnasa, 'Homiletical Exegesis and Theologies of Revelation: Biblical Preaching from Text to Sermon in an Age of Methodological Pluralism', in *Homiletic* 36:1 (2011): pp. 14–25.

Jacobsen, David Schnasa (ed.), *Homiletical Theology in Action: The Unfinished Theological Task of Preaching*, Volume 2: The Promise of Homiletical Theology (Eugene: Cascade, 2015).

Jacobsen, David Schnasa, *Kairos Preaching: Speaking Gospel to the Situation* (Minneapolis: Fortress Press, 2009).

Jacobsen, David Schnasa, '*Schola Prophetarum*: Prophetic Preaching Toward a Public, Prophetic Church', in *Homiletic* 34:1 (2009): pp. 12–21.Janz, Denis R., 'Syllogism or Paradox: Aquinas and Luther on Theological Method', in *Theological Studies* 59 (1998): pp. 3–21.

Jensen, Richard A., *Envisioning the Word: The Use of Visual Images in Preaching* (Minneapolis: Fortress Press, 2005).

Jensen, Richard A., *Telling the Story: Variety and Imagination in Preaching* (Minneapolis: Augsburg Press, 1980)

Johnson, Keith L., 'A Reappraisal of Karl Barth's Theological Development and His Dialogue with Catholicism', in *International Journal of Systematic Theology* 14:1 (January 2012): pp. 3–25.

Johnston, Graham, *Preaching to a Postmodern World: A Guide to Reaching Twenty-First Century Listeners* (Grand Rapids: Baker Books, 2001).

Jüngel, Eberhard, *God's Being Is in Becoming: The Trinitarian Being of God in the Theology of Karl Barth*, trans. John Webster (Edinburgh: T & T Clark, 2004).

Kant, Immanuel, *Critique of Pure Reason*, trans. Norman Kemp Smith (New York: St. Martin's, 1929).

Kay, James F., *Preaching and Theology* (St. Louis: Chalice Press, 2007).

Kay, William K., 'The Ecclesial Dimension of Preaching' (pp. 200–15), in Lee Roy Martin (ed.), *Toward a Pentecostal Theology of Preaching* (Cleveland: CPT Press, 2015).

Kelsey, David, *Eccentric Existence: A Theological Anthropology*, Volume 1 (Louisville: Westminster John Knox Press, 2009).

Kelsey, David, *Uses of Scripture in Recent Theology* (London: SCM, 1975).

Kennedy, Gerald, 'Using Preaching as Teaching', in *Religious Education* 44:4 (1949): pp. 229–32.

Kenner, Hugh, *Paradox in Chesterton* (London: Sheed & Ward, 1947).

Kierkegaard, Søren, *Concluding Unscientific Postscript to Philosophical Fragments*, Volume 1, trans. Howard V. Hong and Edna H. Hong (Princeton: Princeton University Press, 1992).

Kierkegaard, Søren, *Either/Or*, Part I, trans. Howard V. Hong and Edna H. Hong (Princeton: Princeton University Press, 1987).

Kierkegaard, Søren, *Fear and Trembling*, trans. Alastair Hannay (London: Penguin, 2005).

Kierkegaard, Søren, *For Self-Examination* and *Judge For Yourself!*, trans. Howard V. Hong and Edna H. Hong (Princeton: Princeton University Press).

Kierkegaard, Søren, *Philosophical Fragments*, trans. David Swenson (Princeton: Princeton University Press, 1967).

Kierkegaard, Søren, *Practice in Christianity*, trans. Howard V. Hong and Edna H. Hong (Princeton: Princeton University Press, 1992).

Kierkegaard, Søren, *Søren Kierkegaard's Journals and Papers*, Volumes 1–6, ed. and trans. Howard V. Hong and Edna H. Hong (Bloomington and London: Indiana University Press, 1967–78).

Kierkegaard, Søren, *The Concept of Anxiety*, trans. Reidar Thomte (Princeton: Princeton University Press, 1980).

Kierkegaard, Søren, *The Point of View for my Work as an Author*, trans. Walter Lowrie (Oxford: Oxford University Press, 1939).

Kierkegaard, Søren, *The Present Age*, trans. Alexander Dru (London: The Fontana Library, 1969).

Kierkegaard, Søren, *The Sickness unto Death*, trans. Howard V. Hong and Edna H. Hong (Princeton: Princeton University Press, 1980).

Kolb, David (ed.), *New Perspectives on Hegel's Philosophy of Religion* (New York: State University of New York Press, 1992).

Kolb, Robert, *Martin Luther and the Enduring Word of God: The Wittenberg School and Its Scripture-Centred Proclamation* (Grand Rapids: Baker, 2016).

Larsen, Craig Brian (ed.), *Prophetic Preaching* (Peabody: Hendrickson, 2012).

Lauer, Quentin, *G. K. Chesterton: Philosopher without Portfolio* (New York: Fordham University Press, 2004).

Law, David R., *Kierkegaard as Negative Theologian* (Oxford: Oxford University Press, 1993).

Lischer, Richard, *A Theology of Preaching: The Dynamics of the Gospel* (Eugene: Wipf & Stock, 2001).

Lloyd-Jones, D. Martyn, *Preaching and Preachers* (Grand Rapids: Zondervan, 2011).

Logan Jr., Samuel T. (ed.), *The Preacher and Preaching: Reviving the Art* (Phillipsburg: Presbyterian and Reformed Publishing Company, 2011).

Lohse, Bernhard, *Martin Luther's Theology: Its Historical and Systematic Development*, trans. Roy A. Harrisville (Edinburgh: T & T Clark, 1999).

Long, Thomas G., 'And How Shall They Hear', in Thomas G. Long and Gail R. O'Day (eds.), *Listening to the Word: Essays in Honor of Fred B. Craddock* (Louisville: Westminster John Knox Press, 1991).

Long, Thomas G., 'Out of the Loop: The Changing Practice of Preaching' (pp. 115–30), in Mike Graves and David J. Schlafer (eds.), *What's the Shape of Narrative Preaching?* (Atlanta: Chalice Press, 2008).

Long, Thomas G., *Preaching and the Literary Forms of the Bible* (Philadelphia: Fortress Press, 1989).

Long, Thomas G., *The Witness of Preaching* (Westminster: John Knox Press, 1989).

Long, Thomas G. and Farley, Edward (eds.), *Preaching as a Theological Task: Word, Gospel, Scripture: In Honor of David Buttrick* (Louisville: Westminster John Knox Press, 1996).

Long, Thomas G. and O'Day, Gail R. (eds.), *Listening to the Word: Essays in Honor of Fred B. Craddock* (Louisville: Westminster John Knox Press, 1991).

Lowry, Eugene L., *The Homiletical Plot: The Sermon as Narrative Art Form* (Atlanta: John Knox Press, 1980).

Lowry, Eugene L., *The Sermon: Dancing the Edge of Mystery* (Nashville: Abingdon Press, 1997).

Luther, Martin, *The Bondage of the Will*, trans. J. I. Packer and O. R. Johnston (Grand Rapids: Fleming H. Revell, 1997).

Luther, Martin, *Luther's Works*, in 55 Volumes, ed. Jaroslav J. Pelikan and Helmut T. Lehmann (Philadelphia and St. Louis: Concordia Publishing House, 1955–1986).

Luther, Martin, *The Sermons of Martin Luther*, trans. John Nicholas Lenker (Grand Rapids: Baker Book House, 1983).

Luther, Martin, *Table Talk*, trans. William Hazlitt (Grand Rapids: Christian Ethereal Classics Library, 2004).

Luther, Martin, 'To George Spalatin. January 18, 1518' (pp. 111–13), in Theodore G. Tappert (ed.), *Luther: Letters of Spiritual Counsel* (The Library of Christian Classics, Volume XVIII) (London: SCM, 1953).

Macquarrie, John, *Principles of Christian Theology* (London: SCM, 2003).

Maddock, Ian J., *Men of One Book: A Comparison of Two Methodist Preachers, John Wesley and George Whitefield* (Cambridge: The Lutterworth Press, 2012).

Manetsch, Scott M., *Calvin's Company of Pastors: Pastoral Care and the Emerging Reformed Church, 1536-1609* (Oxford: Oxford University Press, 2013).

Marramao, Giacomo, *Kairós: Towards an Ontology of Due Time* (Aurora: The Davies Group Publishers, 2006).

Marshall, I. Howard, et al. (eds.), *New Bible Dictionary* (Nottingham: IVP, 2007).

Martin, Lee Roy, 'Fire in the Bones: Pentecostal Prophetic Preaching' (pp. 34–63), in Lee Roy Martin (ed.), *Toward a Pentecostal Theology of Preaching* (Cleveland: CPT Press, 2015).

Martin, Lee Roy (ed.), *Toward a Pentecostal Theology of Preaching* (Cleveland: CPT Press, 2015).

McClure, John S., *Other-wise Preaching: A Postmodern Ethic for Homiletics* (St. Louis: Chalice Press, 2001).

McClure, John S., *The Roundtable Pulpit: Where Leadership and Preaching Meet* (Nashville: Abingdon Press, 1995).

McCormack, Bruce L., *Karl Barth's Critically Realistic Dialectical Theology: Its Genesis and Development 1910-1936* (Oxford: Clarendon Press, 1995).

McCormack, Bruce L., *Orthodox and Modern: Studies in the Theology of Karl Barth* (Grand Rapids: Baker Academic, 2008).

McGinn, Bernard, *Meister Eckhart: Teacher and Preacher* (New York: Paulist Press, 1986).

McGrath, Alister, *Emil Brunner: A Reappraisal* (Chichester: Wiley Blackwell, 2014).

McKim, Donald K. (ed.), *The Cambridge Companion to John Calvin* (Cambridge: Cambridge University Press, 2004).

Merleau-Ponty, Maurice, *Adventures in the Dialectic*, trans. Joseph Bien (London: Heinemann, 1974).

Metzger, Bruce M., *The Canon of the New Testament: Its Origin, Development, and Significance* (Oxford: Clarendon Press, 1987).

Meuser, Fred W., 'Luther as Preacher of the Word of God' (pp. 136–48), in Donald K. McKim (ed.), *The Cambridge Companion to Martin Luther* (Cambridge: Cambridge University Press, 2003).

Meyers, Robin R., 'Jazz Me Gene: Narrative Preaching as Encore' (pp. 131–44), in Mike Graves and David J. Schlafer (eds.), *What's the Shape of Narrative Preaching?* (Atlanta: Chalice Press, 2008).

Mikkelsen, Hans Vium, *Reconciled Humanity: Karl Barth in Dialogue* (Grand Rapids: Eerdmans, 2010).

Milbank, Alison, *Chesterton and Tolkien as Theologians: The Fantasy of the Real* (London: T & T Clark, 2007).

Milbank, John, 'The Double Glory, or Paradox versus Dialectics: On Not Quite Agreeing with Slavoj Žižek', in John Milbank and Slavoj Žižek, *The Monstrosity of Christ: Paradox or Dialectic?* (London: The MIT Press, 2009).

Monson, Glenn L., 'A Funny Thing Happened on the Way Through the Sermon', in *Dialog: A Journal of Theology* 43:4 (2004): pp. 304–11.

Morris, Colin, *Raising the Dead: The Art of the Preacher as Public Performer* (London: Fount, 1996).

Morris, Colin, *The Word and the Words: The Voigt Lectures on Preaching* (London: Epworth Press, 1975).

Moule, C. F. D., *The Birth of the New Testament* (London: A & C Black, 1981).

Muller, Richard A., *Post-Reformation Reformed Dogmatics: The Rise and Development of Reformed Orthodoxy, ca. 1520 to ca. 1725*, Volume 2: Holy Scripture: The Cognitive Foundation of Theology (Grand Rapids: Baker Academic, 2003).

Myers, Jacob D., 'Preaching Philosophy: The Kerygmatic Thrust of Paul Ricoeur's Philosophy and Its Contributions to Homiletics', in *Literature and Theology* 27:2 (2013): pp. 208–26.

Nichols, Aidan, *G. K. Chesterton, Theologian* (Manchester: Darton, Longman and Todd, 2009).

Niesel, Wilhelm, *The Theology of Calvin*, trans. Harold Knight (Cambridge: James Clarke & Co., 2002).

Nikulin, Dmitri, *Dialectic and Dialogue* (Palo Alto: Stanford University Press, 2010).

Norén, Carol M., 'Crisis Preaching and Corporate Worship', in *Liturgy* 27:1 (2012): pp. 44–53.

O' Collins, Gerald, 'The Inspiring Power of Scripture: Three Case Studies', in *Irish Theological Quarterly* 79:3 (2014): pp. 265–73.

Oddie, William, *Chesterton and the Romance of Orthodoxy: The Making of GKC, 1874–1908* (Oxford: Oxford University Press, 2010).

Ocker, Christopher, *Biblical Poetics Before Humanism and Reformation* (Cambridge: Cambridge University Press, 2008).

Oh, Peter, 'Complementary Dialectics of Kierkegaard and Barth: Barth's Use of Kierkegaardian Diastasis Reassessed', in *Neue Zeitschrift für Systematicsche Theologie und Religionsphilosophie* 48:4 (2007): pp. 497–512.

Old, Hughes Oliphant, *The Reading and Preaching of the Scriptures in the Worship of the Christian Church*, 7 Volumes (Grand Rapids: Eerdmans, 1998–2009).

Olin, Doris, *Paradox* (Durham: Acumen, 2003).

Opitz, Peter, 'The Authority of Scripture in the Early Zurich Reformation (1522–1540)', in *Journal of Reformed Theology* 5:3 (2011): pp. 296–309.

Osborne, Grant R., *The Hermeneutical Spiral: A Comprehensive Introduction to Biblical Interpretation* (Downers Grove: IVP, 1991).

Ottoni-Wilhelm, Dawn, 'New Hermeneutic, New Homiletic, and New Directions: An U.S.–North American Perspective', in *Homiletic* 35:1 (2010): pp. 17–31.

Pagitt, Doug, *Preaching Re-Imagined: The Role of the Sermon in Communities of Faith* (Grand Rapids: Zondervan, 2005).

Pape, Lance B., *The Scandal of Having Something to Say: Ricoeur and the Possibility of Postliberal Preaching* (Waco: Baylor University Press, 2012).

Parker, T. H. L., *Calvin's Preaching* (Edinburgh: T & T Clark, 1992).

Pasquarello III, Mike, *Christian Preaching: A Trinitarian Theology of Proclamation* (Eugene: Wipf & Stock, 2006).

Perkins, Robert L. (ed.), *International Kierkegaard Commentary*, Volume 21: For Self-Examination and Judge for Yourself! (Macon: Mercer University Press, 2002).

Persons-Parkes, Sam, '"The Once and Future Pulpit": Hearing Gerhard Ebeling Again', in *Homiletic* 37:1 (2012): pp. 27–37.

Piper, John, *John Calvin and His Passion for the Majesty of God* (Nottingham: IVP, 2009).

Polk, Timothy H., 'Kierkegaard's Use of the New Testament: Intertextuality, Indirect Communication and Appropriation' (pp. 237–45), in Lee C. Barrett and Jon Stewart (eds.), *Kierkegaard and the Bible, Tome II: The New Testament* (Farnham: Ashgate, 2010).

Pollock, John, *George Whitefield and the Great Awakening* (Oxford: Lion Publishing, 1972).

Popper, Karl R., 'What Is Dialectic?', in *Mind* 49:196 (1940): pp. 403–26.

Pound, Marcus, *Žižek: A (Very) Critical Introduction* (Grand Rapids: Eerdmans, 2008).

Powery, Luke A., 'Nobody Knows the Trouble I See: A Spirit(ual) Approach to the Interpretive Task of Homiletical Theology' (pp. 85–107), in David Schnasa Jacobsen (ed.), *Homiletical Theology in Action: The Unfinished Theological Task of Preaching*, Volume 2: The Promise of Homiletical Theology (Eugene: Cascade, 2015).

Priest, Graham, *In Contradiction: A Study of the Transconsistent* (Dordecht: Martinus Nijhoff Publishers, 1987).

Priest, Graham, 'What's So Bad About Contradictions' (pp. 23–38), in Graham Priest, et al. (eds.), *The Law of Non-Contradiction: New Philosophical Essays* (Oxford: Clarendon Press, 2004).

Priest, Graham, et al. (eds.), *The Law of Non-Contradiction: New Philosophical Essays* (Oxford: Clarendon Press, 2004).

Proctor, Samuel D., *The Certain Sound of the Trumpet: Crafting a Sermon of Authority* (Valley Forge: Judson Press, 1994).

Pyper, Hugh, *The Joy of Kierkegaard: Essays on Kierkegaard as a Biblical Reader* (Sheffield: Equinox, 2011).

Pyper, Hugh, 'The Offensiveness of Scripture' (paper presented at the *Society for the Study of Theology Annual Conference*, April 2011).

Raiter, Michael, 'The Holy Hush: Biblical and Theological Reflections on Preaching with Unction' (pp. 161–79), in Paul A. Barker, et al. (eds.), *Serving God's Words: Windows on Preaching and Ministry* (Nottingham: IVP, 2001).

Ramm, Bernard, *Protestant Biblical Interpretation* (Grand Rapids: Baker Book House, 1970).

Randolph, David, *The Renewal of Preaching* (Philadelphia: Fortress Press, 1969).

Reumann, John, *Variety and Unity in New Testament Thought* (Oxford: Oxford University Press 1991).

Richards, Jay Wesley, *The Untamed God: A Philosophical Exploration of Divine Perfection, Simplicity, and Immutability* (Illinois: IVP, 2003).

Rose, Lucy-Atkinson, *Sharing the Word: Preaching in the Roundtable Church* (Grand Rapids: Westminster John Knox Press, 1997).

Rosen, Michael, *Hegel's Dialectic and Its Criticism* (Cambridge: Cambridge University Press, 1982).

Sánchez, Alejandro Cavallazzi, 'Dialectic' (pp. 165–9), in Steven M. Emmanuel, et al. (eds.), *Kierkegaard's Concepts: Tome II: Classicism to Enthusiasm* (Farnham: Ashgate, 2014).

Sanlon, Peter T., *Augustine's Theology of Preaching* (Minneapolis: Fortress Press, 2014).

Sarlemijn, Andries, *Hegel's Dialectic*, trans. Peter Kirschenmann (Dordecht: D. Reidel Publishing, 1975).

Scharf, Uwe Carsten, *The Paradoxical Breakthrough of Revelation: Interpreting the Divine-Human Interplay in Paul Tillich's Work, 1913–1964* (Berlin: Walter de Gruyter, 1999).

Scharlemann, Robert P., 'The No to Nothing and the Nothing to Know: Barth and Tillich and the Possibility of Theological Science', in *Journal of the American Academy of Religion* 55:1 (1987): pp. 57–72.

Schröer, Henning, *Die Denkform der Paradoxität als theologisches Problem* (Göttingen: Vandenhoeck & Ruprecht, 1960).

Schwöbel, Christophe, 'The Preacher's Art: Preaching Theologically' (pp. 1–20), in Colin E. Gunton, *Theology Through Preaching: Sermons for Brentwood* (Edinburgh: T & T Clark, 2001).

Sinnett, Mark W. *Restoring the Conversation: Socratic Dialectic in the Authorship of Søren Kierkegaard* (Fife: Theology in Scotland, 1999).

Slemmons, Timothy Matthew, *Groans of the Spirit: Homiletical Dialectics in an Age of Confusion* (Eugene: Pickwick, 2010).

Smith, Cyprian, *The Way of Paradox: Spiritual Life As Taught By Meister Eckhart* (London: Darton, Longman, and Todd, 1988).

Smith, John E., 'Time and Qualitative Time' (pp. 46–57), in James S. Baumlin and Phillip Sipiora (eds.), *Rhetoric and Kairos: Essays in History, Theory, and Praxis* (Albany: SUNY Press, 2002).

Snider, Phil, *Preaching after God: Derrida, Caputo, and the Language of Postmodern Homiletics* (Eugene: Wipf and Stock, 2012).

Sorensen, Roy, *Vagueness and Contradiction* (Oxford: Clarendon Press, 2001).

Sproul, R. C., *Essential Truths of the Christian Faith* (Wheaton: Tyndale House, 1992).

Spurgeon, C. H., *An All-Round Ministry: Addresses to Ministers and Students* (London: Banner of Truth, 1960).

Spurgeon, C. H., *Lectures to My Students* (London: Passmore and Alabastar, 1875).

Stackhouse, Ian, 'Charismatic Utterance: Preaching as Prophecy' (pp. 42–46), in Geoffrey Stevenson (ed.), *The Future of Preaching* (London: SCM Press, 2010).

Stephens, W. P. 'Scottish Preachers and Preaching', in *The Expository Times* 105 (1994): pp. 330–35.

Stevenson, Geoffrey (ed.), *The Future of Preaching* (London: SCM Press, 2010).

Stewart, James S., *A Faith to Proclaim: The Lyman Beecher Lectures at Yale University* (London: Hodder & Stoughton, 1953).

Stewart, James S., *Heralds of God: The Warrack Lectures* (London: Hodder & Stoughton, 1946).

Stewart, Jon (ed.), *Kierkegaard's Influence on Theology, Tome I: German Protestant Theology* (Farnham: Ashgate, 2012).

Stott, John, *I Believe in Preaching* (London: Hodder & Stoughton, 1982).

Sullivan, Dale L., 'Kairos and the Rhetoric of Belief', in *Quarterly Journal of Speech* 78:3 (1992): pp. 317–32.

Thiselton, Anthony C., 'Canon, Community and Theological Construction' (pp. 1–32), in Craig G. Bartholomew and Anthony C. Thiselton (eds.), *Canon and Biblical Interpretation* (Milton Keynes: Paternoster Press, 2006).

Thompson, Virgil (ed.), *Justification Is for Preaching* (Eugene: Pickwick Publications, 2012).

Tillich, Paul, 'Kairos' (pp. 32–51), in *The Protestant Era*, trans. James Luther Adams (Chicago: University of Chicago Press, 1948).

Tillich, Paul, *Systematic Theology*, Volume 3 (London: SCM Press, 1978).

Tillich, Paul, 'What Is Wrong with the "Dialectic" Theology', in *The Journal of Religion* 15:2 (1935): pp. 127–45.

Tolstaya, Katya, *Kaleidoscope: F. M. Dostoevsky and the Early Dialectical Theology*, trans. Anthony Runia (Leiden and Boston: Brill, 2013).

Torrance, T. F., *Karl Barth: An Introduction to his Early Theology, 1910–1931* (London: SCM, 1962).

Troeger, Thomas H., *Imagining a Sermon* (Nashville: Abingdon Press, 1990).

Turner, Denys, *The Darkness of God: Negativity in Christian Mysticism* (Cambridge: Cambridge University Press, 1998).

van den Belt, Henk, 'Heinrich Bullinger and Jean Calvin on the Authority of Scripture (1538–1571)', in *Journal of Reformed Theology* 5:3 (2011): pp. 310–24.

Van Dixhoorn, Chad B., *A Puritan Theology of Preaching* (London: St. Antholin's Lectureship Charity Lecture, 2005).

Van Harn, Roger E., *Preacher, Can You Hear Us Listening?* (Grand Rapids: Eerdmans, 2005).

van Liere, Fran, *An Introduction to the Medieval Bible* (Cambridge: Cambridge University Press, 2014).

Van Vleet, Jacob E., *Dialectical Theology and Jacques Ellul: An Introductory Exposition* (Minneapolis: Fortress Press, 2014).

Vanhoozer, Kevin J. (ed.), *Dictionary for the Theological Interpretation of the* Bible (Grand Rapids, Baker Academic, 2005).

von Balthasar, Hans Urs, *The Theology of Karl Barth*, trans. Edward T. Oakes (San Francisco: Ignatius Press, 1992).

Ward, Graham, 'Barth, Hegel, and the Possibility for Christian Apologetics' (pp. 53–67), in Mike Higton and John C. McDowell (eds.), *Conversing with Barth* (Farnham: Ashgate, 2004).

Ward, Koral, *Augenblick: The Concept of the 'Decisive Moment' in 19th and 20th Century Western Philosophy* (Farnham: Ashgate, 2009).

Ward, Maisie, *Gilbert Keith Chesterton* (New York: Sheed & Ward, 1943).

Ward, Timothy, *Words of Life: Scripture as the Living and Active Word of God* (Downers Grove: IVP, 2009).

Warren, Scott, *Emergence of Dialectical Theory: Philosophy and Political Inquiry* (Chicago: University of Chicago Press, 2008).

Webster, John, 'Illumination' (pp. 50–64), in *The Domain of the Word: Scripture and Theological Reason* (Edinburgh: T & T Clark, 2013).

Webster, John, 'The Dogmatic Location of the Canon' (pp. 9–46), in *Word and Church: Essays in Christian Dogmatics* (Edinburgh: T & T Clark, 2001).

Webster, John, *Holy Scripture: A Dogmatic Sketch* (Cambridge: Cambridge University Press, 2003).

Webster, John, 'On the Clarity of Holy Scripture' (pp. 33–67), in *Confessing God: Essays in Christian Dogmatics* II (London: T & T Clark, 2005).

Weiss, Daniel H., *Paradox and the Prophets: Hermann Cohen and the Indirect Communication of Religion* (Oxford: Oxford University Press, 2012).

Westerholm, Stephen and Westerholm, Martin, *Reading Sacred Scripture: Voices from the History of Biblical Interpretation* (Grand Rapids: Eerdmans, 2016).

Whitefield, George, *The Works of George Whitefield*, Volume 4, ed. John Gillies (Edinburgh: Kincaid & Bell, 1771).

Whiting, Robert, *The Reformation of the English Parish Church* (Cambridge: Cambridge University Press, 2014).

Willimon, William H., *Conversations with Barth on Preaching* (Nashville: Abingdon, 2006).

Willimon, William H., *Proclamation and Theology* (Nashville: Abingdon, 2005).

Willimon, William H. and Lischer, Richard (eds.), *Concise Encyclopedia of Preaching* (Louisville: Westminster John Knox Press, 1995).

Wilson, Paul Scott, 'Biblical Studies and Preaching: A Growing Divide?' (pp. 137–49), in Thomas G. Long and Edward Farley (eds.), *Preaching as a Theological Task: Word, Gospel, Scripture: In Honor of David Buttrick* (Louisville: Westminster John Knox Press, 1996).

Wismar, Don Roy, *A Sacramental View of Preaching: As Seen in the Writings of John Calvin and P. T. Forsyth and Applied to the Mid-Twentieth Century* (unpublished doctoral dissertation, Pacific School of Religion, 1963).

Wolfe, Judith, *Heidegger's Eschatology: Theological Horizons in Martin Heidegger's Early Work* (Oxford: Oxford University Press, 2013).

Wood, A. Skevington, *Captive to the Word: Martin Luther, Doctor of Sacred Scripture* (Exeter: The Paternoster Press, 1969).

Wood, Ralph C., *Chesterton: The Nightmare Goodness of God* (Waco: Baylor University Press, 2011).

Žižek, Slavoj, 'The Fear of Four Words', and 'Dialectical Clarity versus the Misty Conceit of Paradox', in John Milbank and Slavoj Žižek, *The Monstrosity of Christ: Paradox or Dialectic?* (London: The MIT Press, 2009).

Žižek, Slavoj, *The Parallax View* (Cambridge: MIT Press, 2006).

Zwingli, Ulrich, 'Of the Clarity and Certainty of the Word of God', in G. W. Bromiley (ed.), *Zwingli and Bullinger* (The Library of Christian Classics, Volume XXIV) (London: SCM, 1953).

NAMES AND THEMES INDEX

SCRIPTURE INDEX